CITIES *to go* ▶

The Top 25 High-Energy,
Make-Every-Minute-Count City Getaways

Rich and Kay Haddaway

JOHN MUIR PUBLICATIONS
A Division of Avalon Travel Publishing

Dedication

In memory of our aunt, Elizabeth Haddaway, who waved her wobbly wand and opened up a world of travel for us. She never packed light, missed dessert, or left a taxi driver uncharmed.

Acknowledgments

We are deeply grateful to our editor, Ellen Cavalli, who kept us focused and afloat through this massive project, and let our voice ring through. And where would we be if Acquisitions Editor Cassandra Conyers hadn't come up with the idea for the book in the first place?

It would have been impossible for us to cover every nook and cranny of 25 cities without the generous help of informed friends, locals, and convention and visitors bureaus. Thank you one and all.

John Muir Publications, 5855 Beaudry Street, Emeryville, CA 94608

Printed in the United States of America.
First edition. First printing 2000.

Library of Congress Cataloging-in-Publication Data
Haddaway, Rich.
    Cities to go: the top 25 high-energy, make-every-minute-count city getaways/by Rich and Kay Haddaway.—1st ed.
        p. cm.
Includes index.
ISBN 1-56261-491-6
        1. United States–Guidebooks. 2. Cities and towns—United States—Guidebooks. I. Haddaway, Kay. II. Title.

E158 .H175 2000
917.304'929—dc21

99-053139

Editors: Ellen Cavalli, Kathleen Hillock, Leslie Miller
Graphics Editor: Bunny Wong
Production: Janine Lehmann
Cover and Interior Design: Janine Lehmann
Maps: Julie Felton
Printer: Publishers Press
Cover photos: Left to right—© Mike Howell/Leo de Wys Inc.; © John Elk III; © Martini/LookLeo de Wys Inc.
Distributed to the book trade by
Publishers Group West
Berkeley, California

CONTENTS

Note to Readers

The most difficult task in writing this book was deciding what to leave out. We cover so much territory in so little space that we're quite sure we've neglected some important stuff.

We need your help. Tell us where we screwed up. Tell us what needs updating. Give us your suggestions for making this an even better book for the next edition. Our e-mail address is rkhaddaway@home.com.

Also, please visit our Web site, www.citiestogo.com. In it, you'll find updates on what's happening in all these cities, plus additions and corrections. This is where many of your comments will appear.

ESCAPE TO THE CITY

WE AWOKE TO A WORLD FULL OF ORANGE AND YELLOW DRAGONS. It was better than a dream.

It was the first morning of a spur-of-the-moment getaway, and we had stumbled into some sort of festival in San Francisco's Chinatown. Nothing major, nothing meant to draw in tourists—it was a street festival for families.

Schoolchildren were the dragons. Several older boys were the accompanists, beating their drums into a rumble of a dragon stampede. You could tell it was children under the costumes—those 12-footed dragons wore sneakers, and the tail of one serpent got the giggles. Proud parents were in the audience, applauding the sneakers they recognized.

Most of the people weren't paying it any mind. Many were across the street, rummaging through a rummage sale. Tables were out along the sidewalk, and people were selling this and that—herbs and teas and suspicious-looking jade pendants, more odds than ends. Locals were selling and locals were buying. Some of the plastic-gold artwork was as gaudy as a velvet Elvis. But the price was right, and it was going fast.

Some people were barbecuing on their balconies, and the dim sum restaurants were opening their doors. The air was sweet and sour with it all, a little burnt, and perfectly delicious.

Less than 24 hours earlier we had been at home, locked in the Rodent Race.

We bet you know all about it. The suburban scurrying: wake the kids, feed the kids, get to work, stay at work, meet the deadline, meet the payroll, meet the train, get home, get dinner, help the kids with homework, sleep. Tulsa, Boise, Akron—the drab days of huffing and puffing are pretty much the same everywhere. It seems like one long treadmill, doesn't it? You press the bar and get your pallid pellet. Every year is the Year of the Rat.

You long for relief, but you don't even have time to *plan* for a decent vacation. What to do?

We've got the answer. A few days in the big city is just the thing to put a little color back in your gray, SUV-driving days.

How's that again? Relaxing in the middle of a big, honking, fuming, teeming city? How could that possibly be a *vacation?*

Simple. Big cities are energizing.

All those new people, many of them fresh from old worlds across the borders, remaking their lives; the clang and clash of youth and all their boisterous art that tingles the ears and stirs the brain; majestic buildings of old, whose shadows hold history; leafy old avenues with vacant-eyed vagrants and strutting pigeons and an art museum that looks like a rocket-propelled grain silo; then, at the corner, streets of commerce, a mad dash of taxis, and all along the way, in almost every store, just about everything's on sale—today only! You've got to buy something, maybe that turquoise bracelet. And what about lunch? That Thai place looked pretty good. And there's a guy playing a saxophone on the corner. A tattoo parlor. The Electric Chair Museum and Gift Shop. A dusty bookstore. A church with gothic trimmings. This way down to the subway. Live nude girls! What about a pesto pizza? A concert in the park tonight. Sunset at the wharves. Let's have an espresso and the chocolate tart.

A city to go. Packaged. Ready to open.

Stand there. Take a bite. Take in all that energy. If that doesn't jolt you out of your treadmill days, nothing will.

Those of you who have traveled very much have probably noticed this unpleasant trend: the franchising of the travel experience.

There are big bucks to be made from showing people a good time, so the big guys move in and take over. The hotels look fresh off the assembly line, and so do all their personnel, the receptionists and bellhops and waitpersons: "Hi, my name's Jason! What's yours?"

It's the amusement park experience. Everything is perfectly convenient, which means it's perfectly planned. Everything is manufactured, from the tidy saloon to the bloodless shoot-out to the made-to-order smile of our old friend Jason, the robo-waitperson: "Howdy, partner, and welcome to Six Flags Over Duluth! My name's Jason. What's yours? How about a sarsaparilla?"

And the results? You feel perfectly manipulated and thoroughly fleeced.

Thankfully, that's not happening too much in the central cities. These are real places full of real people trying to make a living. Shopkeepers and restaurateurs will be kind to tourists, of course, but you're not their mainstay. They're busy with real customers—office workers and whatnot. They don't have time to manipulate you. There's no time to put on a show.

▶▶▶

Think about it. From almost anyplace in North America, you can get to a whole new world in just a handful of hours. You can do it on the spur of the moment, almost—in fact, the closer to the spur, the better your chances of getting a good, last-minute deal from an airline; or maybe you can add a few days' vacation to a convention in a city you've never been to. You can do it without much planning, maybe without renting a car, and all with only one guidebook. (Hint: This is the one!) You can get from the airport into the heart of one of the great cities of the world in nothing flat, and wander to your heart's content.

And it's to a real place, with all new smells and a special pace and people who talk funny and a new weather that brings a wind that catches your attention. There is a sense of otherness, and it hits you like a splash of color, waking you from your drab days with a refreshment that's every bit as good as a dive into a mountain river. Even if you already live in a big city, a trip to another one—a vastly different one— can still be refreshment.

You can walk the cobblestones that Ben Franklin walked, and you can meander through the neighborhood where Martin Luther King Jr. grew up. You can taste a creamy clam chowder in Boston or a grilled trout in Denver or a plateful of barbecued ribs in Fort Worth. You can stop and listen to a doom-saying street-corner preacher in New Orleans or hear the sad truth of the blues in St. Louis. You can walk into Elvis Presley's jungled den in Memphis, or Frank Lloyd Wright's studio in Chicago, or Lawrence Ferlinghetti's bookstore in San Francisco.

And if you're careful, Jason won't be able to find you.

In fact, we've worked hard in this book to make sure that you and Jason don't cross paths. We've tried to direct you to what's authentic about a place—the small hotel, the little restaurant that serves the specialty of the region, the club that plays the music of the city's soul. You'll be more likely to have a grumpy guy named Gus with a dirty apron come out to take your order, and he'll tell you to get the oyster stew—and if you know what's good for you, you will.

Yes, in the center of the city is where the heart beats, and that's where we've tried to direct you, as quickly and as easily as possible.

Like that morning in San Francisco. We had flown in the night before, and we woke up in a whole new world.

Chinatown was only half a hill away from our hotel. We were there in no time, walking through the elaborate gates on Grant Avenue, around corners beside the kite shops and herbal medicine shops and vegetable vendors and little grocery stores with whole fish stranded on mountains of ice. Around one more corner and there we were, in the midst of a swirl of orange and yellow sneaker-footed dragons.

It's closer than you think. Let us show you the way.

PLANNING YOUR GETAWAY

What if you wake up on Monday and realize that the weekend wasn't nearly long enough, and that furthermore you can't take another full week of your boss, your workout routine, or even your kids? By Saturday night, you can be in Chinatown or Beantown, or points in between. We promise. Here's how.

Let's use a real-life example. It's August 30 in Fort Worth, Texas—aka "hotter'n the hinges of hell"—and Mama ain't happy. We start noodling around on the Internet, all the while talking about how nice San Francisco is in August, with daytime temperatures hovering in the 70s. Pretty soon we're on the Travelocity Web site, and in a couple of clicks we've found round-trip airfare for $178 leaving Saturday, September 4, and returning Tuesday, the seventh, which takes in Labor Day. In a couple of more clicks we find a room in one of our favorites, the Hotel Triton, for $179/night. About six blocks from there, the Serrano Hotel offers four-star accommodations for $149/night and is just two blocks from Union Square. We're jazzed.

Just to be on the safe side, we check out a couple more Web sites. Expedia.com has a feature we especially like called Fare Tracker. Enter the pertinent information, and the site checks all the participating airlines for the best fare. We also check hotel deals here and on www.all-hotels.com. Bye-bye "I've-lost-my-will-to-live" Fort Worth in August! We pack. We go. We cool off. Mama's happy again.

But maybe you're not quite that spontaneous. You're new at this travel thing, and you're not ready to plunge in. You need a plan.

Step One: Decide where you want to go.
This book should help you with that. We've picked 25 interesting places for you to consider—our criteria for choosing a city were that it has a central core that's easy to get around in and that it has lots of character. Remember what Gertrude Stein said about Oakland, California? "There is no *there* there." Well, with every city we cover in this book, we guarantee you'll find a *there*—and in it will be unique shops, quirky restaurants, special attractions, and individualized hotels.

So skim through the book. The introductions to each city try to give a sense of the flavor of a place. See what strikes your fancy.

Each of the cities we've covered has a convention and visitors bureau (or similar organization) whose purpose is to help you have a good visit. We've listed those groups. Write, call, or check out their Web sites. They'll send you a package of information that usually includes maps and perhaps some discount coupons.

In trying to decide where you want to go, consider the time of year and the climate. February in Minneapolis can be crisp—and August in Austin can be positively wilting. Sure, off-season travel has its rewards—it's cheaper, and you'll avoid the crowds—but remember the downside. Shoulder season is the time to go just about anywhere. That's usually when the seasons are at their most moderate and the crowds are smaller. Why? Because kids are in school.

This might be a good time to mention that the city getaway is not really designed for children. It's not that you can't take them along—they'll probably have a good time—but you'll have a better chance of having a good family vacation at a theme park or at the beach. Save the big city for yourselves.

Once you've decided where you want to go, it's time for . . .

Step Two: Make your plans.

Now you'll want to research the city. Read the chapter thoroughly. Go back to the Internet and get specific events information and fresh reviews of restaurants and shows. As hard as we've tried to give you up-to-the-minute information, things can change in a hurry. Restaurants close. Hotels raise their rates.

This is also a good time to look for deals. Check out the Web sites such as www.travelocity.com, www.expedia.com, or www.1travel.com. And you *are* saving up your frequent-flier miles, aren't you? We find all kinds of intriguing deals along with our monthly statement from American Airlines.

Our bias in this book is to recommend the smaller boutique hotels, but sometimes the big boys have the best deals. Call the chains such as Hilton or Marriott, and see what kind of deals they're offering.

Also try calling an airline or a hotel chain late at night. The operators are bored stiff. They'll find you a good deal just for the fun of it. One of the best deals we ever got happened this way. We got a room at a Days Inn in Washington, D.C., for $49 a night. We got the deal by prepaying and agreeing that it would be nonrefundable.

We also strongly believe in the value of a good travel agent. Yes, we know they've started charging fees, but what they can save you in time and money will far outweigh their cost.

But our bottom-line advice is, if you want to find a good deal, BE FLEXIBLE. Let's say you've decided you want to go to Philadelphia, but you find a great package deal to Boston. What's wrong with Boston? And while you're at it, check the travel Web sites for package deals, such as a Broadway show package to New York City. Many times these packages can add up to some nifty savings. Just do the math and see if it all makes sense.

Step Three: Get packing.

Pack light. Remember, this is a quick getaway you're going on. One regular suitcase and one carry-on should be plenty for a couple.

The weather, of course, is the main determinant of what you'll pack, and the best way to think about that is to dress yourself in layers: a shirt, a sweater, a coat. One of the most important things you can take is a pair of good walking shoes. You'll be walking in the city as much as you'd be in a hike through the woods. Leave your fashion statements in your closet at home. Don't suffer unnecessarily.

Step Four: Be safe.

The best way to avoid problems with theft or loss is to give yourself plenty of time at the airport. Fear of being left behind can cause you to make mistakes. The one big mistake you're likely to make is to leave your bags unattended or unwatched, even for a minute.

If you're a little afraid of getting lost in your destination city on the way to your hotel, ask your rental car agent for directions. Also, never travel with expensive jewelry—after all, who needs to impress a bunch of strangers at the opera?

As you walk the streets of an unfamiliar city, stay alert. Travel in groups, and stick to the well-lighted, more populous areas. And try to look like you know where you're going.

Step Five: Travel like a local.

Look, we know all about it. We've been there. Almost everybody—everybody except the natives—is intimidated by a big city such as New York. On our first visit, we were deathly afraid of getting lost, of staying lost, of never being heard from again. But think about something for a moment: If a transportation system on the scale of New York's can get millions of people from one place to another every day, there's bound to be some kind of logic to it.

Take it slowly. Don't try to do anything fancy to begin with, such as going from bus to subway to taxi. Start small. Look at your map. Look at all those square streets, and how they're numbered. Hey, it kind of makes sense.

Go ahead and take one of those hokey tourist tours. (You are, after all, just another hokey tourist.) It's a good way to get a lay of the land, to see how landmarks match up with your map.

Buses are a good way to get around because, unlike subways, you can see where you're going. If it looks like you're going the wrong way, you can get off before too much damage is done. Subways are fun, once you get the hang of them. The lines are color-coded, and they're named for the last stop. Is your destination between where you are and the last stop? That's the one you take.

You may find that in the biggest cities, a combination of taxis and public transportation is a much easier way of getting around, and maybe cheaper, than a rental car—and a lot less stressful, too. Let somebody else worry about the traffic and finding a parking place. Plus, just think how incredibly savvy you'll feel once you master a monster of a transportation system. You'll feel like a traveler instead of a tourist. Heck, you'll be well on your way to . . .

Step Six: Have a good time.

Do whatever you need to in order to avoid stressful situations. Find a hotel near the things you're most interested in, and that way you'll avoid too many transportation hassles. If you're a theater buff, for instance, find something close to Times Square. Then you can take the best form of transportation of all, your feet. That's really the best way to get to know a city, anyway.

And this is a vacation, remember. Go ahead and go for cream in your coffee, butter on your croissant, and a luscious apple tart. With all that walking you'll be doing, the calories won't count for much. And for heaven's sake, go ahead and buy that little something or other. We do our Christmas shopping all year long, buying gifts on our travels that can't be found anywhere else. We'll pack a small, empty bag for bringing home all our loot.

The way to get to know a city is to become a part of it. That means talking to people. One of the best conversation starters is, "Listen, we're just visiting, and we're wondering where the best place is to (fill in the blank)." People love to feel like experts, and everybody feels like they're an expert about their own hometown.

Finally, the best way to have a good time is to take it easy. Take the time to wander. Breathe deeply. Give serendipity a chance. Who knows where it might lead—maybe to one of those places of the heart where orange and yellow dragons live.

ABOUT THIS BOOK

We've covered a lot of territory in a small amount of space, so we've had to take a few shortcuts. We haven't listed opening hours or admission prices for most attractions, unless there is something unusual to note—closed Wednesdays, for instance. We've listed the phone number with each attraction, so you can get details if you need them. It's the same with restaurants and nightclubs.

Pricing categories for hotels and restaurants are listed according to the following ranges: For hotels, the price of a room for two per night is denoted by one of four notations—

$ = $75 or less
$$ = $76–$150
$$$ = $151–$250
$$$$ = $251 and up

Restaurants are ranked similarly, with a typical dinner for two (no wine or cocktails) listed as follows—

$ = $25 or less
$$ = $26–$50
$$$ = $51–$75
$$$$ = $76 and up

At press time, the Canadian dollar was pegged to the U.S. dollar at roughly $1 U.S. = $1.40 to $1.50 Can. Shopkeepers will accept U.S. dollars. Canada has two kinds of taxes: The Provincial Sales Tax (PST) is 8 percent on most purchases. Foreign visitors can get the 7 percent Goods and Services Tax (GST) refunded—at least on accommodations and most goods (but not meals). Pamphlets are available at hotels. You can also call 905/712-5813 for more information. The number for U.S. Customs is 604/278-1825.

Another resource for travelers is Beyond Ability International, which makes professional assessments of accessible hotels, attractions, restaurants, and services. Information is free and can be obtained by calling 416/410-3748 or logging on to www.beyond-ability.com.

Finally, if you need medical care while visiting another city, contact **Travelmed Inc.** for doctors, dentists, chiropractors, or board-certified specialists who are available any time for house calls or hotel or doctors' office visits within 30 minutes. You can reach the service at 800/878-3627 (also works with prefixes 888 and 877) or www.travelmedintl.com.

Major Airlines
American Airlines, 800/433-7300, www.americanair.com, www.aa.com
Continental Airlines, 800/525-0280, www.flycontinental.com
Delta Airlines, 800/221-1212, www.delta-air.com
Northwest Airlines, 800/225-2525, www.nwa.com
Southwest Airlines, 800/435-9792, www.iflyswa.com
United Airlines, 800/241-6522, www.ual.com
US Airways, 800/428-4322, www.usairways.com

Rental Car Companies
Alamo, 800/327-9633
Avis, 800/831-2847
Budget, 800/527-0700
Dollar, 800/800-4000
Enterprise, 800/325-8007
Hertz, 800/654-3131
National, 800/227-7368

Major Hotel Chains
Hilton, 800/445-8667
Hyatt, 800/233-1234
Marriott, 800/228-9290
Omni, 800/843-6664
Radisson, 800/333-3333
Ramada, 800/228-2828
Sheraton, 800/325-3535
Westin, 800/937-8461

❶ NEW YORK CITY

to go ▶

If you're bored in New York it's your own fault.
—Myrna Loy

If you want to be a world traveler but just don't have the time, here's an idea for a shortcut: Come to New York City. The whole world is right here, squashed down into one teeming little hustling, bustling global village.

The city as a whole contains more than 7 million people of at least 140 ethnic origins, which makes quite a rich stew in this melting pot. Because you're only going to have time for a taste, we suggest you confine your visit to the savory island of Manhattan. You won't leave hungry.

Manhattan has plenty of people (1.55 million) of all makes and models, and that's not counting the commuters and tourists. This many people of that much diversity in such a small space are bound to get on each other's nerves, and yes, New York is a nervy place. But it's not a zoo. People behave themselves remarkably well. In fact, New York is now the safest large city (1 million or more) in the United States, and the crime rate continues to fall.

The word for New York is energy. It won't take you long to find its rhythm and learn to go with its white-water flow, and then you'll know in your bones the meaning of the term "New York minute." It's about 20 seconds.

New York City

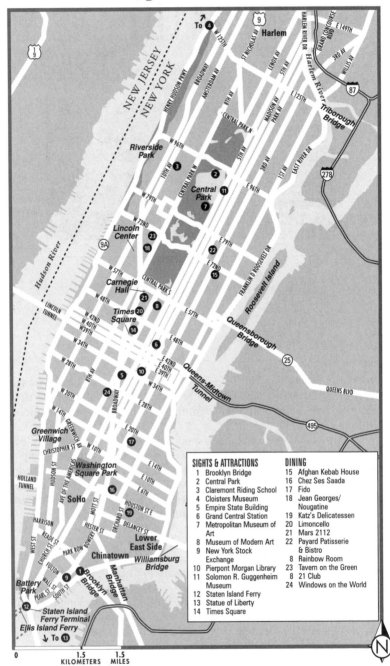

SIGHTS & ATTRACTIONS
1 Brooklyn Bridge
2 Central Park
3 Claremont Riding School
4 Cloisters Museum
5 Empire State Building
6 Grand Central Station
7 Metropolitan Museum of Art
8 Museum of Modern Art
9 New York Stock Exchange
10 Pierpont Morgan Library
11 Solomon R. Guggenheim Museum
12 Staten Island Ferry
13 Statue of Liberty
14 Times Square

DINING
15 Afghan Kebab House
16 Chez Ses Saada
17 Fido
18 Jean Georges/ Nougatine
19 Katz's Delicatessen
20 Limoncello
21 Mars 2112
22 Payard Patisserie & Bistro
8 Rainbow Room
23 Tavern on the Green
8 21 Club
24 Windows on the World

0   1.5   1.5
KILOMETERS   MILES

GETTING AROUND

The three major airports are **John F. Kennedy** (718/244-4444) and **LaGuardia** (718/476-5000), both in Queens, and **Newark** (New Jersey, 973/555-1212), and there are lots of ways to get into the central city. You can get door-to-door transportation on the **SuperShuttle**, 212/209-7000, for $14 to $17 from the airport to your hotel. **Taxis** are metered, and fares are based on distance and time. Bridge and tunnel tolls are extra. From LaGuardia you can take the bus. To **subway** connections, the fare is $1.50.

Don't rent a car. There's no place to park it, and if you find a place, it'll cost you an arm and two legs. You'll need those two legs for walking. It's the best way to get around the city, and the most fun.

The layout of Manhattan is kind of fun to figure out because it makes sense. Apart from two big exceptions (the lower part of the island and the diagonaling boulevard known as Broadway), Manhattan streets are laid out in a grid.

Avenues run north-south, and streets run east-west. The even-numbered streets tend to run one-way eastward, and odd-numbered streets run westward. Fifth Avenue is the dividing line between east and west, and the numbered streets get higher as you go north. The other avenues that run north and south are also numbered like Fifth Avenue, with the exception of Madison, Park, and Lexington, which are between Third and Fifth Avenues. Sixth Avenue is also known as Avenue of the Americas.

Both the subways and the buses are easy, once you get the hang of the grid. Buses and subways are $1.50; buses take exact change, and both take tokens. (Tokens are being phased out. What makes sense is the **MetroCard**—for $15, as an example, you get 10 rides on either the bus or the subway. Get the cards at subway stations and some retail outlets.) Buses are slow, but at least you can see where you're going. The subways will zip you to your destination, if you are lucky enough to have gotten on the right one. Don't ride the subway after 11 p.m. The **Metropolitan Transportation Authority (MTA)**, 718/330-1234, www.mta.nyc.ny.us, runs the subways and buses.

Taxis are everywhere and easy to find (they're yellow), except at rush-hour and in the rain—in other words, when you really need one. You can find a taxi stand in front of hotels, hail one with a wave and a whistle, or call 212/302-TAXI. At night, a taxi is available when the sign on the roof is illuminated.

SIGHTS AND ATTRACTIONS

Manhattan is 12 miles long and 3 miles wide, and every inch of it is interesting. And you're planning to see it all in a few days? Whataya, nuts? Fa-gedda-bout-it!

Since we've got to start somewhere, let's start in the middle. You can't be more centrally located in New York than **Central Park,** Fifth Ave. between 59th and 110th Sts., 212/794-6564. It's an island of serenity within this whirl of honking horns and wailing sirens and all that diesel-coated air. If you've been walking in the city, you'll need a break. If you're about to enter the city, this will help prepare you.

If you can't find it, you're way lost. Central Park is huge—840 acres bordering Fifth Avenue—and filled with trees and fountains, lakes and paths, fields and gardens, and even a castle. Get a map of the park before you venture in. They're available at information centers at the park.

To see the park in style, take a horse-drawn carriage ride. The carriages line up along 59th Street. If you want to skip the carriage and go straight to the horsepower, you can hire a horse at **Claremont Riding School,** 175 W. 89th St., 212/724-5100. There are six miles of riding track in the park.

Bordering Central Park, along Fifth Avenue, is Museum Mile, which is roughly from 82nd Street to 104th Street. Here are some of the world's greatest museums, including the Museum of the City of New York, the Jewish Museum, the Whitney Museum of American Art, and the Frick Collection. But what you absolutely cannot miss is the **Metropolitan Museum of Art,** Fifth Ave. at 82nd St., 212/535-7710, www.metmuseum.org.

The Met contains the largest holding of art and antiquities in the Western Hemisphere, with well over a million objects in 248 galleries. You'll need help, plus some good shoes. This place is one big humility lesson.

Connect with one of the docent tours and hit the highlights. (Don't miss the American Wing with its glassed-in garden, Tiffany windows, and a Frank Lloyd Wright room.) Then check out the current special exhibits. Afterward, go get a snack at one of the restaurants and rest your feet. And don't forget the museum store for some of the best shopping in New York.

If you're not careful, you'll blow one entire day at the Met. So leave already. Two other museums you dare not neglect are the **Solomon R. Guggenheim Museum,** 1071 Fifth Ave. near 89th St., 212/423-3500, www.guggenheim.org—Frank Lloyd Wright's corkscrew salute to modern design—and the mind-stretching **Museum of Modern Art (MOMA),** 11 W. 53rd near Fifth Ave., 212/708-9400, www.moma.org. MOMA is closed on Wednesdays.

Admission is free at the **Cloisters Museum,** Fort Tryon Park at 190th St., 212/769-5000, www.cloisters.org, a somewhat neglected museum because it is so far away from the center of town. Masterpieces of medieval art are housed in a group of monasteries high on a woodland hill overlooking the Hudson River. Concerts of medieval music are common.

A center of energy is **Times Square,** Seventh Ave. and Broadway at W. 44th St. The once-seedy corner, where the New Year makes its

Be ready for an inexperienced cabbie—he or she is likely to be as much of a greenhorn as you are, and not know English very well, either. When you give an address, know the cross street. If you're going to a rough part of town, get in first and then announce your destination. Cabbies aren't allowed to turn down any request based on destination.

It's easy to hail a taxi at night with a **Taxiwand,** 212/767-WAND, www.taxiwand.com, a hand-held device with a flashing red light. You can get them at the major department stores and at many hotels.

During rush hour, you may want to hire a "gypsy" cab—one that is not officially sanctioned by the city. The cabs don't have meters, but don't worry about that. The driver will ask you how much you're willing to pay once you meet your destination—usually between $5 and $10, depending on traffic and distance.

If you're worried about crime, Jackie Mason and Raoul Felder's *Survival Guide to New York City* (Avon Books) helps tell you how to get from here to there without getting mugged—all of it told with great Big Apple humor.

Manhattan can be horridly hot in the summer, when the humidity is high and the sun bakes the canyons of buildings. Bone-chilling winds whip among those same canyons during the winter. If you can, go in the spring or the fall, when the weather is moderate and the crowds aren't as bad.

City Survival Tips

most famous debut, is cleaning up its act with the help of Uncle Walt and the Disney Machine. You might as well tour the theater district while you're in the vicinity, and don't miss West 46th Street, which is also known as Restaurant Row. Surely you're hungry by now.

Check out the newly refurbished **Grand Central Station,** 42nd St. between Lexington and Vanderbilt Aves., 212/340-2345. Shops and sights galore are here. Catch a train or eat a bagel or simply stare at the zodiac ceiling. The whole place recently underwent a $196 million redo.

The **Pierpont Morgan Library,** 29 E. 36th St. at Madison Ave., 212/685-0008, is a much-overlooked treasure trove of art. Its garden restaurant is superb, and its next-door museum shop and restaurant are outstanding.

You certainly can't go to New York and miss King Kong's jungle gym, also known as the **Empire State Building,** 350 Fifth Ave. at 34th St., 212/736-3100. This symbol of the Big Apple is still among the tallest buildings in the world—at 1,015 feet—and attracts about

2.5 million gawkers a year. The best time to visit is sunset. You can watch the city turning itself on as darkness falls.

From there, and if the sky is clear, you should be able to see the other potent symbol of the city, **Brooklyn Bridge.** It took 600 men 14 years to construct, and it was completed in 1883. Twenty people died building it, and even more have jumped to their deaths from it. Don't jump. You can walk across it in about 20 minutes, starting from Park Row.

Then there's that last of the Big Three symbols, the **Statue of Liberty** (Liberty Island, 212/363-3200, www.libertystatepark.com). (Bet you didn't know that Ms. Liberty weighs 225 tons, and each eye is two-and-a-half feet wide.) She attracts huge crowds, especially in the summers, so arrive early and get ready for a long wait. For a good, easy view, you can take the **Staten Island Ferry,** Gangway S, Battery Park, 212/269-5755, for only 50 cents and just stay on the boat.

While you're downtown, drop by the **New York Stock Exchange,** 20 Broad St., 212/656-5167, www.nyse.com. You want energy? Here's energy. You can watch the daily riot of stock trading on the floor of the exchange from the safety of the visitors' gallery above.

LODGING

Intimate, European-style boutique hotels are all over Manhattan. None of them are cheap—don't expect to pay less than $150 a night for a double—but the character, the sense of place, is worth it.

The first four hotels listed here feature complimentary breakfast, a free dessert buffet every evening, and all-day espresso and cappuccino. CD players and VCRs are in each room, and classic movies can be borrowed for free.

The Shoreham, 33 W. 55th St. near Fifth Ave., 212/247-6700, $$$, is popular with the fashion and film crowd. It has original art deco murals in the lobby, Japanese shoji screens in the suites, and down duvets on the beds. It is minutes from Central Park, Rockefeller Center, and 57th Street shopping.

The Franklin, E. 87th St. between Lexington and Third Aves., 212/369-1000, $$, is in a quiet neighborhood near antiques and auction galleries. Guest rooms feature cherrywood paneling and polished black granite. Canopies for the beds are suspended by steel rods from the ceiling, and the lighting is dramatic. The hotel has a Left Bank feel for a lot less money.

Amid historic mansions in the Museum Mile district is the **Hotel Wales,** Madison Ave. at 92nd St., 212/876-6000, $$$. It has harp recitals every evening and chamber music on Sundays, plus afternoon tea. Quite British.

The Mansfield, W. 44th St. between Fifth Ave. and Avenue of the Americas, 212/944-6050, $$$, was once a gentlemen's club, with oval

Big Apple's Little Gems

Besides the big-name museums, New York has some lesser known jewels that shouldn't be missed. Try to drop by at least one of these.

The *Intrepid* **Sea-Air-Space Museum,** Pier 86 on the Hudson River at the end of W. 46th St., 212/245-0072, contains what its moniker suggests—planes and rockets and weaponry—but it's all inside an aircraft carrier.

The Lower East Side Tenement Museum, 90 Orchard St. near Allen St., 212/431-0233, www.tenement.org, offers a slice of nineteenth-century New York life with walking tours and hands-on exhibits.

The Abigail Adams Smith Museum, 421 E. 61st St. near First Ave., 212/838-6878, is an intimate little place that promises personal guided tours showing life in New York circa 1800. This area used to be far in the country, and people would come to a place like this for a breath of fresh air.

The African American Wax Museum, 316 W. 115th St. near Frederick Douglass Blvd., 212/678-7818, is as if Madame Tussaud's had come to Harlem, with likenesses of Booker T. Washington, Martin Luther King Jr., Duke Ellington, and others. Visit by appointment only.

The National Museum of Lesbian and Gay History, 1 Little W. 12th St. near Greenwich St. in the Village, 212/620-7310, is full of gay-themed art and photography.

Listen and watch programs that cover 70 years of media history at the **Museum of Television & Radio,** 25 W. 52nd St. near Fifth Ave., 212/621-6600.

mahogany staircase and floors of yellow limestone. Now it comes furnished with Victorian sleighbeds.

Sculptor James Knowles owns the **Roger Smith,** Lexington Ave. and E. 47th St., 212/755-1400, $$$, which features a gallery with changing art exhibits. Rooms have features such as two-line phones, voice mail, and dataports.

And we'll always have Paris . . . er, New York, at the **Casablanca Hotel,** 147 W. 43rd St. near Broadway, 888/922-7225, $$$, which sports Moroccan-style decor and a rooftop garden. You also get free continental breakfast, evening wine, on-line concierge service, and a VCR with videos that will be perfect for looking at you, kid—plus a cybercafé and a complimentary membership at a nearby fitness center.

At the top of the list, think about the opulent **Sherry Netherland,** 718 Fifth Ave. at 59th St., 212/355-2800, $$$$, which overlooks Central Park. This 1927 classic has long been a favorite of Hollywood moguls. You're free to borrow classic movies and best-selling books for snuggling in your high-ceiling room.

And then there's the hotel-as-art, **The Paramount,** 235 W. 46th St. near Broadway, 212/764-5500, $$$. It's way cool, stylish, sleek, dramatic—all done by Philippe Starck. How about a Vermeer print on your headboard? You'll also get your own VCR and fresh flowers in your room. The Paramount has a fitness center and a business center. Its Whiskey Bar is popular.

The budget-minded might try the **Pickwick Arms,** 230 E. 51st St., 800/PICKWIK, $. For single rooms as low as $60 you get room service, air-conditioning, and two restaurants. For other budget rooms, call 800/96-HOTEL.

DINING

Nowhere does the ethnic stew work better than in the city's restaurants, where all those cultures add their special spices to the pot. With 17,000 restaurants in the city, surely you can find something to your liking. Competition to keep up with the fads is fierce. What's hot today is hash tomorrow. Or maybe it's become a classic.

There's help out there. Can't decide what's good on a Moroccan menu? And what about those Korean desserts? **Posh Nosh,** 212/838-4740, www.poshnosh.com, will take you on an eating tour and explain it all. "I'm out there almost every day, tasting," says the owner, Mary Ann Zimmerman. Tough life.

Going Places

Most people need a little help when they try to take in such a big place. Following are some suggestions out of dozens that are available. **Harlem Spirituals,** 690 Eighth Ave., 212/391-0900, www.harlemspirituals.com, helps you feel the spirit of Harlem with tours that feature gospel concerts, the Apollo Theatre, soul food, and jazz. One neat way to see the city is from the water. **Circle Line,** 212/563-3200, sails year-round, with evening cruises and speedboat rides. Another option is to see all of the island on a **Gray Line** double-decker bus, 212/397-2600. Tours start every 15 minutes in peak season. Hop on, hop off. Do the wheel thing with **Central Park Bicycle Tours/Rentals,** 2 Columbus Circle, 212/541-8759, www.nyctourist.com/ad_biketour.htm. Or how about in-line skating? Call **New York Skateout,** 212/486-1919. Opera buffs can get their fix through **Gilded Age Opera Tours,** 800/737-9854. And ladies who lunch should join the **New York Experience,** 212/370-4868, for a day of high tea, gallery-hopping, and boutique shopping.

New York City skyline

If you want to play it safe with good old American cuisine, **Tavern on the Green,** Central Park West at 67th St., 212/873-3200, $$$, still rides the top of the charts. Mustard-glazed salmon, sautéed sweetbreads, and roasted rack of lamb are some of the specialties. Book way in advance.

Other classic places that will be as here tomorrow as they are today are the **21 Club,** 21 W. 52nd St. near Broadway, 212/582-7200, $$$, a former speakeasy where the power brokers do lunch. Count on a peak experience at the **Rainbow Room,** 30 Rockefeller Plaza near Fifth Ave., 212/632-5000, $$$. And the view of views is from **Windows on the World,** 1 World Trade Center, 212/524-7011, $$$. It offers new interpretations of American classics, with a renowned wine cellar (this high up?).

So where are the celebrities noshing? **Limoncello,** 777 Seventh Ave. near Broadway, 212/582-7932, $$$, a classical Italian restaurant in the Michelangelo Hotel that is winning raves from the critics. It serves standard Italian fare with flair.

Freshness of ingredients is a big deal at **Jean Georges,** 1 Central Park West at 61st St., 212/299-3900, $$$, and at its adjoining café, **Nougatine.** They've hired a botanist to hunt down wild herbs for dishes such as poached filet of turbot with a sauce of caramel, walnuts, lemons, and figs, and pheasant soup spiked with pomegranate seeds and pistachios.

Fido, 1608 Third Ave., 212/423-0654, $$, is a Middle Eastern restaurant in the Village that has nothing to do with dogs. It's pronounced *feedo.* Get the falafel.

A hip place in the East Village is **Chez Ses Saada,** 42 E. First St. near Second Ave., 212/777-5617, $$, a Moroccan restaurant. The bar is on the first left; the restaurant is below and is reached by a rose-petal winding staircase.

Manhattan cab drivers seem to like the **Afghan Kebab House,**

1345 Second Ave. near E. 71st St., 212/517-2776, $. You'll get lots of spicy kebabs and rice for your money.

If you want to have what she's having, you can get it at **Katz's Delicatessen,** 205 E. Houston St. near Orchard St., 212/254-2246, $. This is the restaurant that was made moaningly famous by the movie *When Harry Met Sally.* (And what *was* she having? Pastrami on rye.)

And finally, how about the ultimate in ethnic dining—Martian. You can transcend time and space at **Mars 2112,** 51st St. and Broadway, 212/582-2112, $$, where you can fantasize about exploring the mysterious Mars landscape or taste its super-exotic food (solar system fusion), sip a Martian brew, and even do a little Martian shopping. They take you to your seat on an "aircraft" after a stop-off at the Mars Bar.

How about dessert? Try **Payard Patisserie & Bistro,** 1032 Lexington Ave. at E. 74th St., 212/717-5252, $$, for the chocolate and caramel mousse. Eat in or take out.

SHOPPING

So, you want to shop till you drop. In New York, that's easy. Start downtown in **South Street Seaport's mall**, 12 Fulton St., 212/748-8600, and the **Fulton Market,** Water St. to the Hudson River, 212/SEA-PORT, which feature big chain stores, unique boutiques, and antique shops. These two shopping areas are at the south end of Manhattan Island near the Brooklyn Bridge.

Then it's on to **SoHo,** where you'll find cutting-edge art and clothes to match, plus some of the city's most popular flea markets, such as the one on Sixth Avenue at MacDougal. The area is bounded by Houston, Lafayette, and Canal Streets. The radically chic will want to browse through the **East Village** between Houston and 14th Streets, where funk reigns supreme.

Now it's on to **Chinatown,** which spans from Canal Street to Mott Street and is home of silks and ceramics. **Orchard Street,** in the Lower East Side south of Houston, is one big designer outlet. Move on to Broadway and the **Canal Jean Co.,** 504 Broadway, 212/226-1130, for the brand called Authentic New York.

Chelsea, roughly from 14th Street to 23rd Street, is where you'll find that center of discounted high style, **Loehmann's,** 101 Seventh Ave., 212/352-0856, and lots of other national-brand emporiums. Stop by the **Chelsea Market,** W. 15th St. between 9th and 10th Aves., 212/243-6005, a complex of 20 shops. You can get anything and everything related to food, from cookies to lobster to kitchen supplies.

Also of note is **Macy's at Herald Square,** W. 34th St. between Sixth and Seventh Aves., 212/695-4400, and the nearby **Manhattan Mall,** 34th St. and Sixth Ave., 212/465-0500. The latter used to be Gimbel's, Macy's famous rival. Oh, and don't forget **Fifth Avenue,** with **Saks** (at 50th St., 212/753-4000), **Lord & Taylor** (at 39th St.,

There is nothing more thrilling than New York at Christmas. The festivities begin with the famed **Macy's Thanksgiving Day Parade** and include the must-see *Holiday Spectacular* at Radio City Music Hall, an over-the-top rendition of the holiday featuring ice skating, dancing Santas, and live camels for the manger scene. Then there's the traditional lighting of the huge Christmas tree at Rockefeller Center and the annual performance of *The Nutcracker* by the New York City Ballet at Lincoln Center.

You just can't miss seeing the Baroque Neapolitan crèche and the candle-lit eighteenth-century Christmas tree at the Metropolitan Museum of Art. And stores go all-out to make their windows really show off their wares at this time of year. But call way ahead. Hotels fill up fast and so do Broadway shows. For peak-season hotel reservations, call the New York Convention & Visitors Bureau, 800/846-ROOM.

new york
HOLIDAY

212/391-3344), **Henri Bendel** (at 56th St., 212/247-1100), and, of course, glittering **Tiffany & Co.** (at 56th St., 212/755-8000), and the kid-conscious **FAO Schwarz** (at 58th St., 212/644-9410).

Bloomingdale's, Lexington Ave. at E. 59th St., 212/705-2000, remains the center of New York fashion and flair, and there are loads of upscale stores along nearby **Madison Avenue.** And not to be forgotten are the museum stores. The **Design Shop,** 11 W. 53rd St. near Fifth Ave., 212/708-9400, at the Museum of Modern Art is a prime source for posters, art books, and imaginative jewelry.

Finally, for the finest in understated elegance, you must stroll through **Takashimaya,** 693 Fifth Ave. near W. 54th St., 212/350-0100. This Japan-based store is simply dripping with cashmere and hand-painted silk scarves. It also offers difficult-to-find scents, baskets, china, vases, lamps, and, in the lobby, flowers and garden items from Paris florist Christian Tortu. Buy something here—you'll get to take it home in a three-cornered, yarn-handled bag.

SPORTS AND RECREATION

For those who'd rather do than see, roll into **NY Skateout,** 212/486-1919, www.nyskate.com, for in-line skating instruction and year-round tours. Joggers might want to check out **New York Road Runners Club,** 9 E. 89th St., 212/860-4455, the people who organize the New York Marathon. You can also go bowling at the newly renovated, 42-lane **Bowlmor Lanes,** 110 University Pl., 212/255-8188.

For spectator sports, New York has it all. The thoroughbreds are racing at **Aqueduct Racetrack** in Queens, 718/641-4700, from October to May. The **New York Knicks** (NBA), 212/465-6741, the **Rangers** (NHL), 212/465-6741, and the **Liberty** (WNBA), 212/465-6741, play at two-block-long Madison Square Garden, 4 Pennsylvania Plaza (Seventh Ave. and W. 37th St.).

You don't want to miss seeing the **New York Yankees,** 718/293-6000, www.yankees.com, major league baseball team play at Yankee Stadium, 161st St. at River Ave., Bronx. The **New York Mets,** 718/507-TIXX, www.mets.com, play at Shea Stadium, 126th St. at Roosevelt Ave., Queens. And you can watch the **New York Jets,** 201/507-8900, and **New York Giants** (NFL) play at Giants Stadium, 201/935-8222, in East Rutherford, New Jersey.

ENTERTAINMENT

If you've got plenty of money and all night to party, this is your kinda town. Most of the dance clubs don't really get warmed up until midnight, and cover charges range from $10 to $20.

Relive your youth and dance the night away at **Decade,** 1117 First Ave. near E. 61st St., 212/835-5979, where classic hits from the '70s, '80s, and '90s (yes, the '90s; it doesn't take long these days for a song to become a classic) draw droves of attractive over-30 singles.

Go back to the glory days of cabaret at the glamorous **Supper Club,** 240 W. 47th St. near Broadway, 212/921-1940, a swanky cocktail lounge with a continental menu and dancing to 1940s-style big bands.

It might be hard to eat and laugh at the same time, but why not try it? **Carolines Comedy Nation Comedy Club and Restaurant,** 1626 Broadway between W. 49th and W. 50th Sts., 212/757-4100, the stand-up comedy club that helped launch Jerry Seinfeld, Jay Leno, and Rosie O'Donnell, serves eats and laughs. Also worth a visit is **Duplex Cabaret & Piano Bar,** 61 Christopher St. near Seventh Ave., 212/255-5438, where female impersonators camp it up.

Jazz and more jazz are available at the **Blue Note,** 131 W. Third St. near Avenue of the Americas, 212/475-8592, and **Sweet Basil,** 88 Seventh Ave. near W. 15th St., 212/242-1785. Both are intimate Greenwich Village clubs that have hosted such greats as Dizzy Gillespie and B.B. King. The Blue Note serves a mean Sunday brunch, and Sweet Basil serves jazz every day of the year, says the manager. You can also find jazz in the theater district at **Birdland,** 315 W. 44th St. near Eighth Ave., 212/581-3080. It also offers Southern American cuisine like catfish and fried chicken.

The Big Apple even has country music. You can also get free dance lessons every night at **Denim & Diamonds,** 511 Lexington Ave. near E. 48th St., 212/371-1600.

It's always Carnival at **S.O.B.'s,** 204 Varick St. at W. Houston St.,

Dragon parades, fireworks, and great food mark the **Chinese New Year** on Mott Street in Chinatown. It's held the first full moon between January 21 and February 19.

The **Empire State Building Run-Up** is held in early February, during which runners move up the 1,575 steps to the 86th floor. The best time is something around 12 minutes. Gasp!

All those 140 ethnic varieties mentioned at the beginning of the chapter become Irish for the **St. Patrick's Day Parade**, which is held March 17. The parade begins at 11 a.m. at Fifth Avenue and 44th Street, and it proceeds up to 86th Street. Also in the same general location is the **Columbus Day Parade**, which is held on October 10 each year.

You'll hear **Mostly Mozart** at the same-named festival at Avery Fisher Hall in Lincoln Center, Broadway and W. 65th St., 212/875-5030. The event is held in July and August. And come back to the same place for the **Messiah Sing-in**, which is usually held a week before Christmas. Everybody in the hall (3,000 people) gets to sing Hallelujah!

events
HORIZON

212/243-4940, where Latin, African, reggae, and world beat music are king. The restaurant features Caribbean food.

The famed **Radio City Music Hall,** 1260 Sixth Ave. at W. 50th St., 212/632-4000, is undergoing a $30 million restoration. But don't worry—it's the infrastructure that's getting the redo, not the fabled entertainment palace's art deco look. The marquee has six miles of new neon tubing, the stage has gotten a new hydraulic system (remember, there are a lot of Rockettes that need lifting), and the 144-foot-wide stage has a new gold curtain with fiberoptic lighting embedded in it.

For the fine arts, check out the schedule at **Lincoln Center,** W. 64th St. at Broadway, 212/LINCOLN, where the Metropolitan Opera and New York City Ballet perform. Also find out what's happening at the **Alvin Ailey American Dance Theater** (211 W. 61st St. near Amsterdam Ave., 212/767-0590), the **Apollo Theatre** (253 W. 125th St. near Frederick Douglass Blvd., 212/864-0372), and **Carnegie Hall** (154 W. 57th St. near Seventh Ave., 212/247-7800).

Seeing New York in a few days is going to wear you out. You can get back in the swing of things with the help of a licensed masseuse through **Back to Basics Massage Ltd.,** 315 W. 57th St., Suite 209, 212/974-0988. They'll come to your hotel, or you can drop by their midtown office.

Or how about West meeting East at the **Kozue Aesthetic Spa,** 705 Madison Ave., 212/724-8600? This Japanese day spa offers body treatments, massage, makeup, nail care, waxing, oxygen therapy, and Ki therapy.

CITY BASICS

The **New York Convention & Visitors Bureau,** 810 Seventh Ave. at 53rd St., 212/484-1222, www.nycvisit.com, will provide maps and any other information you may need for your visit. For problems with your airline tickets, contact the **airline ticket office,** 100 E. 42nd St. at Park Ave., 212/986-0888. Search around **www.citysearch.com** for updated info on restaurants, shopping, hotels, and entertainment. For a list of New York–related Web sites, try www.nycmaiug.org/newyork.htm.

City Lights, 212/737-7049, and **Abode Bed and Breakfast,** 212/472-2000, are central booking companies for bed-and-breakfasts in the city. (B&Bs charge only the New York City sales tax of 8.25 percent, not the full hotel tax of 15.25 percent.) You can also get any hotel room through **Room Finders,** 800/473-STAY, www.roomfinders.com.

The disabled can get toll-free access information though **Hospital Audiences,** 888/424-4685. A guide to cultural sites, *Access for All,* is $5. Gay visitors can get help, information, and advice from the **Gay Switchboard,** 212/989-0999.

You can save 50 percent and avoid ticket lines with the **CityPass** booklet, 707/256-0490, www.citypass.net, which includes admission to the Metropolitan Museum of Art, the Empire State Building Observatories, the Museum of Modern Art, the American Museum of Natural History, the *Intrepid* Sea-Air-Space Museum, and the Top of the World Trade Center. The booklet is good for nine days and can be purchased at the attractions listed. The price for adults is $26.75; for youths (13–17), $21.00; and for seniors, $18.00.

Discount tickets for Broadway performances are available the day of the show at the **TKTS** booth at West 47th Street and Broadway. They only take cash; prepare for long lines. Another outlet at the World Trade Center usually has shorter lines.

Try **Theatre Direct,** www.theatredirect.com, for the latest theater information. And don't forget the ticket brokers such as **Edwards & Edwards** (800/223-6108), **New York Concierge** (888/NY-SHOWS), and **Actors' Fund of America,** 212/221-7300.

Media outlets where you can find entertainment listings include *The New York Times,* the *New York Post,* the *Daily News,* the *Village Voice,* the *New York Free Press,* and *Where New York.* The **Official NYC Guide,** 212/484-1200, provides an events calendar; information on hotels, restaurants, and attractions; discounts offers; and a pullout map. The *City Guide* offers extensive Broadway and off-Broadway coverage, with expanded coverage of the Harlem area.

Outer boroughs information:

Brooklyn, www.brooklynx.org or www.brooklynchamber.com
Bronx, www.nypl.org/branch/bronx/bronxweb.html
Queens, www.queens.nyc.ny.us
Staten Island, www.si-web.com

*We must, indeed, all hang together,
or most assuredly we shall all hang separately.*
—Benjamin Franklin, before signing the
Declaration of Independence, 1776

Yo!
—Rocky Balboa

And that, friends, is Philadelphia—patriotism and cheesesteak, in equal abundance.

In fact, there's no reason why you can't gaze on the Liberty Bell and munch on a mustard-dipped pretzel at the same time. It's called "the pursuit of happiness," and there's lots of it to pursue here in the City of Brotherly Love.

The ghosts of history are alive and well and walking on the cobblestones. Art is everywhere. Commerce is thriving. Neighborhoods of particular ethnic pungency aren't melting in the melting pot, but helping instead to keep America's immigrant past alive.

Aren't all these things America? Isn't this what our forepersons had in mind—a place of egalitarianism, consisting of an unstuffy, non-British reverence for the past and a preponderance of good cheer?

We think so. Welcome to America's most American city. Yo!

Downtown Philadelphia

SIGHTS AND ATTRACTIONS

1 Academy of Natural Sciences Museum
2 African American Museum in Philadelphia
3 Carpenter's Hall
4 Christ Church
5 City Hall
6 City Tavern
7 Congress Hall
7 Independence Hall
8 Independence National Historic Park
9 Liberty Bell Pavilion
10 Mantua Maker's Museum House
11 National Museum of American Jewish History
12 Penn's Landing
13 Philadelphia Doll

14 Museum Physick House
15 Quaker Information Center
16 Reading Terminal Market
17 Visitors Center

DINING

18 Brasserie Perrier
19 City Tavern
20 Famous 4th Street Delicatessen
16 Fisher's
21 Le Bec-Fin
16 Salumeria
21 Striped Bass
21 Susanna Foo Restaurant and Bar

Delaware River

Penn's Landing

Independence National Historic Park

Washington Square

GETTING AROUND

Philadelphia, which is 100 miles south of New York and 55 miles west of the Atlantic Ocean, is the second largest city on the East Coast and the fifth largest in the nation. Its metropolitan area population is 5.8 million.

After you've arrived at **Philadelphia International Airport,** 800/PHL-GATE, www.phl.org, which is about eight miles from Center City (that's what locals call downtown), you can take the **SEPTA** (Southeastern Pennsylvania Transportation Authority) **Airport Rail Line** to Center City, 16th St. and John F. Kennedy Blvd. (Visitors Center), 215/937-6800 (Airport Line), 215/580-7800 (buses and subways). The train runs every half hour from 5:30 a.m. to 11:25 p.m. Cost is $5 and trip time is 25 minutes. One-way cab fare from the airport to downtown is about $20 with **City Cab Co.,** 215/238-5000. And there are several airport shuttles. Try **SuperShuttle,** 800/246-0770. You don't want to get in a car and compete with 5.8 million people for a parking space. Forget the car.

Almost everything that's important in Philadelphia is concentrated in Center City. It's an area bounded by the Delaware River on the east and the Schuylkill (SKOO-kul) River on the west. Vine Street is the northern border, and South Street is the southern border. And almost all of the area within Center City is laid out on a perfect grid. Market Street is the main east-west street bisecting the area, and Broad Street is the north-south dividing line. The two streets meet in the middle at City Hall.

Two **subway lines**—the Market-Frankford (east-west) Line and the Broad Street (north-south) Line crisscross the city. Cash fare on most routes is $1.60 (exact change required). What makes sense is SEPTA's **Day Pass,** which provides one day of unlimited transportation on all city transit vehicles, plus a one-way trip on the Airport Line. It's $5 and can be purchased at the Visitors Center. Specific travel instructions are available from SEPTA.

Crime has been falling in Philadelphia as it has in all the big cities, but that doesn't mean you shouldn't be careful, especially on the subway and in blighted areas. (The North Philadelphia Station in particular should be avoided at all times.) Don't take the subway late at night. Get a cab.

Probably the best way to get around Center City is on the **Phlash Downtown Tourist Loop** shuttle bus service, 215/4-PHLASH or 800/4-PHLASH. The buses (they're purple) run in a continuous loop from Logan Circle through Center City to the waterfront and South Street. You can ride one-way for $1.50 or all day for $3.

The **RiverLink Ferry,** 215/925-LINK, departs hourly at Penn's Landing near Walnut Street. This is a good way to see some New Jersey sights. For $5 round-trip, it will take you across the Delaware River to Camden and the New Jersey Aquarium.

Going Places

You can get the lay of the land and maybe even learn something through one of the many tours offered in the city.

Philadelphia Trolley Works, 215/925-TOUR, will take you on a 90-minute, fully narrated tour of Center City. There are 20 stops with the all-day pass, which includes on-off privileges, and they'll pick you up at your hotel. **Philadelphia On Foot**, 800/340-9869, will show you the Colonial era with tours such as "Ben Franklin's Philadelphia." See the sights from the Delaware River on a paddle-wheel riverboat with **Liberty Belle Cruises**, Penn's Landing, 333 N. Front St., 215/629-1131. Lunch and dinner cruises are available. Or see it all from a horse-drawn carriage with the **Philadelphia Carriage Co.**, 215/922-6840.

With **Nubian Tours & Travel**, 215/879-7777, you can trace African American history in Philadelphia from the Revolutionary War through the Civil Rights struggles of the 1960s. You'll learn the roots and legends of Italian cooking on the **Chef's Tour of the Italian Market**, 215/772-0739. Reservations are necessary. And the **Foundation for Architecture**, 215/569-3187, offers 42 architectural tours of the city and its neighborhoods, including City Hall tower.

SIGHTS AND ATTRACTIONS

America's most historic square mile is the **Independence National Historic Park.** There reside two of the nation's most important monuments to freedom—the Liberty Bell and Independence Hall, where the Declaration of Independence was adopted on July 4, 1776, and where 55 delegates developed the U.S. Constitution in 1787. Start your visit at the **Visitors Center,** Third and Chestnut Sts., 215/597-8974, where a short documentary film by John Huston will get you in the patriotic spirit. You can get maps and other material to help you through the park. Everything is in walking distance.

The **Liberty Bell Pavilion** is on Market Street between Fourth and Fifth Streets, and **Independence Hall** is across an expanse of lawn on Chestnut Street, a block over, between Fifth and Sixth Streets. You can get free tickets for the ranger-led tour adjacent to the hall. These are good for the same day only, set for a specific time. Get there a few minutes early.

Close by, on Chestnut Street are **Congress Hall** (between Fifth and Sixth Sts.), where the U.S. Senate and House met from 1790 to 1800, and **Carpenter's Hall** (between Third and Fourth Sts.), where the First Continental Congress met in 1774. Nearby is the **City Tavern,** 138 S. Second St., 215/413-1443, a reconstructed tavern where meals and ales were served as the nation was born. Also, you should stop by **Christ Church,** Church St. between Second and Third Sts., an active Episcopal church since 1695. This is where Ben Franklin, George Washington, and Betsy Ross worshipped. Old Ben is buried in the church cemetery nearby; tradition says you'll have good luck if you throw a penny on his grave.

Elfreth's Alley is the oldest continuously occupied residential street in the nation, historians say. The streetscape holds 33 Colonial- and Federal-style homes, and No. 126 is the **Mantua Maker's Museum House,** 215/574-0560, which once belonged to eighteenth-century dressmakers.

Penn's Landing, east of Columbus Blvd. between Market and South Sts., 215/923-8181, is Philadelphia's waterfront park where more than 70 events take place from May to September. Nearby are several ships that have been converted into museums.

A townhouse built in 1786, the **Physick House,** 321 S. Fourth St., 215/925-7866, was home to the father of American surgery, Dr. Philip Syng Physick and contains a nineteenth-century garden, eighteenth- and early nineteenth–century furniture, silver and porcelain.

City Hall, Broad and Market Sts., 215/686-2840, is in the middle of everything. Its tower is 548 feet tall, topped by a 37-foot bronze statue of William Penn. Visitors can go to the top of the tower, where the view is gorgeous.

The **National Museum of American Jewish History,** 55 N. Fifth St., 215/923-3811, is dedicated to documenting the American Jewish experience. The museum tells the history of Jews in America from 1654 to the present. Nearby is the **African American Museum in Philadelphia,** 701 Arch St., 215/574-0380, which was established during the Bicentennial in 1976. It contains four galleries for comprehensive art exhibits and presentations, which have included such topics as early African American life in Philadelphia and black women sculptors.

Ben Franklin Parkway is Philadelphia's Champs-Elysees, a grand boulevard along which are some fine buildings and major museums—the greatest being the **Philadelphia Museum of Art,** 26th St. at Ben Franklin Pkwy., 215/763-8100, a grand, classic Greco-Roman building on a hill. (Its steps are the ones that Rocky climbed in the movie.) Inside is a world-class collection of art spanning 2,000 years. Nearby is the **Rodin Museum,** 22nd St. at Ben Franklin Pkwy., 215/763-8100, containing the largest collection of Rodin sculptures outside of Paris.

Don't neglect the **Academy of Natural Sciences Museum,** 1900 Ben Franklin Pkwy., 215/299-1000. Founded in 1812, it's the oldest science research institute in the Western Hemisphere. If you're big on dinosaurs, this is the place for you. Also of note are the dolls from around the world that fill the **Philadelphia Doll Museum,** 12253 Broad St., 215/787-0220, including more than 300 black dolls chronicling the story of how black people have been perceived throughout world history.

At the **Quaker Information Center,** 1501 Cherry St., 215/241-7024, you can see a meetinghouse built in 1856 and get information on Quaker history and beliefs.

Kooky Collections

Edgar "Painless" Parker was a nineteenth-century dentist who collected thousands of teeth he pulled, and they're now part of the display at **Temple University's Dental Museum**, Broad St. and Allegheny Ave., 215/707-2816, along with antique dental instruments.

See the tumor removed from President Cleveland's jaw, the death cast of Siamese twins, and a vast collection of skeletons and skulls at the **Mutter Museum**, 19 S. 22nd St., 215/563-3737, ext. 242.

View the most complete (and maybe only) collection of garbage disposals in America at **Dave's Electric**, 2745 Kensington Ave. near Lehigh, 215/423-1027.

Find out all you've ever wanted to know about the history of pretzels at **PretzCo Soft Pretzel Bakery & Museum**, 211 North Third St., 215/413-3010.

The Shoe Museum contains a collection of more than 500 types of footwear, including Eskimo snowshoes and burial sandals. It's at the Pennsylvania College of Podiatric Medicine, Eighth and Race Sts., 215/629-0300.

The Mario Lanza Museum—at the Settlement Music School, 416 Queen St., 215/468-3623—has a collection of records, tapes, statues, and other documentation tracing the life of the famed opera singer.

And if you missed the Mummers Parade, you can still see the collection of outlandishly colored, feathered, and sequined costumes that are the highlight of the annual New Year's Day event. Visit the **Mummers Museum**, Second St. and Washington Ave., 215/336-3050.

Fairmount Park—with 8,900 acres of gardens, meadows, and jogging trails—is one of the nation's largest landscaped city parks. Located on the banks of Schuylkill River between Ford Road, Lehigh Avenue, I-13, U.S. 676, and Lancaster Avenue, it contains the finest group of authentic early American houses in the nation. One of those houses is **Lemon Hill**, 215/232-4337, an eighteenth-century, Federal-style mansion noted for its unusual oval rooms with curved doors and fireplaces. It's on the east side of the park on Poplar Drive.

The **Philadelphia Zoo,** 34th St. and Girard Ave., W. Fairmount Park, 215/243-1100, which opened in 1874, is America's oldest. At least 1,700 animals from around the world live in natural habitats here. The zoo is set in a 42-acre Victorian garden, and some of its trees date from the eighteenth century.

You could classify the **Italian Market,** Ninth St. between Christian and Wharton Sts., under Dining and Shopping, but the overall effect merits its mention as an Attraction. It is an open-air market where you can buy fresh fruits and vegetables from pushcarts. Stores offer hand-made sausages, suckling pigs, homemade pasta, cheeses, bread and pastries, and gourmet coffees and teas. You'll also find cookware, handbags, flowers, and kitchen gadgets. Restaurants and luncheonettes abound, offering the famous South Philly cheesesteak sandwiches.

Similarly, you can watch the butchers and fishmongers at work at the **Reading Terminal Market,** 12th and Arch Sts., which has been an institution since 1893. Get a home-cooked lunch that might include local favorites such as snapper soup, cheesesteak, pretzels, and Bassett's ice cream.

Seven miles northwest of Center City is Manayunk, a historic district that has become Philadelphia's hottest neighborhood. Most of the action is on Main Street, where dozens of restaurants and boutiques are situated. Nearby is the **Morris Arboretum,** 100 Northwestern Ave., 215/247-5777, of the University of Pennsylvania, a 92-acre public garden that includes roses, a swan pond, meadows, and woodlands. It's landscaped in a Victorian style and listed on the National Register of Historic Places.

Finally, you've simply got to see the collection of modern art at the **Barnes Foundation,** 300 N. Latches Ln., in the suburb of Merion, 610/667-0290—200 Renoirs, 65 Matisses, 100 Cézannes, and 35 early Picassos hung eccentrically between tools and whatnot in the Barnes mansion, preserved just as Alfred Coombes Barnes demanded in his will.

LODGING

A hotel anywhere in Center City will put you within walking distance of all the best places. Philadelphia is generally light on the number of hotel rooms, which means you'll have a tough time during big events such as the Army-Navy game or the July 4 festivities. Reserve early. For help with accommodations, contact the **Greater Philadelphia Hotel Association,** 215/557-1900. Likewise, **Bed and Breakfast Connections—Philadelphia,** 800/448-3619, can find you a room among more than 100 B&Bs and inns.

One of the newest hotels in town has gone green. The **Sheraton Rittenhouse Square Hotel,** Locust and 18th Sts., 800/325-3535, $$$, stresses its environmental friendliness with a 40-foot-high bamboo garden to oxygenate the air in the lobby and furniture made of recycled material. Each room has high-speed Internet access. The hotel has four non-smoking restaurants.

Penn's View Hotel, Front and Market Sts., 800/331-7634, $$$, is a historic European-style hotel that overlooks the Delaware River. Some rooms have fireplaces and jetted tubs. Its Ristorante Panorama

Philadelphia Region

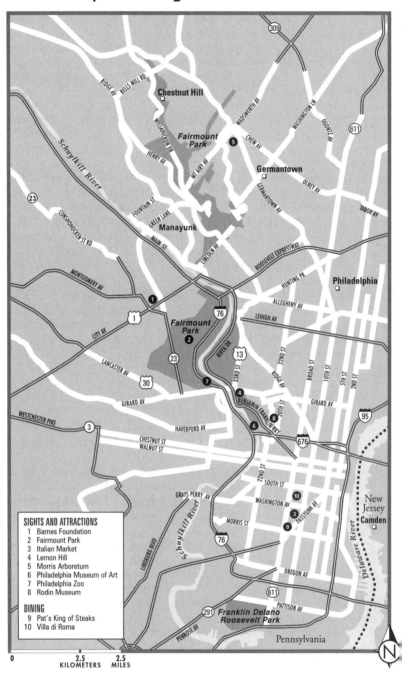

Chestnut Hill

Fairmount Park

Germantown

Manayunk

Philadelphia

Fairmount Park

New Jersey

Camden

SIGHTS AND ATTRACTIONS
1 Barnes Foundation
2 Fairmount Park
3 Italian Market
4 Lemon Hill
5 Morris Arboretum
6 Philadelphia Museum of Art
7 Philadelphia Zoo
8 Rodin Museum

DINING
9 Pat's King of Steaks
10 Villa di Roma

Franklin Delano Roosevelt Park

Pennsylvania

Delaware River

Schuylkill River

0   2.5   2.5
    KILOMETERS   MILES

N

serves contemporary Italian cuisine. Free continental breakfast is included as part of the accommodations.

The **Society Hill Hotel,** 301 Chestnut St., 215/925-1919, $$, was built in 1832 and offers 12 rooms with brass beds, flowers, and a continental breakfast served in your room. The **Shippen Way Inn,** 416–18 Bainbridge St., 800/245-4873, $$, is even older—it was built in about 1750—and offers nine rooms with private baths. It has a colonial garden; the reception room has a fireplace. Breakfast, afternoon tea, and wine and cheese are included.

The **Thomas Bond House,** 129 S. Second St., 800/845-BOND, $$, the former residence of a prominent eighteenth-century Philadelphia physician, is located within Independence National Historic Park and is a historical landmark. The circa-1769 house has 12 rooms with private baths, plus free breakfast and free evening wine and cheese. Another hotel that is a historic landmark is **Independence Park Inn,** 235 Chestnut St., 800/624-2988, $$. It has 36 rooms in a Victorian building. Breakfast is included.

The **Park Hyatt Philadelphia at the Bellevue,** Broad and Walnut Sts., 800/233-1234, $$$, has been around for almost a century and is one of the most elegant hotels in town. Lavish public areas include a seven-story atrium. The Founders restaurant has marvelous views from 19 stories up. Also consider **The Latham** near Rittenhouse Square, 135 S. 17th St., 800/LATHAM-1, $$$, one of the finest European-style hotels in town. The rooms have Louis XV desks and marble-top bureaus, and a concierge is on duty daily.

If you're interested in a B&B, **Antique Row Bed and Breakfast,** 341 S. 12th St., 215/592-7802, $$, is situated in a 180-year-old townhouse on a tree-lined street off historic Antique Row. It has cable TV.

DINING

Condé Nast Traveler readers say Philly is the top restaurant city in the country. The center of fine dining is the Rittenhouse Row area, which is on Walnut Street from Broad through 17th Streets. Manayunk, a neighborhood seven miles northwest of Center City, is another hot area for upscale dining. Chinatown—which is bounded by 9th and 11th Streets, and Vine and Arch Streets—is another area worth exploring. And you can't go wrong wandering through the Reading Terminal and Italian Markets. This is where Philly is at its home-style best.

City Tavern, 138 S. Second St., 215/413-1443, $$, brings the eighteenth century to life with a re-creation of a 1773 tavern. The staff looks authentic, the music is pure harpsichord, and the food comes right out of the history books—Martha Washington's turkey stew, for instance, which can be washed down with a tankard of ale.

Everybody talks about **Le Bec-Fin,** 1523 Walnut St., 215/567-1000, $$$$, all of it in raves. Some say it's the best restaurant in the

United States. A prix-fixe dinner of an appetizer, fish course, entrée, cheese or salad, and unbelievable dessert cart will cost you more than $100 per person. (The famous pressed lobster is $27 extra.) For the meal of a lifetime, you'll eat in elegant surroundings with classical guitar music in the background. Reservations for a Saturday night will need to be made two months or so in advance. Jacket and tie are required.

Le Bec-Fin's founder also has a less formal version of his famous French restaurant. **Brasserie Perrier,** 1619 Walnut St., 215/568-3000, $$$, is a high-energy place for contemporary cuisine, such as salmon in pastry with lime sauce.

Another restaurant that is making waves in Philly is the **Striped Bass Restaurant and Bar,** 1500 Walnut St., 215/732-4444, $$$. It's in a former brokerage house with 28-foot ceilings, massive columns, and a huge sculpture of—guess what?—a striped bass. What to order? How about the striped bass. It comes with ruby chard, porcini, and sage.

Susanna Foo, 1512 Walnut St., 215/545-2666, $$$, is the name of the restaurant and its award-winning chef. The restaurant specializes in Chinese food updated with modern techniques. Mongolian lamb is a favorite, as is the Sunday dim sum brunch. Jackets are required. Reservations are essential.

You can't say you've been to Philly if you don't try a genuine Philly cheesesteak sandwich, and **Pat's King of Steaks,** 1237 E. Passyunk Ave. at Ninth and Wharton Sts., 215/468-1546, $, serves the ultimate. On a roll are shaved slices of beef, grilled onions, and your choice of cheese. You'll want some greasy fries with that, also topped with a heap o' melted cheese. Pat's doesn't take credit cards; it's open around the clock.

In the heart of the Italian Market area is **Villa di Roma,** 936 S. Ninth St., 215/592-1295, $, a classic Philly place that serves up some basic southern Italian cooking. For dessert, get the *tartufo,* a ball of chocolate ice cream dipped in cocoa. No credit cards are accepted.

The **Famous 4th Street Delicatessen,** 700 S. Fourth St., 215/922-3274, $, which was established in 1923, is a Philly landmark. Its specialties are corned beef, roast beef, and award-winning chocolate chip cookies.

At the Reading Terminal Market at 12th and Arch Streets, you've got to try these Philly specials: **Fisher's,** 215/592-8510, $, serves wonderful soft pretzels, which are brushed with butter as they emerge from the oven. And at **Salumeria,** 215/592-8150, $, the hoagie sandwich is raised to a whole new level with such ingredients as roasted pimientos. No credit cards are accepted.

SHOPPING

Wednesday evening is "Make It a Night" in Philadelphia, when many stores stay open late and feature special discounts on shopping, dining,

The City of Brotherly Love's LOVE sculpture, by Robert Indiana

and parking. On the first Friday of each month, art galleries stay open for special exhibits and events.

Jeweler's Row, 700 block of Sansom St., contains more than 350 jewelry-related businesses. Some of the companies have been owned by the same families for five generations. Also, a city with this much history is bound to have some of it for sale, and sure enough, **Antique Row,** Pine St. between 9th and 12th Sts., has loads of wonderful shops. Nearby, **Giovanni's Room,** 345 S. 12th St., 215/923-2960, is among the oldest and best of the nation's gay, lesbian, and feminist bookstores.

More than 300 stores, many of them on the cutting edge, can be found on **South Street,** just south of Society Hill. New Age books, health food, high fashion, low-brow tattoos—they're not your typical mall shops.

On **Walnut Street,** between Broad Street and Rittenhouse Square, are lots more individual shops, most of a high-end sort, but you'll run into some interesting street vendors and artists. **Newman Galleries,** 1625 Walnut St., 215/563-1779, specializes in twentieth-century American art, specifically by Bucks County Impressionists. And nearby is **Daffy's,** 17th and Chestnut Sts., 215/963-9996. It offers "clothing bargains for millionaires," featuring designer duds at big discounts. The store is set in a 1920 art-deco building.

But if you want mall shopping, **Franklin Mills,** off I-95 at Woodhaven Rd., 800/336-6255, is the place for you. It has over 200 outlet stores, 30 designer stores, food courts—the whole nine yards. It's in northeast Philadelphia.

You can find 50 varieties of fresh and frozen pastas among many other Italian specialties at **Talluto's Authentic Italian Foods,** 944 S. Ninth St., 215/627-4967. Also in the Italian Market area is **Fante's Gourmet Cookware Shop,** 1006 S. Ninth St., 800/878-5557. This is where the experts have been coming since 1906 for the best in cooking implements. And **DiBruno Bros. House of Cheese,** 930 S. Ninth St.,

888/DB-CHEESE, has been selling more than 400 different types of cheese and other gourmet foods for more than 50 years.

SPORTS AND RECREATION

Welcome, sports fan. Philadelphia is your kind of city. Spectator sports may be bigger here than in any other city in America.

The First Union Complex, Broad St. and Pattison Ave., 215/336-3600, is home to lots of teams: **76ers** (basketball), 215/339-7600; **Flyers** (National Hockey League), 215/465-4500; **Phantoms** (American Hockey League), 215/465-4522; and **KIXX** (soccer), 888/888-KIXX. Veterans Stadium, where Major League Baseball's **Phillies,** 215/463-1000, and the National Football League's **Eagles,** 215/463-5500, play, is at the same address. This is also the place to see the annual December clash between America's military academy football teams—the Army-Navy game.

The huge **Fairmount Park,** 215/685-0000, has a variety of recreational facilities, including 78 baseball diamonds, 115 all-weather tennis courts, 13 football fields, 14 soccer fields, 2 cricket fields, 2 field hockey fields, a rugby field, bocci courts, 5 golf courses, 6 recreation centers, 5 indoor pools, 75 miles of bridle paths and hiking trails, 25 miles of paved bikeways, a rowing course, a fishing stream stocked with trout each season, and the first and only fish ladder in Pennsylvania. You can rent a bicycle starting at $30 a day from **Trophy Bike Tours,** 311 Market St., 215/625-7999.

There are also many golfing opportunities in and around Philadelphia. One useful resource is the *Pennsylvania Golf Course Guide.* For a copy send a stamped, self-addressed envelope to PGO, 121 Narragansett Dr., McKeesport, PA 15135; 412/751-3379. For a calendar of sports events, call 215/636-1666 or log on to www.libertynet.org/phila-visitor.

ENTERTAINMENT

South Street, between Front and Ninth Streets, is one of the centers of nighttime entertainment in the city. Here's where the night rocks. Another happening place is Main Street in Manayunk, and there are lots of new clubs along the Delaware River near the Ben Franklin Bridge. Cultural events are prominent on Broad Street, where the Avenue of the Arts cultural district sports 16 facilities that display talents of all sorts, from local to international, traditional to innovative.

The **Academy of Music,** Broad and Locust Sts., 215/893-1999, is home to the Philadelphia Orchestra, the Pennsylvania Ballet, the Opera Company of Philadelphia, and Peter Nero and the Philly Pops. Nearby is also the **Curtis Institute of Music,** 1726 Locust St., 215/893-7902, a world-renowned center for training young musicians. Students perform

The **Mummers Parade** is a unique Philadelphia event held each New Year's Day. There are 30,000 spectacularly costumed Mummers who march and dance north on Broad Street to City Hall.

The annual spring tour of private homes, gardens, and historic sites through the city is known as **Philadelphia Open House**. It's in April or May.

Plan ahead if you want to attend the **Sunoco Welcome America** event, which celebrates the nation's birthday in America's birthplace with parades, hot-air balloon races, a drum-and-bugle contest, and of course, fireworks.

Yo! Philadelphia gives the city's neighborhoods a chance to strut their stuff with music, food, and performances. It's in September. Or celebrate Halloween and the legacy of Edgar Allan Poe with a scary candlelight tour of the **Edgar Allan Poe National Historic Site**, 532 N. Seventh St. Poe lived here from 1843 to 1844 and wrote "The Tell-Tale Heart" among other ghastly stories during his stay.

In December, the Colonial mansions in **Fairmount Park** sparkle with old-fashioned holiday decorations. **Candlelight tours** are offered in the evenings.

For information on these and many other annual events, contact the Philadelphia Convention and Visitors Bureau.

events HORIZON

free public recitals most Monday, Wednesday, and Friday evenings during the school year. See a classical star in the making.

One of the largest outdoor amphitheaters in a major U.S. city is in Fairmount Park. The **Mann Center for the Performing Arts,** George's Hill near 52nd St. and Parkside Ave., 215/546-7900, presents classical, pop, jazz, and rock concerts outdoors during the summer. You can also see cutting-edge dance, jazz, theater, poetry, and gallery and performance work by internationally recognized artists at the **Painted Bride Art Center,** 230 Vine St., 215/925-9914.

The **Forrest Theatre,** 1114 Walnut St., 215/923-1515, offers the best in Broadway productions. And the city's leading producer of contemporary American theater is the **Philadelphia Theatre Company,** 1714 DeLancey St., 215/735-0631. The **Society Hill Playhouse,** 507 S. Eighth St., 215/923-0210, presents the best of off-Broadway theater.

Zanzibar Blue, 200 S. Broad St., 215/732-5200, offers live jazz seven nights a week by some of the hottest names in the industry. Or find some southern comfort and lots of blues at **Warmdaddy's,** 4 S. Front St., 215/627-2500.

Go back in time at **Polly Esther's Night Club,** 1201 Race St., 215/851-0776, where disco fever is catching and the walls are covered with the Brady Bunch. Yet another option for your evening is **David Brenner's Laugh House,** 221 South St., 215/440-4242, a new comedy club co-owned by the Philly-born comedian. It's open Thursday through Saturday.

Upstages, 1412 Chestnut St., 215/735-0631, offers tickets to many of the city's music, theater, dance, and museum events.

CITY BASICS

Information about the city is available from the **Philadelphia Convention and Visitors Bureau,** 800/537-7676, 215/636-3403 (TDD), www.libertynet.org/phila-visitor. When you're in the city, the place to go for information is the **Visitors Center,** 16th St. and John F. Kennedy Blvd., 215/636-1666. It's open 9 a.m. to 5 p.m. (6 p.m. during the summer) every day except Thanksgiving and Christmas. For information on the city's overall cultural events, call the **Greater Philadelphia Cultural Alliance,** 215/735-5577.

The weather here is about what you'd expect—cold in the winter, hot and humid in the summer, and pleasant during the shoulder seasons. Philadelphia averages 21 inches of snow during the winter. For up-to-date forecasts, call the **Weather Channel Connection,** 900/932-8437. It will cost you about $1 a minute.

The major daily newspapers include the *Philadelphia Inquirer* and the *Daily News. Philadelphia Magazine* and *Where Philadelphia* will help you find the city information you seek, as will the *Philadelphia Weekly* and the *City Paper.* The **Share the Heritage Guide** helps set the record straight on Philadelphia's rich African American history, culture, and nightlife. Get a copy from the Convention and Visitors Bureau.

to go ▶

> *The more I observed Washington, the more frequently I visited it, and the more people I interviewed there, the more I understood how prophetic L'Enfant was when he laid it out as a city that goes around in circles.*
> —John Mason Brown

Paris has a baby brother. His name is George.

If you've seen one city, you've seen them both—the same broad, tree-shaded avenues; the architectural splendor; the statues, fountains, and gardens everywhere; a museum around every corner; the hordes of tourists. It's the city as a work of art.

The similarities are not surprising. Parisians designed both cities. Pierre Charles L'Enfant, an army engineer who fought for the Americans in the Revolutionary War, grandly laid out the city of Washington.

The result is inviting to the pedestrian. The boulevards pull you along. The great, columned buildings open their arms to you. The city's 50-plus museums are brimming with treasures.

Behind those doors, beside those countless monuments, and within those hallowed halls of government lie stories—where heroes died or scandals brewed or great minds hammered out another grand compromise. It is history come alive and history in the making.

How can you resist? You can't. You shouldn't. Let's go.

The Mall

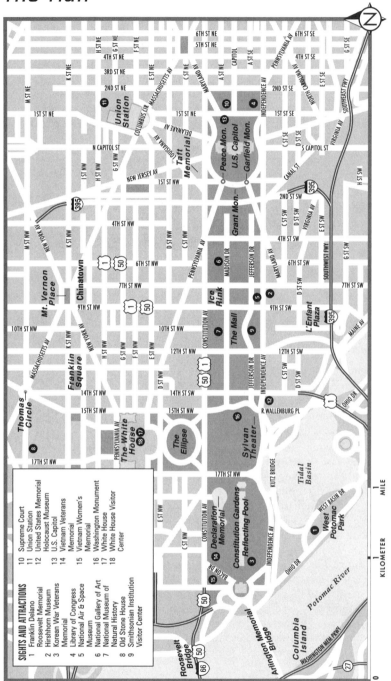

SIGHTS AND ATTRACTIONS

1 Franklin Delano Roosevelt Memorial
2 Hirshhorn Museum
3 Korean War Veterans Memorial
4 Library of Congress
5 National Air & Space Museum
6 National Gallery of Art
7 National Museum of Natural History
8 Old Stone House
9 Smithsonian Institution Visitor Center
10 Supreme Court
11 Union Station
12 United States Memorial Holocaust Museum
13 U.S. Capitol
14 Vietnam Veterans Memorial
15 Vietnam Women's Memorial
16 Washington Monument
17 White House
18 White House Visitor Center

GETTING AROUND

Washington is served by three airports: **National,** 703/661-2700, which is just south of the city on the Potomac; **Dulles,** 703/661-2700, 26 miles west; and **Baltimore/Washington International,** 410/859-7111, about 40 minutes away. From National, you can take a shuttle bus to the Metro station, or go by taxi for $12 to $15. Taxi fare from Dulles is about $40, and from Baltimore/Washington it's about $45. **SuperShuttle,** 703/416-7873, also serves the airports.

Washington has one of the finest subway systems in the world. It's safe, clean, convenient, and user friendly. That's reason enough to leave your car at home or skip the rental agencies. And how about two more reasons: the traffic is horrendous and parking is impossible.

Metro stations open at 5:30 a.m. weekdays and 8 a.m. weekends, and close at midnight. After hours, there are basically three options: travel on foot (bad idea), get around by taxi (better idea), or plan to arrive at your final destination before midnight (best idea). Base fare is $1.10, and you have to buy farecards in the stations. If you're going to be moving around a lot, you might want to get a One Day Pass, which gives you unlimited rides for $5.

If you're going beyond the subway routes, the **Metrobuses** are also $1.10. Exact change is required. Contact 888/METRO-INFO or www.wmata.com for information on buses and subways.

Cabs operate on a zone system. The base fare for one zone is $3.70, with extra charges for each additional passenger and for rides during rush hour. Call for a cab and it will cost you an extra $1.50, but hailing a cab after hours is not always easy. **Checker Cab** is at 202/398-0532.

Washington is divided into four quadrants—NW, NE, SW, and SE—with the U.S. Capitol in the center. Lettered streets run east-west. (There are no J, X, Y, or Z Streets.) Numbered streets run north-south. Diagonal streets are named for states.

Easy enough, right? Yep, just as long as you make sure you've got one of those quadrant indicators locked onto an address—because if you want to go to 500 C Street, for instance, there are two of those in the city. But there's only one 500 C Street SW.

SIGHTS AND ATTRACTIONS

You've got the whole world of Washington in a two-mile-long rectangle. It's called **The Mall,** bounded by First St. NW/SW, Constitution Ave., 23rd St. NW/SW, and Independence Ave. Start your visit on the steps of the Capitol. There—looking westward and spreading out at your feet—are the long squares of grass; that giant obelisk called the Washington Monument; the reflecting pools; and at the far end, a sad-eyed, grandfatherly Abe Lincoln in his armchair of stone, looking back at you.

So, you think, how hard could it be to do this whole little Mall in, maybe, a day? Stop at a museum or two, have lunch, saunter down to Abe's place and then back?

Are you kidding?

What you will soon discover is that each of those little dots of buildings, mostly branches of the Smithsonian complex of museums, will draw you in and not let you go. Every one of them contains an astonishing array of beautiful and/or interesting things sure to captivate your imagination.

Another thing you'll discover is that Washington has places of real courage. It has not chosen to hide the tragedies of the past, and sites such as the Holocaust Museum, the Vietnam Memorial, and Arlington Cemetery will draw you in and challenge your heart.

So don't kid yourself. You're not going to make good time. You won't be able to cover it all. It doesn't matter.

Count on coming home tired, but it will be a good tired. You will have been filled, informed, and maybe even transformed. Washington does that to people.

The **United States Memorial Holocaust Museum,** 100 Raoul Wallenberg Pl. SW, 202/488-0400, is a sacred place. It requires courage just to visit, and yes, you will be horrified by what you see and hear. But you will also be uplifted and empowered. It is a place of great dignity and stark beauty.

The story of the Holocaust builds as the visitor moves from the fourth floor downward, viewing artifacts, films, photographs, and oral histories. Be sure to plan quiet time, such as a walk in the park, at the conclusion of your visit.

Although admission is free, timed tickets are required to view the permanent collection. These are given out each day beginning at 10 a.m. and are usually gone by noon. For advance tickets, call ProTix at 800/400-9373; the service charge is $1.75 per ticket, and the handling fee is $1.00 per order. The museum is just off the Mall next to the Bureau of Engraving and Printing.

Another center of somberness is the **Vietnam Veterans Memorial,** Constitution Gardens, Constitution Ave. and Henry Bacon Dr. NW, 202/634-1568. A stark, V-shaped wall of black granite contains the names of 58,192 people missing or killed in the Vietnam War. It seems like an acre of names. Only 300 feet away is the **Vietnam Women's Memorial,** Constitution Ave. and Henry Bacon Dr. NW, 202/634-1568, a bronze statue of three servicewomen with a wounded soldier. Both are near the Lincoln Memorial.

A new site is the **Korean War Veterans Memorial,** between Independence Ave. and the Lincoln Memorial, 202/619-7222, a sculptured column of 10 foot-soldiers arrayed for combat. A wall beneath contains 2,500 etchings of nurses, chaplains, crew chiefs, and other support personnel who symbolize the vast war effort. It's also near the Lincoln Memorial.

Going Places

DC Ducks: The Boats on Wheels, 202/832-9800, will take you on a narrated tour of the nation's capital by land, followed by a splash into the Potomac for a river cruise. All of this happens in the same vehicle: a rebuilt WWII amphibious vessel. **Old Town Trolley Tours**, 202/832-9800, offers two-hour narrated tours with free reboarding at 16 sites. **Tourmobile Sightseeing**, a subsidiary of Universal Studios, 202/554-5100, has been providing narrated sightseeing shuttle tours for the National Park Service since 1967. It hits most of the top sites, and offers separate tours to Mount Vernon and Frederick Douglass National Historic Site.

For a specialty tour of African American historical sites, among others, try **Capital Entertainment Services**, 202/636-9203. Or Scandal Tours, 800/758-TOUR, can give you an irreverent look at Washington's sites of shame, provided by actors who know their monkey business. Every political persuasion gets equal grilling. "It [the scandal business] is a growth industry," says John Simmons, self-styled Idiot-In-Charge of the comedy troupe known as Gross National Product, which sponsors **Scandal Tours**. "It can only get worse." Tours run from April Fools' Day to Thanksgiving weekend.

The **Washington Monument,** 15th St. and Constitution Ave. NW, 202/426-6841, has recently been refurbished. This majestic obelisk was dedicated in 1885. Take a free elevator ride for a spectacular view. It's in the middle of the Mall.

The **Smithsonian Institution** is a world unto itself, and most of that world is on the Mall. You can get oriented at the **Visitor Information Center,** 1000 Jefferson Dr. SW, 202/357-2700. This is the castle where founder James Smithson is buried. From your orientation you can decide an agenda for yourself—far more museums exist than you can visit in one day. Just don't miss the **National Air & Space Museum,** Independence Ave. and Seventh St. SW, 202/357-2700, which houses the Wright Brothers' 1903 *Flyer*, Lindbergh's *Spirit of St. Louis*, and the *Apollo 11* lunar module. The **National Museum of Natural History.** Constitution Ave. and 12th St. NW, 202/357-2700, has the Hope Diamond, lots of dinosaur fossils, and the world's largest African bush elephant. (Don't worry, it's dead.) The cylindrical **Hirshhorn Museum,** Independence Ave. and Seventh St. SW, 202/357-2700, has modern art galore. And especially enjoyable is the sculpture garden, a wonderful place to stroll through an outstanding collection of Henry Moore's *Reclining Figures.*

The **National Gallery of Art,** Constitution Ave. between Third and Fourth Sts. NW, 202/737-4215, contains a permanent collection of European and American paintings, sculpture, decorative arts, and works on paper.

A Capital Christmas

This is one of the world's most beautiful places during the holidays. Not only are the decorations up, but most of the politicians have gone home, giving the city a peaceful, bombast-free feel.

Each year, early in December, the **People's Christmas Tree** is lit, accompanied by concerts and various ceremonies. At about the same time, the president lights the **National Christmas Tree** in the Ellipse near the White House. Besides the big tree, there are little ones for each state, which makes for quite a festive forest. Special concerts are conducted through the season.

Mount Vernon puts on a special program in which the first president's home is decorated as it would have been when George was around. The White House, too, is specially decorated, and evening tours take place from 5 to 7 p.m.

The National Cathedral has special concerts and services, plus an exhibit featuring nearly 100 nativity scenes from around the world.

Union Station is a place you shouldn't miss. The huge building is decked out grandly for the holidays with big red bows and hundreds of twinkle lights.

Also, you can count on special holiday performances at the **Folger Shakespeare Library**, 201 E. Capitol St. SE., 202/544-7077. Ford's Theatre, 511 10th St. NW, 202/347-4833, www.fordstheatre.org, usually has special performances as well, such as *A Christmas Carol*.

Next on the list for the visitor is the **White House,** 1600 Pennsylvania Ave. NW, 202/456-7041. But before you go, get oriented at the **White House Visitor Center,** 1450 Pennsylvania Ave. NW, which has a film and exhibits about the architecture, furnishings, and social events of the White House. Free tickets to the White House are issued on the morning of the tour only—first-come, first-served—starting at 7:30 a.m. at the visitors center. Be there. The tickets go fast. You can obtain up to four tickets.

The **U.S. Capitol,** entrance on E. Capitol and First Sts. NW, 202/225-6827, is the center of L'Enfant's grand plan for Washington. You've got to at least walk under the huge rotunda and across the white marble disc in the center of the floor where presidents have lain in state. Paintings and statues depict scenes from American history. Free guided tours leave every 15 minutes from the Rotunda.

The **Library of Congress,** 10 First St. SE, 202/707-8000, is the world's largest, with 111 million items in three buildings. Check out (bad pun) the 1897 Thomas Jefferson Building, recently reopened after more than a decade of restoration. It houses one of the world's three perfect copies of the Gutenberg Bible.

When court is not in session at the **Supreme Court,** First St. and Maryland Ave. NE, 202/479-3211, you can hear a lecture about it every half-hour, 9:30 a.m. to 3:30 p.m.

Union Station, 40 Massachusetts Ave. NE, 202/289-1908, is a must. This working train station has been restored to its former beaux-art glory and contains 125 stores and restaurants.

The new **Franklin Delano Roosevelt Memorial** is on 7.5 acres between the Tidal Basin and the Potomac River. Four gallery rooms feature sculptures depicting events from the Great Depression and World War II. Its parklike setting includes waterfalls, quiet pools, and granite upon which many of President Roosevelt's most memorable words are carved.

Also worth a visit is the **Old Stone House,** 3051 M St. NE, 202/426-6851, the oldest house in Washington, built in 1765.

The nation's premier museum devoted to architecture and the building arts is the **National Building Museum,** 401 F St. NW, 202/272-2448. A permanent exhibit chronicles the building of the nation's capital; it's located in the Old Pension Building, designed by Civil War general Montgomery Meigs in 1881.

Don't neglect the **National Zoological Park,** 3000 block of Connecticut Ave. NW, 202/673-4717—a beautiful place just to walk through; the animals are a bonus. The giant panda Hsing-Hsing died in 1999, but there are many other animals to view.

A place of great beauty on a wooded hill above the fray is the **Washington National Cathedral,** Massachusetts and Wisconsin Aves. NW, 202/537-6200, a monumental Gothic-style edifice with gorgeous stained-glass windows. See this if you possibly can. Guided tours are available during the week. Call for times of Sunday services, which are ecumenical in nature.

LODGING

Remember one word: Metro. If your hotel is close to a Metro stop—and almost all of them are—then you are close to everything. It's not necessary to find accommodations close to the Mall.

And guess which city is the most-visited in the nation? Yep. This one, with about 20 million tourists a year. You'd better plan ahead.

The **Hotel Lombardy,** 2019 Pennsylvania Ave. NW, 800/424-5486, $$, offers 125 European-style rooms and suites on a prestigious avenue. Rooms feature fully-equipped kitchens and minibars.

A restored inn that preserves the ambiance of the bygone Victorian era is the **Morrison-Clark Inn,** 1015 L St. NW, 800/332-7898, $$. Free breakfast, fitness center, newspaper, and shoe shine are included.

At the top of the list is the venerable, old-world, grand-but-not-glitzy **Hay-Adams Hotel,** 800 16th St. NW, 800/424-5054, $$$$, which is just across the street from the White House. The hotel, which was

D.C. Region

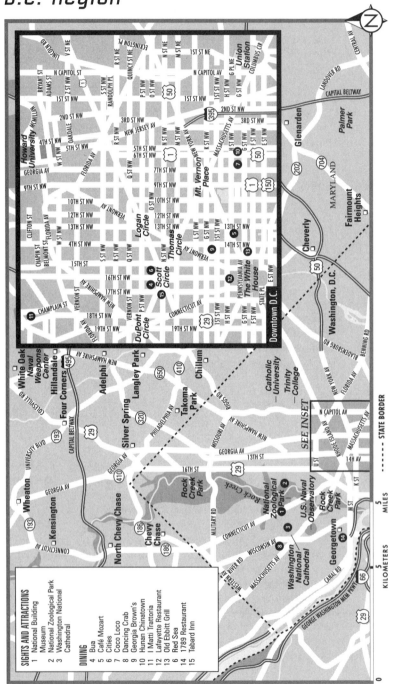

SIGHTS AND ATTRACTIONS
1 National Building Museum
2 National Zoological Park
3 Washington National Cathedral

DINING
4 Bua
5 Café Mozart
6 Cities
7 Coco Loco
8 Dancing Crab
9 Georgia Brown's
10 Hunan Chinatown
11 I Matti Trattoria
12 Lafayette Restaurant
13 Old Ebbitt Grill
6 Red Sea
14 1789 Restaurant
15 Tabard Inn

opened in 1928, has 143 rooms and 32 suites. Nearly every president since Calvin Coolidge has visited or stayed here. The Lafayette dining room is where Washington's power brokers and society mavens meet.

Another of the top-dollar hotels is **The Madison,** 15th and M Sts. NW, 202/862-1600, $$$, which houses the world-renowned antique collection of hotel proprietor Marshall B. Cone. It's also near the White House.

Why not sleep where history was made? The Watergate is not nearly as shabby as the scandal that made it famous. (Actually, the bungled burglary was in the office complex nearby.) More recently, Monica Lewinsky maintained a suite there that was subsequently purchased by none other than Bob Dole. Go figure. The **Watergate Hotel,** 2650 Virginia Ave. NW, 202/965-2300, $$$, has kitchenettes in some rooms, an indoor pool, and a world-famous restaurant. It's adjacent to the Kennedy Center.

The **Dupont at the Circle,** 1606 19th St. NW, 202/332-5251, www.dupontatthecircle.com, $$, is an 1870s Victorian townhouse turned into a B&B. It's in a residential area within walking distance of the White House. It has six rooms with high ceilings, fireplaces, and marble bathrooms with jetted tubs. It has double parlors in the common area. It's a no-smoking establishment.

At the budget end of the spectrum, try the **Adams Inn,** 1744 Lanier Pl. NW, 800/578-6807, $, downtown in the Adams-Morgan area. You might have to share a bath if you want a bargain. Another place to try is the **Woodley Park Guest House,** 2647 Woodley Rd. NW, 202/667-0218, $, near the National Zoo. Again, rooms with a shared bath are the cheapest, of course.

For help in making reservations, try the following resources: **Bed and Breakfast Accommodations,** 202/328-3510, has 130 rooms available, ranging in price from $50 to $250 per night. Many properties are historic. Another service is **Bed & Breakfast League/Sweet Dreams & Toast,** 202/363-7767, which offers lodging in private homes and apartments. Most are in historic districts. Also worth a call is **Accommodations Express,** 800/974-7666, which offers free discount hotel reservations. Another place for discount rooms is **Capital Reservations Tour & Travel Services,** 202/452-1270. Also try **Hotel Reservations Network,** 800/964-6835.

DINING

As befitting the capital of the nation, Washington offers cuisine of every taste and ethnicity. And nowhere else is that diversity more prevalent than at **Cities,** 2424 18th St. NW, 202/328-7194, $$$. Each year this restaurant features a different city from around the world to honor, with decor and menu to match. It's open daily. Jazz is offered in the evenings, and brunch is served on Sundays.

I Matti Trattoria, 2436 18th St. NW, 202/462-8844, $$, is known for homemade bread, pastas, game, and items from the grill. Lunch and dinner are served Monday through Saturday; brunch is served on Sunday. Reservations are suggested.

The Ethiopian restaurant **Red Sea,** 2463 18th St. NW, 202/483-5000, $$, specializes in vegetarian selections. It also offers lamb and beef spiced with cardamom, ginger root, and mace. It's open daily. Reservations are suggested.

Coco Loco, 810 Seventh St. NW, 202/289-2626, $$, offers two different menus—Mexican tapas are served at the bar, and for a big meal, rotisserie beef, lamb, pork, chicken, and turkey are served in Brazilian-steakhouse style. The restaurant also offers live music and dancing.

Hunan Chinatown, 624 H. St. NW, 202/783-5858, $$, has been named as one of the Best 50 Restaurants in *Washingtonian* magazine for

Contact your congressman's or senator's office at least two months in advance for special tickets to guided tours of the White House, U.S. Capitol, FBI, and Bureau of Engraving and Printing. These tours usually are given in the early morning, before regular tour hours begin.

Don't visit Washington when everybody else does, in mid- to late summer. It's a steambath, and all of those tourists are sweating. When the British sent troops to fight Americans in the War of 1812, soldiers who went to Washington got Tropical Pay. (Also, remember: The city is built on a swamp. The founding fathers didn't want to give away any of their good land for a city.) The best time to visit is in the spring or fall, when the weather is gorgeous and crowds aren't so bad. The lowest hotel rates are on weekends and around holidays.

When you check into your hotel during the winter (Thanksgiving through Valentine's Day), ask for a WinterARTS Passport. It contains more than 45 discounts at D.C.'s cultural venues, such as two-for-one theater tickets and discounts at museum shops.

Don't go to the Pentagon. People there are very uptight about showing you around the place.

Also know that the Capitol Hill area can be especially hostile at night, so walking in that area is not recommended. And remember that aggressive panhandling is discouraged by D.C. law. Report harassment to the police.

City Survival Tips

the last dozen years or so. Signature dishes include Crispy Whole Fish, Two-Flavor Lobster, and Crispy Pan-Fried Noodles.

Café Mozart, 1331 H St. NW, 202/347-5732, $$, offers schnitzels, sauerbraten, and other traditional German favorites. Gourmet items are available in the deli.

Georgia Brown's, 950 15th St. NW, 202/393-4499, $$, pays homage to Washington's southern roots with cooking inspired by the South Carolina low country.

The menu at the **Lafayette Restaurant,** 800 16th St. NW, 202/638-6600, $$$$, at the Hay-Adams Hotel combines French savoir faire with American ingenuity. Try the fricassee of guinea breast or the grilled Virginia bison. Seven floor-to-ceiling windows look out onto the White House.

Another seat of power-dining is the **Old Ebbitt Grill,** 675 15th St. NW, 202/347-4801, $$$. This is Washington's oldest bar, established in 1856. It serves up all sorts of American favorites ranging from juicy burgers to succulent rack of lamb. Reservations are suggested.

Bua, 1635 P St. NW, 202/265-0828, $$, in a townhouse in Dupont Circle, is known for creative Thai cuisine. Don't miss it.

You say you want fresh ingredients? The **Tabard Inn,** 1739 N St. NW, 202/785-1277, $$$, uses much of its own produce from its own farm. Dine outside when the weather is good.

For fine dining in Georgetown, try the **1789 Restaurant,** 1226 36th St. NW, 202/965-1789, $$$$, which serves regional game, fish, and produce in a country-inn atmosphere. An on-site bakery prepares fresh breads and desserts. Jacket and tie are suggested. Call for reservations.

Finally, consider a visit to the **Dancing Crab,** 4611 Wisconsin Ave. NW, 202/244-1882, $$, an old-fashioned Maryland crab house that has brown paper on the tables and hammers available to assist your shell-cracking efforts.

SHOPPING

The best shopping is on Connecticut Avenue NW, from K Street north through Dupont Circle. If antique jewelry is your thing, visit the **Tiny Jewel Box,** 1143 Connecticut Ave. NW, 202/393-2747. Or for old, out-of-print books, look at the selection at **Second Story Books**, 2000 P St. NW, 202/659-8884. And the bread is simply marvelous at **Marvelous Market,** 5035 Connecticut Ave. NW, 202/686-4040. You can also get takeout food.

One of the world's largest **Chanel** boutiques is here, 1455 Pennsylvania Ave. NW, 202/638-5055. Handbags, cosmetics, and those famous Chanel suits are available.

Get political gifts and memorabilia such as campaign buttons and bumper stickers at **Political Americana,** 685 15th St. NW, 202/547-1871.

Besides Union Station, another concentration of shops is at the **Old Post Office Pavilion,** 1100 Pennsylvania Ave. NW. You can get a dramatic view of the city from the 315-foot clock tower.

Also of note are the **Galleries of Dupont Circle,** 1710 Connecticut Ave. NW, 202/328-7189, representing 21 private art dealers. The galleries hold joint evening open houses the first Friday of each month.

SPORTS AND RECREATION

Once locals get tired of making fun of politicians for sport, they turn to several spectator sports. The **Washington Redskins,** 301/276-6050, play at RFK Stadium, 2400 E. Capitol St. SE. Regular-season games usually sell out, but tickets to preseason games are often available. Also playing at RFK Stadium is **DC United Soccer,** 703/478-6600, a Major League Soccer franchise. The **Washington Wizards,** 301/NBA-DUNK, provide NBA action at the MCI Center, 601 F St. NW.

At the MCI Center, in the **MCI National Sports Gallery,** 202/628-3200, you'll find the most significant collection of sports memorabilia in the world. It's also home to the American Sportscasters Association Hall of Fame and Museum.

Golfing is available at several courses in the area. Try the **Rock Creek Golf Course** at Rock Creek Park, 16th and Rittenhouse Sts. NW, 202/882-7332. Or if you want to paddle in the shadow of the Jefferson Memorial, contact **Tidal Basin Pedal Boats,** Ohio Dr. and the Tidal Basin NW, 202/484-0206. You can also take a historical jog on the **Mount Vernon Trail,** 703/289-2530, where 19 miles of paths wind along the Virginia side of the Potomac between Theodore Roosevelt Island and George Washington's home at Mount Vernon.

ENTERTAINMENT

The museums can be hard work—worth it, of course, but you'll need a break.

Capitol Steps Political Satire, 1505 King St., Alexandria, Va., 703/683-8330, has performed its special brand of satire on all the networks and for a half-dozen U.S. presidents. Live performances are held every Friday and Saturday night. Catch more political satire from **Mrs. Foggybottom & Friends,** 2853 Ontario Rd. NW, 202/332-1796. Joan Cushing and six members of her comedy troupe take on Washington high society.

Dinner theater is alive and well at the **Burn Brae Dinner Theatre,** 3811 Blackburn Ln., Burtonsville, Md., 800/777-BBDT. You'll get a buffet plus a Broadway musical.

See the best of opera, drama, dance, ballet, music, and films at the

Discover the monuments and history surrounding the Mall

John F. Kennedy Center for the Performing Arts, 2700 F St. NW, 800/444-1324, which is composed of six theaters. Also, *Shear Madness* has been playing at the Kennedy Center for over a decade. It's a hilarious whodunit in which the audience gets a chance to solve the crime. Free guided tours are offered daily 10 a.m. to 1 p.m. The center also has gift shops and restaurants.

The works of Shakespeare and other classical playwrights are performed in an intimate 449-seat **Shakespeare Theatre,** 450 Seventh St. NW, 202/547-1122.

And consider a visit to **Blues Alley,** 1073 Wisconsin Ave., 202/337-4141, the nation's oldest continuously operating jazz supper club. When Charlie Byrd and Sarah Vaughn came to town, this is where they performed. Reservations are required.

Still another entertainment option is **Kramerbooks & Afterwords Café,** 1517 Connecticut Ave. NW, 202/387-1462, a bookstore with a full-service restaurant and live music Wednesday through Saturday nights.

CITY BASICS

As for weather, remember how far south you are. Spring, fall, and early summer are generally temperate. It usually snows in January and February. Late summer can be unbelievably stifling.

For more information about D.C. and its national parks, contact **Washington, D.C. Convention and Visitors Association,** 202/789-7000, www.washington.org, and **National Park Service Dial-A-Park,** 202/619-7257. For free brochures on lodging and attractions, or for a map, write to **Tourist Information,** 1212 New York Ave. NW, Suite 600, Washington, D.C. 20005.

Ticketplace, 1100 Pennsylvania NW, 202/TIC-KETS, is the

Picture Perfect

The nation's capital is one of the most photogenic cites in America. Here are a couple of suggestions for shutterbugs:

Go across the Potomac to Arlington, Virginia, and specifically to the Iwo Jima Memorial Park. Stand on the hill near the Netherlands Carillon and snap a picture looking across the river toward the Lincoln Memorial. Also, the view at dawn with the sun rising over the Capitol is another nifty shot.

At night, climb the steps of the Capitol building, turn around, and take a photograph looking west down the Mall toward the Washington Monument, which is dramatically lighted.

w a s h i n g t o n ,   d . c .

place for half-price day-of-show theater tickets. Check out the booth in the Old Post Office Pavilion.

Washington is one of the most accessible cities for visitors with disabilities; contact the **Smithsonian Institution,** 202/357-2700 or 202/357-1729 (TTY), for information on accessing its museums. Call the Metro system at 202/635-6434 for a guide on accessibility to subways and buses. Also, call the Convention and Visitors Association on general accessibility of hotels, restaurants, malls, and attractions.

Washingtonian magazine is a good source for entertainment news, as are the entertainment sections in the *Washington Post* and the *Washington Times.* An alternative weekly in town is called the *Washington City Paper.*

④ BOSTON

to go ▶

*The New England conscience does not stop you from doing
what you shouldn't—it just stops you from enjoying it.*
—Cleveland Amory

Boston is heavy with history. Some very serious people have lived here—intellectuals and writers, rebels and firebrands, poets and ideologues.

The Puritans, with their starched souls, started it all. Then came Paul Revere and his tea-party raiders. They were followed by the transcendentalists, the abolitionists, the integrationists, and the Vietnam protesters—as well as the blue bloods, blue noses, and book burners. For good or for ill, this is the home of America's conscience.

Boston is a good place to get serious. You can come here and retrace those leaden steps that led to change in America.

But if you think that's all there is to this city—one long history lesson—then you don't know beans about Boston. The Puritans died out ages ago. Those conscientious people who have been spoiling everybody's fun for so long are history. Boston has learned to loosen up.

Boston

SIGHTS AND ATTRACTIONS
1 Charles Hayden Planetarium
2 Computer Museum
3 Faneuil Hall Marketplace
4 Isabella Stewart Gardner Museum
5 John F. Kennedy Library and Museum
6 Lewis and Harriet Hayden House
7 Museum of Fine Arts
8 Museum of Science
9 New England Aquarium
10 Robert Gould Shaw and 54th Regiment
   Memorial

DINING
11 Bay Tower
12 Durgin-Park
13 Galleria Umberto
14 Grand Chau Chow
15 Jacob Wirth Company
16 Legal Sea Food
17 Mike's Pastry
18 Milk Street Café
19 Realto
20 Ye Olde Union Oyster House

GETTING AROUND

Logan International Airport, 800/23-LOGAN, is just two miles outside the city center and across Massachusetts Bay. Take the subway into town. You can ride the Blue Line of the Massachusetts Bay Transit Authority (MBTA, and known as the T for short) from Airport Station to downtown or practically anywhere else.

Something you may want to invest in right off is the T's **Visitor Passport,** 617/222-3200. You can get unlimited travel on subways, trolleys, and buses for one day ($5), three days ($9), or seven days ($18), as well as discounts on popular attractions. A Visitor Passport is also available at the visitors center on Boston Common. Fares are 85 cents within Boston proper and 85¢ to $2 for zone changes. The T starts running at 5 a.m. (6 a.m. on Sundays), and the last trains leave downtown Boston at 12:45 a.m.

To get yourself oriented, find Park Street, which is next to Boston Common. The Park Street subway station is the hub of the system. You can hop on or transfer to any of the four lines that can take you anywhere you want to go. When a subway route says *inbound*, it means it's headed for Park Street. *Outbound* means it's heading out from the Park Street stop.

Taxis are a little harder to hail in Boston than, say, New York. The best advice is to find a taxi stand near a hotel. Fares are $1.50 minimum plus 20 cents for each 1/7 mile thereafter, plus all toll fees. There's an additional fee of $1.00 for cabs originating at the airport. **Checker Taxi** is at 617/536-7500.

SIGHTS AND ATTRACTIONS

One of the top attractions in Boston is the **Faneuil Hall Marketplace,** bounded by North, State, and Congress Sts., 617/338-2323, a complex of historic buildings that houses shops, bars, restaurants, and food stands both inside and outside. Merchants sell fine handicrafts from the region and tacky souvenirs. Street performers are everywhere. This is tourist heaven.

The **Museum of Fine Arts,** 465 Huntington Ave., 617/267-9300, is one of the finest in the world, and a whole world of art resides within it. The museum is known for its Asian and Egyptian art, medieval sculpture, and some of the best of the Impressionists, including 34 Monets. It also has a fine gift shop, with many art books, plus restaurants and a cafeteria. Consider taking the free guided tour of the place.

If you don't have time to take the full tour of the Black Heritage Trail, at least stop by the **Lewis and Harriet Hayden House,** 66 Phillips St., 617/742-5415. After the Fugitive Slave Law was established in 1850, this became a stop along the Underground Railroad.

— Neighborhood Watch

Boston's neighborhoods are a patchwork of distinct personalities. We can't cover them all, and neither can you, but here are a few choice areas worth exploring.

Beacon Hill, which includes Boston Common and the historic area to the north, is full of eighteenth- and nineteenth-century townhouses and mansions among red-brick sidewalks and cobblestone streets, with gas street lights and wrought iron work. The hill itself used to be much higher, but its ground was used as fill dirt for **Back Bay**, an area that was under the Charles River a century ago and is now a mixture of Victorian townhouses, chic shopping areas, and trendy restaurants. It is to the west of Beacon Hill and borders the Charles River.

Newbury Street is crowded with high-dollar galleries and boutiques. This area is just to the south of Back Bay.

The Fenway, to the west of the Newbury area, is the must-see neighborhood for sports fans and garden lovers.

The **South End** is lined with brick bow-front townhouses, and restaurants and jazz clubs predominate. It's south of Back Bay near Columbus Avenue and Tremont Street.

The **Seaport District** is home to lots of hotels and condos along the waterfront, along with the Tea Party Ship and the New England Aquarium. It's south of downtown along Northern Avenue.

The oldest neighborhood in Boston is the **North End**, north of downtown, a predominately Italian enclave where the heritage is most evident in the area's many restaurants.

Testifying to the contribution of African Americans in the Civil War is the **Robert Gould Shaw and 54th Regiment Memorial.** This was the first black regiment to be formed. The memorial is at the entrance to the Boston Common.

Don't neglect the **John F. Kennedy Library and Museum,** Columbia Point, W. Fourth St., and I-93, 617/929-4523. Within are a film biography that is narrated by Kennedy himself by means of clips; a film about the Cuban Missile Crisis; and a darkened chamber in which news reports of the assassination and funeral are played. The I.M. Pei–designed building offers soaring views of the waterfront and Boston's skyline.

The **Isabella Stewart Gardner Museum,** 280 The Fenway, 617/566-1401, is housed in the Venetian–style palace that the eccentric millionaire completed in 1901. Inside is her vast art collection, much of it European classics, and a courtyard that is kept abundant with blooming flowers.

Here's a museum that looks forward instead of backward. One exhibit of the **Computer Museum,** 300 Congress St. on Museum Wharf, 617/426-2800, is a model of a modern computer big enough to walk through, so you can get a clear view of all of those tiny components that make the thing go. Also included are exhibits on virtual reality and the information superhighway. Get some microchip jewelry in the museum's store.

The **Museum of Science,** Science Park at the Charles River Dam, 617/723-2500, works hard to make the unseen forces of nature such as gravity understandable through participatory exhibits. One outstanding component of the museum is the **Charles Hayden Planetarium,** Science Park at the Charles River Dam, 617/723-2500, which will take you deep into space or rock your world with a rock-music laser show. Take the Lechmere branch of the T's Green Line and exit at Science Park.

A city this close to the ocean is almost obligated to have an aquarium, and the **New England Aquarium,** 617/973-5200, is first class all the way. This one is huge, with more than 7,000 fish and aquatic mammals. The central tank attracts the biggest crowd when, five times a day, scuba divers bring food to a gang of sharks. It's at the Central Wharf, which is three blocks from Faneuil Hall Marketplace next to the Aquarium T stop on the Blue Line.

LODGING

Find a hotel near the subway line in Boston and you're minutes away from just about everything. Your hotel doesn't have to be centrally located. But Boston is very popular with tourists, especially in the summer, so be warned. Reservations are vital.

The **Eliot and Pickett Houses**, 6 Mt. Vernon Pl., 617/248-8707, www.vva.org/ep/, $$, offer 20 guest rooms in the heart of historic Beacon Hill. These are very popular places because of location and moderate prices. A self-serve breakfast is included.

Two brick townhouses from the 1880s make up the **Newbury Guest House,** 261 Newbury St., 617/437-7666, $$, a moderately priced little inn in an area teeming with boutiques. A buffet breakfast is included.

The **Fairmont Copley Plaza,** 138 St. James Ave., 800/527-4727, $$$$, is a grand hotel of the first order. It was built in 1912 in the Renaissance revival style, and features large guest rooms with reproduction Edwardian antiques and all the modern amenities.

If theater is what you like, you can't be in a better location than at the **Tremont House Hotel,** 275 Tremont St., 800/331-9998, $$$, a 15-story brick beauty that has been restored to the elegance of its

1924 origins. The huge lobby sports original gold-leaf decorations and an ornate ceiling. A dozen or so rooms are designed for people with disabilities.

The **Regal Bostonian Hotel,** Faneuil Hall, bounded by North, State, and Congress Sts., 800/343-0922, $$$$, is housed in two wings— one an old warehouse that dates to 1824, and another a more modern building, which goes back to 1890. But don't worry. It's been updated— to luxury standards. You get on-demand videos, safes, two-line phones, and a marvelous location just across from the Faneuil Hall Marketplace.

Nearby and also built from a renovated nineteenth-century warehouse is the **Harborside Inn,** 185 State St., 617/723-7500, $$. Guest rooms, which surround an atrium, have hardwood floors, Oriental rugs, and Victorian-style furniture.

So why not spend the night in a rocking bed? **Constitution Yacht Charters,** 28 Constitution Rd., 617/241-9640, www.marinemart.com /constitution.html, $$$, has a bed-and-breakfast aboard a yacht that's moored in Boston Harbor (no boat B&B accommodations available in the winter, though).

There's no reason you can't stay in Cambridge and be whisked into town on the subway. Visitors to Harvard should consider the **Inn at Harvard,** 1201 Massachusetts Ave., Cambridge, 800/458-5886, $$$, a hotel with a high IQ. The four-story, skylighted atrium has backgammon and chess tables, plus lots of bookshelves with Harvard University

___The Cambridge Quilt___

Cambridge, just across the Charles River, is something like Boston's version of the Left Bank. Two world-renowned universities dominate the town—Harvard University and the Massachusetts Institute of Technology—but Cambridge is far more than one big college town. A diversity of cultures is woven into its social fabric.

This is a city of squares, much like Europe, each serving as an independent center of residents, restaurants, markets, and merchants. The subway's Red Line stops at each, so they're easy to get to.

From Boston, the first stop after you cross the Charles River is **Kendall Square**, the home of MIT. A museum on campus helps explain its role as the world's center of computer science. Next stop is **Central Square**, home to more international restaurants than any other area of the city. **Harvard Square**, the next stop, is an absolute must for the visitor to Boston. Besides more than 100 restaurants and street performers on every corner, the area has one of the largest concentrations of bookstores of anyplace in the world. Stop by one of the many coffeehouses where folk artists such as Joan Baez got their start. If you stop by the Information Center at Harvard, you can join a tour of the campus conducted by one of the students.

Shop, eat, and browse at Faneuil Hall Marketplace

Press publications. Guest rooms have work areas with tables and arm-chairs, and on the wall are paintings from the Fogg Art Museum.

A Bed and Breakfast in Cambridge, 1657 Cambridge St., Cambridge, 800/795-7122, $$, offers antiques, fresh flowers, down comforters, and home-baked goodies. It's only two blocks to Harvard Yard.

DINING

If you don't like seafood, don't come to Boston. This is where it's fresh, and this is where they've learned how to cook it right.

A block from Faneuil Hall, **Ye Olde Union Oyster House,** 41 Union St., 617/227-2750, $$, specializes in New England lobster and grilled meats. And they ought to know what they're doing—they've been in business since 1826, making the establishment the oldest continuously operating restaurant in America.

"Fresh" is the byword at **Legal Sea Food,** 800 Boylston St., 617/266-6800, $$$, as the Boston chain makes sure that only top-quality fish and shellfish are served every day. (What's on the menu is what the boats brought in.) Try the smoked bluefish pâté, or the salmon baked in parchment. One location is in the Prudential Center of Back Bay.

One of Boston's favorites is **Durgin-Park,** 340 Faneuil Hall Marketplace, 617/227-2038, $$, as you will soon see by the long line waiting to get in. Don't despair. The line moves quickly because you're likely to be seated at a long table with others; and Durgin-Park knows how to cook fast—they've been doing it since 1827. If you've always wanted to try Boston baked beans, this is the place. They don't take reservations.

Let's have some Boston seafood with an entirely different accent. **Grand Chau Chow,** 45 Beach St., 617/292-5166, $$, is a Cantonese restaurant in Chinatown with fish tanks in which your dinner swims. Specialty of the house is clams with black bean sauce.

If you want a meal with a view—and a very good meal at that—consider the **Bay Tower,** 60 State St., 617/723-1666, $$$$. It's on the 33rd floor of the Sheraton World Headquarters building, and every seat in the place has a wonderful view of the Faneuil Hall Marketplace and the harbor. If you've had so much seafood that you're worried you might grow scales, ask about the pan-seared veal with fava bean cassoulet and morel mushroom sauce.

The **Milk Street Café,** 50 Milk St., 617/542-2433, $, is a kosher restaurant in the financial district that specializes in vegetarian dishes. This is also a nice place for breakfast, with tempting offers such as scones, pastries, fruit salad, and herbal teas.

The North End is an Italian enclave, and where there are Italians, there are people who know how to cook. The area has lots of tiny restaurants that are perfect for coffee and a dessert—try any one of several on Hanover Street, such as **Mike's Pastry,** 300 Hanover St., 617/742-3050, $$. What's also good about Italian food is that the cheap stuff is just as good as the expensive stuff, and nowhere is that more true than at **Galleria Umberto,** 289 Hanover St., 617/227-5709, $. The crowds are trying to tell you something. It's a cafeteria-style place with no item more than about three dollars. Get a slice of pizza or maybe a calzone with spinach and sausage.

Jacob Wirth Company (33–37 Stuart St., 617/338-8586, $$)—Bostonians have been calling it "Jake's" for the 130 years it's been in business—is a great little German place in the theater district. It has all that you'd expect—Wiener schnitzel, knockwurst—plus blackboard specials and great sandwiches.

Realto, in the Charles Hotel at 1 Bennet St., Cambridge, 617/661-5050, $$$$, gives a Mediterranean accent to the fresh fish of the area. The Provençal fisherman's soup with rouille, Gruyère, and basil oil is not a bad choice. Big windows overlook Harvard Square in Cambridge.

SHOPPING

Boston has four clusters of marvelous shopping—Downtown Crossing, Back Bay, Faneuil Hall Marketplace, and Haymarket.

Downtown Crossing, Washington and Winter Sts., is Boston's center of shopping. It's right in the middle of town, a mall of cobblestone and brick streets that is blocked off to traffic and contains the city's most talked-about store, the original **Filene's Basement,** 426 Washington St., 617/542-2011. Filene's Basement is legendary, and it attracts up to 20,000 shoppers a day (even more when that madhouse of a wedding dress sale is held once a year). Everything gets marked down after so many days on the shelves, and big bargains are popping up all the time. Get ready to lunge for what you want. Also at the center is **Macy's East,** 450 Washington St., 617/357-3000, a new addition to the area. Vendors are out and about hawking hot dogs, pretzels, and what not.

The Patriot's Path

The **Freedom Trail** is the way to see Boston—as a walk through history. Just follow the three-mile-long red brick trail across streets and sidewalks, and you'll wander into 16 historic sites. You'll have no need for a tour guide.

Boston Common, on Tremont St. between the Park St. and Tremont St. subway stations, is the oldest public park in the country and where you begin the trail. Just outside, near the Park Street Church (Park and Tremont Sts.) is the **Granary Burying Ground**, the resting place of John Hancock, Paul Revere, and Ben Franklin's parents.

They say American independence was born in the **Old State House**, at the corner of State and Washington Sts. Built in 1713, it's the oldest public building in Boston and the place where the Declaration of Independence was read from the balcony.

Continue across State and Congress Streets to **Faneuil Hall**, built in 1742. This was the site of many fiery town meetings.

The **Paul Revere House**, 19 N. Square, was built around 1680 and is the oldest building in Boston. The famous midnight rider lived here from 1770 to 1800.

Across the Charles River on the North Washington Street Bridge and to your right is the Charlestown Navy Yard. Docked there is a frigate, nicknamed Old Ironsides, which is the **USS _Constitution_ and Museum**. Old Ironsides was undefeated in a succession of 42 battles with the British fleet in the War of 1812. It's the oldest commissioned warship afloat in the world.

Proceed out of the Navy Yard to Adams Street toward Monument Square. There you'll find **Bunker Hill Monument**, a towering obelisk marking the site of the first major battle of the American Revolution. It's dedicated to those who fought and died in the famous battle of June 17, 1775.

There are dozens of art galleries along Newbury Street, which is the heart of high-end Back Bay shopping. The **Copley Society of Boston,** 158 Newbury St., 617/536-5049, was founded in 1879, when its exhibitors back then were James Whistler and John Singer Sargent. Today, many of its artists come from New England. Also worth a look are the New England crafts such as jewelry, glass, and ceramics that are featured at the **Society of Arts and Crafts,** 175 Newbury St., 617/266-1810.

Faneuil Hall Marketplace, at North and Union Streets, is probably the busiest place in town. It's housed in three restored nineteenth-century buildings on Boston's historic waterfront and contains 125 shops and 21 restaurants. Under the north and south canopies in the

Quincy Market Building at Faneuil Hall are the **Bull Market Push-carts,** 617/338-2323, which showcase the wares of more than 100 New England artisans.

Haymarket, I-93 between Quincy Market and the North End, is an open-air fruit and vegetable market held Fridays and Saturdays. Many of the merchants are true characters. This is what real life looks like in Boston.

Upscale shops populate **Copley Place,** 100 Huntington Ave., 617/369-5000, and the adjacent **Prudential Center,** 800 Boylston St., 617/859-0648 (observation deck), 617/236-2366 (customer service). Here's where the big names are. Gucci and Tiffany at the Copley, Saks and Lord & Taylor at the Pru Restaurants, and pleasant places to stroll can make these shopping centers an all-day event.

You'll find a concentration of antique shops along Charles Street, at the foot of Beacon Hill. **Boston Antique Cooperative I & II,** 119 Charles St., 617/227-9810, has everything from vintage clothing to photographs and porcelain.

For shopping in the North End, get a culinary tour through Little Italy with **Michele Topor,** 6 Charter St., 617/523-6032, a professional chef who is one of Boston's foremost authorities on Italian food, wine, and culture.

For books, it's Harvard Square. Try **The Coop,** 1400 Massachusetts Ave., Cambridge, 617/499-2000, (rhymes with "hoop"), not your average college bookstore. You'll find Harvard merchandise, texts for Harvard classes, and lots of tomes worth browsing through.

And why not have a live lobster shipped home to a hungry friend? Several places will do it for you. Try **Bay State Lobster,** 379–395 Commercial St., 617/523-7960.

SPORTS AND RECREATION

One of Boston's main attractions is the 1912-built **Fenway Park,** Brookline Ave. and Massachusetts Turnpike, the oldest baseball park in the major leagues, with character to match. The problem is that it's small, and **Red Sox** fans are loyal, which makes getting tickets difficult. Tickets go on sale in December, and the earlier you order, the better your chances. Call 617/267-8661 (information), 617/267-1700 (tickets), www.redsox.com. There are no-alcohol sections and special seating for people with disabilities.

The new **FleetCenter,** 150 Causeway St., is home of the NBA's famed **Boston Celtics,** 617/624-1000, www.bostonceltics.com. For tickets, call Ticketmaster, 617/931-2000. The FleetCenter is also the home of the NHL's **Boston Bruins,** 617/624-1000, and tickets and information are available from the same numbers. Good luck getting tickets for either team. The NFL's **New England Patriots,** 800/543-1776, play at Foxboro Stadium, which is a 45-minute drive south.

Boston is noted for **First Night**, 617/542-1399, www.firstnight.org, an annual celebration of the arts that is held every New Year's Eve. More than 1,000 artists are featured in over 250 performances of all sorts throughout the city.

The city puts on lots of historic events. One is the **Boston Massacre Re-enactment**, 617/720-3290, which is held at the Old State House in March.

If you think you qualify for the **Boston Marathon**, 617/236-1652, call the Boston Athletic Association. The race is held the third Monday in April, and the crowds are huge. The finish line is at the Boston Public Library.

The ***Boston Globe* Jazz and Blues Festival**, 617/929-2000, is usually the third week in June.

The **Head of the Charles Regatta** takes place in late October, attracting 4,000 participants who race down the Charles River. 617/864-8415.

In December, you can watch a re-enactment of the **Boston Tea Party**, 617/482-6439. It's at the Old South Meeting House.

events
HORIZON

The Esplanade, between the Charles River and Back Bay, is the place for in-line skating. You can rent equipment from **Back Bay Bikes & Boards,** 333 Newbury St., 617/247-2336. Details from the **InLine Club of Boston** are available at www.sk8net.com/icb.

OK, so you probably won't break out in a big sporty sweat, but riding the pedal-powered **Swan Boats,** 617/522-1966, is a lot of fun. You can find them in the lagoon at the Public Garden from April through September. You can also ice skate there in the winter.

ENTERTAINMENT

So you've done the history thing—you've walked the Freedom Trail and read a thousand museum captions and even bought a patriotic T-shirt. Now you're ready to party. So where does Boston let its hair down?

Lots of places. Try the **Alley Cat Lounge,** 1 Boylston Pl., 617/451-6200. Here's where Boston's twenty-somethings go for great tunes and wild drinks. Even old Ben Franklin could learn to kick up his heels if he wandered into **Avalon,** 15 Lansdowne St., 617/262-2424, a high-tech dance club with total surround-sound and the hottest DJs. And why settle for a drab old tea party when you can hoist a brewsky at **Mama Kin,** 36 Lansdowne St., 617/536-2100, a rockin' dance club with a super-cool light show.

Lots of comedians got their first big breaks in Boston—Jay Leno and Rosie O'Donnell, for instance. One of the oldest comedy clubs in

Boston bars must close by 1 a.m. and clubs by 2 a.m. The T quits running soon after midnight. So if you're going to do a night on the town, start early.

You might get a discount on accommodations if you're willing to schedule your quick getaway over a weekend, and a really good deal if you'll visit during the snow season—January, February, and March. It can be difficult to find a room during the shoulder seasons of fall and spring because of big conventions.

Get a Boston CityPass and save 50 percent off combined museum admissions. The advance ticket booklet is good for six attractions—the Museum of Fine Arts, the Museum of Science, the New England Aquarium, the Isabella Stewart Gardner Museum, the John F. Kennedy Library and Museum, and the John Hancock Observatory. The pass is good for five days from the first date of use and is $26.50 for adults, $20.50 for seniors 65 and over, and $13.50 for youths 12 to 17. Entrance for children under 12 is available on a per attraction basis, and is either free or very reasonably priced. Buy the passes at the visitors center at Boston Common or call 888/SEE-BOSTON to get them in advance.

If you're going to be in Boston from May through mid-October, consider taking a whale-watching trip with the New England Aquarium, 617/973-5281. It's $24 for adults and $17 for seniors and students (cash only), but reservations can be made by means of a credit card.

The city of Boston is currently conducting the "Big Dig," an excavation project throughout town. Officials say the road work should not disrupt any tourist activities, but check out www.bigdig.com if you want to know what's going on.

City Survival Tips

Boston is the **Comedy Connection,** 617/248-9700, at Faneuil Hall. It lures big-name acts and talented newcomers.

Lots of good Irish people reside in Boston, which means lots of good Irish bars. The **Black Rose,** 160 State St., 617/742-2286, www.irishconnection.com, is a really popular place, with genuine Irish fiddle music and songs that are easy to sing along to.

Folk music has always been big here, and you might catch a rising star (Tracy Chapman started here) on a corner at Harvard Square. The coffeehouse where Joan Baez got her start is the **Club Passim,** 47 Palmer St., Cambridge, 617/492-7679, and new talent is still being nurtured here. It's in a basement near the Harvard Coop. For rock and folk music, try the **Lizard Lounge,** 1667 Massachusetts Ave., Cambridge, 617/547-0759, next to Harvard Law School. Also, lots of students and professors like **Casablanca,** 40 Brattle St., Cambridge, 617/876-0999, as a watering hole. The food's not bad either.

One of the world's best orchestras is the **Boston Symphony Orchestra,** 617/CONCERT, which performs in Symphony Hall (301 Massachusetts Ave. at Huntington Ave., 617/266-1492), as does the famed **Boston Pops,** 617/CONCERT, when it's not performing outdoors. And in the summer, there's a concert or performance of some kind almost every night at the **Hatch Shell,** 617/727-9547, an amphitheater on the Esplanade (Charles River off Storrow Dr.). This is where the Boston Pops performs its Fourth of July blowout concert.

The **Waterfront Jazz Series,** 617/635-3911, presents amateurs and veterans at the Christopher Columbus Park on the waterfront. The series takes place on Friday evenings in the summer. Additionally, the Museum of Fine Arts, 465 Huntington Ave., 617/267-9300, presents **Concerts in the Courtyard** on Wednesday evenings from June through September. Folk and jazz artists perform at 7:30 p.m. Bring a picnic dinner or buy it there.

For some really good music at a price that's hard to beat (it's free) try to attend a performance by one of the students or faculty members at the **New England Conservatory of Music,** 290 Huntington Ave., 617/585-1100. Performances are held during the academic year.

The **Boston Ballet,** 270 Tremont St., 617/482-9393, and visiting dramatic, dance, and music companies perform at the Wang Center for the Performing Arts, 270 Tremont St., 617/482-9393, an art deco beauty of a building.

Boston also has many repertory theaters. Try the **American Repertory Theater,** 64 Brattle St., Cambridge, 617/547-8300, www.amrep .org, which performs at Harvard University's Loeb Drama Center.

BosTix, 617/482-BTIX, offers half-price, day-of-show tickets to Boston's best arts and entertainment. BosTix kiosks are in Copley Square, Faneuil Hall, and Harvard Square. Other alternatives are **Ticketmaster,** 617/931-2000, and **Next Ticketing,** 617/423-NEXT.

CITY BASICS

For up-to-date visitor information call the **Greater Boston Convention & Visitors Bureau,** 617/536-4100 or 888/SEE-BOSTON, www.bostonusa.com. At the same numbers, try **Boston By Phone,** a one-stop shopping and reservation service connecting your call directly to hotels, restaurants, museums, attractions, sports and recreation facilities, theaters, nightclubs, shops and galleries, sightseeing tour companies, and travel services.

The Boston Common **Visitor Information Center,** 617/497-1630, www.bostonusa.com, is on the Tremont Street side of Boston Common. (Exit at the Park Street subway station.) It's open Monday to Saturday 8:30 a.m. to 5 p.m., Sunday 9 a.m. to 5 p.m. Another visitors

Trail of Heritage

The Black Heritage Trail is a walking tour that explores the history of Boston's black community, which settled in a part of Beacon Hill between 1800 and 1900. To see the sites properly, you must be part of an arranged tour, which is conducted by the Boston African American National Historic Site, 617/742-5415.

At the entrance to the **Boston Common**, Park and Beacon Sts., is the Robert Gould Shaw and 54th Regiment Memorial, a testimony to the service of blacks in the Civil War.

The **George Middleton House**, 5 Pickney St., is the oldest home built by a black person on Beacon Hill. Middleton, a colonel in the American Revolution and leader of an all-black company, built the home in 1797.

The **Charles Street Meeting House**, Mt. Vernon and Charles Sts., served as the pulpit for abolitionists Frederick Douglass, Sojourner Truth, and Wendell Phillips.

The **Lewis and Harriet Hayden House**, 66 Phillips St., was a stop along the Underground Railroad after the Fugitive Slave Law of 1850 was passed.

Another key stop along the trail is the **African Meeting House**, 89 Smith Ct. Established in 1806, it is the oldest black church building still standing in the United States.

center is in the Prudential Center. A third is at Harvard Square adjacent to the MBTA.

Citywide Reservation Services, 617/267-7424 or 800/HOTEL-93, is a one-call source for hotels, inns, guest houses, and short-term condos. You can also get information on accommodations packages, transportation, car rentals, restaurants, and events. For help with hotel reservations, contact the Greater Boston Convention & Visitors Bureau's **hotel hot line,** 800/777-6001. Choose a guest room in historic Federal and Victorian townhouses and restored 1840s waterfront lofts. Ask about the Winter Special—stay three nights, pay for two. You can also contact **Bed & Breakfast Agency of Boston,** 617/720-3540 or 800/CITY-BNB, www.boston-bnbagency.com, a directory of Boston B&Bs.

For 24-hour medical visits to hotels or for dental service, call **Inn-House Doctor,** 617/859-1776.

Major daily newspapers include the *Boston Globe* and *Boston Herald*. Other newspapers and magazines that will help you with information on your visit include *Boston Magazine*, *Where Boston*, *Panorama Magazine*, and the *Beacon Hill Visitor.*

⑤ MONTREAL

Spring comes into Quebec from the west. . . . In Montreal the cafés, like a bed of tulip bulbs, sprout from their cellars in a display of awnings and chairs.
—Leonard Cohen, *Beautiful Losers*

Sitting in a café, you might hear the locals call it *Le Grand Croissant.* "I'll have two of those," you might say, "and a café au lait."

What you'd be ordering is an island. Le Grand Croissant is a nickname for Montreal and refers to the island city's crescent shape. But where you wouldn't be wrong is in believing that Montreal is as exotic- and delicious-sounding as its moniker.

This is, after Paris, the second largest French-speaking city in the world. And the French goes deeper than a few suave turns of phrase. Montreal is French to its toes: It has the food, of course, in all its rich, creamy goodness; but it also has the flair for fashion and the flourish in the architecture (churches and cafés are everywhere) and great, lusty joie de vivre in one and all.

The Francophiles are not totally in charge, though, which means that although most of the signs are in French, they're also in English; and speaking English is not a crime, as long as you're friendly about it.

What you've got here, bottom line, is Paris without the rudeness—and at half the price and less than half the distance away. There may be a little extra snow, but what does it matter?

So what are you waiting for, *mon ami?* Order Le Grand Croissant to go . . . and go!

Montreal

SIGHTS AND ATTRACTIONS

1 Basilique Notre-Dame-de-Montreal
2 Biodome
2 Chalet du Mont-Royal
3 Insectarium
3 Jardin Botanique
4 Musee d'Archeologie Pointe-a-Calliere
2 Musee Juste pour Rire
2 Observatorie de l'Est
2 Oratoire St.-Joseph
2 Parc du Mont-Royal
5 Place Jacques-Cartier
6 Quartier Latin
7 Stade Olympique/Tour Olympique
3 Vieux-Montreal

DINING

8 Bacca d'Oro
9 Beaver Club
10 Brasserie Magnan
11 Fairmount Bagel Bakery
12 Katsura
13 Le Caveau
14 Le Taj
15 Mediterraneo Grill & Wine Bar
16 Toque
17 Zen

PIERRE DE COUBERTIN AV

125

SHERBROOKE ST

134

Jacques Cartier Bridge

Île Ste-Hélène

Notre Dame Island

Concordia Bridge

Parc des îles

Old Port

MOUNT-ROYAL AV

BERRI ST

ROY ST

DULUTH AV

ST. DENIS ST

VIGER ST

RENÉ-LÉVESQUE BLVD

ST-ANTOINE ST

ST-PAUL ST

ST-LAURENT ST

ST-URBAIN ST

LAURIER BLVD

PARK AV

PRINCE ARTHUR ST

STE-CATHERINE ST

Victoria Bridge

ST-VIATEUR WEST

FAIRMONT ST

AYLMER

UNIVERSITY ST

METCALFE ST

STANLEY ST

MAISONNEUVE BLVD

CÔTE STE-CATHERINE ST

ST-JACQUES ST

PEEL ST

DE LA MONTAGNE ST

CRESCENT ST
BISHOP ST
MACKAY ST
GUY ST

Mt. Royal Park

112

BONAVENTURE E

ST-VIATEUR WEST

QUEEN MARY RD

CÔTE-DES-NEIGES

SHERBROOKE ST

ATWATER AV

DU FORT ST

Lachine Canal

0   1.5   1.5
KILOMETERS   MILES

NOTE ABOUT PRICES

The prices listed below are roughly translated from Canadian to U.S. values. The exchange rate, which changes daily, is a moving target, so check the rates in the newspaper before you go. But based on favorable rates prevalent at press time for this book, you'll be pleasantly surprised. Canada is a real bargain. See the section "About This Book" in the "Planning Your Trip" chapter for more information.

GETTING AROUND

You'll be flying into **Dorval International,** 514/394-7377, which is about 14 miles west of the city. A taxi into town costs roughly $25. Base fares are about $2.25, plus $1.00 per each half-mile afterward. Generally taxis easy to find. When the white or yellow light is on up top, the taxi is available. One cab service is **Albee Limousines,** 514/594-4114. **Autocar Connaisseur,** 514/934-1222, a shuttle from the airport, is about $9 to town, and it runs every half-hour.

Don't get a car if you're staying within the city. Although the city is easy to get around in (except for the narrow cobblestone streets of the old city), parking is a major hassle.

The parking signs are in French, and you will encounter many restrictions. If you read the sign wrong, you could get towed—or, worse, if you're parking in the wrong spot during winter, the plows will make sure your car gets buried in a pile of snow. You'll have to tell Avis you'll bring the car back in April.

Who needs a car, anyway? Montreal has one of the best subway systems in the world. For one thing, the cars are extra quiet because they run on rubber wheels. And each of the 65 Metro stops is clean and specially decorated. You can get to all the top tourist stops this way, but if you need to take the bus, you can get a transfer just beyond the ticket booths in the Metro stations. Call **Metro** at 514/288-6287 for information on one-, three-, or seven-day passes.

You'll want to concentrate your visit in two areas—downtown and Vieux-Montreal (the old city). Hotels are abundant in both areas, and getting from one place to the other is a snap on the subway.

Downtown Montreal *(centre-ville)* is much like any other big city of skyscrapers and churches, until you discover that much of the life of the city is underground in a vast area known as the **Cite Souterrain.** It includes 19 miles of passages linking office buildings, hotels, a skating rink, three universities, an art museum, a church, 1,600 shops, and 200 restaurants.

This is where the natives go to escape the heat of the summer and the onslaught of winter. You could live a fine life of a mole here, perfectly plugged into the life of the city and yet never seeing the light of day. You can access the area through the McGill Metro station.

SIGHTS AND ATTRACTIONS

Montreal is an island, yes, but there are so many bridges to it, and the city itself is so full of skyscrapers, that the only way you can see the St. Lawrence River running on either side of it is to get to a tall, tall place and look out.

The very big heart of Montreal is the **Parc du Mont-Royal,** a 494-acre gathering of woods and jogging trails off Côte-des-Neiges that was designed by Frederick Law Olmsted, the genius behind New York's Central Park. You can get there by subway and bus.

The **Observatorie de l'Est,** within Parc du Mont-Royal, is the place to see the wide beauty of the city and the river that runs through it. On the eastern side of Mont-Royal is the 100-foot steel cross that is the icon of the city. The nearby baronial building **Chalet du Mont-Royal** is another place for a lookout, and inside are murals that depict Canadian history. It's on the park grounds. Next to the park and also worth a visit is the **Oratoire St.-Joseph,** 3800 Queen Mary Rd., 514/733-8211, a domed church dedicated to the earthly father of Jesus. This shrine attracts many pilgrims looking for miracles from the saint. Displayed on the walls are crutches left by those who found a cure.

A wonderful area for strolling is **Vieux-Montreal,** bounded by St. Lawrence River, rue McGill, avenue Viger, and rue Berri. *Vieux* means "old" in French, and Vieux-Montreal is where the city began back in 1642 as a fur-trading center on the banks of the St. Lawrence River. Later, stone buildings and streets were built, along with fortifications against invaders; and later still the city moved out and away from its source, leaving the old area to rot. It didn't. It's been resurrected, and today it's the center of government and cultural activity.

Vieux-Montreal is easily worth half a day's visit. Be sure to take in the **Place Jacques-Cartier,** rue Notre-Dame at Pl. Jacques-Cartier, which is at the heart of things. The stone buildings around the square are fascinating, and in the summer the square becomes a marketplace.

Another must is the **Basilique Notre-Dame-de-Montreal,** 116 rue Notre-Dame Ouest, 514/849-1070, an enormous Gothic structure that was built in 1829, replacing previous churches that had been on this site since 1642. Its twin towers are more than 200 feet high, and the organ has more than 7,000 pipes. Stained glass is everywhere. Walking into this huge space will bring a hush to the soul.

The area has several museums, but one not to be missed is the **Musee d'Archeologie Pointe-a-Calliere,** 350 Pl. Royale, 514/872-9150, which concentrates on Montreal's history in a place where the city began. Inside are excavated remnants of original buildings among a maze of stone walls and corridors.

Don't miss the **Olympic Park** area on the eastern side of the city.

Place Jacques-Cartier, heart of Vieux-Montreal

In this area (get ready to walk your legs off) is the **Stade Olympique,** 4141 avenue Pierre-de-Coubertin, which was built in 1976 for the summer Olympics. If you get a chance, take the cable car up to the top of the 890-foot tower at the **Tour Olympique.** You can see for 50 miles. Nearby is the **Biodome,** 4777 avenue Pierre-de-Coubertin, 514/868-3000, a natural-history exhibit that encompasses four ecosystems—from a rain forest to a polar environment—that will leave you hot and cold.

Jardin Botanique, 4101 rue Sherbrooke Est, 514/872-1400, which is also in Olympic Park, is one of the major gardens of the world, 181 acres of lavish gardens that can be visited at any time of the year because of the 10 greenhouses that contain many of the garden's 26,000 species of plants. You'll want to take the little tram on a tour of the place. A fascinating component of the gardens is the **Insectarium,** 4101 rue Sherbrooke Est, 514/872-1400, a bug-shaped building that contains more than 250,000 bugs, alive and dead.

With the Olympic Park's "Get an Eyeful" pass, you can visit the tower, the Biodome, the botanical garden, and the Insectarium for one low price. Call 514/252-8687 for more information.

Another fascinating area of Montreal is the **Quartier Latin,** rue St.-Denis and blvd. St.-Laurent, near the University du Quebec. To get there, take the UQAM subway stop and roam around the area just west of rue St.-Denis and along boulevard St.-Laurent. You'll find lots of coffee shops, designer boutiques, antique shops, and art galleries, not to mention rows of ethnic and French restaurants. This is a happening place.

If you get a chance, drop by the fascinating **Musee Juste pour Rire** (the Just for Laughs Museum), 2111 blvd. St.-Laurent, 514/845-2014. Inside are lots of exhibits, some rather serious. If you've got some jokes you'd like to try out on an audience, bring them. There's a cabaret inside that will let you perform. Opening times are erratic, so call ahead.

LODGING

Montreal has 23,000 rooms, and you should be able to find something unless you happen to cross paths with the Montreal Jazz Festival, which always overwhelms the city with visitors.

The **Bed and Breakfast Downtown Network,** 800/267-5180, can help you find a place to stay either in a Victorian home in a neighborhood or in a downtown apartment. A similar organization is **Bed and Breakfast of Montreal,** 800/738-4338.

The **Auberge du Vieux-Port,** 97 rue de la Commune Est, 888/660-7678, $$$, is ideally located near the Old Port in a stone building dating back to the 1880s. Rooms have exposed beams and brass beds. Included is a full breakfast in the hotel's fine French restaurant.

Chateau Versailles, 1659 rue Sherbrooke Ouest, 800/361-3664, $$, is loaded with charm. Antique paintings and tapestries are all over the lobby and hallways, and the big rooms have fine moldings. The hotel is made up of four mansions all in a row.

Trendy and delightful are the words to describe the **Auberge de la Fontaine,** 1301 rue Rachel Est, 800/597-0597, $$. The walls are yellow, the ceilings are green, and somehow it all works. The hotel comprises two residences built at the turn of the last century, and the location is wonderful—just across from the Parc Lefontaine in the Plateau Mont-Royal district.

Going Places

Gray Line, 1001 Sq. Dorchester, 514/934-1222, offers a complete range of sightseeing tours on board a replica of Montreal's street cars of the old days. You can also rent a bike and be part of a tour with **Velo-Tour Montreal**, 514/236-VELO. Or **Heritage Montreal**, 514/286-2662, will take you on an architectural walking tour downtown and in Montreal's neighborhoods and surrounding area, but only in the summer.

You can have a jet boat give you a quick view of the city from the Lachine rapids. Contact **Saute-Mouton Jet-boating**, 514/284-9607, www.jetboating montreal.com. Prepare to get wet. Or take it much slower with **Rafting on the St. Lawrence**, 514/767-2230. If the weather is right, take a snowmobile tour in the hills 80 minutes north of Montreal with **Randonneige Quebec**, 800/326-0642, www.randonneige.com.

La Reine Elizabeth, 900 blvd. Rene-Levesque Ouest, 800/441-1414, $$$, is the reigning queen of Montreal hotels. Chintz and rumpled style abound in this old Canadian Pacific hotel on top of the Gare Centrale train station.

On the west side of town, in a residential neighborhood close to some fabulous shopping at the Fauborg Ste.-Catherine, is the **Hotel du Fort,** 1390 rue du Fort, 800/565-6333, $$$. The Canadian Center for Architecture is right around the corner.

Auberge les Passants du Sans Soucy, 171 rue St.-Paul Ouest, 514/842-2634, $$$, is a small inn made from an 1836 fur warehouse. There are brass beds, stone walls, soft lighting, and a full breakfast.

If you want to be in the middle of Montreal's nightlife in the St.-Denis area, try the **Hotel Lord Berri,** 1199 rue Berri, 888/363-0363, $$. The decor is bright and modern, and the hotel has a popular Italian restaurant. Another, more modestly priced hotel in the same area is the **Hotel St.-Denis,** 1254 rue St.-Denis, 514/849-4529, $.

Finally, the **Ritz-Carlton Kempinski,** 1228 rue Sherbrooke Ouest, 800/223-6800, $$$$, is consistently rated as one of the finest hotels in Montreal. Its Le Café de Paris is also highly rated.

DINING

Montreal has more than 5,000 restaurants representing over 75 ethnic groups—but the French dominate, as well they should. If you want food that even *sounds* delicious, give it a French accent.

Here, the Gallic influence goes deep, into the soul of the food. Start with croissants and café au lait for breakfast, drop by a deli and have them make you a sandwich from the city's famous smoked meats for lunch, and for dinner, anything with cheese will be wonderful. Why not go all the way and ask for cheese fondue?

Toque, 3842 rue St.-Denis, 514/499-2084, $$$$, is French without being stuck in tradition. Its chefs dare to go out on a culinary limb with different combinations and bright colors—all of the fare emphasizing fresh ingredients, such as the abundant salmon in the area.

The **Beaver Club,** 900 blvd. Rene-Levesque Ouest, 514/861-3511, $$$$, at Le Reine Elizabeth hotel is strong on classic French cuisine, such as roast prime rib au jus. The atmosphere resembles a nineteenth-century men's club.

A traditional French restaurant without the high prices is **Le Caveau,** 2063 avenue Victoria, 514/844-1624, $$, where you can get the traditional appetizer of snails and a main course of rabbit, and of course those creamy desserts.

Zen, 1050 rue Sherbrooke Ouest, 514/499-0801, $$, is an adventuresome Asian restaurant, where the cuisine of several cultures comes together in unexpected ways. It's in Le Westin Mont-Royal.

A restaurant that defies category and dares to stretch the limit is

Mediterraneo Grill & Wine Bar, 3500 blvd. St.-Laurent, 514/844-0027, $$$. Order the duck with sweet potatoes.

Le Taj, 2077 rue Stanley, 514/845-9015, $$, specializes in the cuisine of northern India, which is less spicy than what you might expect.

An extensive menu is the hallmark at **Bacca d'Oro,** 1448 rue St.-Mathieu, 514/933-8414, $$$, an Italian restaurant with a reputation for friendliness and quick service. With your dessert you get a bowl of walnuts that you can crack at your table.

The sushi at **Katsura,** 2170 rue de la Montagne, 514/849-1172, $$$, a Japanese restaurant, centers around the freshest ingredient nearby—salmon. Try it, you'll like it.

They don't mess around at **Brasserie Magnan,** 2602 rue St.-Patrick, 514/935-9647, $$. This is a steak place. The decor is early warehouse and the crowd sort of matches, although just as many business people as dockworkers seem to be attracted to the place. In warm weather, you can eat out on the parking lot.

Locals say the bagels are better in Montreal than anyplace in the world. See for yourself: the bagels are cooked in a wood-burning oven at **Fairmount Bagel Bakery,** 74 rue Fairmount Ouest, 514/272-0667, $.

SHOPPING

Shopping is a year-round pastime in Montreal, thanks to the 19-mile underground network downtown that connects all kinds of boutiques, shopping centers, restaurants, and more. Out in the sunshine, you'll find many antique stores along rue Notre-Dame; elegant shopping is in the Quartier du Musee on rue Sherbrooke; and downtown has many chic boutiques devoted to local designers.

Rue Notre-Dame Ouest, between rue Guy and avenue Atwater, is a center of antique shopping. Montreal also has many fine secondhand bookstores. The book you've been looking for could well be in the huge and dusty **Russell Books,** 275 rue St.-Antonoine Ouest, 514/866-0564.

Two words go together—French and fashion. Some of the city's finest boutiques can be found along rue Sherbrooke. This is a place to wander. But for the very fashion-conscious, the place to go is **rue Chabanel.** It's in the northern part of the city and is the center of Montreal's garment industry. Every Saturday, many of the manufacturers and importers in the area open their doors to the retail trade in a kind of makeshift bazaar. You'll find fine leather goods, men's suits, winter coats, and linens in this area of hundreds of tiny stores. It's an eight-block stretch just west of boulevard St.-Laurent.

Downtown is simply brimming with art galleries, fashion boutiques, and jewelry stores. On and around rues Sherbrooke and Ste.-Catherine is the place to be. Be sure to stop by the major downtown shopping malls of **Le Centre Eaton** (677 rue Ste.-Catherine Ouest, 514/284-8411), **Les Promenades de la Cathedrale** (625 rue Ste.-Catherine Ouest, 514/849-

The end of January brings **La Fete des Neiges** (Winter Carnival) to the Parc des Iles. But June is the month when Montreal really comes alive. **RockFest**, a series of free outdoor rock concerts featuring top local groups and others from around the world, takes place downtown. There's also **Les FrancoFolies de Montreal**, a French cultural festival featuring local and international performers, and the **Worldwide Kite Rendez-vous**, a four-day celebration of wind, color, and free flight.

Perhaps the grandest event of them all is in July, when the **Festival International de Jazz de Montreal** tunes up. It's the biggest street festival of the summer. Get your hotel reservations early.

At the end of July is the **Just for Laughs Festival**, which attracts 650 comedians from 14 countries playing in more than 1,000 shows and performances all over the city.

And food gets top billing at **Les Fetes gourmandes internationales de Montreal** in August.

For additional information on all of these events, contact Tourisme Montreal, 514/844-5400, www.tourism-montreal.org.

events
HORIZON

9925), and **Place Montreal Trust** (1500 McGill College Ave., 514/843-8000). The city's leading department store is Eaton, which was founded in 1925. You can get just about anything there, including a nice meal at its fine restaurant.

There are also some magnificent shopping centers. You don't want to miss **Complexe Desjardines,** blvd. Rene-Levesque and rue Jeanne Mance, a beautiful area of fountains and plants housing 80 stores that run all the way from the budget outlet to top-of-the-line clothing stores. Another is **Les Cours Mont-Royal,** 1550 rue Metcalfe, where almost all of the stores cater to the rich.

You're in the fur capital of the world, and if that's what makes you happy, this is the place to get that coat. Many of the retail outlets for manufacturers are concentrated along rue Mayor and boulevard de Maisonneuve between rue de Bleury and rue Aylmer. Probably the top of the line in furriers is **Birger Christensen,** 1300 rue Sherbrooke Ouest, 514/842-5111. Be sure to check with U.S Customs first before you buy a fur; it may belong to an endangered species.

Vieux-Montreal has lots of tacky tourist shops, but there are a few treasures among the trash. **Desmarais et Robitaille,** 60 rue Notre-Dame Ouest, 514/845-3194, has some very nice Quebecois carvings and handicrafts.

And why not go to the **post office** for a different sort of gift—

Montreal 101

The first European to wander though the area was Jacques Cartier, who was looking for a shortcut to the Orient. He didn't find one. That was in 1535. Samuel de Champlain established a temporary fur trading post in 1611, but it was not until 1642 that the city became more than an outpost. In an effort organized by a French religious society, Paul de Chomedey brought 53 French colonists to establish a missionary colony.

By 1763 Montreal had 60,000 residents, and it was then, as part of the French and Indian War, that Britain captured it. Later, during the U.S. War of Independence, America occupied the city briefly. Montreal was incorporated as a city in 1832, and developed into a major economic center after Canada was formed in 1867.

cities to go

colorful stamps, maybe, or collectible coins from the Royal Canadian Mint. They even have T-shirts. Call 800/267-1177 for help in finding the nearest postal outlet.

SPORTS AND RECREATION

You can watch the major-league **Montreal Expos,** 514/790-1245, www.montrealexpos.com, play baseball at the Stade Olympique (Olympic Stadium), 4549 avenue Pierre-de-Coubertin, 514/790-1245. Likewise, you can catch the **Montreal Impact,** 514/328-FOOT, play soccer both indoor in the winter (Molson Centre, 1260 de la Gauchetiere St. W.) and outdoors in the summer (Centre Claude-Robillard, 1000 Emile Journault, 514/872-6911). And not to be forgotten are the **Montreal Canadiens,** 514/932-CLUB, who have won the Stanley Cup hockey championship more than two dozen times. They play from September to June at the Molson Centre.

You think the French don't play football? Wrong. The **Montreal Alouettes,** 514/871-2266, play professional football as part of the Canadian Football League. Games take place at McGill University Stadium, 475 Pine Ave. W., from June to November.

You can also see the finest horses and the best drivers in exciting harness-racing action at the **Hippodrome de Montreal,** 7440 Decarie Blvd., 514/739-2741.

But why watch? Get out on the ice yourself at **L'Amphitheatre Bell,** 1000 rue del la Gourchetiere Ouest, 514/395-0555, where indoor ice skating is popular all year long. Then in good weather, you can rent bicycles and in-line skates at **Velo Aventure Montreal,** Old Port of Montreal, King-Edward Dock, 514/847-0666.

ENTERTAINMENT

The city's nightlife is a constantly shifting thing—what's hot one day isn't so cool the next. Much of the best bars and dance clubs can be found on the city's east side, along rue St.-Denis and vicinity. Another center of action is on rue Bishop, downtown.

The **Casino de Montreal,** 1 avenue du Casino, 800/665-2274, is one of the finest in the world and is only 10 minutes from Old Montreal. It has more than 110 gaming tables and nearly 3,000 slot machines. What's more, there are no taxes on winnings in Quebec, and jackpots are paid in full on site. The **Cabaret du Casino** is a first-class dinner theater, and the casino's upscale restaurant, **Nuances,** has been awarded a five-star rating from *Mobil Travel Guide* three years in a row. The casino is part of the **Parc des Iles,** 514/872-6222, islands in the St. Lawrence River that include an amusement park, acres of gardens, and a clean beach. Call for more information on activities.

Dance is big in Montreal, both classical and contemporary. Many groups perform at the **Place des Arts,** 175 rue Ste.-Catherine Ouest, 514/285-4270 (information), 514/842-2112 (tickets). Call for details on dance performances, as well as other activities at the five theaters that are housed here. Canada's only professional folkloric dance troupe is **Les Sortileges,** 514/274-5655. And **Les Grands Ballets Canadiens**, 514/849-8681, has been performing classical and contemporary ballet for 40 years.

The world renowned **Orchestre Symphonique de Montreal,** 514/842-9951, performs regularly at the Place des Arts when it is not on tour. Often, many concerts are performed free in Montreal's parks during the summer. Check the *Gazette* listings for time and place.

The city has a thriving group of theaters, but many of them perform in French. One of them is the **Theatre du Nouveau Monde,** 84 rue Ste.-Catherine Ouest, 514/866-8668, which presents French classics of yesterday and today. The premier English-language theater in town is the **Centaur,** 453 rue St.-Francois-Xavier, 514/288-3161, which stages contemporary productions, classics, and Broadway hits.

One of the better jazz clubs is **L'Air du Temps,** 191 rue St.-Paul Ouest, 514/842-2003, in Vieux-Montreal. And to find out what Montreal is laughing about these days, stop by the **Comedy Nest,** 1740 blvd. Rene-Levesque Ouest, 514/932-6378.

CITY BASICS

You can get lots of help from the **Centre Info-Tourist,** 1001 Sq. Dorchester, 514/873-2015, or **Tourisme Quebec,** 800/363-7777. To make hotel reservations, visit or call 174 rue Notre-Dame Est at Pl. Jacques-Cartier, 514/873-2015. For more tourist information, check the Web sites for the **Greater Montreal Convention and Tourism Bureau** (www.tourism-montreal.org), the **Quebec government** (www.tourisme.gouv.qc.ca), and the **Greater Quebec Area Tourism and Convention Bureau** (www.quebec-region.cuq.qc.ca). Information for **people with disabilities** is also available at 514/252-3104, www.craph.org/keroul/.

You can get a unique, live view of Montreal though the **LiveCam,** www.montrealcam.com. Eleven cameras bring different views of the city, and you can get weather information, too.

For currency exchange, try **Currencies International,** 1250 Peel St., or the **National Bank of Canada,** 895 de la Gauchetiere St. W., with several locations including the Central Train Station. Don't forget that you can get a rebate of the 7 percent GST (Goods and Services Tax) on most products and accommodations. Get the details in a brochure called *GST Rebate for Visitors,* 902/432-5608.

A **museum pass** will get you into any of 19 Montreal museums. A day pass is $15, and a three-day pass is $28. Passes are available at any of the museums or at Info-Touriste. Tickets to sports and cultural events are available through **Montreal Reservation Centre,** 505 de Maisonneuve Blvd. E., Suite 205, 514/284-2277. And **ski information** is available at www.skinetcanada.com.

The *Montreal Gazette* has entertainment news, as do the weeklies *AfterHour* and *Mirror.*

⑥ TORONTO

Toronto is New York run by the Swiss.
—Peter Ustinov

About a century ago, and for many years thereafter, the Scots—not the Swiss—were in charge of Toronto. These flint-hearted men pinched the pennies and built the banks and made sure that all was godly and sober. Things, in fact, were so prim back then that you couldn't rent a horse on Sunday for pleasure rides in the family buggy, and shopkeepers drew the curtains on their windows to prevent Sunday window shopping.

Then the non-Anglo immigrants came, and so did the fun.

Today Toronto, with a metropolitan area population of 4.4 million, is among the top 10 cities in terms of size in North America. It's also one of the most ethnically diverse—80 groups speaking 52 languages. In fact, in 1989 the United Nations declared Toronto the world's most multicultural city. Among the main groups represented are a half-million Italians, the largest concentration of Chinese in eastern Canada, and more Portuguese than any place in North America.

Those stiff upper Anglo-Saxon lips have loosened as they've learned to slurp up the pasta and chow down on the dim sum. And the curtains have been raised on some of the grandest shopping in the world.

Yet there seems to be an underlying sense of Scotch order and good manners in Toronto, which is what makes it seem Swiss. It's clean. The mean streets are few and far between.

What you've got here, in other words, is the Big Apple with a lot more polish.

Toronto

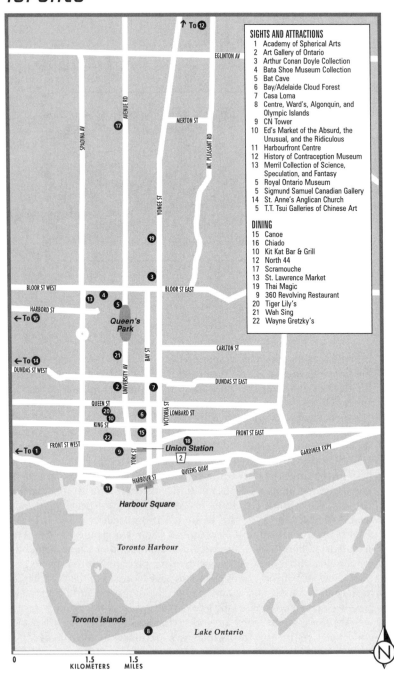

SIGHTS AND ATTRACTIONS
1 Academy of Spherical Arts
2 Art Gallery of Ontario
3 Arthur Conan Doyle Collection
4 Bata Shoe Museum Collection
5 Bat Cave
6 Bay/Adelaide Cloud Forest
7 Casa Loma
8 Centre, Ward's, Algonquin, and Olympic Islands
9 CN Tower
10 Ed's Market of the Absurd, the Unusual, and the Ridiculous
11 Harbourfront Centre
12 History of Contraception Museum
13 Merril Collection of Science, Speculation, and Fantasy
5 Royal Ontario Museum
5 Sigmund Samuel Canadian Gallery
14 St. Anne's Anglican Church
5 T.T. Tsui Galleries of Chinese Art

DINING
15 Canoe
16 Chiado
10 Kit Kat Bar & Grill
12 North 44
17 Scramouche
13 St. Lawrence Market
19 Thai Magic
9 360 Revolving Restaurant
20 Tiger Lily's
21 Wah Sing
22 Wayne Gretzky's

NOTE ABOUT PRICES

Many of the prices listed below are roughly translated from Canadian to U.S. values based upon the exchange rate at press time.

GETTING AROUND

If you're flying in, you'll arrive at the **Lester B. Pearson International Airport,** 416/247-7678, which is in the northwest corner of Toronto about 40 miles from downtown. The **Airport Express Aeroport,** 905/564-3232, operates a shuttle service between the airport and 35 locations downtown. You can buy a ticket from one of six locations in the airport; an adult ticket costs about $10. Be aware that it can take an hour to get downtown during heavy traffic.

Cabs to downtown are about $35, and they are easy to flag down. When the light up top is on, the taxi is available. Try **Diamond Taxi-cab Association,** 416/366-6868.

Toronto's public transit system, operated by the **Toronto Transit Commission,** 416/393-4636, is one of the best in the world. It's safe and clean, with a subway system, buses, streetcars, and light rail. For about $5 you can get a day pass that allows unlimited trips for up to two adults and four children.

So why worry with a car? Parking is terrifically expensive—about $2.00 to $3.50 for the first hour, and a little less for each hour after that. If you situate yourself in a central location, you won't need a car, and public transit is hardly needed either—so very much is bunched into downtown. However, if you do need a lift, why not try a pedicab? They're operated by young, athletic, sweating men and women. You'll find them along Yonge Street, in Yorkville, and around the theater district.

To get to the middle of things in Toronto, go to **Union Station,** which is on Front Street and only a few blocks from Lake Ontario and the rebuilt dock area called **Harbourfront.** Two blocks west of Union Station is the **CN Tower**—go up there to get your bearings. It's the tallest free-standing structure in the world.

A block to the east of Union Station is **Yonge Street,** the main drag of Toronto and the center of fun. It's the longest street in the world and runs through the middle of the central business district area, which is bounded by Front Street to the south, Bloor Street to the north, Spadina Avenue on the west, and Jarvis Street on the east. Stay within this area, or nearby, and you won't be far from all that matters in Toronto.

SIGHTS AND ATTRACTIONS

Toronto's museums are as sprawling as its metropolis. Yours to explore are the unusual world of Canadian art.

One of the finest art museums in North America is the **Art Gallery of Ontario,** 317 Dundas St. W., 416/979-6648. It contains 50 new and renovated galleries and houses the world's largest collection of Henry Moore's sculptures. You'll also find finely crafted art of the Eskimo (Inuit), the roots of which go back thousands of years in Canada.

The **Royal Ontario Museum,** 100 Queen's Park, 416/586-8000, calls itself "Canada's single greatest cultural asset." It has more than 6 million items—everything from porcelain to dead bats—and all under one roof.

Within the museum is the **T.T. Tsui Galleries of Chinese Art,** which explores more than 5,000 years of history with 1,200 objects. It is one of the top 10 Chinese art collections in the world, outside China. And don't neglect the **Sigmund Samuel Canadian Gallery,** which includes paintings, furnishings, and costumes that demonstrate the role played by French and British cultures in the development of Canada from the late 1600s to the early 1900s. Oh, and there's the **Bat Cave,** which contains 4,000 freeze-dried and artificial bats.

Walk, don't run, through the **Bata Shoe Museum Collection,** 327 Bloor St., 416/979-7799, which contains 10,000 items of footwear covering 4,000 years of trodding.

Harbourfront Centre, 410 Queens Quay W., 416/973-3000, is a 100-acre collection of shops and entertainment, and is the center of activity in the city. This is a must. Events include dance, theater, and musical performances; festivals; craft shows; ice skating; boat trips; and a market representing 100 antique dealers.

CN Tower, 301 Front St. W., 416/362-5411, is another icon of Toronto—at 1,815 feet, it is the highest free-standing structure in the world. You can get up near the top in an elevator in about a minute, which is about as fast as a jet plane, and from the observation deck called the Skypod, on a clear day, you can see all the way to Rochester, New York. The Skypod has a glass floor, by the way, and when you're in it you can see about 1,200 feet straight down. It's not for the faint-hearted.

Stop by the **Academy of Spherical Arts,** 38 Hanna Ave., 416/532-2782, to see an impressive collection of antique billiard tables. The place is so popular, though, you may have to queue up to get in.

You'll see every kind of prop imaginable at **Ed's Market of the Absurd, the Unusual, and the Ridiculous,** 276 King St. W., 416/977-3935. The collection of theater impresario Ed Mirvish includes costumes from the Old Vic in London and some worn by stars such as Maggie Smith and Peter O'Toole. And all of it's for sale. To get there, you'll have to go through Old Ed's restaurant, itself something of a museum of the unusual. In the restaurant is a three-ton, 25-foot jade boat, for instance.

St. Anne's Anglican Church, 270 Gladstone Ave., 416/536-1202, is a 1907 beauty built in the Byzantine style. Inside is every bit as beautiful, with murals, bronze reliefs, and mosaics done by some of Canada's lead-

Going Places

You can see the whole wide world though the panoramic windows of the *Empress of Canada*, 416/260-8901, a luxury yacht. **Jubilee Queen Cruises**, 416/203-7245, offers sweeping staircases, Tiffany lamps, and on-board dining in its 120-foot river showboat. You'll see the harbor in style. You can also hop on and off the double-decker London-style sightseeing buses of **Olde Town Toronto Tours Ltd.**, 800/350-0398. Start or stop your tour at any of 15 stops at the city's major attractions and shopping areas.

    SkyDome Tour Experience will give you a behind-the-scenes look at the world's first domed stadium with a fully retractable roof, 416/341-2770.

    Magnotta Winery, 271 Chrislea Rd., Vaughan, 800/461-WINE, has won lots of awards for its wines. The tours are free. It's about a 20-minute drive from Toronto.

ing artists. You can only see the inside on Sundays, during services that begin at 10 a.m.

It's always cloudy at the **Bay/Adelaide Cloud Forest,** Richmond and Yonge Sts., 416/392-1111, a 3,000-square-foot glass conservatory in the financial district that contains a lower level of shade plants, a mid-story of tree ferns, and a canopy of trees, typical of the cloud forests in South America and Asia.

You must visit **Casa Loma,** 1 Austin Terr., 416/923-1171, the 98-room turn-of-the-last-century castle filled with secret panels and long passageways. And don't neglect the gardens outside the opulent home, which have recently undergone a five-year restoration. The grounds are magnificent.

With a little detective work, you can find "the best collection of Sherlockiana available to the public anywhere." The **Arthur Conan Doyle Collection,** 789 Yonge St., 416/393-7000—part museum and part library—captures the ambiance of Baker Street in London with its Victorian decor and the detective's deerstalker and slippers beside the fireplace. The collection includes some rare editions. It's at the Metro Reference Library of Toronto.

You can't miss the **History of Contraception Museum,** 19 Greenbelt Dr., North York, 416/449-9444—it claims to be the only museum of its kind in the world. The 580-piece exhibit includes such artifacts as ancient dung-and-honey tampons, dried beaver testicles, and animal membrane condoms. It's in North York, a suburb in northern Toronto.

The **Merril Collection of Science, Speculation, and Fantasy,** 239 College St., Third Floor, 416/393-7748, was originally known as the Spaced Out Library. It contains 54,000 sci-fi items, including information on parapsychology, UFOs, and Atlantean legends.

One of the treats of Toronto is the group of four islands out in Lake Ontario. They're easy to get to—it's just a few minutes on one of the little ferries to **Centre, Ward's, Algonquin, and Olympic Islands.** The ferries leave from the dock behind the Westin Harbour Castle. The nice thing about the islands is that no motorized transportation is allowed. There's a boardwalk that goes all the way across the interconnected islands, but it's a long walk—about a mile and a half. There are a total of 550 acres of parkland. You may want to rent a bicycle, go to the beach (prepare for a chill), or ride on a turn-of-the-last-century merry-go-round.

LODGING

It makes sense to stay downtown, within easy reach of most of the attractions and theaters. Although most of the downtown accommodations are in the upper cost range, there are a few budget choices, too.

The **Royal York Hotel,** 100 Front St. W., 800/663-7229, $$$, is both a main attraction in the city and an elegant place to stay. It was originally a train station hotel, so of course it's right near Union Station. The 1929 lobby has been carefully restored.

They call the **King Edward Hotel** (37 King St. E., 800/225-5843, $$$) the "King Eddie." Have high tea in the understated lobby, among the marble pillars and palm trees. The hotel's two restaurants—Chiaro's and the Café Victoria—are top choices among the well-heeled high-rollers of Toronto. Ask about the weekend rates and theater packages.

A hotel that's right in the middle of the best of everything is the **Metropolitan,** 108 Chestnut St., 800/323-7500, $$$, a contemporary beauty with modern furniture and king-size beds. It has eight rooms for travelers with disabilities. Nearby is the Eaton Centre and the theater district.

Possibly the best view of any hotel is from the **Westin Harbour Castle,** 1 Harbour Sq., 800/228-3000, $$$$, which looks out onto Lake Ontario and is next to the Harbourfront entertainment and shopping complex. Ask about weekend rates, and maybe you can slice off one of those dollar marks.

The **Delta Chelsea Inn,** 33 Gerrard St. W., 800/243-5732, $$$, is Toronto's largest hotel. Because of its location near the theater district, it's a good place to go if theater is your top interest. Ask about packages that include theater tickets.

A Victorian (built in 1882), midtown, 67-room, European-style hotel is the **Selby,** 592 Sherbourne St., 800/387-4788, $$. Continental breakfast is included. The hotel's suites have fireplaces, and it offers health club privileges and air-conditioning. Another European-style

Toronto skyline

hotel is the **Sutton Place,** 955 Bay St., 800/268-3790, $$$, which has 230 guest rooms and 62 suites.

On the lower end of the price scale but at the upper end of cleanliness and location is the **Hotel Victoria,** 56 Yonge St., 800/363-8228, $$, a Victorian beauty just a block east of Union Station. It has 48 rooms and is located in the heart of the theater and financial districts. Another budget choice is the **Quality Hotel Downtown,** 111 Lombard St., 800/228-5151, $. It has 196 newly renovated rooms and offers free continental breakfast.

Yet another option is **Victoria's Mansion,** 68 Gloucester St., 416/921-4625, $$, a mini-hotel with 23 rooms, all with private baths and refrigerators. Museums and theaters are a walk away.

For something different, stay in a private home in Toronto. The **Abodes of Choice Bed & Breakfast Association,** 416/537-7629, will link you up with everything from a room in a house to a private suite. Another choice for those interested in a B&B is **Clarence Square Bed and Breakfast,** 13 Clarence Sq., 416/598-0616, $$, an elegant historic home in the heart of the entertainment district. It features private baths and whirlpool tubs, and a sumptuous breakfast.

DINING

Listen to this: Little Italy, a sprawling Chinatown, Little India. What do you think you'll find in these small worlds that populate the big world of Toronto, the most ethnically diverse city in the world? Some of the best, most diverse cuisine in the world, that's what.

So if we're going to Canada, let's eat like the natives do—or at least the rich natives. At **Canoe,** 66 Wellington St. W., 54th Floor, Dominion Bank Tower, 416/364-0054, $$$$, you can dine on breast of

Neighborhood Watch

An area of astounding architecture is the **financial district**, around Yonge and Bay Streets, just north of Union Station. And just as fascinating as the historic and modern buildings above is the Underground City below, a maze of tunnels that link it all.

One of the best neighborhoods for strolling about at night is **Little Italy**, especially College Street between Bathurst and Grace. Here you'll find lots of streetside cafés and bars, from little cappuccino bars to boisterous bistros.

Another neighborhood where things are buzzing is **Greektown**, on Danforth Avenue between Broadview and Coxwell. The area is also known as the Danforth. Here's where Torontoans are gathering, thanks to all the lively restaurants with patios spilling out onto the street, plus an eclectic collection of stores.

Baldwin Street, one block north of the Art Gallery of Ontario, is also hopping. You'll find over 30 restaurants here, from Mexican to Malaysian.

And don't forget **Little India**, in the east end of Toronto, along Gerrard Street E. between Highfield and Coxwell Avenues. It's an area of six blocks crowded with restaurants, music stores, and shops, including 20 boutiques that specialize in traditional saris and other brightly colored silk creations. Sunday is one of its busiest days. Take the College Street streetcar from downtown.

Ontario pheasant, or Yukon caribou. If you've always had a hankering for Portuguese food, try **Chiado,** 864 College St., 416/538-1910, $$$$, where fish from the Azores is the specialty.

Tiger Lily's, 257 Queen St., 416/977-5499, $$, is a tiny Chinese noodle shop offering 15 different noodle plates, plus shrimp dumplings. The cooking is light and flavor-balanced. In the eclectic Kensington Market is **Wah Sing,** 47 Baldwin St., 416/599-8822, $$, which often has a two-for-one lobster special. Try it with black bean sauce. And ask for extra water when you order the Hurricane Kettle, a fiery seafood soup, at **Thai Magic,** 1118 Yonge St., 416/968-7366, $$.

Expect a warm welcome (and a big crowd) at the **Kit Kat Bar & Grill,** 297 King St. W., 416/977-4461, $$, which specializes in large portions of southern Italian food. The restaurant has a long history of additions over the years, which accounts for its long, thin shape.

The menu is quite inventive at **North 44,** 253 Yonge St., 416/487-4897, $$$$. Start with the roasted garlic and cylinder of goat cheese studded with beet chips and sage sprigs. The 17-page wine list will surely have something to your liking.

You can't beat the view at the **360 Revolving Restaurant,** 301 Front St. W., 416/362-5411, $$$$, which does pretty much what its name says it does, way up high in the CN Tower. Try the blackened quail or, for the bigger appetite, how about an ostrich steak? Contemporary cuisine is the hallmark of **Scramouche,** 1 Benvenuto Pl., 416/961-8011, $$$. A popular item is the scallop sausage. Jackets are required.

Wayne Gretzky's, 416/979-7825, $$, a restaurant owned by the legendary retired hockey star, has lots of real mementos among the decor, and a menu that has more than the typical sports bar's. It's at 99 Blue Jay Way (his jersey number was 99), a block north of the Sky-Dome stadium.

Bacon on a Bun is a Toronto favorite, a salt-and-sugar–cured slab of extra-lean ham on a sandwich that's served with a strong cup of coffee. You'll find it at the **St. Lawrence Market,** located in the former City Hall, 92 Front St., $.

SHOPPING

Toronto has all the top stores, as you would expect in such a big place, but it also has a secret world of ethnic wares and native designers who have everything from quilts to carvings to offer. With the favorable exchange rate, Americans can't go wrong.

The Kensington Market is where all the ethnic flavors of Toronto come together, and should not be missed. Check out the unbelievable variety of spices, plus bargain coffees and teas, at the **House of Spice,** 190 Augusta Ave., 416/593-9724. Another shop worth browsing here is **Perola's,** 247 Augusta Ave., 416/593-9728, which offers products from Central and South America such as cactuses in cans and an array of rare chiles and dried herbs.

The **Eaton Centre,** 220 Yonge St., 416/598-2322, is more than a shopping center—it's an event. As you rise in the levels, the shopping gets higher-end. Here you'll find lots of food and movies and every kind of shopping in a stunning building. Its graceful glass roof arches 17 feet over the mall. This is Toronto's top tourist attraction.

Prime shopping abounds in the **Yorkville Avenue** area, which is known as the Fifth Avenue of Toronto. It's bordered by Avenue Road, Yonge Street, and Bloor Street. A few stores that have a familiar ring to Americans include Banana Republic, Eddie Bauer, Hermes, and Lacoste.

You'll be greeted with a cup of tea when you visit **Ten Ren Tea,** 454 Dundas St. W., 416/598-7872, a shop that sells dozens of Asian varieties of tea, plus many handcrafted imported teapots. It's in the downtown Chinatown market.

Some of the best shopping in the world is at museum stores, and located here are three shops worth browsing. The store at the **Royal Ontario Museum,** 100 Queen's Park, 416/586-8000, has native-made crafts, jewelry, and sculptures. You can get contemporary Canadian art, including Inuit works, at the **Art Gallery of Ontario** shop, 317 Dundas St. W., 416/979-6610. And finally, the **Hockey Hall of Fame,**

BCE Pl., 30 Yonge St., 416/360-7765, is a great place for mementos of the game and hockey apparel.

Fashion Crimes, 395 Queen St. W., 416/592-9001, takes the elegance and romance of the past and gives it a modern twist with such items as velvet gowns, opera capes, beaded purses, and striking corsets. This is where the local trendy arts-and-film industry crowd can be found.

Antique lovers will enjoy the treasures on sale every Sunday afternoon at the **St. Lawrence Market,** Front and Jarvis Sts. And if a life-size mannequin is what you've always wanted, go to **Locomotion,** 1122 Queen St. E., 416/778-8499. It's part of a number of neat little antique shops on the street.

A legend in art nouveau–inspired French design, **Lalique,** 131 Bloor St. W., 416/515-9191, has its first North American boutique in Toronto, near other high-end shops such as Chanel and Hermes.

Toronto is also home to the largest gay and lesbian bookstore in Canada, the **Glad Day Bookshop,** 598A Yonge St., 416/961-4161.

SPORTS AND RECREATION

Welcome to Jock City (with a Canadian accent). Toronto is home to four professional sports teams—hockey, baseball, football, and basketball. And when Toronto residents aren't watching the game, they're in it, especially during the warmer months when bicycling, jogging, skating, and walking are hotly pursued. In the winter, locals enjoy ice skating and ice hockey.

Get out your clubs, your rackets, your paddles, and your oars: Toronto is the place for you. For information about golf courses, contact **Toronto Parks and Recreation** at 416/392-8186; call the **Ontario Tennis Association** at 416/426-7135 for details about indoor tennis courts in town. Also, one of the largest canoeing and rowing regattas is held every July 1 on Toronto Island's Long Pond. **Canoe Ontario,** 416/426-7170, has the details.

The **Toronto Blue Jays** baseball team, 416/341-1111, can be found at the SkyDome, Front St. next to CN Tower. Games usually sell out, so plan way ahead. The NBA team is the **Toronto Raptors,** 416/366-3865, who've recently moved to the Air Canada Centre behind Union Station, 40 Bay St. The **Toronto Maple Leafs** hockey team, 416/977-1641, has moved there, too. The **Toronto Argonauts,** 416/314-1234, of the Canadian Football League play at the SkyDome.

Learn the ropes—or the rocks—at **Joe Rockhead's Climbing Gym,** 20 Frazer Ave., 416/538-7670, which has 11,000 square feet of artificial rock surface. A three-hour beginner's course, which covers knots and other basics, is about $40.

On September 5, 1914, Babe Ruth hit the first home run of his professional career on **Hanlan's Point** on the Toronto Islands. The 19-year-old pitcher threw a one-hit, 9-0 shutout against the old

Trip to the Falls

If you can spare an extra day, get down to Niagara Falls and see it from the Canadian side. You can rent a car and drive—it's 81 miles south on the Queen Elizabeth Way—or you can take one of the many tours offered in Toronto. Try **Niagara Tours**, 416/868-0400, which will pick you up at your hotel and take you down on a 14-passenger minibus.

Toronto Maple Leafs and hit a three-run homer during the game. A plaque commemorates the event.

ENTERTAINMENT

Toronto is the world's third-largest theater center, just behind New York and London. There are an average of 50 different productions each month, and more than 7 million tickets are sold each year. You'll find everything from mainstream Broadway to fringe productions.

The **Elgin & Winter Garden Theatre Centre,** 189 Yonge St., 416/314-2901, built in 1913–14, is the last remaining and operating double-decker theater complex in the world. Be sure you see the Winter Garden, which is seven stories above. On its ceiling are thousands of leaves, columns disguised as tree trunks, a glowing moon, and trellised walls. Also of note is the **Ford Centre for the Performing Arts,** 5040 Yonge St., 416/872-2222—which contains several smaller, intimate theaters—and the **Factory Theatre,** 125 Bathurst St., 416/504-9971, which is devoted to experimental work.

The **National Ballet of Canada,** 416/872-2262, and the **Canadian Opera Company,** 416/872-2262, make their home in the Hummingbird Centre for the Performing Arts, 1 Front St., 416/872-2262. You'll also find Broadway musicals and rock concerts here. And a striking round structure known as Roy Thomson Hall, 60 Simcoe St., is the home of the **Toronto Symphony,** 416/872-4255.

The club scene is hopping in the warehouse district of Richmond, Adelaide, and John Streets. One place to check out is **The Joker,** 318 Richmond St. W., 416/598-1313, a $1.5-million, four-floor plaza with jester decor. It has 6 bars, 15 bartenders, a dance floor, pool tables, and high-tech lighting.

For lots of simulators and interactive games, many of which feature virtual reality, try the **Sega City Playdium,** 99 Rathburn Rd., Mississauga, 905/273-9000.

For a romantic winter interlude, do the oh-so-Toronto thing and go **ice skating** at City Hall, Bay and Queen Sts. You can also go skating at Harbourfront Centre, 410 Queen's Quay W., or in the beautiful forested setting of High Park, just west of downtown on Colborne

Caught on Film

They call this city North Hollywood, and with good reason. At any one time between 18 and 40 media productions are under way—films, made-for-TV movies, and TV shows (not including commercials and music videos).

Here are a few of the famous films that have been shot in Toronto: *Mrs. Soffel*, with Mel Gibson and Diane Keaton; *Gorillas in the Mist*, with Sigourney Weaver; *The Killing Fields*; *Moonstruck*; *Three Men and a Baby*; and *The Santa Clause*. Parts of *Murder at 1600* with Wesley Snipes were shot at the Royal York Hotel. Casa Loma, a 98-room mansion, played a part in *Extreme Measures* and *Johnny Mnemonic*. And the University of Toronto served as the setting for *Good Will Hunting* with Robin Williams.

toronto

Lodge Dr., south of Bloor St. W.

You're pooped. You're stressed. What you need to do is take a deep breath, and the place to take it is at the **o2 Spa Bar,** 2044 Yonge St., 416/322-7733, where you can get a 20-minute session of breathing 99.9-percent pure, tangerine-scented oxygen. It really clears your head.

CITY BASICS

For more information on Toronto, contact **Tourism Toronto,** 416/203-2500 or 800/363-1990, www.tourism-toronto.com. Information on the Province of Ontario is available through the **Ontario Ministry of Tourism's Travel Centre,** 800/ONTARIO, www.travelinx.com. Also, **Beyond Ability International,** 416/410-3748, www.beyond-ability.com, makes free professional assessments of accessible services.

Leave your Nanuk suit at home. The average temperature ranges from 32 degrees Fahrenheit in January to 77 degrees Fahrenheit in July. That's really not too bad. Get the weather forecast from 416/661-0123, www.theweathernetwork.com.

If you want to know the latest about Toronto's many art galleries, look for a copy of the ***Stride Art & Gallery Guide,*** which is available free at hotels, galleries, and other locations. You can also get one sent to you by calling Tourism Toronto.

Newspapers include the *Toronto Star* and the *Globe and Mail*. Weeklies and magazines that can help you with updated entertainment news include *eye, Now,* and *Where Toronto.*

⑦ CLEVELAND

to go ▶

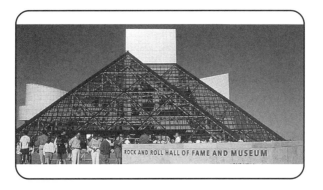

ROCK AND ROLL HALL OF FAME AND MUSEUM

When you're introduced to someone in other cities, they may ask what you do. But when you're introduced to someone in Cleveland, they are more likely to ask what you are.
—John Grabowski, Western Reserve Historical Society, commenting on Cleveland's ethnic diversity

We know what you're thinking.

Cleveland? Do we *have* to?

No, you don't have to, but you just might *want* to after you update your image of the place. It's not just some big old hulk of a city, sitting there rusting into urban ruin. Cleveland has turned to the future.

For one thing, it's been getting a head-to-toe redo—to the tune of $7 billion in capital investment in the last few years—with a revamp of its spirit to go along with it. For another, it's built one of the coolest museums in the country—the Rock and Roll Hall of Fame and Museum, which hasn't got a single Egyptian mummy inside. Consequently, Cleveland calls itself the New American City. We'll go along with that. It has shored up its strikingly beautiful neighborhoods and is celebrating its remarkable patchwork of ethnic variety.

For instance, Cleveland is home to 80 ethnic groups—from Greek and German to Czech and Chinese—speaking more than 60 languages. The city seems to have learned a most valuable lesson: there is strength and beauty in diversity. That's how you make the American quilt, and it's an art.

Cleveland

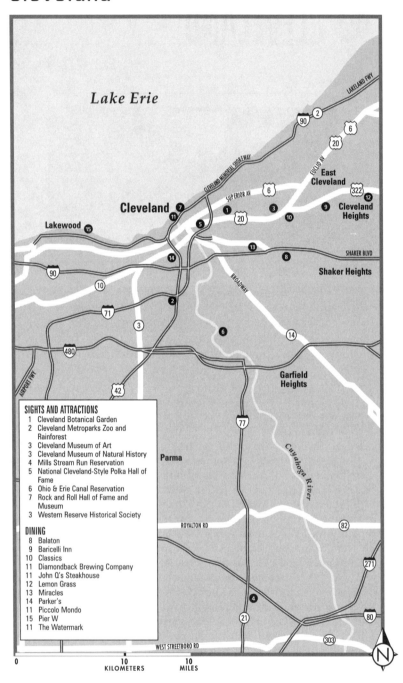

Lake Erie

LAKELAND FWY

CLEVELAND MEMORIAL SHOREWAY

SUPERIOR AV

EUCLID AV

East Cleveland

Cleveland

Cleveland Heights

Lakewood

Shaker Heights

SHAKER BLVD

BROADWAY

Garfield Heights

Cuyahoga River

Parma

ROYALTON RD

WEST STREETBORO RD

SIGHTS AND ATTRACTIONS
1 Cleveland Botanical Garden
2 Cleveland Metroparks Zoo and Rainforest
3 Cleveland Museum of Art
3 Cleveland Museum of Natural History
4 Mills Stream Run Reservation
5 National Cleveland-Style Polka Hall of Fame
6 Ohio & Erie Canal Reservation
7 Rock and Roll Hall of Fame and Museum
3 Western Reserve Historical Society

DINING
8 Balaton
9 Baricelli Inn
10 Classics
11 Diamondback Brewing Company
11 John Q's Steakhouse
12 Lemon Grass
13 Miracles
14 Parker's
11 Piccolo Mondo
15 Pier W
11 The Watermark

0   10   10
   KILOMETERS   MILES

N

GETTING AROUND

A key part of the new life in Cleveland is at **Hopkins International Airport,** 216/265-6030, which has recently undergone a $500 million renovation. You'll find improvement to the baggage claim, passenger terminals, concourse connectors, and mall area, with added specialty shops and restaurants. Continental is the major carrier here. The airport is 10 miles southwest of downtown.

A Tourist Information Center is located on the ticketing level of the main terminal. The Hotel Courtesy Phone Center, which is in the middle of the baggage claim (lower) level, provides information and reservations for area hotels, many of which offer shuttle service. This is also where limo and car rental agencies are located.

Cab companies operate at exits two and four of the baggage claim level. Taxi phones are at each end of the exit vestibule. Try **Yellow Cab,** 216/623-1550. It has wheelchair-accessible vehicles available.

The **Greater Cleveland Regional Transit Authority (RTA)** is a county-wide system with more than 100 bus routes and 4 rapid-transit rail routes. You can take the RTA from the airport to the Tower City Center in downtown's Public Square for $1.50. You can get to the Flats Entertainment District and the North Coast Harbor attractions such as the Rock and Roll Hall of Fame by means of the light rail system from Tower City Center. Get route and schedule information during regular hours from the **RTAnswerline,** 216/621-9500. Recorded information is available from the **RTA RIDEline** at the same number 24 hours a day.

Should you rent a car? Sure. Cleveland is not that difficult to get around.

A good way to get oriented is to go to the observation deck of the **Terminal Tower** downtown. You're 42 stories up, and the view is breathtaking. Besides that, there's a **Visitor Information Center,** 50 Public Sq., 216/621-7981.

SIGHTS AND ATTRACTIONS

Like we said, you'll be surprised. Pleasantly. Cleveland has a life. The **Rock and Roll Hall of Fame and Museum,** 1 Kay Plaza, 888/764-ROCK (information), 800/493-ROLL (tickets), is a world exclusive, and it's playing all the time right here in Cleveland. The $92 million museum, designed by world-renowned architect I. M. Pei, towers above the Lake Erie shoreline at North Coast Harbor. Those spotlighted by the hall of fame are honored by a multimedia production combining film footage, music, interviews, animation, and still photography. There are also computer kiosks, jukeboxes, video monitors, and inductee signatures etched in glass.

The **Cleveland Museum of Art,** 11150 East Blvd., 216/421-7340, contains more than 34,000 works of art that go back 5,000 years.

Going Places

An excellent way to see the city at ground level is on the **Trolley Tours of Cleveland**, 216/771-4484. Tours cover 20 miles and more than 100 points of interest. Or why not see Cleveland from the water? Try the *Goodtime III*, a 1,000-passenger, triple-deck ship that sails on the Cuyahoga River and Lake Erie. Pick it up at North Coast Harbor, 825 E. Ninth St. Pier., 216/861-5110. Another option is the *Nautica Queen*, which can serve up to 400 passengers. It docks at the Flats Nautica Entertainment Complex, 1153 Main Ave., 216/696-8888.

Among its best-known collections are those of medieval European art and Asian art.

The **Cleveland Museum of Natural History**, 1 Wade Oval Dr., 216/231-4600, integrates the sciences of astronomy and geology in an updated, multisensory way. With the help of electronic gadgetry, you can fly around the planets, feel the vibes of an earthquake, and walk through a cave. Besides some real moon rocks, the museum has a fabulous gem collection, including pearls, opals, and colored diamonds.

The **Western Reserve Historical Society**, 10825 East Blvd., 216/721-5722, founded in 1867, is Cleveland's oldest cultural institution. Exhibits re-create the Western Reserve of the Pre–Revolutionary War era through the early twentieth century with costumes, farming tools, manuscripts, and period rooms. The society's library contains one of the largest collections of genealogical resources in the Midwest. It is also home to the Crawford Auto-Aviation Museum.

A new exhibit at the **Cleveland Metroparks Zoo and Rainforest**, 3900 Wildlife Way, 216/661-6500, is called Wolf Wilderness. In a 22,000-square-foot area that depicts animal and plant life of a northern temperate forest, a pack of Great Plains wolves share the space with beavers, bald eagles, and other wetlands species. The rain forest features a jungle path into an area containing 600 animals, simulated tropical thunderstorms, and a 25-foot water curtain.

Cleveland has 19,000 acres in its various parks across the city, and its newest gem is the **Ohio & Erie Canal Reservation**, E. 49th St., Cuyahoga Heights, 216/351-6300. Amid this 315-acre park are trails, picnic areas, spots for fishing, and the 4.5-mile Towpath Trail that stretches along the 166-year-old Ohio and Erie Canal. Another park is the **Mills Stream Run Reservation**, Valley Pkwy. between Bagley and Drake Rds., in Strongsville, 216/351-6300, which operates the Chutes to Thrill toboggan run in the winter. Riders climb aboard a wooden toboggan that takes them for a speedy ride down an icy 800-foot-long chute with a 70-foot drop.

The **Cleveland Botanical Garden,** 11030 East Blvd., 216/721-1600, is undergoing a $37 million facelift, transforming it into a year-round educational and tourist attraction. The centerpiece is a 70-foot-tall conservatory that will contain—in addition to innumerable exotic plants—such rare animals as the poison arrow dart frog from Costa Rica.

Hop to it and get on down to the **National Cleveland-Style Polka Hall of Fame,** Shore Cultural Center, 291 E. 222nd St., 216/261-FAME, a tribute to Cleveland's greatest polka artists that is sponsored by the American Slovenian Polka Foundation. It's at the Shore Cultural Center on the east side.

LODGING

Cleveland has pleasant lodgings scattered all over the place, but we think you'll be happiest staying downtown, close to the action and the lakefront. The **Ritz-Carlton,** 1515 W. Third St., 216/623-1300, $$$, is ideally located at the Tower City Center downtown. Easy chairs and china cabinets add a Victorian flourish to the modern elegance. It offers an indoor pool, afternoon tea, and health club privileges.

The **Renaissance Cleveland Hotel,** 24 Public Sq., 216/696-5600, $$$$, is another top choice downtown. This historic structure began life in 1815 as a log tavern, and after several rebirths has become a historic hotel of the first order. It has an indoor pool, complimentary coffee, and in-room modem links.

The **Baricelli Inn,** 2203 Cornell Rd., 216/791-6500, $$, is situated in an 1896 brownstone in the University Circle area. It features paintings and stained glass throughout, and a continental breakfast is included. Its restaurant is first-rate. The **Glidden House,** 1901 Ford Dr., 216/231-8900, $$$, originally was a 1910 French Gothic mansion, and now has eight Victorian-style suites. A guest wing built in 1988 added 52 rooms with private baths. It's also in the University Circle area.

The **Cross Country Inn,** 7233 Engle Rd., Middleburg Heights, 440/243-2277, $, is a low-priced motel in Middleburg Heights. It has a heated pool, cable TV, and free coffee in the lobby. The **Harley Hotel West,** 17000 Bagley Rd., Middleburg Heights, 800/321-2323, $$, is a motor hotel in the same area. It offers free airport transportation, cable TV, two swimming pools, and a sauna.

The main attraction of **Inn of Chagrin Falls,** 87 West St., Chagrin Falls, 440/247-1200, $$, is the charming village in which it is located, just 18 miles east of downtown Cleveland. The inn has 15 rooms, all of which have different decors and many of which have fireplaces. The inn's main building goes back to the 1920s. Breakfast is complimentary.

For help with B&B accommodations in Cleveland, contact **Private Lodgings,** 216/321-3213.

DINING

Ethnic dining reads like a map of the world here, but there's plenty of traditional fare as well. Also, proximity to the water makes fish a specialty. For some fine seafood in the Flats, try **The Watermark,** 1250 Old River Rd., 216/241-1600, $$. It has an excellent seafood buffet on Fridays. And you'll have a wonderful view of Lake Erie and Cleveland at **Pier W,** 12700 Lake Ave., in the Lakewood area, 216/228-2250, $$$. Enjoy good seafood in a room with nautical decor. Fresh fish and homemade soups are the specialties at **Miracles,** 2391 W. 11th St., 216/623-1800, $$. It offers casual dining in a nineteenth-century building, plus outdoor dining when the weather's nice.

—— Neighborhood Watch ——

They call it **University Circle**. In one square mile centered on Euclid Avenue, and just four miles east of downtown, are museums, theaters, gardens, and shopping. Everything's within walking distance in a parklike setting. Visitors can obtain a map and more details about the area by calling 216/791-3900.

Little Italy, which is also known as Murray Hill, is just east of University Circle and is centered on Mayfield Road. The neighborhood was first settled in the late nineteenth century by skilled Italian artisans. It has kept much of its Old World charm and sense of tight-knit community.

Ohio City, which was founded as a separate town in 1836, is west of West 25th Street, opposite downtown across the Cuyahoga River. Today it's known for its ethnically diverse population and the historic West Side Market, a landmark since 1912. You'll be charmed by the many Victorian-era homes in the neighborhood.

The place for shopping in Cleveland is **Shaker Square/Larchmere**. You'll find all kinds of antique shops, specialty boutiques, fine and folk art galleries, and restaurants. It's centered on Shaker Boulevard.

Fairfax, an area of Victorian homes and turn-of-the-last-century churches, has been the center for African American social life and culture for several decades. It's in east Cleveland, centered on Euclid and Quincy Avenues.

The hippies used to hang out in **Coventry Village** in Cleveland Heights, and it still has a counterculture feel. If you want unusual shopping, this is the place.

The well-heeled settled in **Edgewater**, and it remains one of Cleveland's most prestigious addresses. Many of the houses retain the vestiges of their Gilded Age roots. This area is on the near west side and includes Edgewater Park.

Gaze down at Jacobs Field stadium from Terminal Tower, on the left

Beef tenderloin and lobster-and-crab ravioli are the specialties at the restaurant in the **Baricelli Inn,** 2203 Cornell Rd., 216/791-6500, $$$. The decor is stunning, with fireplaces, stained glass, and paintings. **Classics,** 2065 E. 96th St., 216/791-1900, $$$, is another upscale restaurant, this one in the Omni International Hotel in the University Circle area. Try the rack of lamb or the steak Diane. Jackets are required.

You can't go wrong with a good old steak, and **John Q's Steakhouse,** 55 Public Sq., 216/861-0900, $$, has some of the best in town. Try the 16-ounce pepper steak.

The **Diamondback Brewing Company,** 724 Prospect Ave., 216/771-1988, $$, specializes in just what you'd expect. It also has a champagne bar and some of the best tapas in town.

Veal scallopini and brick-oven pizza are the specialties at **Piccolo Mondo,** 1352 W. Sixth St., 216/241-1300, $$, an Italian restaurant that will remind you of a Mediterranean villa. Or consider **Parker's,** 2801 Bridge Ave., 216/771-7130, $$$, which serves French and American food in a tavern atmosphere that is totally non-smoking. Jackets are required.

What about Thai? Then try **Lemon Grass,** 2179 Lee Rd., in Cleveland Heights, 216/321-0210, $$, which will light up your life with some red-hot curry dishes. And if you've always had a hankering for Hungarian food, **Balaton,** 13133 Shaker Sq., 216/921-9691, $, is the place for you. We recommend the stuffed cabbage or the homemade dumplings with gravy, and a nap afterwards.

SHOPPING

Cleveland has been a crossroads for centuries, which makes it a great gateway for products. That means shopping, lots of it. Some of the best shopping is in the heart of downtown at the $400 million development

Many of Cleveland's major cultural activities are reflections of the city's ethnic diversity. In February, which is **Black History Month**, a black film festival is held at John Carroll University. February also marks a full month of gospel performances at the Rock and Roll Hall of Fame. If you visit Cleveland in mid-March, you can participate in **Buzzard Sunday**. People go to the nearby town of Hinckley for food, festivities, and a chance to see the turkey vultures returning to their summer homes.

The city's most recognizable community is Little Italy, on the east side. In July, **Our Lady of Mount Carmel's Festival** includes Italian food, music, rides, and games. The Holy Rosary Church has a similar **Feast of the Assumption** celebration each August.

The Irish do their thing at the **West Side Irish Club** in June, and the **Puerto Rican Friendly Days** take place at Tremont Valley Park in late July. For the **St. John Kanty Church Polish Heritage Festival**, you'll need to come to Cleveland in September.

For details on all these events, contact the Convention & Visitors Bureau of Greater Cleveland.

events
HORIZON

known as the **Avenue at Tower City Center,** located in Terminal Tower on Public Square, between Prospect Ave. and W. Huron Rd., 216/771-0033. The tower itself rises 52 stories, but at its base is an old train depot that was renovated into the upscale retailing center that includes 120 shopping, dining, and entertainment establishments.

Another downtown shopping center is the **Galleria at Erieview,** E. Ninth St. and St. Clair Ave., 216/861-4343, a glass-enclosed collection of more than 60 shops and restaurants. Here's where you'll find the Cleveland Indians Team Shop.

The Arcade, Euclid Ave. and E. Fourth St., 216/621-8500, was the country's first enclosed shopping center. It was built in 1890 and is an architectural masterpiece. Inside are three levels of specialty shops in an atrium-style structure.

Larchmere Boulevard is a 10-block shopping district with more than 15 antique shops and art galleries, plus European pastry shops and fine restaurants.

Chinatown, several blocks east of downtown and centered on Rockwell Avenue, is home to the Asian Plaza, a mix of Asian food and gift shops.

For souvenirs of Cleveland and the Rock and Roll Hall of Fame, go to **Daffy Dan's Rock 'N Roll Heaven,** 800/579-ROCK. There are 10 locations in town.

In Chagrin Falls, **Angels and Other Folk,** 14 N. Main St., 440/247-2270, has folk art, whimsical antiques, and of course, angels. Nearby you'll find eighteenth- and nineteenth-century furniture, accessories, porcelains, and paintings at **Erythea Antiques and Works of Art,** 100 N. Main St., Chagrin Falls, 440/247-1960. Also stop by the **Village Herb Shop,** 26 S. Main St., Chagrin Falls, 440/247-5029, a country cottage filled with garden gifts. Have some tea in the herb gardens.

SPORTS AND RECREATION

The **Cleveland Browns,** 440/891-5000, www.clevelandbrowns.com, are back as part of the American Football Conference. They've recently moved into a new $283 million Cleveland Stadium, 1085 W. Third St.—which features seating for 72,000 people, is 12 stories tall, extends a half-mile in circumference, and includes the largest scoreboard in football.

The **Cleveland Indians,** 216/420-4200, play baseball at Jacobs Field, 2401 Ontario St. And two teams play at the Gund Arena, One Center Ct.: the **Cleveland Cavaliers** (basketball), 216/420-2000, and the **Cleveland Lumberjacks** (hockey), 216/420-0000. See thoroughbred racing in an enclosed grandstand at **Thistledown Racing Club,** 21501 Emery Rd., 216/662-8600.

Rent in-line skates and jet skis at **Cleveland Jet Ski,** 216/391-5593, at state beaches and marinas (call 440/286-2146 for details). Also, more than 300 golfing facilities are in Greater Cleveland and northeast Ohio. **Quail Hollow Resort & Country Club,** 11080 Concord-Hambden Rd., 800/792-0258, has a Bruce Devlin–designed course with several particularly challenging holes. It's home to the Cleveland Nike Open. The top public course in Cleveland is considered to be **Fowler's Mill Golf Course,** 13095 Rockhaven Rd., 440/729-7569.

Because of its high nutrient levels and warmer temperatures, Lake Erie produces a wider variety of fish than any other Great Lake. It has some of the best walleye, perch, and bass fishing in the world. One of the better places to try your luck is at **Cleveland Lakefront State Park,** 216/881-8141, which has long stretches of beautiful beaches, bike paths, nature trails, picnic areas, and fishing piers.

ENTERTAINMENT

Cleveland rocks, of course. The museum sees to that. But it also rolls with the more sophisticated beat of the classics.

America's most frequently recorded symphony orchestra is the **Cleveland Orchestra,** 216/231-7300. It's been making music since 1918, and it hangs out in the beautiful Severance Hall, 11001 Euclid Ave., except during the summer, when it performs outside.

The **Playhouse Square Center,** 1501 Euclid Ave., 216/241-6000, which was built in the 1920s, is home to the opera and the ballet. The center has four magnificently restored theaters—the State, the Palace, the Ohio, and the Allen. This is where you'll find Broadway productions.

The Flats Entertainment District, once an industrial district along the winding west banks of the Cuyahoga River at Main Avenue, has been converted into a popular dining and entertainment center that includes 60 riverside cafés, restaurants, nightclubs, and bars. The **Nautica Entertainment Complex,** 2000 Sycamore St., in the Flats, 216/861-4080, covers 28 acres on the west bank of the river and includes an amphitheater and a riverfront boardwalk.

Cleveland has more than 90 venues for jazz and blues. Check out **Wilbert's Bar and Grille,** 1360 W. Ninth St. at St. Clair Ave., 216/771-BLUE, which offers southwestern cuisine with the best of the blues. And you had better get there early if you want room to dance at **Mirage on the Water,** 2510 Elm St. in the Flats, 216/348-1135. By midnight, the dance floor is so crowded that all you can do is sway. The music is heavy on R&B and hip-hop. This upscale club attracts a clientele that consists mostly of African American professionals.

Although everybody is welcome at **The Grid,** 1281 W. Ninth St., 216/623-0113, the crowd is primarily gay men. Located in the warehouse district, the club has plenty of room for dancing, with video games and pool downstairs.

CITY BASICS

Cleveland's weather has the moderating influence of Lake Erie. In the summer, cool lake breezes keep temperatures generally below 90 degrees Fahrenheit. And the lake seems to moderate the winter temperatures, too. However, Lake Erie also helps to produce plenty of snow, so bring your boots in the winter. For **road condition** updates call 216/606-6423 or 800/FYI-ROAD.

The **Convention & Visitors Bureau of Greater Cleveland,** 216/621-5555, www.travelcleveland.com, has a number of visitors centers and "Touch Cleveland" visitor information kiosks around the city, including at the Terminal Tower downtown and the Rock and Roll Hall of Fame and Museum. For visitor information and hotel/motel reservations and packages, call the **Cleveland Hot Line,** 800/321-1004. For information about the state, call the **Ohio Office of Travel and Tourism,** 800/BUCKEYE.

Get tickets to sports and entertainment events through **Advantix,** 216/348-5323, or **Ticketmaster,** 216/241-5555.

The *Cleveland Plain Dealer* is the major daily newspaper in the city. You can get information on events from the *Free Times,* a weekly, or from *Cleveland Magazine.*

❽ CHICAGO

to go ▶

Big plans, elaborate schemes, and grand designs sort of messily bleeding into one another [have] created Chicago's reputation for rawness. But that rawness is just ambition—sometimes ambition run amuck— that has acquired a life of its own.
—Pat Colander, *The New York Times*

Carl Sandburg once called Chicago the "City of Big Shoulders" for its meat and wheat, but that was long ago. Today, although the city isn't doing as much hog butchering and wheat stacking, it is still a raw, muscular place.

You'll see it right off. Downtown ripples. The wind comes in off Lake Michigan—an oceanic force in itself—and the people and traffic seem to be swept along. The energy of commerce keeps things flexed. Go to a Cubs or Bulls game, and you'll see rawness.

With about 3 million people in Chicago proper and more than 6 million in the metropolitan area, it can't help but be energetic. Today most of these people are coat-and-tied into the business services and health care fields, but many of them work in some of the truly magnificent buildings that Chicago's brawn has created—the birthday-cake-looking Wrigley Building of 1924, for instance, or the sky-rocketing Sears Tower.

The visitor will instantly recognize what Chicago is known for: it's the city that put the art in architecture.

But that's just the tip of the skyscraper. This vigorous place has

Chicago Region

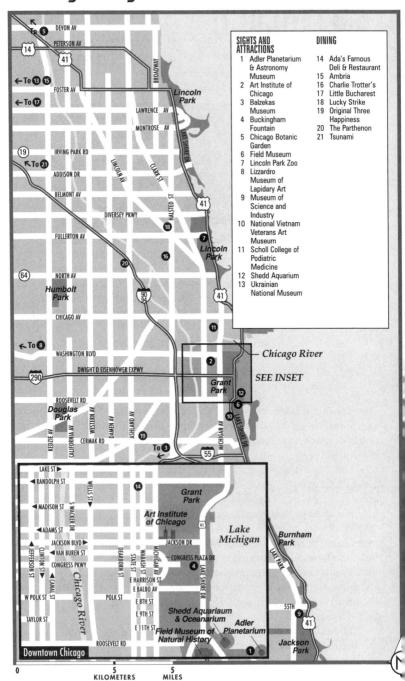

SIGHTS AND ATTRACTIONS
1 Adler Planetarium & Astronomy Museum
2 Art Institute of Chicago
3 Balzekas Museum
4 Buckingham Fountain
5 Chicago Botanic Garden
6 Field Museum
7 Lincoln Park Zoo
8 Lizzardro Museum of Lapidary Art
9 Museum of Science and Industry
10 National Vietnam Veterans Art Museum
11 Scholl College of Podiatric Medicine
12 Shedd Aquarium
13 Ukrainian National Museum

DINING
14 Ada's Famous Deli & Restaurant
15 Ambria
16 Charlie Trotter's
17 Little Bucharest
18 Lucky Strike
19 Original Three Happiness
20 The Parthenon
21 Tsunami

Chicago River

SEE INSET

Downtown Chicago

0   5   5
   KILOMETERS   MILES

plenty of brains, too, as it is home to some of the greatest museums in the world.

Chicago, however, doesn't intend on intimidating visitors with its muscular and mental acumen. Chicagoans like to walk in the park, shop, eat hot dogs, cheer-on their teams, and listen to the blues. And they don't mind sharing their city with you.

GETTING AROUND

You will probably land at **O'Hare International Airport,** 773/686-2200, the busiest in the world. But don't freak out. O'Hare is well organized. The three domestic terminals are linked. Information booths are everywhere. Somebody will help you.

Taxi service, 312/TAXI-CAB, is on the lower level of each terminal. A ride to downtown takes about 30 minutes and will cost you between $25 and $30. A shared-ride program will get you there for about $15. Consider **Continental's Airport Express,** 312/454-7799, which provides van service to all downtown hotels and the North Shore and Oak Brook suburbs. One-way tickets are about $14, and vans leave every five minutes. Ticket counters are across from the baggage claim areas. You don't have to fly Continental Airlines to use this service.

The cheap seats are provided by the **Chicago Transit Authority,** 312/836-7000, www.transitchicago.com. Rapid transit trains leave from inside the terminal on the lower level every 5 to 10 minutes days and evenings, and every 30 minutes from 1 a.m. to 5 a.m. All trains to downtown connect free to all other trains. It takes about 35 minutes to get downtown, and the ride will only set you back $1.50.

Midway Airport, 773/838-0600, is 20 minutes from downtown, and the same transportation is available, only a little cheaper. The rapid transit train, however, is still $1.50.

Don't rent a car. The traffic is one big unfriendly snarl, and parking is a beast. Take a taxi in the central city. They're easy to find (but call if you can't find one).

For unlimited rides on buses and trains, get a **CTA Visitor Pass** from the Chicago Transit Authority. You can get one-, two-, three-, and five-day passes at the airports, Union Station, the visitors centers, and some museums. If you get lost, call CTA and a staffer will tell you how to get from here to there by public transportation.

The heart of Chicago is called the Magnificent Mile. It's essentially Michigan Avenue from Oak Street to the Chicago River. Get there. Camp there. Center your stay there among the burly buildings. There are plenty of interesting sites within walking distance, and if you want to go to the cluster of major museums near the lake, grab a cab or take the bus. It's as easy as pie.

It probably wouldn't be a bad idea to get the lay of the land with the help of a tour. See Chicago from the water (try **Uglyduck Cruises,**

312/396-2220), by sightseeing bus (try **Chicago Trolley Company,** 312/663-0260), or via a somewhat different mode (check out **Windy City Blues Cruise,** 773/348-6546).

SIGHTS AND ATTRACTIONS

Chicago is home to some of the finest museums in the world. Bring your walking shoes. And call ahead: many of the museums have days during the week when admission is free.

Several museums are located on Chicago's lakefront museums' campus, on Lake Shore Drive. One such place is the **Field Museum,** next to Soldier Field at S. Lake Shore Dr. at Roosevelt Rd., 312/922-9410, where you can see the bones of the biggest T-Rex ever found, an Egyptian sarcophagus, and the person-eating lions of Tsavo (safely stuffed). Nearby is the **Shedd Aquarium,** 1200 S. Lake Shore Dr., 312/939-2438, the world's largest indoor aquarium, which holds 6,000 aquatic animals and a coral reef exhibit where divers hand-feed sharks, sea turtles, and eels daily.

The **Adler Planetarium & Astronomy Museum,** 1300 S. Lake Shore Dr., 312/322-0304, is another must-see. Sky shows transport visitors to planets, moons, stars, and distant galaxies. You'll ascend to the domed Sky Theater via the 77-foot "Stairway to the Stars" special-effects escalator. Likewise, consider a visit to the **Museum of Science and Industry,** 57th St. at Lake Shore Dr., 773/684-1414, which offers more than 800 interactive exhibits, a space center, and an Omnimax theater showing science and technology films.

The **Art Institute of Chicago,** 111 S. Michigan Ave., 312/443-3600, is one of the premier art museums in the world, and should not be missed. If you've got a whole day, this place can handle it. Besides 5,000 years worth of art from throughout the world, the institute contains a fabulous shop and three restaurants. Come to think of it, this wouldn't be a bad place to *live.*

And then there are the museums of the unexpected. Everything you ever wanted to know about Lithuania is at the **Balzekas Museum,** 6500 S. Polaski Rd., 773/582-6500. Or how about the **Ukrainian National Museum,** 721 N. Oakley St., 312/421-8020? Easter eggs and dolls in native costumes are spotlighted.

If you ever put your foot in your mouth, you can learn how to extract it at the **Scholl College of Podiatric Medicine,** 10001 S. Dearborn St., 312/280-2487. You'll find plenty of hands-on —or is that feet-on?—exhibits.

Learn all about gemstones and see a world-famous collection of Chinese jade at the **Lizzardro Museum of Lapidary Art,** 220 Cottage Hill, Wilder Park, Elmhurst, 630/833-1616.

Also deserving a visit is the **National Vietnam Veterans Art Museum,** 1801 S. Indiana Ave., 312/326-0270, which contains more

Enjoy an outdoor concert on Navy Pier

than 500 pieces of fine art created by artists who served in the Vietnam War.

Watch the dance of water and light at the **Buckingham Fountain,** Congress Pkwy. and Columbus Dr., 312/742-7529, in Grant Park. Or take a break from the hurly-burly city with a visit to the world-famous **Lincoln Park Zoo,** Cannon Dr. at Fullerton Pkwy., 312/742-2000. It's a garden oasis of 35 acres right in the heart of the city. Christmas is the best time to come here—the zoo is decorated in an extravagance of lights, and citizens come to sing carols to the animals.

Worth a trip is the **Chicago Botanic Garden,** Lake Cook Rd. east of the Edens Expressway, 847/835-5440, which is 25 miles north of Chicago. It is composed of 385 acres of 20 different gardens, including the English Walled and Rose Gardens, the Japanese Islands, and the Waterfall Garden.

LODGING

The Magnificent Mile has plenty of sterling hotels. Consider staying in one of them and waking up in the magnificent middle of things. One such place, **The Drake,** 40 E. Walton Pl., 800/55-DRAKE, $$$$, is the grande dame of Chicago hotels. A $20 million renovation has taken nothing away from its Old World charm, with rooms that are spacious and windows that are wide. There's even a proper settee in the elevator. The hotel has three restaurants and the Palm Court tea room, and it is listed in the National Register of Historic Places. It's just off Michigan Avenue.

The Blackstone, 636 S. Michigan Ave., 312/427-4300, $$, is another of the national landmark hotels on the Magnificent Mile, but this one is less expensive than The Drake and is closer to the museums. Continental breakfast is included.

Another well-located hotel in the middle of the Magnificent Mile is **Lenox Suites,** 616 N. Rush St. at Ontario St., 800/44-LENOX, $$, a European-style hotel that offers continental breakfast and ready-to-brew coffee in each room. Just as much in the middle of things, but at a more reasonable price, is **Cass Hotel,** 640 N. Wabash Ave., 800/787-4041, $. Cable TV, a lounge, a café, voice mail, and electronic key-card entry are offered.

Neighborhood Watch

Chicago is much more than its magnificent canyons of buildings downtown. It's a network of distinctive neighborhoods that are definitely worth exploring.

Two of the oldest buildings in Chicago, the Glessner and Clarke houses, which were built right after the Great Fire of 1871, are on the **Near South Side**. This is also where **Comiskey Park** is, and the **Bronzeville** area nearby is rich with its African American heritage.

Colorful pagoda towers and the Chinatown Gate greet visitors a bit farther south in **Chinatown**. And the biggest Mexican American settlement is in **Pilsen**. **Little Italy** is beneath the shadow of the University of Illinois at Chicago, around Taylor Street. **Greektown** is west of the Chicago Mercantile Exchange inside the Loop. (The Loop is the part of downtown encircled by the original elevated train, or El).

River North, encompassing West Ontario Street and surrounding blocks, houses a chic district of art galleries, trendy new restaurants, and clubs.

As for another of Chicago's neighborhoods, the name of a street says it all: **North Astor**. This is the heart of Chicago's Gold Coast, an area of wealth teeming with wonderful examples of late-nineteenth- and early-twentieth-century architecture. The **Gold Coast** is on the Near North Side.

Don't miss **Old Town**, which is noted for its Victorian homes and cobblestone streets. And the "off-Loop" theater district is thriving along Halsted Street in the **Lincoln Park** area. This is also the home of the Second City comedy troupe.

Chicago's hottest neighborhood is **Bucktown/Wicker Park**, which is just west of the Lincoln Park area. You'll find cutting-edge galleries, coffee houses, and poetry readings.

Want more ethnic flavor? Asian restaurants, bakeries, and shops abound in the **Argyle/North Clark Street** area. Farther north is the Scandinavian community of Andersonville. And north up Devon Avenue is the International Marketplace, where more than 60 ethnic restaurants, bakeries, and shops thrive.

You can explore these neighborhoods on your own or hook up with **Chicago Neighborhood Tours**, which depart from the Chicago Cultural Center, 77 E. Randolph St., 312/742-1190.

A downtown hotel bright and lively in design is **The Allegro,** 171 W. Randolph St., 312/236-0123, $$$, which boasts in-room CD boom boxes, in-room faxes, and two-line speaker phones.

Steps from Bloomingdale's and the Museum of Contemporary Art is the **Regal Knickerbocker Hotel,** 163 E. Walton Pl., 312/751-8100, $$$, which has recently undergone an $18 million renovation. It offers 305 elegant rooms in traditional European style. Also consider **The Talbott,** 20 E. Delaware Pl., 312/944-4970, www.talbotthotel.com, $$, a boutique hotel of the first order. It is a small, European-style Gold Coast hotel that offers turndown service and free continental breakfast and morning newspaper.

The **Seneca Hotel,** 200 E. Chestnut St., 800/800-6261, $$, which was built in 1924, features high ceilings and Queen Anne decor, but it's been updated with voice mail and dataport phones. It has three restaurants and a Gold Coast location.

The **House of Two Urns,** 1239 Greenview Ave., 773/235-1408, $$, is a B&B in the with-it neighborhood of Wicker Park. You get slippers and a robe, and scones with your breakfast. Book way ahead because there are only five rooms.

DINING

A husky city like Chicago is going to have a hearty appetite. Its vast number of restaurants attest to that. So whaddaya think Chicagoans want when they're hungry? Beef, deep-dish pizza, and hot dogs—and OK, maybe a seared tuna kabob with wild mushrooms. You can get 24-hour dining information through **Let's Eat,** 773/4-DINING.

First, let's talk beef. The **Chicago Chop House,** 60 W. Ontario St., 312/787-7100, $$, says of itself: "Where the city that works eats." Prime aged beef and succulent chops head up the menu, but they're not afraid of chicken and seafood.

Gene & Georgetti, 1928 Rush St., 312/527-3718, $$$, has been a Chicago landmark for more than half a century. It boasts big steaks and whole roasted chicken and ribs. It also has a lively piano bar.

Morton's of Chicago, 1050 N. State St., 312/266-4820, $$$$, is the place for prime aged steaks, served in a clubby atmosphere. And Chicagoans have also put this place on their list of favorite steak houses: football great Mike Ditka's **Iron Mike's Grille,** Tremont Hotel, 100 E. Chestnut St., 312/587-8989, $$$. Ditka's restaurant serves all-American food with "all-pro service in a hall of fame atmosphere." After your pot roast, you can move to the cigar lounge for a Mike Ditka Signature Cigar.

Charlie Trotter's, 816 Armitage, 773/248-6228, $$$$, is one of the finest restaurants in Chicago, and reservations are recommended far in advance—they are taken up to six months ahead of time. However, it doesn't hurt to call at the last minute to see if a cancellation has occurred. Trotter's is known for its multicultural fusion.

Pizzeria Due, 619 N. Wabash Ave., 312/943-2400, $, established in 1943, is the birthplace of Chicago deep-dish pizza. No, wait, **Pizzeria Uno,** 29 E. Ohio St., 312/321-1000, $, says *it's* where the pizza first went deep. This could mean war.

For a memorable hot dog, try **Downtown Dog,** 804 Rush St. 312/951-5141, $. These dogs are meaty and include a buttered bun, tomatoes, mustard, and celery salt. It's a meal. Get a famous corned beef sandwich at **Ada's Famous Deli & Restaurant,** 14 S. Wabash St., 312/214-4282, $, which has been around since 1948. Or if you like game at dinner, and we don't mean deer, try the **Lucky Strike,** 2747 N. Lincoln Ave., 773/549-2695, $, which features eight bowling lanes and a swanky restaurant.

For variety, Chicago's melting pot is cooking up a storm. The cuisine scene is an ethnic masterpiece. The **Original Three Happiness,** 209 W. Cermak Rd., 312/842-1964, $, is famous for its dim sum and Cantonese-Szechwan cuisine. Outstanding sushi and innovative Japanese cuisine are the hallmarks of **Tsunami,** 1160 N. Dearborn Pkwy., 312/642-9911, $$, a restaurant hot spot on the Gold Coast. And we loved the low-cost fusion cuisine at **Big Bowl,** 159 W. Erie St., 312/787-8297, $$. You'll get all of Asia—Thailand, Vietnam, China, Japan—and maybe a few other countries, in the same bowl if you like. Here's some fusion for you: the Mongolian pizza has chicken, peanuts, and lemon grass.

A restaurant consistently getting raves is **Ambria,** 2300 Lincoln Park W., 773/472-5959, $$$$, which specializes in French cuisine using the freshest ingredients. Also consider **The Parthenon,** 312 Halsted St., 312/726-2407, $$, everybody's favorite Greektown restaurant. Specialties include suckling pig, Greek sausage, and codfish.

Yet another offering in the ethnic culinary array is **Little Bucharest,** 3001 N. Ashland Ave., 773/929-8640, $, which serves cuisine of Romania such as chicken paprikash. The place is casual and quaint, and they'll pick you up and take you back to your hotel.

SHOPPING

If your idea of a vacation is an excuse to shop, welcome to the biggest excuse of all. Chicago is your kind of town. Shopping puts the "magnificence" in the Magnificent Mile of Michigan Avenue. It is home to three spectacular multistory shopping malls containing more than 200 shops, restaurants, and cinemas.

Let's start at 700 N. Michigan Avenue. **Chicago Place** is anchored by Saks Fifth Avenue and is home to Talbots, Louis Vuitton, and Ann Taylor. Bloomingdale's is the main attraction at the **900 N. Michigan Shops,** a complex that contains six stories of other, smaller shops including Gucci. And just down the street is the **Water Tower Place,** N. Michigan Ave. between E. Pearson and E. Chestnut Sts., featuring Chica-

Near North Chicago

DINING
1 Big Bowl
2 Chicago Chop House
3 Downtown Dog
4 Gene & Georgetti
5 Iron Mike's Grille
6 Morton's of Chicago
7 Pizzeria Due
8 Pizzeria Uno

Milton Lee Olive Park

Gateway Park

South Pier

LAKE SHORE DR

E OHIO ST

E GRAND AV

N WATER ST

N MCCLURG CT

N FAIRBANKS CT

LOWER ILLINOIS ST

Chicago River

Lake Shore Park

DEWITT PL

MIES VAN DER ROHE WY

N ST. CLAIR ST

N MICHIGAN AV

N RUSH ST

N WABASH ST

Oak Street Beach

41

E ELM ST

E CEDAR ST

E BELLEVUE PL

E OAK ST

E WALTON PL

E DELAWARE PL

CHESTNUT ST

PEARSON ST

N STATE ST

N ASTOR ST

N STATE PKWY

N RUSH

Washington Square

DEARBORN PKWY

W CHESTNUT ST

DEARBORN PKWY

N CLARK ST

N LA SALLE ST

DIVISION ST

64

W ELM ST

W MAPLE ST

W OAK ST

W HILL ST

N WELLS ST

N FRANKLIN ST

N ORLEANS ST

W CHESTNUT ST

CHICAGO AV

SUPERIOR ST

HURON ST

ERIE ST

ONTARIO ST

OHIO ST

GRAND AV

ILLINOIS ST

HUBBARD ST

W KINZIE AV

Seward Park

N HUDSON ST

N CLEVELAND ST

N CAMBRIDGE ST

N LARRABEE ST

N KINGSBURY ST

Chicago River

JEFFERSON ST

DES PLAINES ST

W OHIO ST

N UNION ST

Stanton-Schiller Park

N KINGSBURY ST

North Branch Canal

HALSTED ST

MILE

KILOMETER

go's home-grown Marshall Field's, plus Lord & Taylor and dozens of other shops and boutiques.

Don't stop. Don't drop. Keep going down Michigan Avenue to the 600 block, where Eddie Bauer, Marshall's, and Linens 'n Things have found a home along with a nine-screen movie theater. And at the corner of Michigan and Chicago Avenues is a huge version of Pottery Barn and a Banana Republic store.

Before you leave Michigan Avenue, stop in at the **City of Chicago Store,** 700 N. Michigan Ave., at the Chicago Water Works Visitor Information Center. Here you'll find gifts with distinctive Chicago flavor, such as works by local artisans.

Just west of Michigan Avenue and around the corner on Oak Street is a route lined with intimate buildings that cater to international tastes—**Ultimo's** (114 E. Oak St., 312/787-0906), **Gianni Versace** (101 E. Oak St., 312/337-1111), and **Giorgio Armani** (113 E. Oak St.,

Wright Pilgrimage

If you've never walked through one of his doors, you can't really appreciate the mastery of Frank Lloyd Wright. Pictures in a book don't do it. He knew how to make walls talk. Wright's buildings are scattered across the world—and across Chicago, too—but there's a concentration of them in the western suburb of **Oak Park**. It's worth a trip.

Go to the **Frank Lloyd Wright Home and Studio**, 951 Chicago Ave., 708/848-1976. This is where the master began his career, in a home he designed for himself in 1889. As the years went by and the children accumulated, he added on, and in the yard he built a studio where he and his employees came up with all those designs.

For eight dollars you can get a tour of both buildings by a volunteer docent. Additionally, you can pick up information to help you take a self-guided tour of other Wright-designed homes in the neighborhood. For further assistance, contact the **Oak Park Visitors Center**, 158 N. Forest Ave., 708/848-1500.

One of Wright's masterpieces, the **Robie House**, 5757 S. Woodlawn Ave., 773/834-1361, is next to the campus of the University of Chicago in the south part of town. The residence was built in 1910 and is one of the most striking examples of Wright's daring style. It is three stories of horizontal planes, with recesses and unexpected angles. After nearly a century, it still looks revolutionary. The house is worth the struggle to find. And once you get there, docents will give you a tour.

The Robie House and the Oak Park Studio are unoccupied, but residents do live in the other Oak Park homes. Some people allow tours; others don't. If there's not a sign out front, don't go barging in.

312/787-5500). You'll need your Gold Card for all that Gold Coast shopping. For discounted versions of the same thing, check out **Designer Resale,** 658 N. Dearborn St., 312/587-3312, nearby.

State Street, in the center of the Loop, is the location of the original **Marshall Field's,** 835 N. Michigan Ave., 312/641-7000, which opened in 1852. State Street is also home to another famous Chicago department store, **Carson Pirie Scott,** 1 S. State St. The ornate grillwork at the entrance was designed by architect Louis Sullivan in 1899. You might also want to check out the **Jeweler's Center,** 5 S. Wabash Ave., 312/853-2057, www.jewelerscenter.com, headquarters for 165 fine jewelers and where the jewelers themselves shop.

Fanning out a bit, visit River North, a neighborhood north of the Chicago River and west of Michigan Avenue. You'll find art galleries, furniture stores, and specialty shops. Clothing boutiques, antique shops, and unique home accessory stores are abundant in the Lincoln Park neighborhood along Lincoln Avenue, Clark Street, Armitage, and Halsted. Check out the **Lincoln Antique Mall,** 3141 N. Lincoln Ave., where 60 dealers have come together to offer Victorian, mission, art-deco, and 1950s designs in furniture, art, and everything else.

In the Lakeview area, along Broadway between Diversey and Belmont Avenue, you'll discover shops and people that are a bit off the beaten franchised path. Belmont Avenue is full of antique shops and vintage clothing stores. **Antique Resources,** 1741 W. Belmont Ave., 773/871-4242, specializes in seventeenth- to nineteenth-century works and has more than 300 chandeliers for sale.

In the Hyde Park neighborhood near the University of Chicago are stacks of bookstores. Or check out the **Library Store,** Harold Washington Library, 400 S. State St., 312/747-4130. You'll find library-theme gifts, cards, stationery, and handcrafted jewelry by local artists.

SPORTS AND RECREATION

This is a baseball town, a BIG baseball town. The **Chicago White Sox,** 312/831-ISOX, play at Comiskey Park, 333 W. 35th St. The **Cubs,** 312/831-CUBS, play at Wrigley Field, 1060 W. Addison St.

Da **Bears** (NFL), 847/615-BEAR, play at Soldier Field, McFetridge Dr. and Lake Shore Dr. The **Bulls** (NBA), 312/559-1212, can be seen at the United Center. And Chicago has two hockey teams: The **Chicago Wolves,** 312/559-1212, play in the Rosemont Horizon, 6920 N. Mannheim Rd., Rosemont. The **Chicago Blackhawks,** 312/455-4500, compete at the United Center, 1901 W. Madison St.

The 26-mile-long sweatfest known as the **Chicago Marathon,** 888/243-3344, begins in Grand Park and winds its way through many neighborhoods; it usually takes place in mid-October.

Bike Chicago, 800/915-BIKE, will deliver a bike to your hotel for

— Skyward Bound —

Chicago was home to the world's first skyscraper, which was designed by William Le Baron Jenney in 1885. Although the Home Insurance Building no longer stands, today Chicago is home to three of the world's 10 tallest buildings.

Sears Tower, located in Chicago's Loop at 233 S. Wacker Dr., is still considered by many to be the world's tallest building at 1,450 feet. (The office building in Malaysia doesn't count because they're counting the flagpole and that's not fair, say the Sears backers.) Enter on Jackson Street and take a gander at the skyline from the Skydeck. 312/875-9696.

The second-highest building in town is the slender **BP-Amoco Building**, 200 E. Randolph Dr., which was opened in 1974. 312/856-5111.

Third highest is the **John Hancock Center**, 875 N. Michigan Ave., which features an outside Skywalk, the Midwest's highest open-air experience. How high? On a clear day, you can see three states—Illinois, Indiana, and Wisconsin. 888/875-VIEW.

The **Chicago Architecture Foundation** has 60 tours available, Santa Fe Building, 224 S. Michigan Ave., and at the John Hancock Center, 312/922-TOUR.

daily rentals. It provides maps and free group tours, and you can drop off the bike at any of four locations on the 18-mile lakefront bike route.

Call **EZLinks Tee Time Network**, 630/794-8500, for golf tee time reservations for individuals and groups.

You can also get instructions on in-line skating, plus all the gear, just blocks from Navy Pier. For skate rental, call **PPT**, 847/934-9772.

ENTERTAINMENT

Chicago covers the spectrum in the area of entertainment—from the down-home basics like the blues to some of the most sophisticated and avant-garde theater performances anywhere.

The **Navy Pier**, at the end of E. Grand Ave., 312/595-PIER, www.navypier.com, is a Chicago landmark with more than 50 acres of parks, gardens, shops, restaurants, and attractions. Ride the Ferris wheel and carousel or visit **Joe's Be-Bop Café & Jazz Emporium**, 600 E. Grand Ave., 312/595-5299.

Chicago is big on dancing. To find out what's happening, call the **Chicago Dance Coalition**, 312/419-8383. One place for the dance-minded is the **Joffrey Ballet of Chicago**, 312/739-0120, at the Auditorium Theatre, 50 E. Congress Pkwy. Another venue is the **Athenaeum Theatre**, 2936 N. Southport Ave., 773/935-6860, also a kick-up-your-heels kind of place. Additionally, the Athenaeum is a major center for live theater, and the building itself is a landmark. It was built in 1889 by Dankmar Adler and Louis Sullivan. The theater's extraordinary sight lines and fine acoustics make it one of the world's greatest performance arenas. And don't forget the famed **Steppenwolf Theatre Company,** 1650 N. Halsted St., 312/335-1650, where some of the finest actors in America (John Malkovich, Gary Sinise) cut their teeth on its cutting-edge drama. Also worth a listen is Daniel Barenboim leading the **Chicago Symphony Orchestra,** 312/294-3000, in the refurbished Symphony Center, 220 S. Michigan Ave.

Second City, 1616 N. Wells St., 312/337-3992, is a Chicago institution. Since 1959 it's been presenting its signature brand of sociopolitical satire, and it has been the breeding ground of many famous actors, writers, and directors.

For something entirely different, take to the skies in a balloon with FAA-licensed **Windy City BalloonPort,** 100 Ski Hill Rd., Fox River Grove, 847/639-0550. Included is a bottle of champagne for toasting the heavens.

Screenz Digital Universe, 2717 Clark St., 773/348-9300, offers 45 networked computers with which you can surf the Internet, play the hottest games, or check in at the office. Sip a latte in the café.

Or get your pulse racing at **Whirly Ball,** 1880 W. Fullerton Ave., 800/894-4759, a fast-paced combination of hockey, lacrosse, and basketball, played in a high-tech bumper car.

One sure way to get the blues is to go to Chicago and not hear any of this soulful music. Buddy Guy's **Legends,** 754 Wabash Ave., 312/427-0333, offers one of many such opportunities to do so. You'll hear top national and local blues bands seven nights a week at this nightclub owned by the Grammy Award winner. Another spot is **B.L.U.E.S.,** 2519 N. Halsted St., 773/528-1012, which *Chicago Magazine* called "perhaps the world's premiere blues bar." Music gets going about 9 p.m. every night. Yet another highly recommended center for blues is **Rosa's Blue Lounge,** 3420 W. Armitage Ave., 773/342-0452, where some of the best in the business can be heard.

And not to be forgotten is the **Green Mill Jazz Club,** 4802 N. Broadway, 773/878-5552, where Al Capone and his cronies gathered. It's still the most famous nightclub in town.

CITY BASICS

For a free visitor information packet, call 800/2CONNECT. You can also contact the **Chicago Office of Tourism** or visit its Web site, 312/744-2400 or 312/744-8500 (TDD), www.ci.chi.il.us/tourism.

Additionally, the Office of Tourism has three information centers. One is at the Chicago Water Works at Michigan Avenue and Pearson Street. Another is at the Chicago Cultural Center at 77 E. Randolph

Entertainment Aids

Need help in deciding on entertainment options? Try these numbers, all area code 312: **Art Dealers Association**, 649-0065; **Live Concert Hotline**, 666-6667; **Music Alliance** (classical concerts, opera), 987-9296; **Dance Hotline**, 419-8383; **Jazz Hotline**, 427-3300; **Ticketmaster**, 559-1212; **Hot Tixx Hotline**, 977-1755.

Hot Tixx sells half-price day-of-performance theater tickets and full-price tickets to all Ticketmaster events. Hot Tixx accepts MasterCard, Visa, and American Express, and Ticketmaster takes cash only. However, you can only get Hot Tixx tickets in person, at these locations: Chicago Loop, 198 N. State St.; Chicago Place, 700 N. Michigan Ave., Sixth Level; and 1616 Sherman Ave. in Evanston. You can also find Hot Tixx at Tower record stores.

chicago

Street. This location is where you can learn about architecture, cultural attractions, and public art. A third center is at the Illinois Market Place in Navy Pier at 700 E. Grand Street. All three are open daily except on major holidays.

For hotel reservations, call the **Illinois Reservation Service,** 800/491-1800. Other useful services are **Room Finders,** 800/473-STAY, www.roomfinders.com, and **Hotel/Motel Association of Illinois,** 800/978-7890. For information on B&Bs, call the **Heritage Bed and Breakfast Registry of Chicago,** 800/431-5546. Contact the **Illinois Restaurant Association** at 312/787-4000.

Information on just about everything in Chicago—restaurants, nightclubs, museums, and gambling locations—is available through the *Chicago Sun-Times* **Infoline,** 630/231-4600. For up-to-date information on what's going on, also look at the freebie weekly called *The Reader*, which is available everywhere and also on-line, www.chireader.com. *Windy City Times*, another free weekly, caters to the gay community.

First in booze, first in shoes, and last in the American League.
—Unattributed saying about St. Louis
at the turn of the last century

When something as big as the Mississippi flows by your front door every day, it does something to people. It makes them want to get a move on.

People around here have been doing that from the beginning—moving to the city, moving away from it, bringing things in, taking things away. It's called a crossroads. There's always lots of traffic at a crossroads.

First were the Native Americans. Then came French fur traders and Spanish explorers, Lewis and Clark and the pioneers, slaves and cotton, steamboats and barges, trains and aviation, and the blues. That's a lot of stuff, lots of different people, and lots of new ideas—and all of it moving in and out and rubbing elbows with one other. A couple of hundred years of that—of making shoes and brewing beer and playing baseball—and you're going to remain vital. And your baseball team might eventually get pretty good, too. But mainly what you're going to do is create an interesting place.

So why not go with the flow?

Meet me in St. Louie, Louie, and bring your sense of adventure.

St. Louis

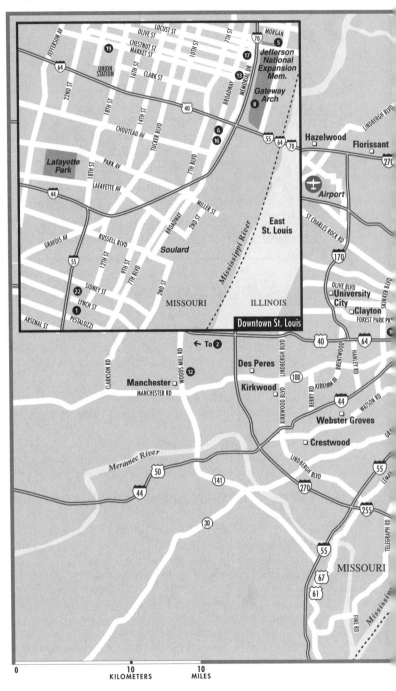

Downtown St. Louis

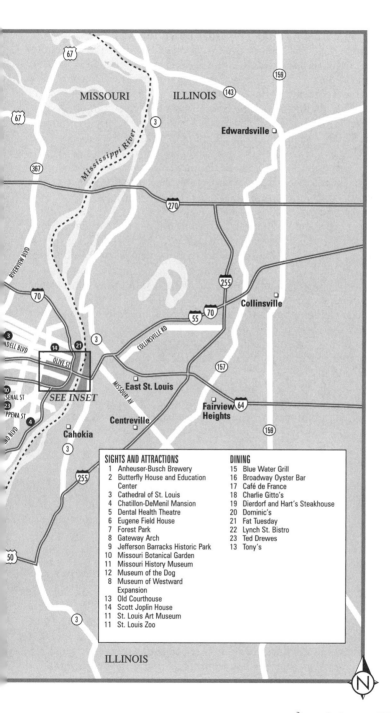

MISSOURI ILLINOIS

Edwardsville □

Mississippi River

Collinsville

East St. Louis

Fairview
Heights

Centreville

Cahokia

SEE INSET

SIGHTS AND ATTRACTIONS
1 Anheuser-Busch Brewery
2 Butterfly House and Education
   Center
3 Cathedral of St. Louis
4 Chatillon-DeMenil Mansion
5 Dental Health Theatre
6 Eugene Field House
7 Forest Park
8 Gateway Arch
9 Jefferson Barracks Historic Park
10 Missouri Botanical Garden
11 Missouri History Museum
12 Museum of the Dog
8 Museum of Westward
   Expansion
13 Old Courthouse
14 Scott Joplin House
11 St. Louis Art Museum
11 St. Louis Zoo

DINING
15 Blue Water Grill
16 Broadway Oyster Bar
17 Café de France
18 Charlie Gitto's
19 Dierdorf and Hart's Steakhouse
20 Dominic's
21 Fat Tuesday
22 Lynch St. Bistro
23 Ted Drewes
13 Tony's

ILLINOIS

N

GETTING AROUND

The Lambert–St. Louis International Airport, 314/426-8000, www.lambert-stlouis.com, is just 15 minutes from downtown. You can take the light rail **MetroLink**, 314/231-2345 or 314/982-1555 (TDD), from the airport to downtown and the center of activity. MetroLink is a 17-mile system that begins at the airport and goes by all the major tourist stops, ending across the river in East St. Louis, Illinois. A one-way ticket is $1.25, or an all-day pass is $4.00. From the airport to downtown is $3.00. The light rail also connects to three shuttle services—one goes to Forest Park, one to the Botanical Garden, and another to Washington University. Shuttles cost $1.25 for an all-day ticket.

You can take the **Airport Express** shuttle, 314/429-4950, from the airport to major hotels for $10 one way, $15 round-trip.

Sorry, you can't hail a cab in St. Louis. The only way to get one is to go to a taxi stand near either the major hotels or the convention center, or you can call for one. Try **Harris Cab,** 314/535-5087, or **Yellow Cab Co.,** 314/361-2345. To ride in style, contact **Style Limousine,** 314/521-6506.

Should you get a car? You can get along without one, but it would not be much of a hassle to get one.

If you can find the Arch, you can find St. Louis. Almost everything that's anything is nearby, or within reach of the MetroLink.

Downtown streets are laid out on a grid with alternating northbound and southbound streets. Parking is abundant in high-rise garages, and meters go for two hours. You can ride free around downtown St. Louis on the MetroLink from 11:30 a.m. to 1:30 p.m. weekdays. There's no charge if you stay within the stops of Laclede's Landing, Union Station, St. Louis Centre, and Busch Stadium.

SIGHTS AND ATTRACTIONS

There's more here than the **Gateway Arch,** St. Louis likes to say about itself. And that's well and good, but it doesn't mean you should neglect this silver rainbow that has become the city's icon. This monument to Thomas Jefferson and the Louisiana Purchase—gateway to the West—is 630 feet high and America's tallest monument. You can take a tram to the top.

A visitors center at the Arch, at the riverfront between Third St. and Lenore K. Sullivan Blvd., 314/425-4465, contains a theater that shows films about construction of the Arch. The center also houses a gift shop and the **Museum of Westward Expansion,** 314/982-1410, which focuses on Lewis and Clark and the struggles of pioneer life. Best times to avoid long lines are right after the 8:30 a.m. opening and just after 5 p.m. Also, you can buy tram tickets early in the morning for specific times later in the day.

Going Places

You can get more than a narrated sightseeing tour with an hour-long cruise on **Gateway Riverboat Cruises**, at St. Louis Levee below the Gateway Arch, 314/621-4040 or 800/878-7411. The old-fashioned riverboats—the *Tom Sawyer* and the *Becky Thatcher*—offer **Dixie Dinner Cruises** complete with live bands and prime rib dinners.

Besides the riverboat tours, you might consider **St. Louis Carriage Company**, 314/621-3334, which will pick you up at most major downtown hotels in a horse-drawn carriage for a tour of the town. **Grayline**, 314/421-4753, will get you around to the major stops in a bus with a tour guide.

The other central spot in St. Louis is **Forest Park,** bounded by I-64, Kingshighway, Lindell Blvd., and Skinker Blvd. At 1,300 acres, it's even larger than New York's Central Park. Besides the usual—biking and running trails, ball fields, lakes, golf, skating, and tennis—the park is home to several cultural institutions, including the St. Louis Art Museum, the Missouri History Museum, and the St. Louis Zoo.

The **St. Louis Art Museum,** 1 Fine Arts Dr. in Forest Park, 314/721-0072, www.slam.org, is one of the best in the world, and contains art from seven continents and thousands of years. The **Missouri History Museum,** 5700 Lindell Blvd., 314/746-4599, features exhibits on Lewis and Clark, the American West, Charles Lindbergh, and the 1904 St. Louis World's Fair. The **St. Louis Zoo,** 100 Government Dr. in Forest Park, 314/781-0900, www.stlzoo.org, has more than 6,000 animals and is considered one of the best anywhere.

Don't neglect the **Missouri Botanical Garden,** 4344 Shaw Blvd., 314/577-9400, www.mobot.org, which features the largest Japanese garden in the world, as well as a rain forest, a Chinese garden, and the Kemper Center for Home Gardening.

The **Jefferson Barracks Historic Park,** 533 Grant Rd., 314/544-5714, is devoted to military history. Robert E. Lee and Ulysses S. Grant served here. The site is a national cemetery. It's closed Mondays.

Stroll through a three-story conservatory filled with tropical plants and more than 2,000 butterflies that roam freely in the **Butterfly House and Education Center,** Faust Historic Park, 18175 Olive Blvd., Chesterfield, 314/530-0076. Outside is a sculpture garden planted to attract wild butterflies.

The **Cathedral of St. Louis,** 4431 Lindell Blvd., 314/533-0544, is a Romanesque-Byzantine building that is decorated with one of the world's largest collections of mosaic art. The cathedral has a museum and a gift shop. Take a tour with a docent for only two dollars, or wander through on your own for free.

A fine example of St. Louis's gloried past is the **Chatillon-DeMenil Mansion,** 3352 DeMenil Pl., 314/771-5828, a Greek Revival beauty built in 1848. The house is furnished with authentic period pieces and is a national landmark. After your tour, have lunch in the restaurant.

The **Anheuser-Busch Brewery,** I-55 and Arsenal St., 314/577-2626, is the world's largest. Take a tour and see the inside of the lager cellar, the packaging plant, and the Brew House, and then visit the stables where those magnificent Clydesdale horses are kept. The hospitality room passes out free samples.

Now here's something to sink your teeth into: the **Dental Health Theatre,** 727 N. First St., Suite 103, 314/241-7391, which features 16 three-foot-high fiberglass teeth, in addition to films and puppets. Call for reservations, but floss first.

And here's something that might sink it's teeth into *you:* the American Kennel Club **Museum of the Dog,** 1721 S. Mason Rd., 314/821-DOGS. You'll find out all about canine history and see sculptures, paintings, decorative arts, and photos that celebrate man's best friend.

Eugene Field was the children's poet who wrote such chestnuts as *Little Boy Blue* and *Winken, Blinken, and Nod.* The **Eugene Field House,** 634 Broadway, 314/421-4689, has been turned into a museum filled with antique toys and dolls. Field's father, Roswell M. Field, was the lawyer for Dred Scott, the slave who sued for his freedom; the case further drove the country to Civil War.

St. Louis's picturesque **Old Courthouse,** 11 N. Fourth St., 314/655-1600, was built between 1839 and 1862. Two galleries depict local history, and two courtrooms have been restored to their original nineteenth-century appearance. This is where the Dred Scott trial took place, and re-enactments of the drama take place regularly. You can also see a movie about early St. Louis.

The **Scott Joplin House,** 2658 Delmar Blvd., 314/340-5790, is where the King of Ragtime spent some of his most creative years. It's a restored, post–Civil War home that showcases a music room and galleries.

LODGING

In the shadow of the Arch is where you want to stay. That's where all the action is. The premier spot to lay your weary head is the **Hyatt Regency St. Louis,** 1820 Market St., 800/233-1234, $$$. The hotel is part of historic Union Station, one of the world's largest train stations that is now also home to a huge shopping area of 100 stores, several restaurants, and entertainment venues. And it's right in the middle of everything, next to the MetroLink.

A hotel with a great location and a reasonable rate is the **Regal Riverfront Hotel,** 200 S. Fourth St., 314/241-9500, $$. Right out your

Gateway Arch

window is the Gateway Arch, riverboat casinos, and Busch Stadium. The **Omni Majestic,** 1019 Pine St., 800/THE-OMNI, $$$, is another well-situated downtown hotel in a historic building that's been around since 1914. It has a well-regarded restaurant, the Majestic Grill.

Ask about the gambling package at the **Adam's Mark,** Fourth and Chestnut Sts., 800/444-2326, $$, a moderately priced downtown hotel. You get a shuttle and free entrance to the *Casino Queen* casino, plus a buffet breakfast and health club privileges.

Drury Inn, 20th and Market Sts., 800/378-7946, www.drury-inn.com, $$, is a chain hotel with three locations downtown, plus several more in outlying areas. Breakfast is included, and most of the hotels have swimming pools and cable TV. One of the locations is at Union Station.

How does Jacuzzi by candlelight sound? The **Park Avenue Bed & Breakfast,** 945 Park Ave., 800/430-2506, $$, has four rooms, all with private baths and jetted tubs. It's located downtown.

The **Lehmann House Bed & Breakfast,** 10 Benton Pl., 314/231-6724, $$, is in a historic mansion downtown, and its rooms have fireplaces and antiques. Two of its four rooms have private baths.

Napoleon's Retreat, 1815 Lafayette Ave., 800/700-9980, $$, promises luxurious accommodations in Lafayette Square, a neighborhood known as the Victorian Heart of St. Louis because of its many stately homes that date back to the 1870s. It has five rooms, all with private baths.

An upscale B&B is the **Parker Garden,** 2310 State St., 888/298-3834, www.bbonline.com/il/parkergarden, $$$, which has fireplaces and whirlpool tubs. Its two rooms have private baths, and it's located across the river in East St. Louis.

DINING

Think about it: this is the place that, at the 1904 World's Fair, merchants plopped some chunks of ice in tea and called it iced tea; wrapped a waffle around a frozen dairy dessert to create the ice cream cone; and popularized hot dogs and hamburgers. St. Louis knows its food.

Everybody who comes to St. Louis has got to try the Concrete—it's a milkshake so thick that you can turn it upside down and not lose a drop. Taste one at **Ted Drewes,** 6726 Chippewa St., 314/481-2652, $, a St. Louis landmark on a stretch of Old Route 66.

Another food specialty of St. Louis is an addictive little appetizer known as the toasted ravioli. The meat-filled ravioli is rolled in breadcrumbs, deep fried, and served with meat sauce. **Charlie Gitto's,** 5226 Shaw Blvd., 314/772-8898, $$, is where the toasted ravioli was invented in 1947. Your best bet for a great dining experience at this establishment is "the trio," a sample of three items from the menu chosen by the chef. And for dessert, ask about the tiramisu. It's Charlie's mama's recipe.

In the same neighborhood is **Dominic's,** 5101 Wilson Ave., 314/771-1632, $$$$, an award-winning restaurant that *Condé Nast Traveler* readers say is one of the best in the nation. Specialties are fresh fish and homemade pasta. **Blue Water Grill,** 2607 Hampton Ave., 314/821-5757, $$, is one of the few non-Italian restaurants in the same neighborhood. It's known for its fresh seafood with hints of southwestern and Mexican seasoning.

For some authentic Cajun cuisine, try the **Broadway Oyster Bar,** located two blocks south of Busch Stadium downtown, 736 S. Broadway, 314/621-8811, $. It has a jazz brunch on Sundays and live music nightly. A restaurant with New Orleans–style food and a specialty bar known for the world's largest selection of frozen daiquiris is **Fat Tuesday,** 700 N. Second St., 314/241-2008, $. It mostly serves appetizers and sandwiches.

S t. Louis, like the rest of the nation, is going casual more and more. Although some people still wear suits and cocktail attire to the theater and the symphony, most tone down to a kind of dressy casual style.

And here's something to remember about St. Louis weather: anything goes. The city sits in the middle of the country, the battleground for conflicting weather—warm air from the south, cold air from the north, and thunderstorms where the masses meet. So be prepared for just about anything, such as a cold snap in early fall or a hot day in the middle of spring, and rain just about any time.

City Survival Tips

The *ZAGAT Survey* has been rating downtown's **Café de France,** 410 Olive St., 314/231-2204, $$$, as St. Louis's top French restaurant for the last two decades. The food and service are elegant. It's closed Sundays. **Tony's,** 410 Market St., 314/231-7007, $$$$, is the only restaurant in Missouri to have won AAA's Five-Diamond Award. The cuisine is Italian and top-drawer all the way.

Hey, tough guy. What you want is a steak from the kitchen of a couple of beefy guys, football stars Dan Dierdorf and Jim Hart. Check out their restaurant, **Dierdorf and Hart's Steakhouse,** 701 Market St., 314/421-1772, $$$.

The **Lynch St. Bistro,** 1031 Lynch St., 314/772-5777, $$, in the Soulard district presents an eclectic menu of New American specialties, such as barbecue-crusted salmon.

You can make dining reservations through the **St. Louis Visitor Information Center,** Seventh St. and Washington Blvd., 314/342-5041.

SHOPPING

More than 100 shops and restaurants have moved into what was once the nation's largest and busiest train station, **St. Louis Union Station,** Market St. between 18th and 20th Sts., 314/421-6655. It was built in 1894, and its Grand Hall reflects the opulence of days gone by.

If antiques are what you're looking for, head over to **Cherokee Street Antique Row,** 1900-2300 Cherokee St., 314/773-8810. There are more than 45 stores in this little neighborhood, with everything from quality furniture to dusty whatnots.

The **Apropos Gallery,** 7750 Forsyth Blvd., 314/212-5500, has one of the region's finest collections of contemporary crafts, including jewelry and sculpture.

And almost 200 artists are represented by the **Componere** gallery in the Loop neighborhood, 6509 Delmar Blvd., 314/721-1181. Specialties include blown glass, printed silk, and painted furniture.

Just down the street is **Coyote's Paw,** 5388 Delmar Blvd., 314/721-7576, a gallery with fine arts and crafts from Africa, Asia, Oceania, and the Americas. You will find ritual objects, musical instruments, and textiles.

Plaza Frontenac, Lindbergh and Clayton Rds., 314/432-5800, is one of the major shopping centers of St. Louis. Stores include Saks Fifth Avenue, Neiman Marcus, and Williams-Sonoma.

Or visit the **St. Louis Centre,** 515 N. Sixth St., 314/231-5913, a shopping center downtown that connects two major department stores—Dillard's and Famous-Barr. One of the shops in the complex is **St. Louis Stuff and Company,** 314/231-9711, which specializes in souvenir items such as Cardinals, Rams, and Blues apparel.

If you've always wanted to construct your own teddy bear, the place for you is **Build-A-Bear Workshop,** 314/423-8000. You stuff, stitch, fluff, name, dress, and take home your own stuffed animal. It's in the **St. Louis Galleria,** Brentwood Blvd. and Clayton Rd., an upscale mall with 165 stores.

SPORTS AND RECREATION

Let's see. There's what's-his-name . . . Mark somebody. McGwire? Yeah, that's the ticket. To get tickets to see McGwire and the **St. Louis Cardinals** in action, call, write, or check the baseball team's Web site: Cardinals Ticket Office, 300 Stadium Plaza, St. Louis, MO 63102; 314/421-2400 (for tickets); 314/421-3060 (for information); www.stlcardinalstickets.com.

Now here's a double play: the **International Bowling Museum,** 111 Stadium Plaza, 314/231-6340, and the **Cardinal Hall of Fame Museum,** 111 Stadium Plaza, 314/231-6340, all under one roof. You'll see trophies, videos, and mementos chronicling both the 100-plus years of Cardinals baseball and the highlights of the history of professional bowling. And hey, you can go bowling, too—either on an old-fashioned lane or on one of the new high-tech alleys.

You don't have to go to the grand **Busch Stadium,** 300 Stadium Plaza, 314/241-3900, only when the Cards are playing. It's available for tours, too. And you can visit the Cardinals gift shop or wander over to the Family Pavilion for some interactive games. You might meet a past or present Cardinal star.

The **St. Louis Blues,** 314/622-2500, play hockey from September through May at the Kiel Center, 1401 Clark St. And the National Football League's **St. Louis Rams,** 314/425-8830, play at Trans World Dome, 701 Convention Plaza.

When you want to get physical yourself, one of the best places to take a hike is around the Gateway Arch. There are several paths in the national park, one of which borders the Mississippi and all of which include green space, reflecting ponds, and a close-up look at the Arch.

There are several interesting paths through Forest Park, including a 7.5-mile bike path. Bikers and walkers who want to get acquainted with the many different trees found in the park can obtain a free copy of the Tree Walk map from the **St. Louis Park Department,** 314/367-7275. You'll see 25 different trees on the 2.5-mile paved course. Another walk takes you by fountains, contemporary art, and statues and monuments, including depictions of Civil War heroes.

ENTERTAINMENT

The Grand Center Arts and Entertainment District is located on Grand Boulevard between Lindell and Delmar Boulevards. It's St. Louis's Great White Way, featuring popular music, dance concerts, Broadway

Singing the Blues

St. Louis has always been a center for popular music, but it is probably best known for the blues. Some say the blues got going with the great migration of blacks who came up the river from Mississippi and landed in St. Louis during World War II. Says John May of the St. Louis Blues Society: "Ragtime was very popular in St. Louis, and the integration of blues music from Mississippi created what became known as the St. Louis blues."

But **W.C. Handy** had begun the fusion earlier with his immortal *St. Louis Blues*, which has become the most recorded blues song in history. Handy was a contemporary of **Scott Joplin**, the ragtime king, who was a regular in the nightspots of St. Louis around the time of the 1904 World's Fair. At the same time, jazz was also steaming upriver from New Orleans, and the whole mix has resulted in some of America's best music.

You can still hear this brand of music today in several neighborhoods. Just south of the Gateway Arch are lots of blues clubs tucked away in the red brick buildings of the **Soulard** neighborhood. You'll start finding clubs around Busch Stadium, moving south on Broadway.

Another area to explore for good music is **Laclede's Landing**, where music echoes off the cobblestone streets and bounces between clubs housed in restored nineteenth-century warehouses. This area is near the America's Center convention complex.

shows, and original productions. This is where you'll find the **Circus Flora**, 634 N. Grand Blvd., Suite 10D, 314/531-6273; **Dance St. Louis**, 634 N. Grand Blvd., #1102, 314/534-6622; **Fox Theatre**, 527 N. Grand Blvd., 314/534-1111; **Portfolio Gallery**, 3514 Delmar Blvd., 314/533-3323; **Powell Symphony Hall**, 718 N. Grand Blvd., 314/533-2500; **St. Louis Black Repertory**, 314/534-3807; **Sheldon Concert Hall**, 3648 Washington Blvd., 314/533-9900; and **Vaughn Cultural Center**, 3701 Grandel Sq., 314/371-0040.

The **St. Louis Symphony**, 314/534-1700, is America's second oldest and is ranked among the top in the world. It plays in Powell Symphony Hall. Also of note is the **Opera Theatre of St. Louis**, 130 Edgar Rd., 314/961-0644, which presents new and classic operas.

All you've got to do is cross the river and you can enjoy both spectacular views of the St. Louis skyline and the fun of gambling. The *Casino Queen*, 800/777-0777, offers dining as it chugs up and down the Mississippi 11 times a day. It's docked right across from the Arch in East St. Louis.

The largest dockside casino in the area is *The Admiral*, St. Louis Levee, 800/772-3647, an art deco–style former cruise ship. The Presidential Casino inside has 100 table games and more than 50 video-poker and slot machines.

Blueberry Hill, 6504 Delmar Blvd., 314/727-0880, is a St. Louis landmark filled with pop-culture memorabilia. Inside is an authentic jukebox full of 45-rpm golden oldies, especially those of St. Louis hometown-hero Chuck Berry. You'll also find lots of Elvis and Howdy Doody material. Specialties are hamburgers, and they have a huge beer selection. The **Side Door Music Club,** 2005 Locust St., 314/231-3666, presents the latest alternative rock bands from around the nation as well as local groups.

It's the name of the club and the address, too—**1224 Washington,** 1224 Washington Ave., 314/231-9800. It has three floors that include dancing, a martini lounge, and billiards. The **Casa Loma Ballroom,** 3354 Iowa Ave., 314/664-8000, is the oldest nightclub west of the Mississippi. Its art-deco ballroom has a 5,000-square-foot dance floor. Live music is by local and national bands.

BB's Jazz, Blues & Soups, 700 S. Broadway, 314/436-5222, specializes in St. Louis-style cuisine with local and national jazz and blues acts. And also consider a visit to **Mike & Min's,** 925 Geyer Ave., 314/421-1655, a real St. Louis blues mecca—it was established in 1937. It's a neighborhood bar in Soulard with live blues bands nightly. In Laclede's Landing, try **Hennegan's,** N. Second St., 314/241-8877, built as a replica of the Senate dining room with fine dining during the week and jazz on weekends.

CITY BASICS

Get general information about St. Louis by checking with the **St. Louis Convention & Visitors Commission,** 800/916-0040 or 800/916-0092, www.st-louis-cvc.com or www.explorestlouis.com. Likewise, you can contact hot lines for **accessibility information,** 314/622-3686 or 314/622-3693 (TDD); **special events,** 314/421-2100; **highway conditions,** 800/222-6400; and **weather forecasts,** 314/441-8467.

The *Riverfront Times* has all the listings for current entertainment, such as blues, jazz, rock, reggae, and more. It's free, and you can find it in restaurants and office buildings. Also, the *Post-Dispatch* puts out a section called "Get Out," another way to find out what's happening in the city.

to go ▶

People who think Kansas City is kind of a cow town have not been here,
because it's a graceful city, one of the most graceful in America.
—Garrison Keillor

KC calls itself the Heart of America. Certainly that's true geographically. The East Coast is 1,900 miles to the right. Same with the West Coast, except you go left. But it takes more than location to call yourself a "Heart." It takes soul. Does Kansas City have that? Damn straight.

This city is home to the Three B's—beef, baseball, and the blues. And talk about America—how can you get more American than that? The song we Americans sing has a mellow, jazzy wistfulness. The food we eat is clean and simple. The game we play is the same—three strikes and you're out; fair is fair and foul is foul; hit one over the fence and you're a hero, and a millionaire, no matter what color you are.

But the jazz and blues came from African Americans. Baseball was at its best in the old Negro National League here, before it was absorbed into the all-white major leagues. The beef came to America via the Spanish in Mexico.

Black and white and brown. Sounds American to us. Sounds like a rainbow soul.

Kansas City

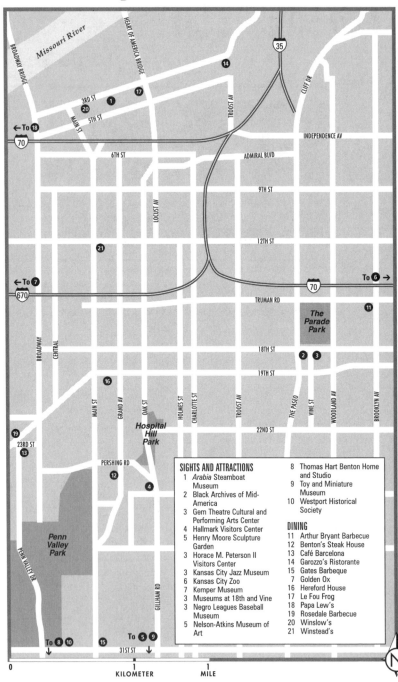

SIGHTS AND ATTRACTIONS

1 *Arabia* Steamboat Museum
2 Black Archives of Mid-America
3 Gem Theatre Cultural and Performing Arts Center
4 Hallmark Visitors Center
5 Henry Moore Sculpture Garden
3 Horace M. Peterson II Visitors Center
3 Kansas City Jazz Museum
6 Kansas City Zoo
7 Kemper Museum
3 Museums at 18th and Vine
3 Negro Leagues Baseball Museum
5 Nelson-Atkins Museum of Art
8 Thomas Hart Benton Home and Studio
9 Toy and Miniature Museum
10 Westport Historical Society

DINING

11 Arthur Bryant Barbecue
12 Benton's Steak House
13 Café Barcelona
14 Garozzo's Ristorante
15 Gates Barbeque
7 Golden Ox
16 Hereford House
17 Le Fou Frog
18 Papa Lew's
19 Rosedale Barbecue
20 Winslow's
21 Winstead's

GETTING AROUND

Kansas City International Airport (KCI), 816/243-5237, is about 25 minutes northwest of downtown. If you hop on a Red Bus, thinking you're on some kind of shuttle to downtown, you're wrong. You'll be taken either to one of the other airport terminals or to the airport parking lots.

You can get door-to-door airport transportation from **Quicksilver Airport Service,** 913/262-0905. For airport shuttles, call **Metropolitan Transportation Services,** 888/471-6050. Taxis are also available from **Kansas City Taxi Drivers Association,** 816/591-4755.

You can contact the **Metro** for information about the city bus service at 816/221-0660, but do get a car. It's the only thing that makes sense. Kansas City's central district, which contains most of the interesting stuff, is long and thin. You don't want to try to walk it.

There's not a whole lot of difference between Kansas City, Kansas, and Kansas City, Missouri—it's just a matter of crossing the street, State Line Road. Most of the interesting sites are on the Missouri side, but most of the people live in Kansas—of about 1.6 million people total, 450,000 live on the Missouri side.

The downtown area of tourist interest is a corridor that begins at the Missouri River and moves south, with Broadway and Main Streets as the primary north-south routes through the middle of it. At the north end is **downtown** proper, which contains the 18th and Vine historic jazz district. Next is **Crown Center,** an area of hotels, shops, and restaurants built around Hallmark Cards headquarters. You'll also encounter **Westport,** once an outfitting post for wagons heading West and now a historic area of shops and art galleries. Yet another area is **Country Club Plaza,** a shopping district that is bedecked in Moorish architecture and that is home to a number of major hotels; it wouldn't be a bad place to set up camp here. To get yourself familiar with the lay of the land, consider taking a one and a half hour grand tour of Kansas City on **Grayline Trolley Tours,** 888/471-6050.

SIGHTS AND ATTRACTIONS

Begin your visit at the **Museums at 18th and Vine,** 1616 E. 18th St., 816/474-8463. This part of town is where baseball, jazz, and good times reigned as part of Kansas City's cultural life in the 1920s and 1930s, and where America's native sound was nourished—so it's only natural that the museums should be combined and put right here. Inside the new $26 million facility, which was opened in 1997, are the **Kansas City Jazz Museum,** 816/474-8463; the **Negro Leagues Baseball Museum,** 816/221-1920; and the **Gem Theatre Cultural and Performing Arts Center,** 816/474-8463. The **Horace M. Peterson II Visitors Center** offers an overview and history of the area and the facility.

— Now You Know —

If it weren't for Kansas City, we wouldn't have these inventions and new products, all of which came from local brain-storming: Teflon, the Eskimo Pie, the melt-in-your-mouth-not-in-your-hands M&M candy coating, the wax-coated ice cream container, the jazz jam session, and the McDonald's Happy Meal.

Imagine Count Basie, Ella Fitzgerald, and Charlie "Yardbird" Parker playing their hearts out and honing their craft in that wide-open, free-wheeling town back then. When you're done pondering it, head on over to the Kansas City Jazz Museum, where you can watch rare performances on a giant video screen or see artifacts such as Parker's sax. In the evenings, the museum cranks up the **Blue Room,** an actual jazz club that features contemporary KC artists. The Jazz Museum is free on Wednesdays.

The Negro Leagues Baseball Museum covers the National Negro League from its beginning after the Civil War to its end in the 1960s. The museum re-creates the look, sounds, and feel of baseball in the height of the league, when games drew as many as 50,000 spectators to games coast to coast and featured such greats as Willie Mays and Hank Aaron, who moved to the white teams after Jackie Robinson made the transition in 1947.

The Gem Theatre was constructed in 1912 as a movie house for African Americans and has been refurbished into a 500-seat cultural and performing arts center. Other areas of interest include the **Kansas City Zoo,** I-435 and 63rd St., 816/871-5700, which recently underwent a $71 million expansion, adding several naturalistic exhibits. The zoo has its own IMAX Theater. Naturally, it shows nature films.

The **Nelson-Atkins Museum of Art,** 4525 Oak, 816/561-4000 or 816/751-1ART (information), housed in a stone neoclassical structure built in 1933, features 30,000 items dating from 3000 B.C. to the present. Notable are its collections of Asian and European art, and twentieth-century sculpture. Outside is the **Henry Moore Sculpture Garden.** The nearby **Kemper Museum,** 4420 Warwick, 816/561-3737, opened in 1994 and features work by international contemporary artists. It, too, has lots of outdoor sculpture.

See over 200 tons of artifacts recovered from a sunken 1856 steamboat at the *Arabia* **Steamboat Museum,** 400 Grand Ave., 816/471-4030, including china, jewelry, hardware, and even food. Or you can take a self-guided tour through the **Thomas Hart Benton Home and Studio,** 3616 Belleview, 816/931-5722. The artist lived here from 1939 until his death in 1975. Also check out the **Black Archives of Mid-America,** 2033 Vine, 816/483-1300, which contains one of the largest Midwestern collections of African American memorabilia, artifacts, and research material.

And 85 years of Hallmark card history is presented through inter-

Kansas City lights up at night and resonates with jazz sounds

active exhibits, displays, and movies at the **Hallmark Visitors Center** in the Crown Center, Level Three, 25th St. and Grand, 816/274-5745. The **Toy and Miniature Museum,** 5235 Oak, 816/333-2055, is in a restored 1911 mansion and contains a fine collection of miniatures, antique dollhouses, and furnishings. But don't neglect **Westport,** Broadway St. and Westport Rd., a historical district in Kansas City dating back to the 1830s where pioneers provisioned themselves before the long trek westward. The **Westport Historical Society,** 816/756-2789, can tell you what you need to know.

LODGING

The **Doanleigh Inn,** 217 E. 37th St., 816/753-2667, $$, is well-situated between Crown Center and the Plaza. It has five guest rooms with private baths, phones, cable TV, fireplaces, and antiques.

Or ask about the getaway weekend rates at the downtown **Historic Suites of America,** 612 Central, 800/733-0612, www.historicsuites.com, $$$. With your room you get a full breakfast buffet plus use of an outdoor pool and Jacuzzi.The **Radisson,** 8787 Reeder Rd., 800/333-3333, www.radisson.com, $$, is listed on the National Register of Historic Places, but it has all the newest amenities, including an indoor/outdoor pool, fitness center, and whirlpool spa.

With a total of 983 rooms, the **Marriott Downtown,** 200 W. 12th St., 800/228-9290, $$$, is one of the largest hotels around. It consists of two towers connected by a skywalk. One tower is actually the Marriott's skillful renovation of the historic Hotel Meuhlebach, once known as the hotel to the presidents, and host to all but one from Teddy Roosevelt to Ronald Reagan. President Truman used the hotel as a second White House.

The **Southmoreland on the Plaza,** 116 E. 46th St., 816/531-

7979, $$, has a four-star rating from *Mobil Travel Guide*. Its 12 guest rooms are in a 1913 Colonial house close to the Country Club Plaza. Each room has private bath, and some have decks, fireplaces, and jetted tubs. You can walk to the Plaza and the Nelson-Atkins Museum of Art from the recently updated **LaFontaine Inn,** 4320 Oak, 816/753-4434, www.lafontainebb.com, $$, which has five elegant rooms in a 1910 Georgian Colonial home. Each room has a private bath, and two have steam rooms.

The **Quarterage,** 500 Westport Rd., 800/942-4233, $$, is a boutique hotel with 23 rooms in the heart of town near restaurants, shopping, and entertainment. Twenty-two rooms have been restored to 1888 elegance at the **Hotel Savoy,** located in the heart of downtown's historic garment district, 219 W. Ninth St., 800/SAVOY-BB, $$. The gourmet breakfast has 32 items from which to choose.

Additional lodging information is available from the **Hotel and Motel Association of Greater Kansas City,** 816/444-7860.

DINING

Kansas City is home to more than 80 barbecue restaurants, each with its own specialty—ribs, pork, mutton, ham, sausage, and even fish.

The king of barbecue in KC is "King Arthur" Bryant, whose barbecue lineage goes back to the early days when Henry Perry, now known as the Father of KC Barbecue, got his pit smoking in the early 1920s. Today **Arthur Bryant Barbecue,** 1727 Brooklyn, 816/231-1123, $, is still going strong. *New Yorker* columnist Calvin Trillin wrote that Bryant's is "the single best restaurant in the world."

Another old-timer in the business is **Rosedale Barbecue,** 600 Southwest Blvd., 913/262-0343, $, which has been around since 1934. And **Winslow's,** 20 E. Fifth St., 816/471-RIBS, $, has been serving barbecue and blues for more than 25 years. Live blues is presented Thursdays.

Gates Barbeque, 1221 Brooklyn; 3201 Main St.; 800/662-7427, $, is a family-owned business with two locations in town. It has a sterling reputation for good food. But they serve more than the usual barbecue at **Papa Lew's,** 1504 Prospect, 816/231-2800, $. How about smothered pork chops, catfish, steak, collard greens, and fresh peach cobbler? They don't take credit cards.

This is a beef town, remember, and some cuts of meat are too good to be barbecued. We're talking steaks here, and one of the better steak houses in Kansas City is the **Hereford House,** 2 E. 20th St., 800/840-1080, $$. It has good food and relaxed Midwestern hospitality. Along with your charbroiled steaks, chops, and seafood, **Benton's Steak House,** Westin Crown Center, One Pershing Rd., 816/391-4460, $$$, brings you art with your dinner. Some original Thomas Hart Benton paintings hang in the restaurant, which also offers spectacular views.

If you want to get an earful, come to the **Kansas City Blues and Jazz Festival**, 800/530-5266, www.kcbluesjazz.org, in July. It draws more than 100,000 people annually to Penn Valley Park with top names in national and local groups.

Another big event is the **Count Basie Birthday Bash**, which takes place each August in the streets of the historic 18th and Vine district. Also, the **Kansas City International Jazz Festival**, 816/931-2022, attracts top names each September. The two-day festival is held at Starlight Theatre in Swope Park.

The American Royal BBQ Contest, held the first weekend in October, is the largest such competition in the world, with several hundred amateur chefs competing in meat, sauce, and entertainment divisions. So where is it held? Just follow your nose—and the smoke. Contact the Kansas City Barbecue Society for more information, 800/963-5227.

Each fall marks the occurrence of a Kansas City tradition that has been going on since 1899. It's the **American Royal Livestock, Horse Show & Rodeo**, 816/221-9800, the largest such combined event in the world, they say. A western art show is held in conjunction with the rodeo, too.

events
HORIZON

The **Golden Ox,** 1600 Genessee, 816/842-2866, $$, is a good steak place in the old stockyards area, and the atmosphere is pure Western.

But Kansas is not just a one-note wonder of a gastronomic town. There are plenty of opportunities to branch out from the beef. **Le Fou Frog**, 400 E. Fifth St., 816/474-6060, $$, is an intimate, romantic, southern French bistro with outside terrace dining. The former chef for Aristotle Onassis prepares Spanish and Italian Mediterranean specialties at **Café Barcelona,** 520 Southwest Blvd., 816/471-4944, $$. **Garozzo's Ristorante,** 526 Harrison, 816/221-2455, $$, is authentically Italian with a cozy, intimate atmosphere.

And **Winstead's,** 1200 Main St., 816/221-3339; 101 Brush Creek, 816/753-2244, $, is a classic 1950s-style soda fountain serving famous steakburgers at two locations in town. They don't accept credit cards.

SHOPPING

Possibly the best area for shopping is **Country Club Plaza,** W. 47th and Broadway Sts., 65 acres of Spanish-style buildings set among more than 40 fountains and 50 sculpted works of art. With more than 180 retail and service establishments, the area is often compared to New

⎯ Kansas City 101 ⎯

Like St. Louis, Kansas City has always been a gateway city. It's where the famous Oregon, California, and Santa Fe trails crossed, and so it was always a natural starting point for westward-hoing.

After traders and trappers developed the town on the southern bank of the Missouri in the early 1800s, thousands of pioneers later came and disembarked from riverboats here to begin their overland journey. The town made sure there were plenty of supplies available, and the city became a major market area. Today the City Market is the Midwest's largest open-air farmers market.

Kansas City has also been a cattle town from way back when. In the late 1800s, as barbed wire closed the Plains to the large cattle drives, the city became a shipping point for cattle, and its stockyards were a major reason for its growth.

From the 1920s to the 1950s, jazz was king in Kansas City, and so was baseball. The Kansas City Monarchs were the equivalent of the New York Yankees in the National Negro League, and this period was the Monarchs' heyday. That's why the Kansas City Jazz Museum and the Negro Leagues Baseball Museum share the same complex at the Museums at 18th and Vine.

York's Fifth Avenue and Rodeo Drive in Los Angeles. Stores such as Saks Fifth Avenue, Brooks Brothers, Ralph Lauren, Gucci, Mark Shale, and Laura Ashley—along with the locally founded Halls—have helped to establish the Plaza as a major fashion center in the Midwest. While at the Plaza, stop by **Trade Wind Gallery,** Country Club Plaza, 440 Ward Pkwy., 816/531-1976, which offers a wide variety of limited-edition prints, ceramics, bronzes, and wood carvings.

The **Crown Center Shops,** 2450 Grand, 816/274-8444, are located in a three-level complex adjoining the international headquarters of Hallmark Cards. Local stores such as Halls Kansas City, Finishings for Her, and Function Junction adjoin national retailers such as Casual Corner and The Limited. You'll also find restaurants and entertainment venues in the complex. The **American Indian Store,** Crown Center, Level One, 2450 Grand, 816/283-0303, has silver and turquoise, plus crafts, pottery, and baskets handmade by Native Americans. For the best of Kansas City, try **Best of Kansas City,** 6233 Brookside Plaza; Crown Center, 2450 Grand; 800/366-8780, which has gift baskets made with local products, plus lots of souvenirs. And they'll ship it home for you. The store has two locations.

The **City Market,** 20 E. Fifth St., 816/842-1271, is the largest open-air farmer's market in the Midwest. It has 37 specialty shops, plus restaurants, nightclubs, and art galleries.

Many interesting shops and galleries are among the city's oldest buildings in Westport. While you're there, stop by **Pioneer Park,** Broadway St. and Westport Rd., 816/756-2789, which traces Westport's role in founding Kansas City and opening the West. You'll find art and fine collectibles by leading African American artists at **Ethnic Art,** 1601 E. 18th St., 816/472-VINE.

SPORTS AND RECREATION

The Truman Sports Complex, I-70 and Blue Ridge Cutoff, about 10 minutes from downtown, is the home of the **Kansas City Chiefs,** 800/676-5488, and the **Kansas City Royals,** 800/6ROYALS, the only twin football-baseball stadiums in the country. Kaufman Stadium, home of the Royals, seats 40,000, and Arrowhead Stadium, home of the Chiefs, seats 79,000.

The **Kansas City Blades,** 816/842-5233, an IHL hockey team, play at Kemper Arena. The **Kansas City Attack,** 816/474-2255, play indoor soccer at the Kemper, too. The **World Team Tennis Explorers,** 913/362-9944, play at the Hale Arena in the American Royal Complex, which is part of the Kemper.

The **Big 12** men's and women's basketball tournaments, usually played in March, are traditions in Kansas City. The women play at Municipal Auditorium downtown, and just a short distance away, the men play at Kemper Arena, 1800 Genessee.

To get a free *Golf Guide* on courses in the area, call the Convention and Visitors Bureau, 800/767-7700. Kansas City has four municipal golf courses, and many parks, including **Swope Park,** 816/871-5600, which, at more than 1,700 acres, is the second biggest urban park in the country.

ENTERTAINMENT

All that jazz is why you're here, and there are lots of ways to hear it besides the Jazz Museum. Jazz and blues pub crawls, in which shuttle buses take patrons from club to club for samplings of local music, are sponsored by local clubs such as the **KC Blues Society,** 913/432-KCBS, and the **KC Jazz Ambassadors,** 816/478-8378.

If you want the real deal in Kansas City jazz, go to the **Mutual Musicians Foundation,** 1823 Highland, 816/471-5212, in the 18th and Vine district. Every Friday and Saturday, local musicians get together and jam all night—just like they did back in the 1920s, when the concept of a jam session was born.

Harling's Upstairs, Main and 39th Sts., 816/531-0303, is the place to find the real blues. Diane "Mama" Ray performs here with her blues band from 1 to 6 p.m. every Saturday. Harling's is on the second floor up some steep wooden stairs in an art-deco building.

The Truman Shows

Independence, Missouri, only 15 minutes east of downtown Kansas City, is best known as the home of Harry S. Truman, the United States' 33rd president. The Truman Library and Museum, at U.S. 24 and Delaware, 800/833-1225, has a re-creation of the Oval Office, right down to Truman's famous "The Buck Stops Here" plaque. His home is a Victorian mansion built in 1885. Tickets are issued on a first-come basis beginning at 9 a.m.; 816/254-2720.

Adolfo's Discotheque, 1111 Grand, 816/221-7650, is located downtown in a historic building, featuring disco music from the 1970s and 1980s. Country music is the thing at the **Beaumont Club,** 4050 Pennsylvania, 816/561-2560, which features a large dance floor, pool tables, and a mechanical bull.

The **Folly Theatre,** 300 S. 12th St., 816/842-5500, first opened in 1900, then became a burlesque emporium in the early 1920s, and today, after renovation, features live theater and a world-class jazz series. One of the grandest theaters around is the **Midland Theater,** 1228 Main St., 816/471-8600, a 1920s movie palace. Nowadays it offers live theater performances. The **State Ballet of Missouri,** 816/931-2232, also performs here.

The **Lyric Opera of Kansas City,** 816/471-4933, is the oldest performing arts organization in town. It and the **Kansas City Symphony,** 816/471-0400, perform at the Lyric Theatre, 11th St. and Central.

For live, off-Broadway theater of a cutting-edge nature, check out the productions of the **Unicorn Theatre,** 3828 Main St., 816/531-PLAY. For Broadway-style performances from musicals to mysteries, try the **American Heartland Theatre** in the Crown Center, Level Three, 2450 Grand, 816/842-9999.

CITY BASICS

For information on the Kansas City area, call the **Convention and Visitors Bureau,** 800/767-7700, www.kansascity.com. The Kansas City, Kansas, side of town is represented by the **Wyandotte County Convention and Visitors Bureau,** 800/264-1563, www.kckcvb.org. For information on recreation spots, call the **Missouri Department of Natural Resources Information Service,** 800/334-6946.

The *Kansas City Star* is the main newspaper in town. You can get alternative and entertainment news from the *Pitch Weekly*. For more in-depth coverage of the city scene, turn to *Kansas City* magazine.

to go ▶

*St. Paul is a wonderful city. It is put together in solid blocks
of honest bricks and stone and has the air of intending to stay.*
—Mark Twain

So what do people do here for entertainment, ice fish?

Actually, yes, they do. And if that sounds like a good reason for you to
visit the Twin Cities, then pack your gear and BYOB—bring your own bait.
But really, there's so much more. You can sit around the fire and listen to
Garrison Keillor on the radio or watch Mary Tyler Moore reruns on television. And gosh darn it, can you pass the lutefisk?

Wait a minute. We've got these cities all wrong. This is a mighty big
place, with 2.68 million people in the metropolitan area. Not all of them
have gone fishing, have they?

They could, we suppose. Minnesota has 90,000 miles of shoreline,
which is more than California, Florida, and Hawaii combined. There are
22 lakes and 170 parks in Minneapolis alone, plus lots of bike and nature
trails. This is a nature-centered metropolis in a natural wonder of a state.

Not everybody has a Lake Wobegon accent, either. Immigrants from
around the world have settled here, and lots of Native Americans never
left. African Americans make up 13 percent of the population; Asians make
up 5 percent.

The cities have 35 museums, almost that many theaters, 275 restaurants, shops and galleries of all kinds, and—to top it all off—the country's
largest enclosed shopping and entertainment complex, featuring more than
500 stores, restaurants, and attractions. They call it the Mall of America.

Minneapolis–St. Paul

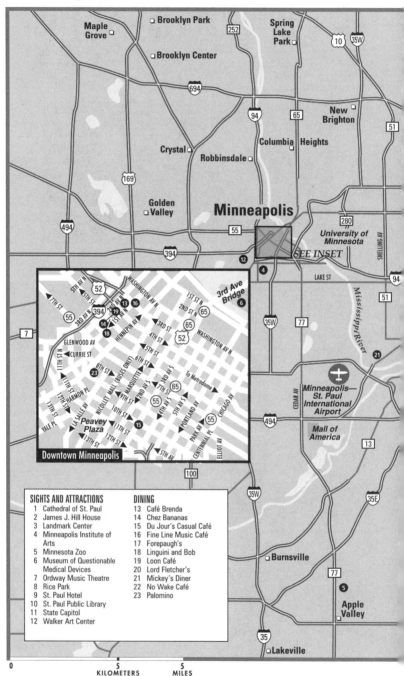

Maple Grove □
□ Brooklyn Park
[252]
Spring Lake Park □
[10] [35W]
□ Brooklyn Center
[694]
[94] [65]
New Brighton □
[51]
Crystal □
Columbia Heights □
Robbinsdale □
[169]
Golden Valley □
Minneapolis
[494]
[55]
University of Minnesota
[280]
SNELLING AV
[394]
12
4
SEE INSET
LAKE ST
[94]
[51]

Downtown Minneapolis

5TH AV N
7TH ST
[52]
5TH ST
WASHINGTON AV N
1ST ST N
3rd Ave Bridge
6
[55]
3RD AV N
[394]
2ND AV N
1ST AV N
19
13 16
2ND ST N
[65]
14
3RD ST
[65]
18
HENNEPIN AV
4TH ST
WASHINGTON AV N
GLENWOOD AV
5TH ST
[52]
N 11TH ST
CURRIE ST
6TH ST
8TH ST
3RD AV S
To Metrodome
23
7TH ST
[65]
11TH ST
HARMON PL
9TH ST
2ND AV S
[55]
5TH AV S
4TH AV S
13TH ST
NICOLLET MALL (BUSES ONLY)
MARQUETTE
10TH ST
PORTLAND AV
PARK AV
[55]
CHICAGO AV
YALE PL
LA SALLE AV
11TH ST
15
12TH ST
CENTENNIAL PL
ELLIOT AV
Peavey Plaza
13TH ST
5TH AV

Mississippi River
[35W]
[77]
21
Minneapolis– St. Paul International Airport
CEDAR AV
[494]
Mall of America
[13]

[100]

SIGHTS AND ATTRACTIONS
1 Cathedral of St. Paul
2 James J. Hill House
3 Landmark Center
4 Minneapolis Institute of Arts
5 Minnesota Zoo
6 Museum of Questionable Medical Devices
7 Ordway Music Theatre
8 Rice Park
9 St. Paul Hotel
10 St. Paul Public Library
11 State Capitol
12 Walker Art Center

DINING
13 Café Brenda
14 Chez Bananas
15 Du Jour's Casual Café
16 Fine Line Music Café
17 Forepaugh's
18 Linguini and Bob
19 Loon Café
20 Lord Fletcher's
21 Mickey's Diner
22 No Wake Café
23 Palomino

□ Burnsville
[77]
[35W]
[35E]
5
Apple Valley □
[35]
□ Lakeville

0   5   5
KILOMETERS   MILES

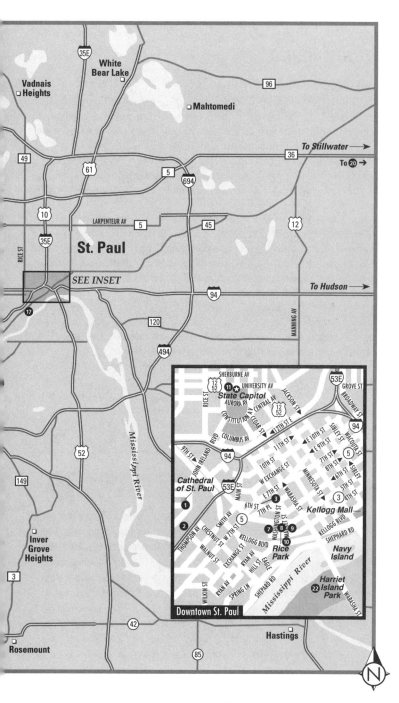

So go ahead and bring your bait. But don't forget your dancing shoes, too. This place is hopping.

GETTING AROUND

The **Minneapolis–St. Paul International Airport,** 612/726-5555, is about 20 minutes away from both cities. The Ground Transportation Center is one floor below the airport's baggage claim area. Adjacent to the baggage area is information about hotels that provide shuttle service. Information on limousine and bus service is available at Travelers' Assistance or the Ground Transportation Center in the main terminal building, where you'll also find the car rental desk. For the true shopaholic, you can go directly from the airport to the Mall of America by shuttle.

Should you get a car? Yes, except in winter. If you aren't a veteran of winter driving, you're likely to get in trouble. For one thing, you'll park where you shouldn't and the plows will bury you in snow. For another, there's this stuff called black ice. That's when the exhaust of cars freezes and hides itself on the roadways. You're likely to find it in a most unfortunate way.

If you're driving, remember that Interstate 35 is the main north-south dividing line between both cities. Interstate 35E branches through St. Paul, and Interstate 35W runs through Minneapolis. The east-west thoroughfare dividing both cities is Interstate 94.

Although the Twin Cities don't have a subway system, the **Metro Transit,** 612/373-3333, has 900 buses that can get you from here to there relatively inexpensively. Fares range from 25¢ for downtown travel in non-rush hours to $2 for express travel in rush hours. For wheel-

Going Places

The **Minneapolis RiverCity Trolley**, 612/204-0000, offers daily 65-minute tours of downtown Minneapolis, highlighting the history of this old milling town. You can get on or off at any time. The trolley runs April through October. Also, you can tour the entire Twin Cities in a motorcoach with **MetroConnections**, 612/333-TOUR or 800/747-8687. And then again, maybe the best view is from the water. Take one of five large riverboats operated by **Padelford Riverboats**, 651/227-1100, on the Mississippi, with landings in both Minneapolis and St. Paul. To get around to the high points of St. Paul, take one of the **Capital City Trolleys**, 651/223-5600—four historic-looking, rubber-tired vehicles that operate Monday through Friday. The ride only costs 50 cents.

Minneapolis's modern skyline

chair and special needs transportation, call **Metro Mobility,** 651/602-1111 or 651/221-9886 (TDD).

Taxis aren't always easy to get. Your only guarantee is to use one of the few designated taxi stands at locations downtown, at MSP International Airport, and at the Mall of America. Otherwise you'll need to call for one. Try **ABC Taxi,** 612/788-1111.

SIGHTS AND ATTRACTIONS

The best thing about the Twin Cities is that they're not identical. You'll find Minneapolis more brash and forward-looking—the entrepreneurial son; St. Paul is a bit more serious and mature, with glasses and a hint of tweed—the history professor. There's much to like about both siblings.

The **Walker Art Center,** 725 Vineland Pl., Minneapolis, 612/375-7622, is a world-class contemporary art center. It features film and video screenings, dance performances, concerts, lectures, and music and theater events. Outside its front door is the mammoth Minneapolis Sculpture Garden. The **Minneapolis Institute of Arts,** 2400 Third Ave., 612/870-3131, boasts an 85,000-piece collection spanning 4,000 years. Specialties include decorative art, textiles, and the art of ancient times.

You don't want to miss the **Museum of Questionable Medical Devices,** 219 SE Main St., Minneapolis, 612/379-4046. It features 250 unbelievable medical "cures," such as a huge neck ring for magnetizing the blood. Get the bumps on your head read for two dollars.

Rice Park, Market and Fourth Sts., St. Paul, is a central location for some of St. Paul's most important attractions. The square block is surrounded by four of the city's most spectacular structures: the **Ordway Music Theatre,** 345 Washington St., St. Paul, 651/224-4222, www.ordway.org, which has been praised for both its programs and its beauty; the **Landmark Center,** 75 W. Fifth St., St. Paul, 651/292-3225, a castlelike structure dating back to 1902 that is now used as headquarters for several arts organizations; the **St. Paul Public Library,** 90 W. Fourth St., St. Paul, 651/292-6311; and the **St. Paul Hotel,** 350 Market St., St. Paul, 800/292-9292, www.stpaulhotel.com.

America's longest span of intact, residential Victorian architecture is on Summit Avenue in St. Paul. Wrought-iron gates, stained-glass windows, white marble, and graceful pillars beckon along the avenue as it stretches 4.5 miles to the Mississippi River. The largest mansion in the Midwest is the home of **James J. Hill,** 240 Summit Ave., St. Paul, 651/297-2555, founder of the Great Northern Railroad. It contains a three-story pipe organ, 22 fireplaces, 13 bathrooms, a ballroom, cut-glass chandeliers, and a two-story art gallery. Nearby is the **Cathedral of St. Paul,** 239 Selby Ave. at Summit Ave., St. Paul, 651/228-1766, modeled after St. Peter's in Rome. Also not far away is the **State Capitol,** 75 Constitution Ave., St. Paul, 651/296-2881, crowned by the largest unsupported marble dome in the world.

The **Minnesota Zoo,** 13000 Zoo Blvd., 612/432-9000, covers 485 acres in the southern suburb of Apple Valley and lays claim to being the second largest zoo in America. It is home to more than 450 species of animals.

LODGING

The place to stay is the **Nicollet Island Inn,** 95 Merriam St., Minneapolis, 612/331-1800, $$, a 24-room inn on an island in the Mississippi that gives the feeling of being in a rural B&B yet is within the heart of Minneapolis. It's housed in a nineteenth-century limestone building that was originally the Island Door and Sash Company. It offers beautiful views of the river from its restaurant, which serves a dynamite brunch.

The **Hyatt Whitney Hotel,** 150 Portland Ave., Minneapolis, 612/339-9300, $$, is housed in the old Standard Mill, which was built in 1879. This European-style hotel has one of the best locations in town—not only is it near many downtown Minneapolis attractions, but its outdoor plaza overlooks the historic Mississippi riverfront.

If you want to be part of the skyway chain and stay out of the cold, check into the **Marquette Hotel,** 710 Marquette Ave., Minneapolis, 612/333-4545, $$$$. It's within walking distance of the Metrodome and the Target Center. The **Regal Minneapolis Hotel,** 1313 Nicollet Mall, Minneapolis, 800/222-8888, $$$, is similarly located. It has a pool, a sauna, and exercise facilities.

For the budget-minded, there's the gay-friendly **Hotel Amsterdam,** 628 Hennepin Ave., Minneapolis, 612/288-0459, $, a 24-room establishment built above a popular gay bar. The location, near theaters and restaurants, is ideal. Many of the rooms have shared baths.

A B&B that is right in the middle of everything—near the Guthrie

The **St. Paul Winter Carnival** draws about 1.5 million people annually. The carnival includes parades, concerts, and competitions in ice carving, snow sculpting, and skating. It's held in January and/or February. Spring is the time for the **Festival of Nations**, the largest multiethnic event in Minnesota. You'll find ethnic food, live music, folk dancing, and arts and crafts. It's in April in St. Paul.

If you've always wanted to try walleye on a stick, go to **A Taste of Minnesota**. It's held over the Independence Day weekend at the state capitol grounds in St. Paul. In the fall, usually in September, St. Paul hosts the **Minnesota State Fair**. The fair offers more than 700 performances, 300 food vendors, exhibits, cows, art, carnival rides, and more. For more information on these events and others, contact the St. Paul Convention and Visitors Bureau, 800/627-6101.

events
HORIZON

Theater, the Walker Art Center, and the Chain of Lakes in Minneapolis—is **Evelo's Bed and Breakfast,** 2301 Bryant Ave. S., Minneapolis, 612/374-9656, $$. It's in an 1897 Victorian house. Similarly located in downtown Minneapolis is **1900 Dupont,** 1900 Dupont Ave. S., Minneapolis, 612/374-1973, $$, a three-story Colonial B&B featuring a library on the second floor, and antiques throughout.

The **Inn on the Farm,** 6150 Summit Dr. N., Brooklyn Center, 612/569-6330, $$, part of the Earl Brown Heritage Center, is located just north of Minneapolis. This B&B consists of four separate homes, each decorated differently and all furnished with private baths that have whirlpool tubs. You'll feel like you're in the country, but you're only minutes from the city.

Theater lovers should think about staying at the **St. Paul Hotel,** 350 Market St., 800/292-9292, www.stpaulhotel.com, $$$, which is just across the street from the Ordway Theatre and historic Rice Park. It was built in 1910 by the same architects—Reed and Stern—who designed New York's Grand Central Station. The hotel is a member of the Historic Hotels of America group.

A prime B&B in St. Paul is the **Como Villa Bed and Breakfast,** 1371 W. Nebraska Ave., St. Paul, 651/647-0471, $$. It features three rooms, each with a private bath, in an 1870s Victorian home that has stayed true to its past. Yet another B&B to consider is the **Covington Inn,** Pier One, H100 Yacht Club Rd., St. Paul, 651/292-1411, $$, located at the front end of the No Wake Café restaurant-boat on Harriet Island. The inn has four rooms with private baths and fireplaces, and the decor is pure Old Navy.

DINING

A great area for grazing is the Minneapolis neighborhood of Nicollet, which is just south of downtown on Nicollet Avenue. A 1.2-mile stretch of road is home to more than 50 food outlets—Latino, Asian, Middle Eastern, German, Greek, and others.

Café Brenda, 300 First Ave. N., Minneapolis, 612/342-9230, $$, is a quaint little place in the Minneapolis warehouse district that features natural food and gourmet vegetarian dishes, along with seafood. Huge bay windows make for great people-watching.

Let's have a sticky bun at **Du Jour's Casual Café,** 89 S. 10th St., Minneapolis, 612/333-1855, $. It's a toasted English muffin topped with brown sugar, cinnamon, and nut sauce; cream cheese; and spiced sliced apples. Du Jour's is open for breakfast and lunch only. Also downtown, the **Loon Café,** 500 First Ave. N., Minneapolis, 612/332-8342, $, specializes in Minnesota wild rice soup, high-stacked sandwiches, and five different sorts of chili set at three different temperatures—mild, medium, and hot.

If you're in the mood for music, the **Fine Line Music Café,** 318 First Ave. N., Minneapolis, 612/338-8100, $$, is where you belong. The music ranges from folk to pop to rock, and on Sunday the brunch is accompanied by live gospel music. At **Chez Bananas,** 129 N. Fourth St., Minneapolis, 612/340-0032, $$, which features Caribbean cuisine, you get toys on your table such as Mr. Potato Head, Etch-a-Sketch, and a magic eight ball. The restaurant is in the warehouse district in downtown Minneapolis.

Linguini and Bob, 100 N. Sixth St., Butler Square Building, Minneapolis, 612/332-1600, $$, is a hip and energetic restaurant-bar that offers classic Italian cuisine in an atmosphere of high ceilings and exposed brick walls. Try the pizza with caramelized onions and hot peppers or the linguini in parchment. **Palomino,** 825 Hennepin Ave., skyway level, Minneapolis, 612/339-3800, $$$, is a Euro-bistro in the heart of downtown Minneapolis that specializes in wood-fired Roma-style pizza, spit-roasted garlic chicken, and Mediterranean pastas.

Or do like the natives do and go out to **Lord Fletcher's,** 3746 Sunset Dr., 612/471-8513, $$, on Lake Minnetonka in the Spring Parkin suburb west of Minneapolis. Patrons dock their boats nearby and come in for a bite to eat. They also sit out on the deck overlooking the lake and watch the trained walking ducks do their thing. In the restaurant, try the walleye and wild rice.

Dining at its finest in St. Paul is at **Forepaugh's,** 276 S. Exchange St., St. Paul, 651/224-5606, $$$, a French restaurant in a restored Victorian house in Irvine Park with a better reputation for its surroundings and service than for its food. You can dine in one of nine nineteenth-century dining rooms, each named for a past governor.

The **No Wake Café,** Pier One, H100 Yacht Club Rd., St. Paul, 651/292-1411, $$, on the Mississippi across from downtown St. Paul, is the area's only floating restaurant. Fresh fish is the specialty. The view of the river and downtown are great. And you can't neglect **Mickey's Diner,** 36 W. Seventh St., St. Paul, 651/222-5633, $$, an architectural classic example of streamline modern design of the 1930s. The jukebox makes a perfect complement to your eggs and hash browns.

SHOPPING

There's no sales tax on clothing here. That may be reason enough to visit.

Downtown Minneapolis claims to have more retail outlets in a four-block area than any other city in the country. There are more than 400 stores and 3 million square feet of retail space, and in the center of that is **Nicollet Mall,** a 12-block thoroughfare with traffic limited to service vehicles and pedestrians. It's just south of downtown along Nicollet Avenue. **Farmers markets** are held from May through September at Nicollet Mall. Flowers, fruits and vegetables, crafts, and clothing are offered each Thursday and Saturday. At **China in the Nude,** Calhoun Sq., 3001 Hennepin Ave. S., Minneapolis, 612/827-2575, you pick out a dish from the selection of ceramic housewares, then draw and paint your own design on it. If you're not that hot at drawing, you can get help with a pre-drawn design.

Grand Avenue in St. Paul is a Victorian-style strolling street that is lined with turn-of-the-last-century residences and storefronts. Bookstores, specialty shops, coffee shops, and ethnic restaurants abound.

For a different shopping experience, try the **50th and France Shops,** 50th St. and France Ave., in the southern suburb of Edina. You'll find home decor stores, boutiques, and bread and coffee shops.

SPORTS AND RECREATION

The climate-controlled Hubert H. Humphrey Metrodome, Chicago Ave. and Fifth St., Minneapolis, 612/332-0386, is the only facility in the country to host a Super Bowl, a World Series, and a NCAA Final Four basketball championship. It's the home to **Minnesota Twins** Major League Baseball team, 612/375-1366; the **Minnesota Vikings** National Football League team, 612/333-8828; and the **University of Minnesota Gophers** football team, 612/332-0386. Try to buy a beer from **Wally the Beer Man,** a legend at Minneapolis sporting events. He even has his own trading card.

The Target Center, 600 First Ave., Minneapolis, 612/337-3865, is home to **Minnesota Timberwolves** National Basketball Association team, 612/673-1600, and has hosted such events as the Davis Cup tennis semifinals, the NBA All-Star Game, and the 1998 World Figure Skating Championships.

Mother of All Malls

The biggest attraction in the Twin Cities is the **Mall of America**, at the intersection of I-494 and 24th Ave. S. in the suburb of Bloomington, 612/883-8800. And when we say big, we mean big. The mall contains more than 4.2 million square feet and includes 400 stores, 25 sit-down restaurants, 27 fast-food restaurants, 9 nightclubs, and 14 theater screens—oh yeah, and a roller coaster and a 1.2-million-gallon aquarium. Anchor stores are Macy's, Nordstrom, Bloomingdale's, and Sears.

Wear comfortable shoes and take plenty of money. The statistics indicate that on average people spend about $100, stay 3 hours and 20 minutes, and complain about their feet hurting about once every 30 minutes.

You can get express bus service from downtown St. Paul and Minneapolis every 30 minutes. If you drive, you'll have 12,700 parking places awaiting you, most of which will be full. Don't worry about remembering where you parked, though—each of the lots is named for a state. Surely you can remember that you parked in South Dakota and not North Dakota, can't you?

The **St. Paul Saints,** 651/644-6659, play minor league baseball at the Midway Stadium, 1771 Energy Park Dr., St. Paul. One of the team's owners is comedian Bill Murray, who may have a hand in some of the team's off-beat events, such as Mary Tyler Moore Night, in which fans have the chance to go out onto the field and toss up their berets. The **Minnesota Wild,** 651/333-PUCK, are a recent addition to the National Hockey League. They play at the St. Paul RiverCentre, 175 W. Kellogg Blvd., St. Paul.

If you'd like to get in on the athletic activity, too, consider winding through Minneapolis on 53 miles of designed walking and biking paths. The eight-foot-wide **Grand Rounds Bike Trail,** 612/661-4800, connects the Chain of Lakes, Lake Hiawatha, and the Mississippi River.

No, on second thought, let's take a canoe. There are 57 miles of scenic waters to navigate on the Mississippi between Anoka and Hastings. Rent a canoe from **Ketter Canoeing,** 612/560-3840, or **Midwest Mountaineering,** 612/339-3433. For general information, call the **Minnesota Department of Natural Resources,** 651/296-6157. Why not try wind surfing? It's quite popular at Lake Calhoun in Minneapolis. For information, contact **Minneapolis Park and Recreation** special services, 612/661-4800.

Minneapolis says that it has more golfers per capita than any other city in the country. For details about tournaments and events, contact the **Minnesota Golf Association,** 612/927-4643.

The Twin Cities area is also the home of Rollerblade and the invention of in-line skating. Popular spots for cruising the trails are the lakes near the Uptown neighborhood of Minneapolis, especially Lake Calhoun. Skate rentals are available at many of the sport shops along nearby Lake Street. Or how about rock climbing? The real deal is along the north shore of Lake Superior and at Taylors Falls. An indoor version is at **Vertical Endeavors,** 519 Payne Ave., St. Paul, 651/776-1430.

Another area for outdoor recreation is **Fort Snelling State Park,** Post Rd., St. Paul, 612/725-2390, which is situated between St. Paul and Minneapolis and contains 18 miles of hiking trails and 5 miles of biking trails, along with canoe and paddle-boat rentals and a beach on Snelling Lake. The park is located at the junction of the Mississippi and Minnesota Rivers next to Fort Snelling, which was established in 1820. To get there, take Minnesota Highway 5 to Post Road.

When winter rolls around, the Twin Cities have hundred of miles of cross-country ski trails within Minneapolis and St. Paul. **Theodore Wirth Park,** Wirth Pkwy., Minneapolis, offers 8.5 miles of hilly trails. Or what about slopes? There are lots of possibilities. Try **Wild Mountain Ski Area,** 37350 Wild Mountain Rd., Taylors Falls, 651/462-7550, which has a 300-foot vertical drop, 21 runs, night skiing, 4 chairlifts, and 1 rope tow.

ENTERTAINMENT

The Twin Cities brag that they have more theater seats per capita than any other U.S. metropolitan area outside New York. Lots of Broadway productions get their tryouts here, at venues such as the historic **State Theatre,** 805 Hennepin Ave., Minneapolis, 612/339-7007, and **Orpheum Theatre,** 910 Hennepin Ave., Minneapolis, 612/339-7007. And more than 30 smaller theaters scattered across the two cities present farcical ballets, cabarets, comedies, and other unique performances.

The jewel of regional theaters in Minneapolis is the **Guthrie Theater,** 725 Vineland Pl., Minneapolis, 612/377-2224, which consistently presents critically acclaimed contemporary shows. It is a theater-in-the-round, which means there's not a bad seat in the house.

The **Uptown Theater,** 2906 Hennepin Ave., Minneapolis, 612/825-8620, shows artistic and alternative films, but you've gotta be hip if you expect to like it. Usually a lot of hoopla surrounds the opening of a new film. Watch out for long lines on opening night—get a ticket early, then take in some sights and food in the Uptown Minneapolis neighborhood while you wait for the show to begin.

St. Paul's **Ordway Music Theatre,** 345 Washington St., St. Paul, 651/224-4222 (tickets), 651/282-3000 (information), is one of the main reasons not to miss the eastern half of the Twin Cities. Liveried footmen greet theater-goers at the lobby entrance, and inside is a sweeping spiral staircase to the Grand Foyer and upper Promenade, both with spectacular views of the city. The Ordway is home to the Minnesota

Opera Company and the world-renowned St. Paul Chamber Orchestra. Broadway shows are often performed in the Main Hall, and there is also a smaller studio theater.

The **Fitzgerald Theater,** 10 E. Exchange St., St. Paul, 651/290-1221, is home to Garrison Keillor's *Prairie Home Companion,* as well as chamber music, films, live radio shows, and other cultural programs.

Want to go to the downtown Minneapolis nightclub where the Artist (formerly known as Prince) filmed *Purple Rain*? That would be **First Avenue,** 701 First Ave., Minneapolis, 612/332-1775, where you'll see concerts from local and national groups. The dance floor is big, and so are the television screens.

In Uptown Minneapolis, **Bryant Lake Bowl Theater,** 810 W. Lake St., Minneapolis, 612/825-3737, does what its name promises—it gives you a place to bowl, plus offers music and theater and independent film showings. It also has a restaurant. **Champs,** Butler Sq., 100 N. Sixth St., Minneapolis, 612/335-5050, is a sports bar that offers a dozen big- and small-screen televisions, huge portions of food, and a wide variety of beers. It also has an outdoor beer garden with live entertainment.

With more casinos than Atlantic City, the state of Minnesota is the largest Native American gaming market in the United States. There are 17 casinos in the state, including **Mystic Lake Casino,** 2400 Mystic Lake Blvd., 800/262-7799 in the Minneapolis suburb of Prior Lake.

CITY BASICS

The **Greater Minneapolis Convention and Visitors Association,** 612/348-7000, www.minneapolis.org has info on Minneapolis. St. Paul's official tourist information outlet is the **St. Paul Convention and Visitors Bureau,** 800/627-6101, www.stpaulcvb.org. Visitor Information Centers are scattered throughout the area. The one inside the airport is in the baggage claim area near carousel number three.

There are two **area codes** covering the Twin Cities: 612 serves Minneapolis and the west metropolitan area; 651 serves St. Paul and the east metropolitan area. To place a local call between area codes, dial all 10 numbers without the 1. You won't be charged a long-distance rate.

Publications include the *St. Paul Pioneer Press,* the *Star Tribune, City Pages, Lavender Magazine, Skyway News,* and *Minnesota Monthly.*

⑫ VANCOUVER
to go ▶

This seems to me the place to live.
—The Queen Mum, 1939

If we hadn't seen Vancouver, then we could say that Rio de Janeiro is the most beautiful city in the world. Now we'll have to call it a tie.

Nothing is more stunning than the embrace of mountain and ocean, the tumbling of evergreen woods down to everblue sea. Put a city right in the middle of that, make sure the city respects its natural beauty enough to give it room to breathe with giant parks and great gardens, and in that sophisticated big city of 1.8 million, turn a United Nations of cultures into a mix of well-mannered Canadians. There you have it. Vancouver.

This is a gateway city. The giant English garden known as Vancouver Island is just a ferryboat ride across the Strait of Georgia; the famed ski resort town of Whistler is a two-hour drive north; and Vancouver itself is where cruise ships depart on more than 250 trips a year to the icy cliffs of Alaska.

Stop at the gate. Give Vancouver some of your time. It will give some sweet memories back to you.

NOTE ABOUT PRICES

Many of the prices listed below are roughly translated from Canadian to U.S. values based upon the exchange rate at press time. Double check the rate before you visit.

Downtown Vancouver

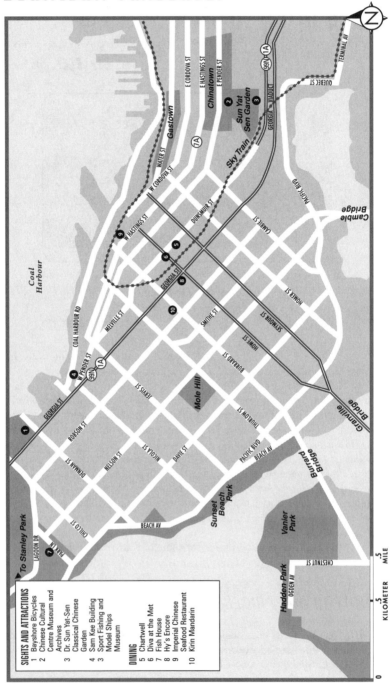

SIGHTS AND ATTRACTIONS
1 Bayshore Bicycles
2 Chinese Cultural Centre Museum and Archives
3 Dr. Sun Yat-Sen Classical Chinese Garden
4 Sam Kee Building
3 Sport Fishing and Model Ships Museum

DINING
5 Chartwell
6 Diva at the Met
7 Fish House
8 Hy's Encore
9 Imperial Chinese Seafood Restaurant
10 Kirin Mandarin

GETTING AROUND

Vancouver International Airport, 604/276-6101, is about 20 minutes from downtown. It'll cost you $10 to get from the airport to downtown by bus, about $30 by limo, and $20 to $25 by taxi. Contact the **Vancouver Regional Transit System,** 604/521-0400; **Airport Limousine Service,** 604/273-1331; and **Yellow Cab,** 604/681-1111, respectively for more information on these transportation options.

Although Vancouver is sufficiently concentrated to make a car unnecessary, we vote that you get one. The city is easy to drive in, and you'll have a hard time resisting the interesting places outside of town that necessitate a car to visit.

Situate yourself downtown—let's say around Robson or Georgia Street—and you'll be right in the middle of the best of Vancouver, especially shopping and nightlife. To your west is the magnificent **Stanley Park,** and to the east are the intriguing areas of **Gastown** and **Chinatown.** Those areas will be enough to keep you busy for several days.

Vancouver's downtown inner harbor is served by floatplanes and helicopters. Call **Seair Services,** 604/273-8900, and **Helijet Airways,** 604/273-4688, for details.

And if you want to take to the water, **BC Ferries,** 250/386-3431, provides service from two terminals. Tsawwassen is south of the city and is the terminal for ferries to Victoria and Nanaimo on Vancouver Island and to the Southern Gulf Islands. Horseshoe Bay, the terminal north of Vancouver, also has ferry service to Nanaimo on Vancouver Island, as well as to Bower Island and the Mainland's Sunshine Coast. Fares to Vancouver Island vary according to the season but are about $9 per person, or $41 for a car and a driver.

SIGHTS AND ATTRACTIONS

At 1,000 acres, **Stanley Park** is the largest city park in Canada. It began in the mid-1800s as a military reserve established to guard the entrance to Vancouver's harbor from aggressive Americans. Today it is an area of forests, gardens, and beaches based on the planning principles of Frederick Law Olmsted, the designer of New York City's Central Park. Stanley Park is north of downtown, overlooking Burrard Inlet and English Bay. Highway 99 (Georgia Street) runs through the middle of it.

A shuttle bus, 604/257-8400, will take you through the huge park in the summers. You'll walk yourself to death if you try to do the whole thing on foot, but do take a stroll down the five-mile seawall path if you can. You can also go by bike or in-line skates, both of which are available for rental at Bayshore Bicycles, 745 Denman St., 604/688-2453.

Within the park are woods, lakes, totem poles, and the **Vancouver Aquarium,** 604/682-1118, www.vanaqua.org, which features tanks big enough to give whales some room to roam.

Vancouver's motto is "Spectacular by Nature," and it certainly lives up to that with the many gardens that add to the natural beauty of its seaside and mountains. The 55-acre **VanDusen Botanical Garden,** 5251 Oak St. at 37th Ave., 604/878-9274, is always in season. It's open daily at 10 a.m. And you can find more natural beauty at the **University of British Columbia Botanical and Nitobe Memorial Gardens,** 6804 SW Marine Dr., 604/822-3928, www.hedgerows.com, which has more than 20,000 species, including the largest collection of rhododendrons in Canada. Also featured on its 70 acres is an authentic Japanese strolling garden.

Chinatown is home to the Western World's first authentic classical Chinese garden—the **Dr. Sun Yat-Sen Classical Chinese Garden,** 604/662-3207. And not to be forgotten is the **Bloedel Floral Conservatory,** 33rd at Cambie, 604/257-8584, in Queen Elizabeth Park, which boasts a huge garden under glass containing many plants, free-flying tropical birds, and koi fish.

Be sure to see the world's first steam-powered clock in Gastown at Water and Cumbie Streets. Its whistle blows every quarter hour, and every hour it exhales a big cloud of steam. It's a gas. Also a must-see is the **Chinese Cultural Centre Museum and Archives,** 555 Columbia St., 604/687-0282. And try to squeeze in a visit to the **Sam Kee Building,** 8 W. Pender, said to be the narrowest building in the world. (It's six feet wide.)

Stop by the **Emily Carr Institute of Art and Design,** 139 Johnson St. on Granville Island, 604/844-3811, which has a contemporary

Going Places

Take a boat/train day trip, a sunset dinner cruise, or a harbor cruise with **Harbour Cruises,** 800/663-1500. **Gray Line,** 800/667-0882, is another major outlet for tours of the city, as well as for tours of Victoria, Whistler, Nanaimo, and the Canadian Rockies. Whale-watching is also offered.

Rocky Mountaineer Railtours, 800/665-7245, www.rkymtnrail .com, will take you on a two-day train trip through the Canadian Rockies in a bi-level dome car.

You can go sightseeing at your own pace with the **Vancouver Trolley Co.,** 888/451-5581, www.vancouvertrolley.com. There are 17 stops on the narrated trips, with pickups at major downtown hotels and on-off privileges.

Take a leisurely tour on the **Stanley Park Horse-Drawn Tours,** 604/681-5115, www.stanleyparktours.com, which feature one-hour narrated rides departing daily from the Information Booth on Park Drive, east of the Rowing Club. Reservations are not required.

Burrard Inlet

gallery inside. Nearby is the **Sport Fishing and Model Ships Museum,** 1502 Duranleau St., 604/683-1939, which includes fishing displays, works of art, and exquisitely detailed model ships, all of which tell the story of British Columbia's coastal way of life.

You've got to take a deep breath and walk across the **Capilano Suspension Bridge,** 3735 Capilano Rd., 604/985-7474. There are only planks between you and the rushing Capilano River 230 feet below. Approximately 800,000 people a year make the walk, so don't be a chicken. An interpretative center tells the 105-year-old story of the bridge.

Also worth viewing is the art of the Northwest Coast First Nations, featured at the **Museum of Anthropology,** 6393 NW Marine Dr., 604/822-3825, in an award-winning building overlooking mountains and sea on the campus of the University of British Columbia.

LODGING

The place to stay is either downtown or near Stanley Park. That will be easy—those areas are home to the best places to stay.

Dominating downtown is the grand **Hotel Vancouver,** 900 W. Georgia St., 800/441-1414, $$$$, which was opened in 1939 by the Canadian National Railway. Mahogany furniture and old-fashioned deep bathtubs contribute to the elegance of a bygone era.

The Metropolitan, 645 Howe St., 800/667-2300, $$$$, is a high-end hotel that has recently been renovated, and everything about the place speaks of quiet luxury—down duvets on the bed, bathrobes for guests, and valet service. As fine as any china is the **Wedgewood Hotel,** 845 Hornby St., 800/663-0666, $$$, which features beveled glass and antiques in the lobby, turndown service, and flowers all about. You'll be pampered.

Greater Vancouver

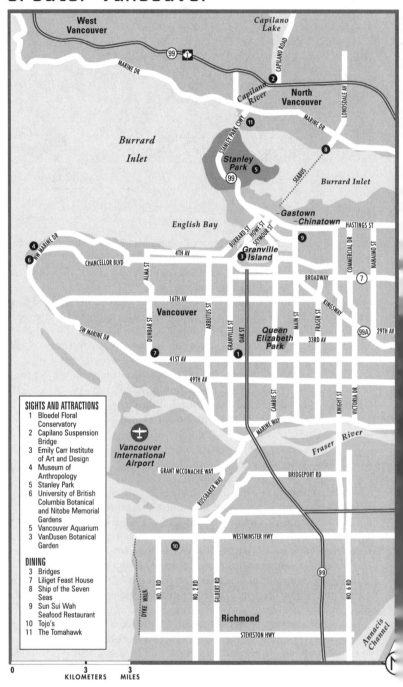

West Vancouver

Capilano Lake

MARINE DR

99

CAPILANO ROAD

Capilano River

North Vancouver

MARINE DR

LONSDALE AV

11

STANLEY PARK CSWY

8

Burrard Inlet

Stanley Park

5

99

SEABUS

Burrard Inlet

English Bay

—*Gastown*
—*Chinatown*

HASTINGS ST

BURRARD ST

HOWE ST

SEYMOUR ST

9

COMMERCIAL DR

NANAIMO ST

4

NW MARINE DR

6

CHANCELLOR BLVD

4TH AV

Granville Island

3

BROADWAY

7

ALMA ST

16TH AV

Vancouver

ARBUTUS ST

GRANVILLE ST

OAK ST

Queen Elizabeth Park

MAIN ST

FRASER ST

KINGSWAY

99A

29TH AV

SW MARINE DR

DUNBAR ST

7

41ST AV

1

33RD AV

49TH AV

CAMBIE ST

KNIGHT ST

VICTORIA DR

MARINE WAY

Fraser River

Vancouver International Airport

GRANT MCCONACHIE WAY

RUSSBAKER WAY

BRIDGEPORT RD

99

DYKE WALK

WESTMINSTER HWY

10

NO. 1 RD

NO. 2 RD

GILBERT RD

NO. 6 RD

Richmond

STEVESTON HWY

Annacis Channel

SIGHTS AND ATTRACTIONS
1 Bloedel Floral Conservatory
2 Capilano Suspension Bridge
3 Emily Carr Institute of Art and Design
4 Museum of Anthropology
5 Stanley Park
6 University of British Columbia Botanical and Nitobe Memorial Gardens
5 Vancouver Aquarium
3 VanDusen Botanical Garden

DINING
3 Bridges
7 Liliget Feast House
8 Ship of the Seven Seas
9 Sun Sui Wah Seafood Restaurant
10 Tojo's
11 The Tomahawk

0   3   3
   KILOMETERS   MILES

Tourism Vancouver is sponsoring a program called **Vancouver's Enter-tainment Season**, 800/663-6000, www.tourism-vancouver.org, in which hotel accommodations at up to 50 percent off summer rates are being offered from October to April. Packages include theater tickets and sightseeing and walking tours. There are two-for-one restaurant deals, lift tickets, and discount shopping coupons.

If you can possibly spare the time, try to get over to **Vancouver Island** and the charming, veddy British city of Victoria. You can get there in two and a half hours by ferry from Vancouver or Seattle. 250/386-3431. The city is full of quaint shops, restored nineteenth-century buildings, and lots of pubs. Be sure to see **Butchart Gardens,** 250/652-5256, which is 13 miles north of Victoria and includes 50 acres of ponds, walkways, and rose gardens, as well as 700 varieties of other flowers in a former limestone quarry. This is one of the great gardens of the world, and a million people a year come here. You can get a free 96-page travel guide for Vancouver Island by writing to Tourism Vancouver Island, 302-45 Bastion Sq., Victoria, B.C., Canada V8W1J1. You can also visit them on the Web at www.islands.bc.ca.

City Survival Tips

Sandman, 180 W. Georgia St., 800/SANDMAN, $$, is a small chain of moderately priced hotels in British Columbia and Alberta. The one at 180 W. Georgia Street is ideally located near Robson Street shopping, Chinatown, and Gastown. The **Oceanside Apartment Hotel,** 1847 Pendrell St., 604/682-5641, $$, is near the English Bay beach, but it is also within walking distance of downtown and only two blocks from Stanley Park.

Ideally located downtown is the **English Bay Inn,** 1968 Comox St., 604/683-8002, $$, a B&B in a five-bedroom 1930s house. Ask about the two-level suite that looks down on the garden from the sitting room. Breakfast is served in the Gothic dining suite. Also consider a stay at the **Thistledown House Bed and Breakfast,** 3910 Capilano Rd., 888/633-7173, $$, a 1920s arts and crafts home in North Vancouver.

And to experience a B&B with a past, reserve a room at **O Canada House,** 1114 Barclay St., 604/688-0555, $$. This is where the first version of Canada's national anthem, O Canada, was written in 1909. It's a restored 1897 Victorian full of antiques but with updated amenities such as VCRs. It's in a quiet residential neighborhood within walking distance of downtown. A lavish breakfast is included.

DINING

Vancouver is known as Lotusland because of the strong Chinese influence in the city. Nowhere is this more evident than in the food. The major influx of Asian immigrants to the area came from Hong Kong, where fresh ingredients and fine dining are emphasized. How fresh? Go into one of the Asian supermarkets and pick out a fish from one of the tanks. They'll deep-fry it for you while you shop.

At the top of the culinary heap is the **Imperial Chinese Seafood Restaurant,** 355 Burrard St., 604/688-8191, $$$. You'll want to try the lobster in black bean sauce with egg noodles and pan-fried scallops. The bird's-nest delicacies are another specialty. The restaurant overlooks Stanley Park.

The **Kirin Mandarin,** 1166 Alberni St., Suite 102, 604/682-8833, $$$, features lobsters and crabs in tanks. Pick the one you want, and you get to choose 1 of 11 different preparations for your selection. The restaurant is downtown near many of the major hotels. When a Chinese radio station in town asked its listeners to vote for their favorite restaurant, they picked the **Sun Sui Wah Seafood Restaurant,** 3888 Main St., 604/872-8822, $$. This is the place for dim sum. And you might just wander into a Chinese wedding.

One of Vancouver's old standbys is **The Tomahawk,** 1550 Philip Ave. near the Lions Gate Bridge, 604/988-2612, $, which has been in business since 1926 serving basics like burgers and big breakfasts (five slices of bacon, two eggs, hash browns, and toast). And what's at the top of the charts? **Chartwell,** in the Four Seasons Hotel, 791 W. Georgia St., 604/689-9333, $$$$. You'll feel like you just set foot in a British club, what with all the wood paneling and plush chairs. Do ask for the rack of lamb, old boy.

So you've just gotten out of the opera and you're famished. How about dessert at **Diva at the Met** (in the Metropolitan Hotel, 645 Howe St., 604/602-7788, $$$)? The Stilton cheesecake might be nice. But when you look at the menu, you'll wish you'd skipped the show and stayed here for dinner. The cuisine is contemporary and the decor is art deco.

One of the finest sushi chefs in the world is Hidekazu Tojo, who will whip up a wonderful dish for you based on the seasons. If it's spring, ask for the salad of scallops and pink cherry blossoms. **Tojo's,** 777 W. Broadway Ave., Suite 202, 604/872-8050, $$$, is in an office tower uptown. Or you can eat like the natives at **Liliget Feast House,** 1724 Davie St., 604/681-7044, $. The menu is based on First Nation cuisine, including such selections as pan-fried oolichans (candlefish), toasted seaweed, and wild blackberry pie.

The **Fish House,** 8901 Stanley Park Dr., 604/681-7275, $$, offers exceptional seafood, an oyster bar, and flaming prawns, along with microbrewed beers, in a garden setting in Stanley Park overlooking English Bay. You can't get any nearer the source of your dinner than at the **Ship of the Seven Seas,** at the foot of Lonsdale Ave. next to the Seabus, 604/987-3344, $$, a floating restaurant in North Vancouver. And more fish, great views, and outdoor dining are the thing at **Bridges,** 1696 Duranleau St., Granville Island, 604/687-4400, $$, on the waterfront.

Finally, if steak is what you want, they've been doing it the right way for 30 years at **Hy's Encore** downtown, 637 Hornby St., 604/683-7671, $$$.

SHOPPING

Vancouver's center of shopping is at the intersection of West Georgia and Granville Streets. On opposite corners are **Eaton's,** 701 Granville St., 604/685-7112, and **The Bay,** 674 Granville St., 604/681-6211. Both have been around for a long time, and both have just about everything on their shelves, from ironing boards to souvenirs.

The Bay is what they call the former Hudson's Bay Company, which was founded more than 300 years ago by King Charles II, making it the oldest commercial establishment in the world. What was created to supply furs to the British empire is today a chain of stores across Canada where you can get the latest from Calvin Klein, choose from a great assortment of Wedgwood and Royal Doulton china, or pick up something with a Canadian flavor, such as Inuit art, smoked salmon, or maple syrup.

On the same corner, but underground, are access points to the underground labyrinth of the **Pacific Centre** and **Vancouver Centre** malls. Not too far away, on Burrard and Hornby Streets, you will find some high-dollar boutiques such as Chanel and Versace. At Hastings and Granville Street, the **Sinclair Centre** is home to some 20 shops specializing in designer clothing and fashionable imports.

In Gastown you'll find specialty items such as Inuit art and crafts, including sweaters, moccasins, and Indian jewelry. Two such shops are the **Inuit Gallery of Vancouver,** 345 Water St., 604/688-7323, and **Images for a Canadian Heritage,** 9164 Water St., 604/685-7046.

There are many exotic little shops in Chinatown offering everything from ginseng to green tea, embroidered linens, silk robes, and Chinese tableware and cooking utensils. This is a place to wander.

Many artisans and craftspeople are concentrated on Granville Island. You'll find potters, weavers, textile artists, and jewelry makers all along the streets in the former warehouses. One place to try is **Crafts Association of B.C.,** 1386 Cartwright, 604/687-6511.

Finally, don't neglect the wonderful shops that you'll find at museums and tourist places. One store where you're sure to find something extraordinary is **The Clamshell,** which is at the Vancouver Aquarium in Stanley Park, 604/659-3413.

— Neighborhood Watch —

One of the main tourist areas, and the oldest part of Vancouver, is known as **Gastown**. It's just to the east of downtown. Gastown was named for John Deighton, a Yorkshire-born saloon owner known as Gassy Jack—not for the beans he ate, but for his talkative nature. In the late 1800s Gassy showed up with a barrel of whiskey on the south shore of Burrard Inlet and told the mill workers there that they could have all the whiskey they could drink if they'd help him build his saloon. Gassy's place was up and running in 24 hours. The area (mainly Water Street and nearby) built up thanks to lumber, railroads, and a gold rush, then went into decline before being declared a historic district and renovated. Today it's a charming (if a bit touristy) area full of cafés, boutiques, and souvenir shops. It's a great place for a walk.

Vancouver's **Chinatown** is the third largest in North America, behind San Francisco's and New York's, and is just three blocks south of Gastown. Head south on Cumbie Street to Pender and east to Carrall. Nearby are fascinating markets and buildings that look like Canton. Go into one of the many little restaurants and point to something that looks good. (The waiter may not speak English.)

So what's hot in Vancouver? The many trendy restaurants and neat boutiques along **Robson Street** are. Another happening street is **Denman**, which gets hot at **Georgia Street** and proceeds to English Bay. There are 20 espresso and juice bars on this strip. Also of note is **Davie Street**, the core of the gay and lesbian community.

Another interesting place for a stroll is **Granville Island**, a small island out in False Creek. You can get there from the south end of Hornby Street downtown, where **Aquabuses,** 604/689-5858, will take you across the water. The island has lots of shops and galleries, boat building shops, a public market, and a whole community of houseboats, all of which can easily be reached on foot.

SPORTS AND RECREATION

Many of Vancouver's spectator sports are played at the General Motors Place Stadium, 800 Griffiths Wy.—namely, the **Grizzlies** (National Basketball Association), the **Lions** (Canadian Football League), and the **Canucks** (National Hockey League). Call Ticketmaster, 604/280-4400, for tickets to their games. The **Canadians,** 604/872-5232, play baseball at Nat Bailey Stadium, 4601 Ontario St.

Or you can fish. **Bonnie Lee Fishing Charters,** 1676 Duranleau St., 604/290-7447, www.bonnielee.com, has the largest selection of guided salmon-fishing vessels in British Columbia. For saltwater fishing information, contact the **Federal Department of Fisheries and Oceans,** 604/666-2828.

Vancouver All-Terrain Adventures, 4191 Dominion St., 604/434-2278, offers white-water rafting trips, eagle-watching tours, off-road sightseeing trips to Whistler, and overnight getaways to secluded natural hot springs. You'll be picked up by the Extreme Limousine. **Lotus Land Tours,** 604/684-4922, will take you on a kayaking adventure at Indian Arm, Canada's most southern fjord. The trip includes a picnic on an uninhabited island. Or if you want to get a close-up look at the eagles in the area, **Outback Adventure Company,** 604/921-7250, will get you there. The best time for seeing eagles is in the winter.

If you love to windsurf, Squamish offers some of Canada's best conditions, with strong thermal winds that blow down the valley and keep things moving. Contact the **Squamish Windsurfing Society** for more information, 604/926-9463.

Golfing amid the natural beauty is big in Vancouver. **Last Minute Golf,** 604/878-1833, will match you up with one of the courses, and might get you a discount. There are almost 200 free tennis courts in town. For information, contact the **Vancouver Board of Parks and Recreation,** 604/257-8400.

ENTERTAINMENT

The greatest percentage of the population (35 percent) is between ages 25 and 45. Also, Vancouver boasts the largest wine consumption of any city in North America. This place knows how to boogie. This is the hometown of Bryan Adams, BTO, Sarah McLachlan, and Loverboy. Cool, dude. It's a town for the young, and the young at heart.

Shed your inhibitions at **Wreck Beach,** off SW Marine Dr. near Totem Pole Park, the unofficial nude beach of the area. It's in a secluded area at the foot of cliffs. Put your clothes back on and take an icy whirl at the **Robson Street Skating Rink,** 300 Robson St., 604/482-1800. It's a small covered area just down the steps from the Vancouver Art Gallery.

As for Vancouver's dance scene, it's as varied as its cultural makeup, and ranges from traditional Japanese and Chinese dance to classical ballet. There are 18 professional dance companies in the area, and many of them gather at the **Conference Center,** 800 Robson St., 604/606-6400. Call for information on upcoming performances. The Vancouver-based **Lorita Leung Dance Association,** 604/261-5918, promotes and preserves Chinese dance, both through its own performances and by sponsoring the North American Chinese Dance Competition.

The city is also a major center for taiko drumming music and is the home of **Uzume Taiko,** 604/683-8240, North America's first professional taiko drumming ensemble. The group's music is "new world," yet based on Japanese traditions. The band is made up of three drummers, a flutist, a cellist, and African and Latin percussionists. Call for performance information. Also a great resource for music information is the hot line of the **Coastal Jazz and Blues Society,** 604/872-5200.

Theater, too, is a vital part of the city scene. The **Queen Elizabeth Theatre,** 600 Hamilton St., 604/665-3050, hosts Broadway musicals, opera, dance, and pop and rock shows. And on the cutting edge is the **Out West Theatre Society,** 604/253-5122, which is dedicated to the celebration of gay perspectives.

Vancouver is home to more than 100 galleries and museums. The **Canadian Craft Museum,** 639 Hornby St., 604/687-8266, showcases excellence in craftsmanship and design from Canada and around the world, from clothing to utensils. It has an excellent museum shop.

The **Hamilton Street Grill,** 1009 Hamilton St., 604/331-1511, in trendy Yaletown brags of having the best martini in town. It's open for dinner only. Also consider checking out **Babalus,** in the Hotel Dakota, 654 Nelson St., 604/681-6341, a popular new bar that has big band sounds, a big dance floor, and a cigar lounge. Get there early on weekends or you'll wait in line to get in.

CITY BASICS

Because of Pacific Ocean currents, Vancouver's weather is the mildest in Canada. The average daytime temperature in the summer is 72 degrees Fahrenheit. In the winter, it's 35 degrees Fahrenheit. Spring comes early, with flowers hitting their stride usually in early March. Late summer and fall (August to October) are usually warm and sunny. Then come the winter rains. (Something has to give all those flowers a boost.) However, it's advisable to bring an umbrella at any time of the year.

Tourism Vancouver operates a visitors center at the Waterfront Centre, Plaza Level, 200 Burrard St. You can also call (604/683-2000) or visit their Web site for information, www.tourism-vancouver.org. Similarly, you can get fast, easy, and free information and **lodging reservations** by phone, 800/663-6000, for all of British Columbia.

For information on dance, theater, music, and exhibitions, call the **ARTS Hotline** or visit their Web site, 604/684-2787, www.culturenet .ca/vca. You can get a *Discover Vancouver on Transit* guidebook at tourist information outlets or by phone, 604/540-3450. **Weather information,** 604/664-9010, is also available by phone. The **Western Institute for Deaf and Hard of Hearing,** 604/736-7391 (voice) or 604/736-2527 (TDD), offers information for visitors.

The *Vancouver Sun* is the major newspaper in town. Its entertainment section comes out on Thursdays. You can also find entertainment news in two free weeklies, *The Georgia Straight* and *City Food.*

⑬ SEATTLE

to go ▶

Seattle is a liquid city. Everything it is famous for is wet. The coffee. The beer. The salmon. Puget Sound and the urban lakes. And of course, the rain.
—*Alaska Airlines* magazine, May 1997

This place is wired, man.

Too much coffee will do that to you. That, and the Internet. And grunge music.

But being wired is not a bad thing. It means you're connected, tuned in, current, with it; pierced and tattooed; awake and aware and riding the crest of a new wave that is overtaking the world. Seattle is the hub of the brave new wired world that we're all moving into.

This is Bill Gates's hometown. Jimi Hendrix was born here, too. Matt Groening sketches *The Simpsons* here. Frasier Crane sips his lattes right around the corner.

Of course, Seattle can be bleak. Dreary skies set in and seldom lift from November to March. And sometimes it seems like too many people have swarmed in here, clamoring to ride the Seattle wave. More than 3 million people reside in the giant metropolitan area that stretches from Tacoma to Everett, about 60 miles long. Good luck finding a parking place.

But the fog always lifts, eventually, and that's when you can see where you are. You are surrounded by majestic mountains, with snow-capped peaks almost circling the city. And water is everywhere; Puget Sound is on one side, Lake Washington on the other.

Seattle

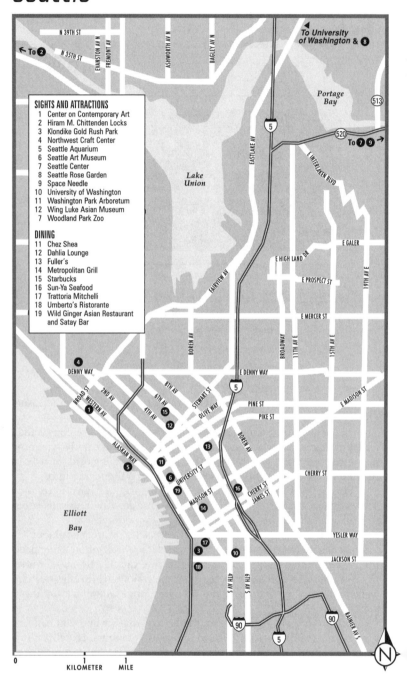

SIGHTS AND ATTRACTIONS
1 Center on Contemporary Art
2 Hiram M. Chittenden Locks
3 Klondike Gold Rush Park
4 Northwest Craft Center
5 Seattle Aquarium
6 Seattle Art Museum
7 Seattle Center
8 Seattle Rose Garden
9 Space Needle
10 University of Washington
11 Washington Park Arboretum
12 Wing Luke Asian Museum
7 Woodland Park Zoo

DINING
11 Chez Shea
12 Dahlia Lounge
13 Fuller's
14 Metropolitan Grill
15 Starbucks
16 Sun-Ya Seafood
17 Trattoria Mitchelli
18 Umberto's Ristorante
19 Wild Ginger Asian Restaurant
   and Satay Bar

To University of Washington & ⑧

Portage Bay

To ⑦ ⑨

Lake Union

Elliott Bay

0 KILOMETER MILE

All of that natural beauty tends to soften the jangled nerves around here. People leave their computers and espressos behind to ride their bikes into the wild world around them.

And that's Seattle—the best of both worlds, wired and wild. What are we waiting for?

GETTING AROUND

Seattle-Tacoma International Airport, 800/544-1965, known as Sea-Tac, is 13 miles south of Seattle off Interstate 5. Information on **ground transportation** is available by phone, 206/431-5906, and ground transportation booths are at each end of the baggage claim area.

Seattle is a cinch to navigate—the heart of it is all downtown, in walking distance or easily reached by bus, streetcar, or monorail. You can do without a car. Downtown is squeezed into a narrow strip of land between Lake Washington on the east and Elliott Bay on the west.

A good place to start your visit and get yourself oriented is 600 feet up on the observation deck of Seattle's **Space Needle,** a remnant of the 1962 World's Fair and Seattle's reigning symbol. If skies are clear, and that's a big if, you can see much of the city, the Cascade and Olympic mountains, and all that water. To get there, take the monorail from Westlake Center downtown at Fifth Avenue and Pine Street.

Most of the major hotels are within a few blocks of the **Pike Place Market,** which is a few blocks west of the Westlake Center. To get there from the Space Needle, pick up the trolley at the foot of Broad Street at Alaskan Way.

You can get back on the trolley to get to a third central area of interest—**Pioneer Square** and the **International District**. Buses can whisk you back to Westlake Center through a tunnel beneath downtown. If you stay downtown, the ride is free.

Outside the downtown ride-free area, regular **bus** fare is $1.25 during peak hours, $1.00 for other times. Fares for the **trolley** are the same as for the bus, but trolleys do not offer ride-free zones. Call 206/553-3000 for information.

Gray Line, 206/626-5208, runs a fleet of motorized trolleys around the main attractions downtown, and you can get on and off.

Taxis usually have to be called. They can't be hailed on the street, but you might find one available at the major hotels or in front of the Westlake Center (Third and Fourth Aves. and Pine St.). Try **Yellow Cabs,** 206/622-6500, or **Farwest Taxi,** 206/622-1717.

SIGHTS AND ATTRACTIONS

Downtown has it all, and if you brought plenty of shoe leather, you can see it all on foot.

Start with the **Pike Place Market.** This is the single most fascinating place in Seattle, where hundreds of farmers, fishermen, craftspeople, and entrepreneurs of every ethnic variety come together every day to hawk their wares. Want a fresh salmon? No problem. She-crabs on ice? Sure. Herbal remedies from China; baguettes; Greek cheese; pork buns; sex toys—it's all here. There are no franchise stores, and all crafts are handmade by locals. The market is off First Avenue, and it's blocks long. Walk down Pine, Pike, or Stewart Street toward the bay. You can't miss it. Don't.

For truly cutting-edge art, drop by the **Center on Contemporary Art** (COCA), 65 Cedar St., 206/728-1980. Perhaps you'll catch some performance art. You won't be bored. Jesse Helms hates this place.

Just below the Pike Place Market (straight down via stairs or an elevator) is the **Waterfront,** a series of piers that make for a nice place to walk and watch the water. There are lots of touristy souvenir places along here. Waterfront Park at Pier 57 is particularly serene. The **Seattle Aquarium,** at Pier 59, 148 Alaskan Wy., 206/386-4320 houses several ecosystems plus a deep-water exhibit full of sharks and octopi. Out back is a salmon ladder and a pool full of seals and otters.

Back up all the stairs (or the elevator, if you can find it) and just west of the retail core of downtown is the **Seattle Art Museum,** 100 University St. at First Ave., 206/654-3100. Don't miss the museum's core collection of Native American folk and tribal art, especially the totem poles, canoes, and masks of the Northwest tribes.

Klondike Gold Rush Park, 117 S. Main St., 206/553-7220, pays tribute to the days when Seattle became the outfitter for the miners in 1897. You can watch a slide show about the old days, and park rangers demonstrate gold panning. The **Wing Luke Asian Museum,** 407 Seventh Ave. S., 206/623-5124, examines the sometimes brutal relationship between Asian and Western cultures in Seattle.

At the north end of downtown (beyond the free zone for buses) is the **Seattle Center,** 219 Fourth Ave., 206/443-2111, formerly the grounds of the 1962 World's Fair and home of the **Space Needle,** 206/443-2111. To zip to the top will cost an adult $8.50, so don't leave the launching pad unless skies are clear. Otherwise you're going to see a lot of expensive fog. Drop by the **Northwest Craft Center,** at the Seattle Center, 206/728-1555, to see works by local craftspeople. It has a nice gift shop.

The **Washington Park Arboretum,** 2300 Arboretum Dr. E., 206/543-8800, is a spectacular collection of gardens, waterfront nature trails, and mature forests. The azaleas are to die for in the spring, and you will also encounter a beautiful Japanese garden.

The **University of Washington,** 4014 University Wy., 206/543-9198 (visitors center), has 35,000 students, and that many young people means lots of liveliness and great but cheap places to eat. The campus is lovely, with stunning views across Lake Washington to Mount Rainier.

© JOHN ELK III

Space Needle, built in 1962

The **Woodland Park Zoo,** 5500 Phinney Ave. N., 206/684-4800, is one of the top 10 in the country. The zoo has been at the forefront of freeing animals to live in their natural habitats. Next to it is the huge **Seattle Rose Garden,** 5500 Phinney Ave. N., a good place to stop and smell the roses.

A fascinating place is the **Lake Washington Ship Canal,** northwest of Seattle proper, where the lake meets the saltwater of Puget Sound. Lots of boats come through here, and at the **Hiram M. Chittenden Locks,** 3015 NW 54th St., 206/783-7059, you can watch the salmon working their way up the fish ladder. The salmon run is from mid-June to September.

LODGING

Because it's such a popular summer tourist destination, as well as a year-round convention site, it's best to plan ahead for a trip to Seattle. Hotels can be quite pricey in the summer, but during the off season (November through March) travelers are in luck. During these months most downtown hotels offer **Super Saver packages,** 800/535-7071, which are generally 50 percent off the standard rack rate. If B&Bs are more to your liking, call the **Seattle B&B Association,** 206/547-1020, for help.

For a great location, it's hard to beat the **Alexis Hotel,** 1007 First Ave. at Madison St., 800/426-7033, $$$, halfway between Pike Place Market and Pioneer Square and two blocks from the waterfront. Each of the 54 rooms are comfortably decorated with overstuffed chairs, reading lamps, and antique tables.

The Edgewater, Pier 67, 2411 Alaskan Wy., 800/624-0670, $$, is Seattle's only waterfront hotel. With its vaulted, open-beam ceiling, deer-antler chandelier, and stone fireplace, the lobby has the feel of a luxury fishing lodge. In fact, not that long ago, guests were allowed to fish from the balconies of their rooms.

If you long to be in the thick of things but with tranquil surroundings, then the **Inn at the Market,** 86 Pine St., 206/443-3600, $$$, is the place for you. Done in French country decor, this elegant inn is in fact the only lodging in Pike Place Market. The guest rooms feature wide bay windows overlooking Puget Sound, along with antiqued furniture, well-lit writing desks, and huge bathrooms.

Hotel Monaco Seattle, 1104 Fourth Ave., 206/621-1770, $$, is one of the city's newest boutique hotels. The building once housed the old Seattle Phone Building and was recently converted into suite-style rooms that are individually and colorfully decorated.

The **Mayflower Park Hotel,** 405 Olive Wy., 206/623-8700, $$, was built in 1927 and features rooms furnished with an eclectic blend

Neighborhood Watch

North of Pike Place Market along First Avenue is an area considered to be the hottest in Seattle—**Belltown**. This used to be the artistic center of the city, where grunge music was born, but lately the toney restaurants and designer boutiques have moved in. It's still cool, and musicians are still around.

Pioneer Square is second only to the Pike Place Market as a worthy choice for your precious time in Seattle. This is where Seattle was born, and nothing much has changed since the turn of the last century. The square itself has a totem pole, but the main appeal is simply strolling the surrounding streets—First Avenue and Cherry Street—among specialty shops, restaurants, and homeless missions. **Yesler Way**, just south of the square, was originally called Skid Road. Logs were skidded down the muddy hill to the pier below. When the area declined and the homeless people moved in, the area became known as Skid Row, and eventually the name become synonymous with all such blighted areas in America. Yesler isn't blighted anymore.

A few blocks south is **Occidental Square**, another park and an area of antique stores, galleries, and coffee houses. To the east, along Jackson Street and spreading out between Fifth and Seventh Avenues, is the **International District**, or the ID, as the natives call it—a politically correct renaming of Chinatown. Although the ID isn't as big and bold as similar areas in San Francisco or Vancouver, there are more Asian cultures represented here than elsewhere. After the original influx of Chinese, others who came include Japanese, Laotians, and Vietnamese, all of whom have added to the vitality of the area. You'll find some interesting shopping here, and some great little restaurants.

Maybe the most interesting neighborhood for strolling is **Capitol Hill**, which is northeast of downtown. The main drag is Broadway, where students, young pierced persons, and gay people combine in a lively mix. Odd shops, ethnic restaurants, and coffeehouses abound. This is the main route for Seattle's passing parade.

of contemporary and traditional European furnishings. It's connected by monorail to the Seattle Center.

Hotel Vintage Park, 1100 Fifth Ave., 206/624-8000, $$, offers complimentary evening wine tastings, and each of its 126 rooms is named after a Washington winery. Furnishings are classic with Italian influences.

You'll always know what time it is at the **Sixth Avenue Inn,** 2000 Sixth Ave., 206/441-8300, $. Behind the front desk is a huge railway clock that covers an entire wall. The hotel lobby and rooms are cozily decorated with wicker furniture.

If a clean, comfortably sized, and moderately priced room in a great location appeals to you, then **Seattle Downtown Travelodge,** 2213 Eighth Ave., 206/624-6300, $, is the place for you. It is located midway between the Washington State Convention and Trade Center and the Seattle Center, and is within walking distance of most major sites.

DINING

Northwestern cuisine is shaped by three factors: an abundance of fresh seafood, the availability of a wide array of fresh fruits and vegetables, and the influence of Asian cooking. Fresh is the key word here, with Asian seasonings giving the fare a unique punch.

The **Dahlia Lounge,** 1904 Fourth Ave., 206/682-4142, $$$, has long been recognized as a pioneer in the evolution of northwestern cuisine. Not to be missed are the Dungeness crabcakes and Dahlia special fried rice. Considered by many to be Seattle's finest restaurant is **Fuller's,** in the Sheraton Seattle Hotel, 1400 Sixth Ave., 206/447-5544, $$$. Examples of entrées include grilled pork loin with apple-mustard sauce and pan-seared kasu cod with soy-ginger vinaigrette.

For a romantic setting and a spectacular view of Puget Sound and the Olympic Mountains, **Chez Shea,** 94 Pike St., Suite 34, Pike Place, 206/467-9990, $$$, is the place to be. Because ingredients such as the day's seafood catch come from neighboring Pike Place Market, they are certain to be fresh.

And although Seattle doesn't boast a large Italian population, it is home to an amazing number of Italian restaurants. A couple of the best are in the Pioneer Square area. **Trattoria Mitchelli,** 84 Yesler Wy., 206/623-3883, $$, is known for good pasta, pizza, and bread. Also, **Umberto's Ristorante,** 100 S. King St., 206/621-0575, $$, features outstanding pasta dishes along with grilled entrées such as pork tenderloin with Madeira sauce and wild mushrooms.

Tired of seafood and/or pasta? Just want a steak? Try **Metropolitan Grill,** 818 Second Ave., 206/624-3287, $$. The dining room features green velvet booths, mirrored ceilings, and historic photos of former Seattle movers and shakers. The perfectly cooked steaks here are considered to be the best in the city.

The Ultimate Memento

Want to really impress your kids, your neighbors, or your co-workers with a genuine souvenir of Seattle? No, not another T-shirt, and certainly not one of those plastic totem poles.

Come home pierced. Or tattooed.

The **Pink Zone**, 211 Broadway E., 206/325-0050, has a reputation for cleanliness and does both tattooing and piercing, in addition to being a place for gay merchandise such as erotic pasta and a board game called Tired Old Queen. Earlobe piercings are $15 each, other body areas are $30. Call ahead for an appointment.

Rudy's, 614 E. Pine St., 206/329-3008, has been around for awhile, and also has a good reputation for cleanliness. Tattooing specialties include Native American and traditional sailor designs. This is also a barbershop, so you can come home with a pink Mohawk, too.

Please note: It is considered impolite to scream during a piercing.

s e a t t l e

Hankering for ethnic? How about **Sun-Ya Seafood,** 605 Seventh Ave., 206/623-1670, $, for some great dim sum. Everybody's been to a sushi bar, but you may not have done the satay scene. Pull up a stool at **Wild Ginger Asian Restaurant and Satay Bar,** 1400 Western Ave., 206/623-4450, $, and the cook will grill anything from seafood to veggies to lamb. Each skewer is served with a dipping sauce and sticky rice.

And finally, lest we forget, Seattle is home to the original **Starbucks.** To make a pilgrimage, go to Pike Place between Virginia and Stewart Streets, 206/448-8762, $.

SHOPPING

You already know that any city that's home base to Nordstrom is a great place to shop. Seattle offers an interesting blend of major chain and department stores along with smaller, locally owned shops.

The downtown shopping scene is dominated by **Nordstrom,** Pine St. at Fifth Ave., 206/628-2111. If your pulse quickens at the thought of a new pair of shoes, then this is the place to be. It's now at a new address with double the retail space. Be sure to check out Nordstrom's new line of housewares. The other major player in the downtown area is Seattle's venerable grande dame, **Bon Marche,** Third Ave. and Pine St., 206/506-6000. It's known to locals as "the Bon" and is Seattle's oldest and largest department store.

REI, I-5 and Stewart St., 206/223-1944, the outdoor gear mega-store, will have you climbing the walls. In fact, it has its own climbing wall, plus a rainstorm shower where you can try out the rain gear. Or you can put on some hiking boots and try them out on the store's trail. If it's something you need out-of-doors, this place has it.

Westlake Center, Fourth Ave. and Pine St., houses many upscale boutiques including Cache, Jessica McClintock, and Williams-Sonoma. The center also features many locally owned shops. Try **Fireworks,** 206/467-1600, offering arts and crafts gifts from regional artisans.

City Centre Mall, Fifth Ave. between Pike and Union Sts., is even more upscale, featuring such tenants as Barneys New York, FAO Schwarz, and Butch Blum. For a local boutique, try **Design Concern,** City Centre Mall, Fifth Ave. between Pike and Union Sts., 206/623-4444, specializing in office toys, soaps, watches, and locally crafted jewelry.

If you just love a bargain—and who doesn't?—**Nordstrom Rack,** 1601 Second Ave., 206/448-8522, has some great deals. It's closer to Pike Place than the main Nordstrom and has great prices on returned and closeout items from the parent store.

Underneath Pike Place Market are dozens of shops to explore. Need a new love potion? The **Market Magic Shop,** 206/624-4271, can fix you right up. Got to have some new Birkies? **MJ Feet's Birkenstock Store,** 206/624-2929, is the place to go. Just a kid at heart or got a couple of them at home? The **Great Wind Up,** 206/621-9370, promises tons of fun with loads of windup toys from which to choose.

SPORTS AND RECREATION

Seattle has just over 6,000 acres of parks. It also has 8 shorelines totaling 24 miles, and 11 swimming beaches. The people here don't just sit around and drink coffee. Seattle has 90 miles of bike routes marked with signs and 13 miles of bike lanes on city streets, and the city has the nation's highest percentage of people biking to work. Rent a bike from **Al Young Bike and Ski,** 3615 NE 45th St., 206/524-2642, where you can also get advice and gear for skiing.

Kayaking is big here, especially in the quiet waters of Puget Sound. Rent a kayak and get instructions on white-water and sea kayaking at **Northwest Outdoor Center,** 2100 Westlake Ave. N., 206/281-9694.

If you want to play tennis and it's raining outside, go to the indoor courts at the **Seattle Tennis Center,** 2000 Martin Luther King Jr. Wy. S., 206/684-4764. The course of choice for golfers is **Jackson Park,** 1000 NE 135th St., 206/363-4747, an 18-hole municipal golf course that's usually crowded on the weekends. It's in north Seattle.

New stadiums are being built at the site of the old Kingdome just

south of downtown. The **Seattle Mariners,** 206/628-3555, play baseball at the new Safeco Field, First Ave. and Royal Brougham Wy. However, the NFL **Seattle Seahawks,** 425/827-9777, won't be getting into
their new stadium until 2002. Call for information on where they'll be
playing in the meantime. The NBA **Seattle Supersonics,** 206/283-
DUNK, play at Key Arena in the Seattle Center, 219 Fourth Ave. The
Thunderbirds, 206/448-PUCK, play hockey in the same arena.

ENTERTAINMENT

Although Seattle's grunge music craze has come and gone, the city is
still a strong supporter of local musicians, and you can find every kind
of music in the world here in lots of small clubs. Although you can find
these small, interesting clubs all over the city, probably the best area for
the hottest nightlife is Capitol Hill, in the area of Broadway where East
Pine and East Pike Streets intersect. So stroll the streets and see what
sounds interesting as you pass by on the sidewalk.

Grunge music is still the thing at **The Comet,** 922 E. Pike St.,
206/323-9853. Play pool, look cool and surly, and you'll fit right in. As
long as you're wandering through the Pike Place Market, stop at the
Pink Door Ristorante, 1919 Post Alley, 206/728-1937, for a glass of
wine and some jazz or accordion music.

Remember Chris, the laid-back DJ on *Northern Exposure?* John
Corbett, the actor who played him, owns **The Fenix,** 315 Second Ave.,
206/467-1111, a club in the Pioneer Square area that plays lots of rock
and alternative music. It's got billiards, a cigar bar, and a dance space
called The Under. For jazz, try **Dimitriou's Jazz Alley** downtown,
Sixth and Lenora Aves., 206/441-9729.

If you want to sit and sip where Allen Ginsberg and Jack Kerouac did, slip into the **Blue Moon Tavern,** 712 NE 45th St. It has no phone; most people in this dive don't want to be found.

Seattle, like Denver, is big on brewpubs—it too has access to lots of clear mountain water. The **Elysian Brewing Company,** 1221 E. Pike St., 206/860-1920, is a nice one. This Capitol Hill establishment has live music on weekends.

Seattle's theater scene is cutting edge, just like everything else. An alternative theater in the Pioneer Square area is the **Velvet Elvis,** 107 Occidental Ave. S., 206/624-8477.

The **Seattle Symphony,** 206/215-4747, has developed into one of the strongest and best in the nation. The symphony performs in the Benaroya Concert Hall downtown, Second Ave. and University St. Also active and excellent is the **Seattle Opera,** 206/389-7676. It performs at the Opera House in the Seattle Center, 219 Fourth Ave. N. Or check out **Summer Nights at the Pier,** 206/628-0888—musical acts performed outdoors in the summer at the Waterfront on Piers 63 and 64.

Seattle has several small cinemas where you can find the unique and obscure in today's filmmaking, but the true film connoisseur should attend the **Seattle International Film Festival,** 206/464-5830, in late May or early June. It includes many U.S. film debuts.

For half-price, day-of-performance tickets, try **Ticket/Ticket,** 206/324-2744. It has booths at Pike Place Market and in the Broadway Market in Capitol Hill.

——Weather or Not———

Seattleites buy more sunglasses per capita than any other city in the nation. And we know what you're saying to yourself: Do those sunglasses come with little windshield wipers? Or maybe they're buying those sunglasses out of hope?

Actually, summers are nice. The days are cool, with average highs between 75 and 85 degrees Fahrenheit. Sure, the clouds often roll in from Puget Sound at night, but then burn off by afternoon. This, however, is when the tourists are abundant.

Spring and fall are the best times, with alternating rain and clear skies common. September and October feature warm days and cool nights.

But why not winter? Why not bring an umbrella and your snow skis? The skiing is glorious, and it's just a hop, skip, and slalom away.

And there are other advantages to coming during this gloomy time of year. The symphony and opera are in full force, working to buoy sagging spirits. And from November through March, you can save up to 50 percent on rooms ranging from luxury hotels to modest inns. You can also get a coupon book for good deals on dining, shopping, and attractions. Bring your galoshes. Call 800/535-7071 for details.

Water Watch

With water, water everywhere, it's no surprise that Seattle counts more boats per capita than anywhere in the country. Boating activity continues from early May—the opening day of yachting season—through mid-summer hydroplane races, to the close of salmon-fishing season in late fall. Plenty of opportunities exist for the traveler to join the fun.

Washington State Ferries, 206/464-6400, is the nation's largest ferry system, serving 10 routes with 25 vessels. You can travel with or without your car—either to get someplace or to just take the ride for an excursion.

Zip over to Victoria on Vancouver Island in less than two hours on the *Victoria Clipper IV*, 206/448-5000, a high-speed passenger-only catamaran. It's the fastest passenger vessel in the Western Hemisphere.

Gray Line, 206/626-5208, offers a two-hour cruise from May through October that includes Elliott Bay and the Lake Washington Ship Canal.

Rent a canoe or rowboat at the **University of Washington Arboretum**, 206/543-9433, and paddle about to your heart's content for four dollars an hour.

CITY BASICS

For a package of Seattle–King County visitor information, call or write to the **Seattle–King County Convention & Visitors Bureau:** Attn: Visitor Informant, 520 Pike St., Suite 1325, Seattle WA 98101; 206/461-5840. You can also go to the **walk-in booth** at the Convention and Trade Center in downtown Seattle, Galleria Level, 800 Convention Pl. (Eighth Ave. between Pike and Union Sts.).

You can get a 50-percent discount on some of Seattle's main attractions by purchasing a **CityPass.** These ticket booklets are available at the attractions, which include the Woodland Park Zoo, the Space Needle, the Pacific Science Center, the Seattle Aquarium, the Seattle Art Museum, and the Museum of Flight. For adults, the pass costs $23.75 ($47.50 value); for seniors 65 and over, $19.25; and for youths 6 to 13, $15. Admission is free for children under 6.

The trends are impossible to keep up with, so check out the performance scene in publications such as the *Seattle Weekly, The Rocker,* and *The Stranger.* The city daily newspapers—the *Seattle Times,* the *Seattle Post-Intelligencer,* and the *Morning News Tribune*—also provide weekly arts listings.

⑭ PORTLAND

to go ▶

Come again and again. But for heaven's sake, don't move here to live.
—Oregon Governor Tom McCall, 1971

Think of Seattle, but make it decaffeinated.

Portland is laid back. Way, way laid back—all the way back to the 1960s, in a way. It's as if the hippies never left. They stayed here and made jewelry and planted rose bushes and got elected to city government. And they did a wonderful job of making this one of the most livable cities in America.

What's not to love about this place? You've got a downtown full of parks, polite citizens who think littering is a major crime, public art everywhere, restored buildings, malls that don't look like malls, a transportation system that moves people quietly around downtown without charge, miles of nature trails, one of the biggest bookstores in the world (and enough well-read customers to keep it going), and a clear river that runs through it all.

With a population of 1.3 million in the metropolitan area, Portland is America's biggest little city. It fights growth, regulates it, is wary of it—thus Governor McCall's request that we not hang around his state.

It's hard to resist, though. Portland sits in the midst of some of the most beautiful scenery in the world. The city is 78 miles from the rocky Pacific coast and 65 miles from the perpetually snow-covered Mount Hood.

Greater Portland

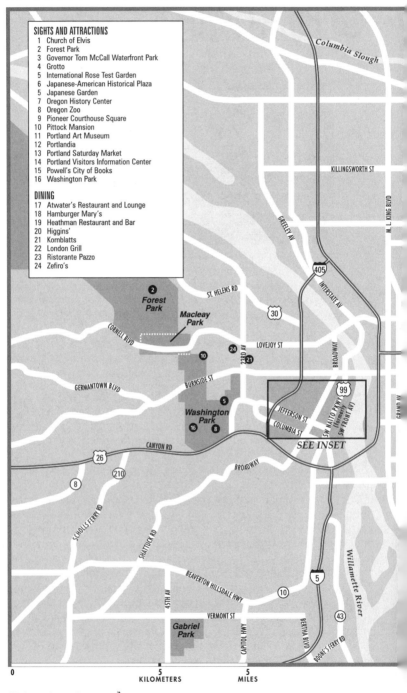

SIGHTS AND ATTRACTIONS
1 Church of Elvis
2 Forest Park
3 Governor Tom McCall Waterfront Park
4 Grotto
5 International Rose Test Garden
6 Japanese-American Historical Plaza
5 Japanese Garden
7 Oregon History Center
8 Oregon Zoo
9 Pioneer Courthouse Square
10 Pittock Mansion
11 Portland Art Museum
12 Portlandia
13 Portland Saturday Market
14 Portland Visitors Information Center
15 Powell's City of Books
16 Washington Park

DINING
17 Atwater's Restaurant and Lounge
18 Hamburger Mary's
19 Heathman Restaurant and Bar
20 Higgins'
21 Kornblatts
22 London Grill
23 Ristorante Pazzo
24 Zefiro's

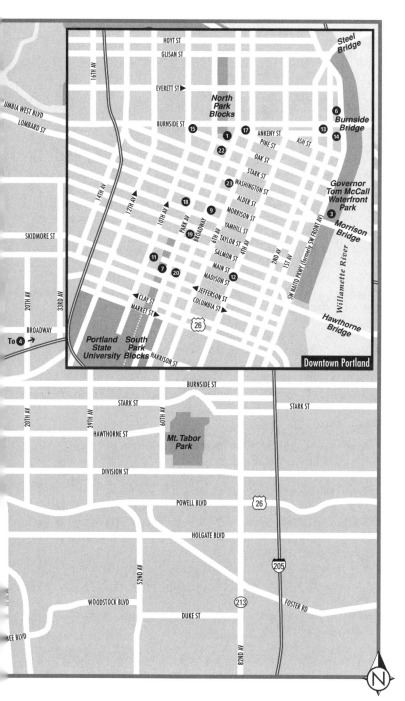

Rose City is Portland's nickname. The city's International Rose Test Garden is the largest and oldest such garden in the United States. It covers four and one half acres of a hillside—symbolizing, softening, and perfuming the city that lies in the river valley below.

A kinder, gentler, rosier place you won't find anywhere.

GETTING AROUND

If you arrive at **Portland International Airport** (PDX), 503/460-4234, you won't have to go far to see something special about Portland. In the middle of the main terminal is the **Oregon Market,** a mall full of shops that specialize in Oregon products. You'll find Nike sportswear, casual clothing from Norm Thompson, and specialty items from Made in Oregon. This is especially nice for last-minute gifts on your way home.

The airport has recently undergone some vast improvements, and getting around is a snap. PDX has video screens that detail the beauty of Oregon's scenery, visual paging systems that display messages for the hearing-impaired, and outdoor artwork.

Portland's **MAX** (Metropolitan Area Express) light rail system is expected to be connected to the airport by the fall of 2001, but until then getting into town isn't that difficult. It's a 20-minute drive, all of it on freeways. A Tri-Met bus (No. 12) leaves the airport for downtown every 15 minutes from 5:30 a.m. to 11:30 p.m.; the cost is $1.00. The **Raz Transportation Downtown Shuttle,** 503/684-3322, will take you downtown for $8.50. A taxi into town is about $25.00. Try **Broadway Cab,** 503/227-1234, or **Radio Cab,** 503/227-1212. You'll want to stay in downtown Portland, and getting around without a car

Portland is as laid back about its **dress code** as it is about everything else. Don't worry about wearing jeans to the symphony—plenty of others will be dressed just like you. But you'll see tuxes and pearls, too, and everyone seems to be just fine with whatever.

If you happen to be walking around downtown and come across a pair of folks in green jackets and blue pants, there's a good chance they're **Portland Guides**. It's their job to answer your questions. Go ahead, grill them.

More than half of Tri-Met's 90 bus lines run through the **downtown transit mall** along SW Fifth and Sixth Avenues. The transit mall streets are filled with sculptures, fountains, and glass-roofed shelters. But beware, drivers: parts of the transit mall are closed to automobile traffic.

City Survival Tips

is simple. Portland has a wonderful transportation system called **Tri-Met,** 503/238-RIDE, which consists of light rail, buses, and electric trolleys. **Fareless Square** is a 300-block area downtown in which rides on the light rail or bus are free. Outside the area, tickets are $1.05 to $1.35. You can take the light rail from downtown to the Oregon Zoo and the International Rose Test Garden. Tri-Met also has a wildly decorated bus called ART (No. 63) that will take you to all the major cultural offerings in Portland. You can get trip-planning information by calling Tri-Met.

Staying anyplace near the light rail or a bus line is going make getting around Portland easy. If you stay downtown, you'll be close to a transportation line.

Pioneer Courthouse Square, right in the middle of downtown, is the perfect place to get oriented. It's beautiful and serene, with waterfalls and trees. And through the double doors beneath the waterfalls is **Tri-Met Customer Service,** where you can get a map and advice. Wherever you want to go, you can get there from here.

Pioneer Courthouse Square is about six blocks south of **Burnside Street,** the main east-west dividing line of Portland. Six blocks east of the square is the **Governor Tom McCall Waterfront Park** and the **Willamette River.**

SIGHTS AND ATTRACTIONS

If you want to plunge into everything that Portland is, all at once, time your visit to begin on the last day of the week, because then you can start in the middle of **Portland Saturday Market,** underneath the Burnside Bridge between SW First Ave. and SW Ankeny St., 503/222-6072. This is said to be America's largest continuously operating open-air crafts market, where up to 300 creative, laid-back tradespeople come together to sell their wares. Just the names of a couple of the booths—Dali Mama, Rainbow Rags—should give you an idea of the kind of stuff that's for sale. The market is held on both Saturday and Sunday.

The market is right in the middle of Portland's historic **Skidmore District,** also called **Old Town.** This is a good place for walking and shopping. **Chinatown** is next door, and you can enter it through a colorful Chinese gate at Burnside Street and Fourth Avenue.

Come back down Burnside to the Willamette River, and walk south through **Governor Tom McCall Waterfront Park,** a place of fountains and trees and serenely rolling river. But first stop at the **Japanese-American Historical Plaza,** which is beside the Burnside Bridge along First Avenue on the park. Granite stones are inscribed with poetry, and another names the 10 WWII internment camps that were set up in the area.

The park goes a long way, about 10 short blocks. Where Salmon Street meets the park, you'll find the **Portland Visitors Information**

Center, 503/275-9799. There you can stock up on maps and brochures and advice. Call for weather, events information, and more.

Go six blocks west on Salmon Street and two blocks north, and you're at the center of downtown, **Pioneer Courthouse Square,** 701 SW Sixth Ave. Wander here beside the waterfalls and soak up the scene.

While you wander, consider a visit to **Powell's City of Books,** 1005 W. Burnside St., 503/228-4651. This place is a slice of heaven. Acres of new and used books—more than a million—invite you to browse to your heart's content. Should you need fortifications, a coffee shop is conveniently located within the store. Be sure to ask for a map before you venture into the stacks.

And here's an idea for contrasting art experiences: the Portland Art Museum and the Church of Elvis. The names give you a pretty good idea of what to expect.

Founded in 1892, the **Portland Art Museum,** 1219 SW Park Ave., 503/226-2811, is the oldest and largest such institution in the region. Inside are 35 centuries of Asian and European art, with a strong emphasis on the art of Native Americans of the Northwest Coast. The masks and totem poles are particularly fascinating.

The **Church of Elvis,** 720 SW Ankeny St., 503/226-3671, is a 24-hour coin-operated gallery. At an altar dedicated to the King you can give your confession, receive psychic counseling, and go through a non-binding wedding ceremony conducted by an Elvis impersonator.

Near the Portland Art Museum is the **Oregon History Center,** 1200 SW Park Ave., 503/222-1741. Learn all about the rugged people who helped settle the Oregon Territory. Displays include artifacts of the old days, such as snow skis, bicycles, dolls, fashions, and a covered wagon.

Portlandia is a hammered bronze babe—second largest of her kind, with the Statue of Liberty being the biggest—that serves as Portland's official symbol. You can see her atop the Portland Building, 1120 SW Fifth Ave.

Worth half a day, unless it's raining, is a visit to **Washington Park,** off Highway 26, which you can get to by light rail or bus. It's in southwest Portland, and all the best gardens and the zoo are here.

You simply can't miss the **International Rose Test Garden,** 400 SW Kingston Ave., Washington Park, 503/823-3636, which is *the* central symbolic home of what Portland is all about. Within it are four and one half acres of roses, including the classics, an area of miniatures, and the Shakespeare Garden, which contains all the roses mentioned in Shakespeare's works. The garden was established in 1917. Blooms are in evidence from late spring to early winter. After your visit, stop by the exquisitely tranquil **Japanese Garden** next door, 503/223-4070.

Formerly called the Washington Park Zoo, the **Oregon Zoo,** 4001 SW Canyon Blvd., 503/226-1561, is known for its elephant breeding program and African habitat. You can ride a miniature train from the zoo to the rose and Japanese gardens. Also consider a visit to **Forest Park,** W. Burnside St. and Newberry Rd., the largest forested city park

Portland's skyline with Mount Hood in the background

in the United States. Within its 4,800 acres are 50 miles of walking trails and more than 100 species of birds.

One of the most visited attractions in Portland is the 62-acre Catholic sanctuary called the **Grotto,** NE 85th Ave. and Sandy Blvd., 503/261-2404, www.thegrotto.org. It features a marble replica of Michelangelo's *Pietà* carved into the base of a 110-foot cliff.

And the view is to die for on the 46-acre grounds of the **Pittock Mansion,** 3229 NW Pittock Dr., 503/823-3623, a 1914 chateau full of eighteenth- and nineteenth-century antiques. The mansion is perched in the West Hills, with a sweeping view of the mountains and rivers and the city below. Have lunch or tea in the caretaker's cottage, and don't forget to visit the gift shop.

LODGING

Portland prides itself on its individuality, and that's reflected in the large number of interesting, non-chain hotels.

Built in 1912 by lumber baron Simon Benson, his namesake hotel exudes Old-World elegance. The palatial lobby features mammoth Austrian crystal chandeliers, walnut-wood paneling imported from Russia, and a marble fireplace and staircase. Rooms have been redone in shades of gray with French furnishings. **The Benson,** 309 SW Broadway, 503/228-2000, $$$$, also houses the gourmet-quality London Grill, which offers a lavish Sunday brunch.

Down the street a few blocks is the **Heathman Hotel,** 1001 SW Broadway at Salmon St., 503/241-4100, $$$$, whose elegance is of the understated sort. Original art is located throughout the hotel—including guest rooms—and ranges from the eighteenth-century works to Andy Warhol prints. The Heathman Restaurant and Bar receives consistent rave reviews.

Are you a stargazer? Ask for a starlight room at the **Hotel Vintage Plaza,** 422 SW Broadway, 503/228-1212, $$$$. These rooms are built in greenhouse style with windows that extend into the ceiling, making for wonderfully romantic views at night and lots of light during the day. The hotel has two-level suites and standard rooms, all done in a luxurious Italian decor in keeping with the style of the hotel's lobby.

For a bargain that's still in the middle of downtown and is clean and comfortable, try the **Mallory Hotel,** 729 SW 15th Ave. at Yarnhill St., 503/223-6311, $$. Because it's one of the best deals in town, you would be wise to book your room far in advance. Several rooms have good views of the city.

If you're a waterbaby, then **Riverside Inn,** 50 SW Morrison Ave., 503/221-0711, $$, is the place for you. As the name suggests, you are only steps away from the Willamette River, but you're also close to restaurants and shopping. Ask for a room with a river view.

Another riverfront option, slightly more upscale and centrally located, is the **RiverPlace Hotel,** 1510 SW Harbor Wy., 503/228-3233, $$$. Situated on the Willamette with a great view of the marina, it's a wonderful place to unwind after a busy day of sightseeing and watch a glorious sunset.

Close to the trendy Nob Hill shopping and dining district is **Heron Haus,** 2545 NW Westover Rd., 503/274-1846, $$$, located in a luxurious English Tudor home built in 1904. This B&B offers great views, nicely furnished rooms, and some pretty amazing bathrooms. One shower has seven shower heads, and another has a whirlpool spa in which you can relax while enjoying a spectacular view of the city.

If you like your B&B experience served up Victorian-style, then **John Palmer House,** 4314 N. Mississippi Ave., 503/284-5893, $$, is where you need to be. Rooms are decorated with massive Victorian furnishings, and stained-glass windows are throughout the house. A gourmet breakfast is served each morning, and high tea is available on Sunday afternoons, complete with waitstaff in Victorian attire. The John Palmer House is located in North Portland.

DINING

Portland's cuisine is much like Seattle's, with the emphasis on fish. The Pacific Rim influence brings an Asian touch.

Combining spectacular views of Portland and the Willamette River with the best in Pacific Northwest cuisine is **Atwater's Restaurant and Lounge,** 503/275-3600, $$$. On the 30th floor of the U.S. Bancorp Tower, 111 SW Fifth Ave., the restaurant offers an elegant setting in which to enjoy chef Mark Gould's creations. Seafood is the obvious choice here, and desserts are equally impressive, so save space.

Greg Higgins, former chef at the Heathman, has set up a new basecamp just a couple of blocks away. Why not try the **Higgins',** 1239 SW

OK, Portland's not perfect.

It takes a lot of moisture to grow all those roses and rhododendrons. And we're not talking about a bunch of guys with watering cans. What you've got here is kind of like a chilly rain forest, and that's perfect for plants. It takes months of misty, bone-chilling, suicidal weather in the winter to build up those bushes for their burst of color in the spring.

Oh sure, sure—technically Portland get less rain than Atlanta or Houston or New York City. But the rain, rather than falling like it does in most places, just sort of hovers in the air here and seems like it won't ever leave.

But then . . . what's that? Blue sky? Yes! And through the summer it often stays that way for days, all the way into the fall.

Broadway, 503/222-9070, $$$, roasted pavæ of salmon with a mustard crumb crust? Consider ending the meal with fresh peach fritters in marionberry sauce.

Believe it or not, one of Portland's finest restaurants is located in a basement. The redeeming features are that the room is elegantly appointed and the basement happens to be underneath the luxurious Benson hotel. The **London Grill,** 309 SW Broadway, 503/228-2000, $$$, has waitstaff schooled in the art of tableside service, producing such classics as steak Diane and crepes Suzette. And don't miss the lavish Sunday brunch.

The menu at the **Heathman Restaurant and Bar,** 1009 SW Broadway, 503/241-4100, $$, changes seasonally to ensure peak freshness of ingredients. The emphasis is on Northwest seafood with a French accent. The restaurant is rather small and therefore has a bistro-like feel to it.

The Italian decor of the Hotel Vintage Plaza would seem to demand an Italian restaurant, and that's exactly what you'll find. But rather than continue the elegant look of the hotel's lobby, the **Ristorante Pazzo,** 627 SW Washington St. at Broadway, 503/228-1515, $$, with its red-and-white checkered tablecloths and hanging hams and sausages, has a rustic Italian countryside look and feel.

Mediterranean with a twist would be one way to describe **Zefiro's,** 500 NW 21st Ave., 503/226-3394, $$. French and Italian dishes dominate, but you can also find Morocco, Spain, Greece, and even Thailand represented here. Sample the cream risotto or tuck into a grilled veal chop or grilled mahimahi with herb salsa verde.

Just want a corned beef sandwich? **Kornblatts,** 628 NW 23rd Ave., 503/242-0055, $, is where you want to be. A dozen tables and a busy take-out counter serve up some really great Jewish soul food. The bagels are terrific, and are even better with lox and cream cheese on them. Don't forget to try at least one of the five different kinds of cheesecake.

If you're craving a burger, **Hamburger Mary's,** 840 SW Park Ave., 503/223-0900, $, will turn you into a happy camper. Thick, juicy burgers, piled high with lettuce and tomatoes and served on whole-wheat buns, will satisfy the most exacting connoisseur.

SHOPPING

Over the past several years, Portland has made a big push to protect and restore its historic architecture. In this process several historic buildings have been reborn as interesting shopping centers. Outstanding among these are **New Market Village,** 50 SW Second Ave., 503/228-2392, and **Skidmore Fountain Square.** The trendsetter shopping scene is to be found primarily in the northwest Nob Hill area.

If all that trekking around Portland has you wishing for a new pair of tennies, head on over to **Nike Town,** 930 SW Sixth Ave., 503/221-6453, a super-flashy showcase for the entire Nike collection. Who says jogging can't be fun?

The **Eye of Ra,** in the Water Tower at John's Landing, 5331 SW Macadam Ave., 503/224-4292, is well known for the ethnic look in clothing, jewelry, and home furnishings. Since the 1970s, the store has specialized in women's clothing from Southeast Asia and India.

And although the name implies a children's store, the **Real Mother Goose,** 901 SW Yamhill St., 503/223-9510, is for the young at heart who love original arts and crafts. Showcasing the finest contemporary work, the store houses everything from ceramics to furniture to jewelry.

Twist, 30 NW 23rd Pl., 503/224-0334, is another place for hand-made jewelry and original crafts. This northwest Portland shopping destination features everything from Thomas Mann techno-romantic jewelry to housewares and handcrafted furniture.

The **Galleria** is a three-story atrium shopping mall located in the heart of downtown Portland. It houses more than 50 specialty shops and restaurants, including a **Made in Oregon** store, 921 SW Morrison St., 503/228-2748.

Pioneer Place, 700 SW Fifth Ave., 503/228-5800, is one of the newest and most upscale shopping centers in Portland. This four-story pavilion is anchored by Saks Fifth Avenue and includes upscale-mall standards such as Williams-Sonoma, Banana Republic, Eddie Bauer, and the city's only Godiva store.

SPORTS AND RECREATION

The **Portland Trail Blazers,** 503/234-9291, www.nba.com/blazers, have been consistently high-achievers on the court, and in 1995 the city built them a state-of-the-art arena called the Rose Garden, just off the Broadway exit of I-5. The **Portland Power,** 503/249-1130, www.portlandpower.com, the women's professional basketball team, play their home games in Memorial Coliseum, 439 N. Broadway. The **Winter Hawks,** 503/238-6366, www.winterhawks.com, play hockey at the Rose Garden or the Memorial Coliseum.

And they're off: Horses race at **Portland Meadows,** 1001 N. Schmeer Rd., 503/285-9144. Greyhounds race at **Multnomah Greyhound Park** in Fairview, 503/669-2283, www.ez2winmgp.com. And Cars race at **Portland International Raceway,** three miles north of downtown, 1940 N. Victory Blvd., 503/823-7223, www.teleport.com /~autorace.pir/.

Bicycling magazine has voted Portland the most bicycle-friendly city in America. And with a comprehensive network of bikeways, bicycle lanes, and secure bicycle parking, it's no wonder. The **Fat Tire Farm,** 2714 NW Thurman St., 503/222-3276, will rent you a mountain bike for $30 a day.

A perfect place for in-line skating is the long and level Waterfront Park. Rent skates at **Sports Works,** 421 SW Second Ave., 503/227-5323. Snow skiing is available all year long. **Timberline Ski Area** is about an hour away; 503/231-7979 (in Portland) or 503/272-3311.

ENTERTAINMENT

Portland claims to have more brewpubs than any other place in the United States, what with the wonderful fresh water from the melting snows of Mount Hood and the access to nearby fields of barley and hops. **BridgePort** is Oregon's oldest microbrewery, and is located in a landmark Portland building, 1313 NW Marshall St., 503/241-7179. Its specialty is firkin (naturally conditioned) ales.

All that beer contributes to an active and varied nightlife scene in Portland. One of the city's favorite characters, drag queen diva Darcelle, is headliner at his/her nightclub called **Darcelle XV,** 208 NW Third Ave., 503/222-5338. The shows sport a variety of dancing, pantomiming beauties who don't take themselves too seriously. That beefy, bawdy babe herself, Darcelle, acts as both emcee and bouncer. Shows are Wednesday through Saturday nights at 8:30, with extra shows at 10:30 on Fridays and Saturdays. The Men of Paradise (manly men) strip show takes place at midnight on Fridays and Saturdays as well. The cover is $10.

They call it the Schnitz, and with great affection—it's short for **Arlene Schnitzer Concert Hall,** 1111 SW Broadway, a 1920s movie palace that has been restored into the elegant art-deco home of the **Oregon Symphony.** The Schnitz is worth a visit, even if the symphony is taking a night off. The nationally recognized symphony performs from September to June.

Across the street from the Schnitz are two smaller theaters, the **Intermediate** and the **Winningstad,** housed together in a gleaming

—— A Toss-Up ——

Portland got its start—and its name—from a coin.

A Tennessee drifter named William Overton and a Massachusetts lawyer named Asa Lovejoy got out of their canoe on the banks of the Willamette River and decided they had found a nice place for a town. Overton wanted to stake a claim, but he didn't have the 25 cents needed for the filing fee. Lovejoy agreed to a loan if he could have half the claim. A deal was struck.

Overton drifted on, selling out his half of the claim to a guy named Francis Pettygrove. Now Lovejoy and Pettygrove were partners, but they couldn't agree on a name. Lovejoy, the Massachusetts native, liked Boston; Pettygrove, from Maine, thought Portland had a nice ring to it.

They tossed a coin, and the Portland penny won.

---

glass box called the **New Theatre Building.** The Intermediate is the home of **Portland Center Stage,** Portland's largest theater company, which puts on classic and contemporary plays. Call the **Center for the Performing Arts,** 503/248-4335, for information on these theaters and the symphony.

The **Oregon Ballet Theatre** performs classic and contemporary ballets at the **Portland Civic Auditorium,** SW Third Ave. at SW Clay St., which is only a few blocks from the Schnitz. The auditorium is also the home of the Portland Opera. Call the Center for the Performing Arts for ballet and opera information.

CITY BASICS

The **Portland Oregon Visitors Association,** 26 SW Salmon St., Portland, OR 97204-3299; 800/962-3700; www.pova.org, is the organization to contact for visitor information. You can also get **weather information,** 503/275-9792, and up-to-date details on **road conditions,** 503/222-6721.

A Web site, www.katu.citysearch.com, also offers the latest in **entertainment news** and more, including activities, restaurants, sports, and businesses.

The Portland Oregon Visitors Association's downtown information center is a one-stop ticketing outlet for arts and cultural performances. They call it **Ticket Central—Portland,** and all of the ticketing agencies work through this office. You can't get tickets by phone, but the office is located downtown, 26 SW Salmon St., 503/275-9750, www.pova.com.

For entertainment news, check out the free publications *Willamette Week* and *Portland Guide,* or buy a copy of the Friday *Oregonian.*

⑮ SAN FRANCISCO

to go ▶

The San Francisco Bay Area [is] the playpen of countercultures.
—RZ Sheppard, *Time* magazine, September 8, 1996

This city is at the top of everyone's list for one reason. Character.

Where does character come from? (Hint: Not from corporations. Sorry, Walt.) It comes from *characters*—people who are not afraid to be individuals, to stand out, to think and act differently, to try something new.

San Francisco has been attracting these kinds of people for decades. Individualism is nourished, diversity is celebrated, and the results have been woven into a rich and flamboyant tapestry . . . with feathers and fringe and a hint of chintz.

These characters have built hotels, restaurants, and nightclubs that appeal to their sense of individuality, and the result is an abundance of odd and special and charming places. Add to that the great diversity of cultures, especially the exotic influence of populations from the East, and what you have is the perfect place for a getaway to the extraordinary.

Wonderful weather doesn't hurt. Temperatures infrequently exceed 75 or drop below 45. Summers are especially nice, with the fog from the Pacific rolling in like a fresh puff of air-conditioning.

And then there's the natural beauty of the place—a dramatic coastline, acres of gardens, and a diversity of terrain with all those hills.

Not a bad place to leave one's heart, or at least to take it on a quick getaway. Hearts need vacations, too, you know.

Downtown San Francisco

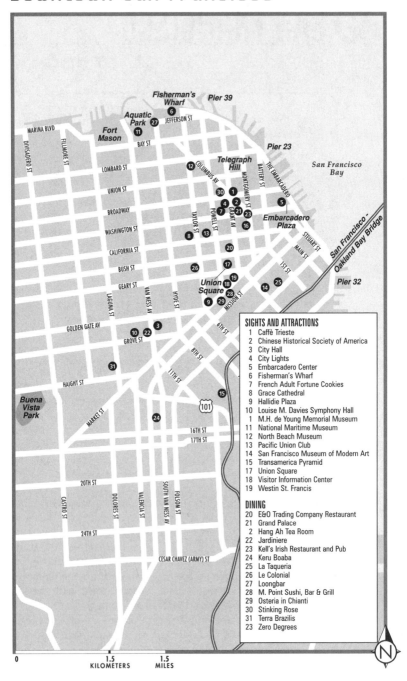

Fisherman's Wharf
Pier 39
Aquatic Park
Jefferson St
MARINA BLVD
Fort Mason
BAY ST
Pier 23
LOMBARD ST
Telegraph Hill
San Francisco Bay
COLUMBUS AV
UNION ST
BROADWAY
GRANT AV
POWELLS ST
Embarcadero Plaza
WASHINGTON ST
TAYLOR ST
CALIFORNIA ST
STEUART ST
BUSH ST
MAIN ST
GEARY ST
Union Square
1ST ST
Pier 32
LAGUNA ST
VAN NESS AV
HYDE ST
MISSION ST
GOLDEN GATE AV
GROVE ST
6TH ST
8TH ST
HAIGHT ST
11TH ST
Buena Vista Park
MARKET ST
101
16TH ST
17TH ST
20TH ST
CASTRO ST
DOLORES ST
VALENCIA ST
SOUTH VAN NESS AV
FOLSOM ST
24TH ST
CESAR CHAVEZ (ARMY) ST
San Francisco – Oakland Bay Bridge
THE EMBARCADERO
DIVISADERO ST
FILLMORE ST

SIGHTS AND ATTRACTIONS
1 Caffè Trieste
2 Chinese Historical Society of America
3 City Hall
4 City Lights
5 Embarcadero Center
6 Fisherman's Wharf
7 French Adult Fortune Cookies
8 Grace Cathedral
9 Hallidie Plaza
10 Louise M. Davies Symphony Hall
1 M.H. de Young Memorial Museum
11 National Maritime Museum
12 North Beach Museum
13 Pacific Union Club
14 San Francisco Museum of Modern Art
15 Transamerica Pyramid
17 Union Square
18 Visitor Information Center
19 Westin St. Francis

DINING
20 E&O Trading Company Restaurant
21 Grand Palace
2 Hang Ah Tea Room
22 Jardiniere
23 Kell's Irish Restaurant and Pub
24 Keru Boaba
25 La Taqueria
26 Le Colonial
27 Loongbar
28 M. Point Sushi, Bar & Grill
29 Osteria in Chianti
30 Stinking Rose
31 Terra Brazilis
23 Zero Degrees

0   1.5   1.5
   KILOMETERS   MILES

N

GETTING AROUND

San Francisco is served by two major airports—**San Francisco International Airport** (SFO), 650/876-2222, which is 16 miles from the center of town (about a 30-minute drive), and **Oakland International Airport,** 510/577-4000, which is 35 miles away. Taxis into San Francisco will cost you at least $30 and $50, respectively.

The fifth busiest airport in the United States is SFO, but help is on the way. Besides a new international terminal, a new Airport Rail Transit (ART) system will accommodate 4,000 passengers per hour around the airport. A new rental car facility is also planned. Direct access on the city's Bay Area Rapid Transit (BART) system from the airport to downtown is expected to be available in 2001. All of these airport improvements are expected to cost $2.4 billion.

Many shuttle services operate from the airports to downtown. Go first class with **All City Limousines,** 800/723-7854. Travel is by sedans, vans, and limos. Or try **Quake City Shuttle,** 415/255-4899, for shared-ride shuttle service. Another operator is **Supershuttle San Francisco,** 800/BLUEVAN, www.supershuttle.com.

Within the city, buses and streetcars (called **MUNI,** 415/673-6864) cost $1.00 for adults and 35¢ for seniors and children. Cable cars are $2.00 for all. Exact change is required. **BART,** 415/989-2278, service costs $1.10 within the city and as much as $4.05 to the far corners of the Bay Area for a one-way fare.

SIGHTS AND ATTRACTIONS

San Francisco is a necklace of neighborhoods. Each has its special feel and glint of light, and contained within each neighborhood are equally special sights that somehow seem to sum up the surroundings. To wander though its neighborhoods is to get to know the city.

A good place to start is **Union Square,** bounded by Powell, Stockton, Geary, and Post Sts. You're within minutes of the best shopping in the city, fine restaurants, many hotels, galleries, Chinatown, and the cable cars. In fact, you could have a wonderful getaway without ever leaving this area.

Union Square itself contains benches and mimes, street preachers and wackos, pigeons and panhandlers—plus tourists.

The stunning **Westin St. Francis** hotel, 335 Powell St., 415/397-7000, is on one side. Do go in, even if you can't afford to stay there. Inside the lobby is the famous Viennese Magneta clock, the one that the locals refer to when they say, "Meet me under the clock."

A few blocks south is **Hallidie Plaza,** Powell St. at Market St., where you can get help from the Visitor Information Center. This is also where one of the cable car lines (the one that goes up Powell Street) begins.

Nob Hill is not far away. Still known as "Snob Hill," this is where the elite of the city used to live—Leland Stanford, Mark Hopkins, Collis P. Huntington. Most of the palatial homes were destroyed in the 1906 earthquake and fire, but luxurious hotels such as the Mark Hopkins, the Fairmont, and the Huntington have taken their place. One original mansion remains, a brownstone building that is now the home of the exclusive **Pacific Union Club,** 1000 California St. And while you're in the area, don't miss **Grace Cathedral,** California and Taylor Sts., 415/749-6300, a Gothic edifice noted for its modern-themed stained-glass windows of people such as John Glenn and Robert Frost—not just the same old saints.

West of Union Square is the **Tenderloin,** a rather shabby area that contains the seat of San Francisco government and some of the most beautiful buildings in town. Take a look at the beautiful beaux-arts-style **City Hall,** Polk St. and McAllister St. Standing out from the period pieces of architecture in this area is the **Louise M. Davies Symphony Hall,** Grove and Franklin Sts., 415/864-6000, a stunning work of modern design.

You mustn't miss **Chinatown,** one of the largest Chinese communities outside of Asia. But don't even think about using a car here. In this area you'll find a density of things to see and smell; they must be savored.

The grand entrance to Chinatown, an archway with a dragon on it, is at Grant and Bush Streets. You'll walk into crowds of people, experience exotic smells from restaurants, and encounter tacky souvenir shops next to legitimate places selling jade or tea or art. Stop by the **Chinese Historical Society of America's museum,** 644 Broadway St., Suite 402, 415/391-1188, which tells all about the early life among the immigrants. Don't neglect one of the many dim-sum eating establishments along the way. And you'll spend a fascinating few minutes watching fortune cookies being made at **French Adult Fortune Cookies,** 56 Ross Alley: Flat pieces of dough come down a conveyor belt. Old women then put a paper fortune in each piece and fold over the dough. They do this day after day. Good fortune, it seems, has not shone on them.

North Beach is an adjoining neighborhood brimming with Italian flavor. It's a great place for wandering and munching among the bakeries and bread shops. Have some cappuccino.

The North Beach neighborhood is also home to **City Lights,** 261 Columbus Ave., 415/362-8193, www.citylights.com, where the heart of the Beat movement still beats. It was founded in 1953 by poet and publisher Lawrence Ferlinghetti and is one of the best independent bookstores in America. It offers an extensive selection of poetry, fiction, music, and more.

For further flavor of North Beach, stop in at the **North Beach Museum,** 1435 Stockton St. in Bayview Bank, 415/626-7070, a little bank-sponsored place that features some fine old photographs, plus a hand-written copy of one of Ferlinghetti's poems. And since you're in the neighborhood, stop by **Caffè Trieste,** 601 Vallejo St., 415/392-6739, for a jolt of Italian coffee and a remembrance of poets past.

Follow Columbus Avenue to the intersection of Washington and Montgomery Streets for a glance at the crown jewel of the **Financial District,** the **Transamerica Pyramid,** 550 Montgomery St., 415/781-7810—a San Francisco icon and the city's tallest building at 853 feet. Although you can't get to the top, you can get a good view from the Virtual Observation Deck in the lobby, which shows the view though cameras mounted on the roof.

Nearby, the **Embarcadero Center,** Clay, Sacramento, and Battery Sts., is a four-tower combination of office buildings, malls, restaurants, and hotels. From the waterfront along Embarcadero at the end of Market Street, you can see the well-lighted **Bay Bridge** at night. Also, a farmers' market is held on Saturdays at the foot of **Market Street**; you can find fresh produce, bread, and ready-to-eat food from restaurants.

The closer you get to the water, the more touristy things get. **Fisherman's Wharf,** near the intersection of The Embarcadero and Jones St., is said to be the second-most visited place in California, next to

Going Places

Get the lowdown on Chinatown with insider **Linda Lee**, 812 Clay St., 415/982-8839. Her unique tour covers history, culture, and traditions of local people. Learn about the Summer of Love and hippie happenings on the **Haight-Ashbury Flower Power Walking Tour**, 415/863-1621. Pot not included. **Sfgaytours.com**, 173 Elsie St., 415/648-7758, specializes in gay dining, nightclubs, theater, shopping, and weddings. Its name is its Web site, which will provide the details.

A tour called **Cruisin' the Castro from an Historical Perspective**, 375 Lexington St., 415/550-8110, www.webcastro.com/castrotour, features entertaining vignettes on gay history and visits to the AIDS memorial quilt museum, the Castro Theatre, and Harvey Milk's camera shop, among other stops.

Living history gets a new meaning on the **Ghost Hunt Walking Tour**, 415/922-5590, a one-hour stroll through the toney Pacific Heights neighborhood to check out documented ghost sightings and haunted houses. History, magic, chills, and thrills.

The Victorian Home Walk, 2226 15th St., 415/252-9485, features a small-group, low-impact walk through San Francisco's lovely Victorian past. Learn about the architecture, lifestyle, and history of the era.

Really in a hurry? Take a jet helicopter and see it all in one swell swoop with **San Francisco Helicopter Tours and Charter**, 800/400-2404.

Disneyland. Walk among the piers. Buy a T-shirt. Bump into a fellow tourist. Say hi to the sea lions who lie about on their equivalent of lawn chairs out in the harbor. Nearby, the **National Maritime Museum,** Beach and Polk Sts., 415/556-3002, www.maritime.org, has a remarkable collection of shipshape artifacts and historical displays.

Ghirardelli Square (GEAR-a-delli), Polk, Larkin, Beach, and North Point Sts., is something special amid the crowds. Among shops and restaurants in an old woolen mill lies the sweet center of the chocolate factory. You can see the wonderful mess being made, and of course have a bite. Take something back—how about a chocolate cable car for Aunt Maude? Recommended is the chocolate soda. It's heaven in a straw.

Across town, **Golden Gate Park,** Stanyan and Fell Sts., 415/263-0991, is easily a one-day event. It's a thousand acres of gardens and hills, bike paths and lakes and museums. Here is a place to retreat from the density of the city. Do not miss the intricate beauty of the **Japanese Tea Garden** within the park.

Two additional must-stops in Golden Gate Park are the **Asian Art Museum,** 415/379-8800, www.asianart.org, which showcases art from 40 Asian countries, and the **M.H. de Young Memorial Museum,** 415/750-3600, www.thinker.org, which has 22 galleries of American art.

While you're in the vicinity, stop by the **Presidio,** bounded by Lincoln Blvd., W. Pacific Ave., Lyons St., and the Bay, an area at the base of Golden Gate Bridge that was once a huge military outpost and has since become a park. It's full of interesting architecture—the post dates back to 1776, when the Spanish got it going—and hiking trails. The **Presidio Museum,** Funston Ave. and Lincoln Blvd., 415/561-4331, will tell you all about it.

If you're driving, be sure to curb your wheels when parking on a hill. Curbing your wheels means turning your tires toward the street when facing uphill, and towards the curb when facing downhill. This serves as an extra brake. (If you plan to get drunk in San Francisco, try to curb your body when you pass out. Otherwise you could roll away.)

Muir Woods, just on the other side of the Golden Gate Bridge, is definitely worth a visit. But to give it a fair shake with a long walk among its giant redwoods, you'll need to use up half a day, at least. You might want to rent a car, buzz across the bridge, and visit the park; 415/388-2070. On the way back, why not stop off for lunch in the beautiful bay town of Sausalito, 415/332-0505. Or why not simply enjoy the ride across the bay? A Golden Gate Ferry ride to Sausalito is $4.70 for adults, 415/923-2000.

City Survival Tips

Cable car in front of Grace Cathedral

Another must-visit neighborhood is the **South of Market** area, or SoMa, bounded by Market, Townsend, and 13th Sts. It's a warehouse district that has been revitalized with art museums and galleries, office buildings, and the convention center. Be sure to see the **San Francisco Museum of Modern Art,** 151 Third St., 415/357-4000, which houses more than 150,000 works of all kinds in a spectacular space. Try the shopping in the MuseumStore and the dining at Caffe Museo.

LODGING

You'll be cheered and charmed when you step into one of this city's many boutique hotels. Nowhere else is San Francisco style so clearly evident as in the decor of its hotels—cool but not cold, a bit of flair, a dash of fun. How can you resist?

Highly recommended is the **Hotel Triton,** 342 Grant Ave., 800/433-6611, $$, a perfect example of that funky chic, right down to the lobby's retro furniture and iridescent pillows. This place is hip, hip, hip. You'll even get a rubber ducky for your tub. It's in a wonderful location in the gallery district, near Union Square and the gate to Chinatown. Complimentary coffee and evening wine are included.

At the top of the list, and on top of Nob Hill, is the **Fairmont Hotel,** 950 Mason St. at California St., 800/527-4727, $$$$. The place is rich with history, but you'll need to be temporarily rich to stay here. At least stop in at the Tonga Room and enjoy a drink, plus a tropical storm.

Where does Luciano Pavarotti stay when he's in San Francisco? The **Inn at the Opera,** 333 Fulton St., 800/325-2708, $$$, of course. It's right next to the culturally rich Civic Center. The inn offers kitchenettes, canopy beds, and fresh flowers. Ask about the symphony, opera, and ballet packages.

Greater San Francisco

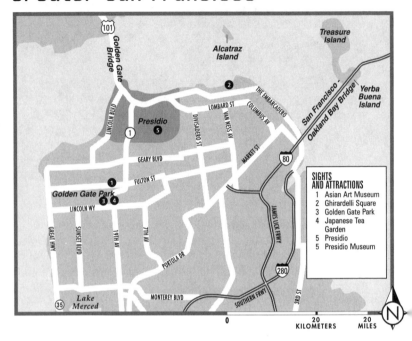

At the **Hotel Metropolis,** 25 Mason St. at Market St., 415/775-4600, $$, you get two-line phones, dataports, and honor bars that provide ginseng and energizing drinks, plus free continental breakfast and evening wine. The hotel is housed in a 10-story, 1930s building.

It's like spending a day at a California beach house when you stay at the **Hotel Del Sol,** 3100 Webster St., 415/921-5520, $$, in the Marina District. It's a renovated 1950s-style motor lodge with coastal colors and comfy fabrics that aim for that bright and airy California look. Surf's up!

If movies are your thing, try the **Hotel Bijou,** 111 Mason St., 415/771-1200, $$, in the Union Square area. A mini-theater, with velvet curtains and antique deco seats, is just off the lobby. The theater plays features from its library of 65 movies that have been made about San Francisco. The interior of the establishment has movie-theater styling, and each guest room is named after one of those movies in the hotel's library.

For a splurge, try the **Sherman House,** 2160 Green St., 415/563-3600, $$$$, in the Lombard area. It's the former palatial home of music store owner Leander Sherman, built in 1876 in the Victorian Italianate style. Rooms feature Persian carpets, fireplaces, and feather beds. Some suites have terraces that look out on the Golden Gate Bridge. Try the fabulous French cuisine from the Dining Room.

A budget suggestion is **The Dakota,** 606 Post St., 415/931-7475, $, well-located in the Union Square area. It offers spacious claw-foot bathtubs and complimentary continental breakfast.

The **Archbishop's Mansion,** 1000 Fulton St., 415/563-7872, $$, is a B&B that was built in 1904. Each of the 15 rooms is named for an opera, and all rooms have fireplaces and private baths.

DINING

San Francisco is second only to Paris as the World Capital of Food. An innovative spirit, fresh ingredients close by, and the influence of other cultures have combined to make this a place of splendid eating. Leave your heart in San Francisco, but leave your diet at home.

Try the dim sum at either **Hang Ah Tea Room,** One Hang Ah St., 415/982-5686, $; or **Grand Palace,** 950 Grant St., 415/982-3705, $; both in Chinatown. Servers bring carts around with tidbits of this and that in little dishes. Try it. Taste it. Who knows what it might be; it will probably be good. At the end of the meal, they count up your empty dishes and that's what you owe.

In the South of Market district is **M. Point Sushi, Bar & Grill,** 55 Fifth St., 415/543-7600, $$, featuring a spectacular black granite sushi bar and cocktail specialties from around the world.

Zero Degrees, 490 Pacific Ave. at Montgomery St., 415/788-ZERO, $$, in the Financial District, is a European-style café that serves desserts, coffee, and drinks, handmade pastries and ice creams plus top-shelf liquors and champagne. It's open morning to midnight, and outdoor seating is offered.

How about some Indonesian fusion cuisine? Give it a try at **E&O Trading Company Restaurant,** 314 Sutter St., 415/693-0303, $$, in the Union Square area.

Or drop into a medieval Tuscan tavern for some pumpkin ravioli, pasta rustica, and Italian wines at **Osteria in Chianti,** 101 Eddy St., 415/447-7497, $$, near Union Square.

Jardiniere, 300 Grove St., 415/861-5555, $$$, a collaboration between restaurant designer Pat Kuleto and star chef Traci Des Jardins, is winning rave reviews for its French-Californian cuisine.

Vampires might want to avoid the **Stinking Rose,** 325 Columbus Ave., 415/781-7673, $$, where all dishes are heavy on the garlic. BYOBM: Bring your own breath mints. It's at the border of Chinatown and North Beach.

For good, authentic Mexican food, stop by **La Taqueria,** 2889 Mission St., 415/285-7117, $, in the Mission District. You'll get tacos and burritos, plus some healthy fruit drinks, at this little place.

And you haven't lived until you've tried the cuisine of Senegal, which includes the Arabic influences of couscous, peanut sauce, marinated onions, and exotic spices. Red snapper is the specialty at **Keru Boaba,** 3386 19th St., 415/643-3558, $$.

An Irish restaurant that has gotten lots of attention in Seattle has opened a branch in San Francisco. **Kell's Irish Restaurant and Pub,** 530 Jackson St., 415/955-1916, $$, specializes in lamb and salmon in pastry. Irish bands entertain several nights a week.

New in Union Square is **Le Colonial,** 20 Cosmo Pl. at Taylor St. between Sutter and Post Sts. (where Trader Vic's used to be), 415/931-3600, $$$, a restaurant that specializes in the cuisine of French colonial Southeast Asia. Among the Vietnamese specialties are Goi Cuon (soft salad rolls with poached shrimp) and Ca Hap (steamed sea bass in banana leaves). Veranda dining is available.

Try the Singapore chili soft-shell crab or the Kung Pao smoked quail at **Loongbar,** 900 North Point St., 415/771-6800, $$, in Ghirardelli Square. You'll see sweeping views and dragons on the wall.

Terra Brazilis, 602 Hayes St. at Laguna St., 415/241-1900, $$, specializes in such regional Brazilian specialties as shellfish stew, braised oxtail, and desserts of tropical fruits. It's near the Opera House and Symphony Hall.

SHOPPING

All of that stylish flair that you see here is probably for sale. Bring some home. The world could use some brightening.

Across the street from Hallidie Plaza is **San Francisco Centre,** Market St. at Fifth St., a breathtaking concentration of shops with a spiral escalator in the middle. Here the shoe aficionado will find the mothership, **Nordstrom.** You'll wade through acres and miles and floors of shoes. You're in shopping nirvana, baby.

Did you notice **Macy's,** 233 Geary St., 415/397-3333, www.macys .com, and **Neiman Marcus,** 150 Stockton St., 415/362-3900, when

San Francisco Freebies

1. Get a cheap chuckle at the Cartoon Art Museum, 814 Mission St., 415/227-8666. The first Wednesday of each month is "pay what you wish" day.
2. You can't keep the change, but you can at least take a long look at it at the Museum of Money of the American West, at the Bank of California, 400 California St., 415/765-0400.
3. Walk across the Golden Gate Bridge. Only the cars get charged.
4. Watch the mimes of the San Francisco Mime Troupe, 415/285-1717. They're out and about July through September. (Note: Some mimes answer the phone with hand gestures. Please be patient.)
5. Take a one-hour history walk compliments of City Guides, 415/557-4266. Walks are in various areas June through September.

The city's largest festival is the **Chinese New Year Celebration**. You'll see a block-long golden dragon and a wonderful parade. It's in Chinatown in late February. 415/982-3000. The **Cherry Blossom Festival** is held somewhere from mid to late April at the Japan Center. 415/563-2313.

The **Cinco de Mayo Festival**, 415/826-1401, is always the first Sunday in May in the Mission District. And you can't believe the fun and extravagance of the **Lesbian, Gay, Bi-Sexual, Transgender Pride Celebration**, 415/864-3733, which is held in the Castro at the end of June.

San Francisco's **Blues Festival**, 415/979-5588, is the oldest such celebration in the United States, and it always attracts the best musicians. It's held in the Great Meadow at Fort Mason on the last weekend of September.

events
HORIZON

you were at Union Square? Macy's has gotten a redo, and Neiman's is as stunning as ever. In its rotunda is a stained-glass sailing ship, decades old, that sheds its amber light on all the shoppers.

On nearby Geary Street are galleries galore, most of them in buildings above street level. The galleries are also on Sutter Street and Grant Avenue. Pick up a free *Gallery Guide* in any of these places for help in finding the kind of art that interests you.

Three floors of fine porcelain—plus Oriental art, carpets, fine furniture, and bronze sculptures—are at **Farinelli Antiques & Fine Art,** 311 Grant Ave., 415/433-4823, in the Union Square area. Also in the Union Square area is **Dreamweaver,** 171 Maiden Ln., 415/981-2040, featuring handknit sweaters in cotton, silk, wool, cashmere, chenille, mohair, and alpaca.

Close by is **Xanadu Tribal Art** gallery, 140 Maiden Ln., 415/392-9999, located in a historic Frank Lloyd Wright building in Union Square. You'll find artifacts, textile, and jewelry from around the world. Another art gallery is **Hang,** 556 Sutter St., 415/434-HANG, which sells and rents a variety of contemporary art at reasonable prices.

Nearby, and a must for gifts, is **Gump's,** 135 Post St., 415/982-1616, www.gumps.com. Asian and European antiquities, crafts, and original jewelry are its specialty. The store has been around for 150 years. For a final stop in Union Square, how about a Kashmir sapphire? Find it at **Amir H. Mozaffarian,** 155 Post St., 415/391-9995.

If you want to take home a genuine piece of San Francisco, stop by the **City Store,** Pier 39, 415/788-5322; and 1000 Great Hwy. at Beach Chalet, 415/831-4758, both of which offer authentic San Francisco

Earthquake!

What to do if an earthquake hits while you're sleeping on the 14th floor of your hotel:

1. Don't panic. Of course that's what they all say, and that's the first thing you'll do.
2. Don't get on the elevator, especially one of those glass ones. Surely you've seen those earthquake movies where the people decide that taking such a route would be the smart thing to do. They usually die in the first reel, and rather spectacularly.
3. If you're already on the elevator when the quake hits, and the thing stops and the lights go out—go ahead and scream. How could it hurt?
4. Seriously, take the stairs. Before you go to bed, check to see where the stairs are in your hotel. And don't forget your flashlight.
5. Once you're on the street, you're on your own. Watch out for falling debris. Watch out for fire trucks and shrieking, fleeing drag queens. Don't run to the ocean—there might be a tidal wave. Don't go up one of the city's quaint hills—there might be a Victorian avalanche.
6. Go to a one-story bar.

memorabilia and local crafts. Take home a brick from Lombard Street and a piece of cable that once pulled cable cars, plus "Clothing Optional" and classic street signs. The store gives at-risk youth a chance to gain retail experience and turn away from drug use, gangs, and homelessness.

SPORTS AND RECREATION

Try out the **Frequent Flyers Bungee Trampoline** at Fisherman's Wharf. Do a back flip, and rocket up to 25 feet in the air. We recommend that you not try this one right after lunch.

How about ice skating with a view? The new **Yerba Buena Ice Skating Center,** 750 Folsom St., 415/777-3727, has huge windows overlooking the skyline. It's like skating outdoors. Or see some of California's most beautiful terrain as you sail over it in a hang glider. Novices go with an instructor. Call **San Francisco Hang Gliding Center,** 510/528-2300, and they'll meet you at the cliff. And good luck.

Saddle up at the **Golden Gate Park Stables,** John F. Kennedy Dr. and 36th Ave. in the park, 415/668-7360. Take one-hour rides through the park, as well as rides along Ocean Beach.

You can have a mountain bike delivered to your hotel with a call to **Four Winds Adventure Mountain Bike Rental,** 888/360-1087. Pedal through the city or take a guided tour to Marin County, Muir Woods, the Sonoma wine country, and more. For $21 per day or $6 per hour, you get helmets, water bottles, and locks included. Call 24 hours a day.

As for spectator sports, the **San Francisco 49ers,** 408/562-4949, play at 3Com Park, eight miles south of San Francisco via the Bayshore Freeway. A new park, Pacific Bell Park, has just opened in the China Basin off Second Street. That's where the **San Francisco Giants,** 800/734-4268, play National League baseball.

ENTERTAINMENT

Heavens, you can get anything you want in San Francisco. Bring your sense of adventure.

They call themselves "gender illusionists"—drag queens, in other words. And they'll be serving you Cal-Asian fusion cuisine at **asia sf,** 201 Ninth St., 415/255-8889. Then from 10 p.m. to 2 a.m. the place becomes a gay or straight dance club, depending on the night. It's in the South of Market district.

Nosh 'n' wash at **Brain Wash,** 1122 Folsom St., 415/255-4866, which offers a combination laundromat/café, and you can listen to music from the acoustic stage during the spin cycle. **Doo Wash,** 817 Columbus Ave., 415/885-1222, has much the same thing, but with pinball, pool, and a TV room.

Beach Blanket Babylon has been keeping things zany for a quarter of a century. The musical revue at **Club Fugazi,** 678 Green St., 415/421-4222, spoofs popular culture with singers in outrageous costumes and enormous hats. Reservations are required.

Holy Cow, 1535 Folsom St., 415/621-6087, one of the most popular bars in the area, is where both locals and tourists congregate. DJs play lots of disco and funk. It's in the South of Market district. Or check out John Lee Hooker's **Boom Boom Room,** 1602 Fillmore St., 415/673-8000, which features down-home blues, with live bands most nights. Credit cards are not accepted.

The world-famous **San Francisco Symphony,** 415/864-6000, features conductor Michael Tilson Thomas and performs at the Davies Symphony Hall in the Civic Center, Van Ness Ave. and Grove St. Also at the Civic Center is the **San Francisco Opera,** 415/864-3330.

If you happen to be in town in early December, why not participate in *The Dance Along Nutcracker.* They'll rent you a tutu and you can jump right in there. It's at the **Yerba Buena Center for the Arts,** Third St. between Mission and Howard Sts., 415/978-ARTS, where there are also exhibits, films, music and dance performances, and other events.

CITY BASICS

For more information on events, activities, transportation, and lodging, contact or visit the **Visitor Information Center,** 900 Market St. at Powell St., Lower Level, Hallidie Plaza, 415/391-2000.

The View From Here

One thing you absolutely must do is take advantage of some of the amazing vantage points in the city. Find a tall place and look out. In one easy survey you will see an ocean, a bay, islands, mountains, and a shimmering city.

Three tall places:

Coit Tower, 415/362-0808, on the tippy-top of Telegraph Hill, has a gorgeous view waiting for you. The tower, built in 1933, is 212 feet high with frescoes inside depicting California scenes.

The cocktail lounge at the top of the Mark Hopkins Hotel, 1 Nob Hill, 415/392-3434, is known as the **Top of the Mark**. You'll pay top prices, but the 360-degree view will be worth it.

Walk across the **Golden Gate Bridge**. You can't miss it. It's the gold one. (Actually, it's orange, and is being repainted continuously.)

san francisco

For visitor literature such as *The San Francisco Book* and the *Lodging Guide*, write to the **San Francisco Convention & Visitors Bureau**, P.O. Box 429097, San Francisco, CA 94142-9097; 415/392-0328 (TDD/TTY); www.sfvisitor.org. Cost is $3 per book for postage and handling. The Convention & Visitors Bureau also has information available via its Web site and offers a **Leisure Reservation Service**, 888/782-9673, which visitors can call to make lodging reservations.

For event information, call the **San Francisco Events Hotline**, 415/391-2001 or 800/220-5747 (to receive information via fax). The hot line is updated weekly. And check out the entertainment events and the latest food gossip in the *San Francisco Examiner* or *Chronicle*. Free publications include the *San Francisco Bay Guardian* and the *SF Weekly*. Two publications that cater to a gay audience are the *Bay Area Reporter* and the *San Francisco Bay Times*.

MUNI operates over 30 accessible bus lines and accessible Metro service for disabled riders. Visitors should request a copy of the *MUNI Access Guide* or call for more information on the services offered, MUNI Accessible Services Programs, 949 Presidio Ave., San Francisco, CA 94115; 415/923-6142. Also, the Convention & Visitors Bureau maintains a TDD/TTY information line, 415/392-0328.

Visitors should also note that San Francisco has an 8.5 percent sales tax, unless you have the product shipped outside of California.

⑯ LOS ANGELES

to go ▶

Fall is my favorite season in Los Angeles,
watching the birds change color and fall from the trees.
—David Letterman

This place is not for wimps. It can intimidate just about anybody.

There are crowds of perfect people, puffed and buffed with smiles that glimmer, the better to spotlight your own imperfections. These people know all the right people, and those people aren't you. The only overweight things about them are their billfolds, their jewels, and their bulging egos. Instead of a map *to* their house, they give their guests maps *of* their house.

There are the monstrous freeways that can eat the faint-hearted for lunch. And then there are the sooty air, windstorms, firestorms, landslides, mudslides, earthquakes; shopping sprees, crime sprees, berserk cops, race riots.

We could go on. But let's not. Let's look at the logic.

If LA is so bad, what are 15.5 million people doing here, then? Are they trapped?

Au contraire, as they say in Hollywood. Maybe these people know something that the uninitiated don't.

The truth about Los Angeles is that it's big. Everything here is big, bigger than life, silver-screen big. That includes the museums, the nightlife, the restaurants, the stores. Who do you think is going to entertain the entertainers?

Sure, the problems are big—the weather, the traffic, the crime.

Los Angeles Area

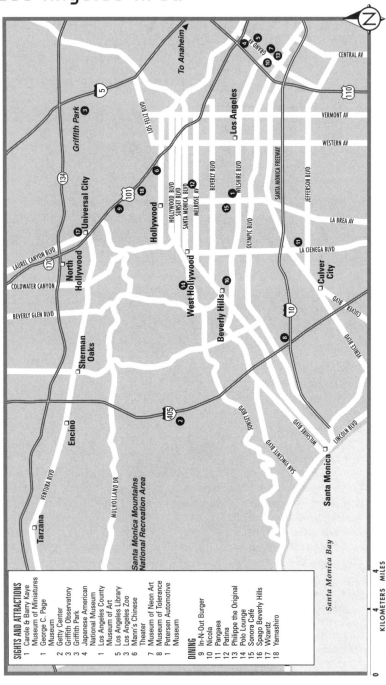

N

CENTRAL AV

VERMONT AV

WESTERN AV

To Anaheim

110

Griffith Park

Los Angeles

LOS FELIZ BLVD

Universal City

Hollywood

North Hollywood

West Hollywood

Beverly Hills

Culver City

Santa Monica

LAUREL CANYON BLVD

COLDWATER CANYON

BEVERLY GLEN BLVD

Sherman Oaks

Encino

Tarzana

VENTURA BLVD

MULHOLLAND DR

Santa Monica Mountains National Recreation Area

BEVERLY BLVD

WILSHIRE BLVD

JEFFERSON BLVD

LA BREA AV

LA CIENEGA BLVD

SANTA MONICA FREEWAY

OLYMPIC BLVD

HOLLYWOOD BLVD
SUNSET BLVD
SANTA MONICA BLVD
MELROSE AV

GRAND

Santa Monica Bay

SUNSET BLVD

SAN VINCENTE BLVD

WILSHIRE BLVD

LINCOLN BLVD

CULVER BLVD

VENICE BLVD

0   4   KILOMETERS
0   4   MILES

SIGHTS AND ATTRACTIONS

1 Carole & Barry Kaye Museum of Miniatures
1 George C. Page Museum
2 Getty Center
3 Griffith Observatory
3 Griffith Park
4 Japanese American National Museum
1 Los Angeles County Museum of Art
5 Los Angeles Library
3 Los Angeles Zoo
6 Mann's Chinese Theater
7 Museum of Neon Art
8 Museum of Tolerance
1 Petersen Automotive Museum

DINING

9 In-N-Out Burger
10 Nicola
11 Pangaea
12 Patina
13 Philippe the Original
14 Polo Lounge
15 Sonora Café
16 Spago Beverly Hills
17 Wizardz
18 Yamashiro

But the rewards are big, too, like big bucks, big dreams, and a sun that breaks through the smog more often than not. How else can you account for all those tans and all those oranges?

Listen, let's give LA a chance. Suck in that gut, rebrush those teeth, shine up that credit card. Let's go see what all the shouting's about.

GETTING AROUND

Los Angeles is one big sprawl of people. The general area of it covers five counties—34,149 square miles—and includes a population (15.5 million) that is larger than most states. You've got beaches, mountains, and the suburban plains in between. You've got the canyons of a major downtown; wide, glitzy boulevards; palm-lined streets; and a mouse-infested castle—everything, in other words, and not enough time to see it all.

So let's stick to one general area, the parts of LA that seem to be the LAest—namely, **Hollywood** and the neighborhoods to its west, plus a few places outside that area.

Once you've landed at **Los Angeles International Airport,** 310/646-5252, aka LAX, you're going to want a car. It's really the only thing that makes sense in this wide-ranging city.

Instead of getting an ordinary rental car at the airport, why not try **Beverly Hills Rent a Car,** 9220 S. Sepulveda Blvd., 310/337-1400, and get yourself a Mercedes, BMW, or Viper. For up to $2,800 a day (for a Lamborghini), you can look like a native. Don't forget the sunglasses.

What about a motorcycle? Call **EagleRider Motorcycle Rental,** 20917 Western Ave., Torrance, 310/320-4008, for everything from helmets to Harleys. You can also take a guided motorcycle tour.

If you want to take a taxi, it's going to be about $30 to downtown or Hollywood, $70 to Disneyland. A limo is going to cost you about $50 an hour. Try **Yellow Cab Co.,** 310/715-1968, or **Fox Limousine,** 310/641-9626, respectively.

The city's trains and buses are operated by the **Los Angeles County Metropolitan Transit Authority,** 213/626-4455. Call for a brochure outlining tours you can take by public transportation. Downtown is served by the **DASH**—Downtown Area Short Hop—system, which consists of minibuses that can get you from City Hall to Chinatown and elsewhere nearby for only 25 cents.

The subway system is growing. The **Red Line,** which begins at Union Station, is expanding into North Hollywood and beyond.

SIGHTS AND ATTRACTIONS

Los Angeles has more museums per capita than any other American city, plus more than 150 art galleries and, it brags, more theaters than New York City.

Going Places

Get the scoop on the city's architecture with a tour from **Architours**, 323/294-5825. **JRT International**, 818/501-1005, will take you hiking through the city or the Santa Monica Mountains.

See the sights from the heights with **Biplane Adventures**, 818/834-5957, which offers barnstormer rides in open-cockpit biplanes, and includes loops and rolls. Don't forget your scarf. Or you can do it all by helicopter with **Helinet Aviation Services**, 818/902-0229, a company known for work in Hollywood films.

Do the town right with **LA Nighthawks**, 310/392-1500, which will take you for a VIP Night-on-the-Town tour by limo to cabarets and comedy and dance clubs. And of course there are those must-see tours of the stars' homes. Try **Starline Tours of Hollywood**, 323/463-3333. Or how about **Tour Shuttle Columbia**, 213/739-5757.

The undisputed museum champion of Los Angeles is the **Getty Center**, 1200 Getty Center Dr., 310/440-7300, www.getty.edu. The $1 billion architectural masterpiece sits on 110 acres in the Brentwood hills and has an endowment of nearly $4 billion. Many paintings by Monet, Renoir, and Cezanne are on permanent display. This is also the home of Van Gogh's *Irises.* The center features a full-service restaurant, two cafés, a bookstore, and garden areas. Visitors to the Getty Center take a scenic five-minute tram ride to the complex from the parking area, through a stunning park. Admission is free, but parking is five dollars. Parking reservations are required, unless you arrive by taxi or bus. The center is closed Mondays.

Many of the museums are clustered into Wilshire Boulevard's **Museum Row.** The **Los Angeles County Museum of Art,** 5950 Wilshire Blvd., 323/857-6111, www.lacma.edu, houses more than a half-million works from ancient times to the present. The **Petersen Automotive Museum,** 6060 Wilshire Blvd., 213/930-CARS, www.petersen.org, is devoted to the history of the automobile, from motorized carriages to the Flintstone's Flintmobile, and contains the largest collection of automobiles in the United States. The **George C. Page Museum,** 5801 Wilshire Blvd., 213/934-PAGE, www.tarpits.org, exhibits fossils unearthed from the La Brea Tar Pits. And, finally, the **Carole & Barry Kaye Museum of Miniatures,** 5900 Wilshire Blvd., 323/937-6464, www.museumofminiatures.com, is a shrink's dream.

The **Museum of Tolerance,** 9786 W. Pico Blvd., 310/553-8403, looks at racism and prejudice throughout history. Try out the Point of

View Diner, a re-creation of a 1950s diner that serves a menu of controversial topics on video jukeboxes.

The **Los Angeles Library,** 630 W. Fifth St., 213/228-7000, built in 1925, combines Byzantine, Egyptian, and Spanish architecture. The new Bradley wing has a stunning glass roof and atrium. And don't forget to check out all those books.

You can walk through history in downtown's **Little Tokyo** by following the neighborhood's commemorative timeline: "*Omoide no Shotokyo*—Remembering Little Tokyo." Text and quotations are etched in the sidewalk, covering Japanese settlement from the 1890 immigration through World War II internment camps. The streetscape fronts 18 historic First Street buildings, including the **Japanese American National Museum,** 369 E. First St., 213/625-0414.

Griffith Park, 4730 Crystal Springs Dr. (Ranger Visitor Center), 323/665-5188, the largest city-run park in the country at 5,000 acres, holds numerous attractions, including the **Los Angeles Zoo,** 323/665-5188; the **Griffith Observatory,** 323/665-5188; a carousel; train rides; and more than 50 miles of bridle and hiking trails.

The **Museum of Neon Art,** located downtown, 501 W. Olympic Blvd., 213/489-9918, will light up your life. The main exhibit space is on the first floor of the Renaissance Tower downtown. Also, you can take a guided bus tour of neon signs, movie marquees, and contemporary neon art in the city.

You can't go to LA and not see the **Hollywood Walk of Fame.** Here you'll see hundreds of stars that have recently made a comeback: two-hundred-plus star panels were removed and reinstalled on Hollywood Boulevard because of work being done on the new subway line. After checking out the Walk of Fame, tiptoe on over to **Mann's Chinese Theater,** 6925 Hollywood Blvd., 323/461-3331, and enjoy a movie.

LODGING

Los Angeles has 93,000 hotel rooms, and that figure is growing every day. Surely you can find something to fit your needs.

The **New Otani,** 120 S. Los Angeles St., 213/629-1200, $$$, in the Little Tokyo section near downtown, has recently renovated its guest rooms and public areas. You can get suites with Japanese- and Western-style decor. The restaurant called A Thousand Cranes serves traditional Japanese cuisine in private tatami rooms overlooking a half-acre rooftop Japanese garden.

The **Hollywood Metropolitan,** 5825 Sunset Blvd., 213/962-5800, $$, is in the heart of the entertainment scene. Its rooms feature wall-to-wall windows offering panoramic views of Hollywood.

If you can possibly afford it, you ought to stay at the legendary **Beverly Hills Hotel,** 9641 Sunset Blvd., 310/276-2251, $$$$, which recently underwent a $100 million restoration so that everything that was old is new again—but looks the same, right down to the pink-and-green banana-leaf wallpaper. This is where Liz Taylor enjoyed a couple of honeymoons. Or was it three honeymoons?

How about something brand new? **L'Ermitage Beverly Hills,** 9291 Burton Wy., 310/278-3344, $$$$, features rooms that are double the size of most, with 40-inch televisions, audio systems, fax machines, and cellular phones. It boasts a staff of 250—2 for every hotel guest.

The Mondrian, 8440 Sunset Blvd., 213/650-8999, $$$, has been reinvented as an "urban resort," emphasizing the idea of hotel as theater—in other words, high drama everywhere. You might rub elbows with celebrities in the hotel's Sky Bar.

The Argyle, 8358 Sunset Blvd., 213/654-7100, $$$, has a rich history. It was built in 1929 in the art-deco style and is listed in the National Register of Historic Places. This is where Marilyn Monroe, Errol Flynn, Jean Harlow, and Clark Gable stayed. It has recently been restored.

A moderately priced hotel near the Hollywood Walk of Fame and chock-full of history is the **Hollywood Roosevelt Hotel,** 7000 Hollywood Blvd., 323/466-7000, $$. Montgomery Clift's ghost supposedly haunts Room 926.

A hotel on the less expensive side, on the Westside, is the **Beverly Inn,** 7701 Beverly Blvd., 323/931-8100, $$. Also consider the **EconoLodge Wilshire,** 3400 W. Third St., 213/385-0061, $$, in Hollywood; the hotel has 100 rooms that have been recently renovated.

Way off the beaten track, but worth consideration, is the **Snug Harbor Inn,** 108 Sumner Ave., 310/510-8400, $$$. It's in the charming town of Avalon, on Catalina Island. It was built in the late 1800s and has recently been restored. Its six rooms feature bay views and hardwood floors.

DINING

LA is home to more than movie stars. These days, chefs come here to make a name for themselves, and some, such as Wolfgang Puck and Joachim Splichal, achieve a kind of stardom themselves. The city has more than 20,000 restaurants, and some of them are among the best—and most expensive—in the world.

The byword of the LA dining scene—and this trend has been around for awhile—is fusion. That means taking aspects of one culture's cuisine and combining them with those of another, such as Thailand's delicate flavors combined with southern California's veal or fish. But the area is also home to some good old American favorites, and those who want to stick to basics can find plenty of places to satisfy them. Southern California is the birthplace of the cheeseburger, the chili dog, the Cobb salad, and the hot fudge sundae.

At the top of the charts is **Patina,** 5955 Melrose Ave., 213/467-

Hollywood is as much a state of mind as a specific area, but if you have to pin it down, go to Hollywood Boulevard. It's a little seedy around here (but improving all the time), so you'll want to branch out into surrounding neighborhoods. Nearby are funky Melrose Avenue, the famous Sunset Boulevard, and an area known as mid-Wilshire, where the museums are congregated.

To the west is ritzy-ditzy Beverly Hills and an interesting area known as West Hollywood, where many of the city's best restaurants, shops, and art galleries are. This is the center of LA's gay community. Nearby are the wealthy areas of Bel Air and Brentwood. Westwood is home to University of California-Los Angeles. Century City, once the backlot of Twentieth Century Fox, is where the Shubert Theatre and many other shops and cinemas can be found.

1108, $$$$, Splichal's signature restaurant in Hollywood. He won the James Beard Award in 1991, and his restaurant has been at the top of the *ZAGAT Survey* for several years running. The atmosphere is casual, the food creatively French, and the prices stratospheric ($200 for dinner for two). However, you can get a two-course spa cuisine lunch for about $20. Reservations are required.

Puck's **Spago Beverly Hills,** 176 N. Canon Dr., 310/385-0880, $$$$, is known as LA's flagship restaurant. This is the guy who instigated the California fusion craze, and it's still going strong here. Needless to say, star-quality is expensive—about $60 per person for dinner.

One of the best new restaurants in LA is **Nicola,** 601 S. Figueroa St., 213/485-0927, $$$$, which is taking fusion dining to new heights in a futuristic dining room at the Sanwa Bank Plaza downtown. Try the Nicola oysters and the pan-fried rice noodles with roast duck.

LA is another one of those giant-melting-pot cities, and something scrumptious is always stirring in the ethnic stew. **Yamashiro,** 1999 N. Sycamore Ave., 323/466-5125, $$$, is a romantic Japanese castle set in gardens high in the Hollywood Hills. Enjoy the view and fresh seafood, sushi, sashimi, and tempura.

Sonora Café, 180 S. La Brea Ave., 213/857-1800, $$$, is a Mexican-Southwestern mix specializing in duck tamales, and crab and wild-mushroom enchiladas. Another specialty is the potent, individually shaken margarita. Try the brunch on Saturdays.

Some of the best restaurants are in hotels. **Pangaea,** in Hotel Nikko, 465 La Cienega Blvd., 310/246-2100, $$$, continues to win raves for its hibachi-style Chilean sea bass and rack of lamb. Try the Big Band Sunday brunch (11:30 a.m. to 3:30 p.m., $32), a buffet set amid the sounds of Tommy Dorsey and Benny Goodman.

January 1 is the famed **Tournament of Roses Parade and Rose Bowl game**, 818/419-ROSE, in Pasadena. Get there before dawn if you want a seat. The first Sunday in March is the time for the **City of Los Angeles Marathon and Bike Tour**, 310/444-5544. If you want to race, you must register in advance.

One of the biggest cultural celebrations in LA is **Cinco de Mayo**, which is held the first weekend in May on Olvera Street. Food, games, and mariachis are the highlights.

If you don't want to brave the crowds for the Rose Bowl Parade, come to Colorado Boulevard in Pasadena the Saturday after Thanksgiving for the **Doo Dah Parade**. It's an irreverent spoof of the many-petaled extravaganza in January.

events
HORIZON

Even if you don't have a lot a power, if you've got the dough you can lunch at the **Polo Lounge** in the Beverly Hills Hotel, 9641 Sunset Blvd., 310/276-2251, $$$. Dine outside and watch the stars stroll by.

And there's something magical about **Wizardz**, 1000 Universal Dr., Suite 217, 818/506-0066, $$$, a magic club and dinner theater at Universal CityWalk. Here you'll encounter a laser show, a psychic reading room, and the Magic Potionz Bar. The staff will perform tricks at your table. Any chance of making the bill disappear?

Fast food is fresh at **In-N-Out Burger** drive-through locations throughout the city, including one near CityWalk, 3640 Cahuenga Blvd., $. Call 800/786-1000 if you can't find one.

When you're downtown, check out **Philippe the Original,** 1001 N. Alameda St., 213/628-3781, $, the place where the French dip sandwich was invented in 1918. For about four dollars per sandwich you can eat your fill.

SHOPPING

Welcome to hog heaven. If you can find **Rodeo Drive,** you've arrived.

Here's where the well-heeled buy shoes from Cole-Haan, suits from Giorgio Armani, luggage from Louis Vuitton, and jewelry from the largest Tiffany & Co. store outside of New York.

But that's only the beginning. Los Angeles County has 49 malls, and surely you can find something among them to suit your taste. The **Beverly Center,** La Cienega and Beverly Blvds., 310/854-0070, is one of the best, with more than 160 shops and restaurants. This is where the stylists go to outfit shows such as *Friends* and *Beverly Hills, 90210.*

Another spot for a shopaholic is the **Fashion District,** formerly known as the Garment District, which is just south and east of downtown. You'll have to hunt, but you should find some bargains here. The **CaliforniaMart** contains 1.4 million square feet of display space for 1,200 showrooms. And although it is primarily a wholesale market, about five times a year it produces "Super Sale Saturdays" that are open to the public. There's a one-dollar admission fee.

Get a map of the downtown shopping district from the **Fashion District of Los Angeles** either by stopping by their office or going to their Web site; office at 110 E. Ninth St., Suite C625 (open Mon–Fri 8 a.m.–5 p.m.), 213/488-1153, www.dpoa.com.

Also worth a visit is a funky little neighborhood on the border of Los Feliz and Hollywood that has been in the spotlight lately. The **Silver Lake District** is a fashion mecca outfitted with trendy boutiques and street vendors and featuring vintage and used clothing—LA's version of New York's SoHo. The area is attracting celebrities, young adults, and world-class designers. It's centered on Vermont Avenue and Sunset Boulevard.

Melrose Avenue is home to the punk and funk look, where the off-beat and high-energy meet. This is a good street for strolling and shopping. One of the shops you'll find is **Aardvark,** 7579 Melrose Ave., 323/655-6769, which has clothes from the 1940s, such as fedoras and wide ties. Or try **LA Eyeworks,** 7507 Melrose Ave., 213/653-8255, for that Hollywood fashion must, designer sunglasses.

Also consider a stop at **Leimert Park** in the heart of the city, where African American artists offer rainbow-colored clothes and exotic artwork, including African masks and statues.

SPORTS AND RECREATION

The **Santa Monica Mountains Recreation Area** is LA's top outdoor spot. The 65,000-acre park runs from the Hollywood Hills to the Ventura County line. The nearby **Peter Strauss Ranch,** at Mulholland Hwy., Agoura Hills, 818/991-9231, offers a mile-long path for hikers.

Biking enthusiasts can use the 22-mile **beach bikeway,** Temescal Canyon Rd. to Palo Verdes Peninsula, which runs from Temescal Canyon Road on the north to the edge of the hilly Palo Verdes Peninsula on the south. Take bike locks and some cash, so that you can stop at Venice Beach for lunch and a look at the street performers. Rental bikes are available from shops along Washington Street at the south end of Venice.

Venice's **Muscle Beach,** on Venice Boardwalk along the Venice Municipal Beach, has recently been refurbished. You can get pumped up or just watch the hunks in action. This is where Arnold Schwarzenegger used to work out. The other beaches have different appeals to different folks. Serious surfers head for **Surfrider Beach** in Malibu. For scuba diving, head for **Santa Catalina Island** and take a gander at the island's Underwater Park.

If you can't snag a spot to golf with the elite at the River Country Club in Pacific Palisades or at Hillcrest south of Beverly Hills, talk to the folks at **Rather Be Golfing,** 1515 Lincoln Blvd, Santa Monica. 310/458-6898, for help with arranging an outing.

The NHL **Kings** (310/673-6003), plus the two NBA teams, the **Lakers** (310/419-3100) and the **Clippers** (213/745-0500), have recently moved into the new Staples Center, 1111 S. Figueroa St.

The **Los Angeles Dodgers,** 213/224-1491, play at Dodger Stadium, 1000 Elysian Park Ave., northeast of downtown. About as famous as the team are the Dodger Dogs, available at the concession stands. **The Galaxy,** 888/657-5425, are the city's soccer team. They play at the Rose Bowl in Pasadena.

ENTERTAINMENT

They call it the see-and-be-scene, and it's endemic to La-La Land. The best place for it is called the Strip—a section of Sunset Boulevard in

— What's New in LA? —

The **Disney Concert Hall**, scheduled to premiere in the fall of 2001, will be the new home of the Los Angeles Philharmonic. Besides a 2,380-seat concert hall, the venue will include an outdoor park, restaurant, bookstore, and gift shop.

The **Japanese American National Museum** has recently tripled its size with a new addition across the street. The museum explores the history of Japanese Americans from their immigrant origins to modern lives.

The $50 million **Cathedral of Our Lady of the Angels**, mother church of the Archdiocese of Los Angeles, opens in 2000. It is designed by Spanish architect Jose Rafael Moneo and will include a 20,000-square-foot plaza and Mission-style colonnades. It's at Temple Street between Grand Avenue and Hill Street downtown.

The Academy Awards will be returning to Hollywood in March 2001 with the multimillion-dollar project to restore **Mann's Chinese Theater** and add a huge entertainment complex housing theaters, a hotel, shops, and a 3,300-seat auditorium. It's all part of a restoration project for **Hollywood Boulevard**, which will include cleaner streets, private security patrols, subway stops, a new **Hollywood History Museum** in the historic Max Factor Building, and a retail village called **Hollywood Marketplace**.

Bike and jog along Santa Monica Beach

West Hollywood where the sidewalks are lined with cafe-goers and gawkers.

Begin with a slow drive down the Strip, Fairfax to Doheny, and check out where the longest lines are. If that's where the biggest crowds are, then that must be the club-of-the-moment. Nearby is public parking for a mere eight dollars, and then you can go and join the scene. Wear black. Wear shades. Be tanned. And make sure all your low-cut parts are as tanned as the rest of you.

You'll find a youthful, pierced crowd in front of Johnny Depp's **Viper Room,** 8852 Sunset Blvd., 310/358-1880. The cover charge is $5 to $10. The **Whisky-a-Go-Go,** 8901 Sunset Blvd., 310/652-4205, is a happening place, too, with lots of leather and alt rock. The cover here is also $5 to $10. Or how about the **House of Blues,** 8430 Sunset Blvd., 323/848-5100, Dan Ackroyd's salute to the Blue Brothers phenomenon and southern culture.

Other favorite hangouts in LA are the comedy clubs. The **Laugh Factory,** 8001 Sunset Blvd., 323/656-1336, always draws a crowd, watching who gets out of the limos that pull up to the front. Could it be a celeb, or is it just another regular person having fun in a rented limo?

All the people who made it big in comedy started in local clubs, and sometimes they'll drop by to hone their delivery or try out new material. One of the best known clubs is the **Comedy Store,** 8433 Sunset Blvd., 213/656-6225, which is owned by Pauly Shore's mom, Mitzi. Roseanne is a prominent returnee here.

Another top name is **The Improv,** 8162 Melrose Ave., 213/651-2583. Although the club's TV show, *Evening at the Improv,* is filmed at the Santa Monica location, this place still attracts some of the best in the business, who sometimes make sneak appearances. Look for Jay Leno, Billy Crystal, and Robin Williams.

With more than 1,100 annual productions and 21 openings every week, more theatrical shows are produced in LA than in any other city

Behind the Scenes

You've come to the movie capital of the world, so the logical thing you'll want is a look at how movies are made. There are several studio tours from which to choose.

Universal Studios Hollywood, 818/622-3801, combines serious tour opportunities with theme-park extras. The studio offers a Backlot Tram Tour that visits some of the most famous sets in the world, such as *Jaws*, *Back to the Future*, and *The Sting*. You'll be briefed on the rich history of the studio, and you may bump into a genuine movie star on the way. The tour costs $38 for adults.

The **Warner Bros. Studios VIP Tour**, 818/954-1744, is among the most detailed of the Hollywood tours. You'll see some of the top TV shows being made, such as *E.R.* Reservations are required.

The **Paramount Studios** visitors center, 860 N. Gower St., 213/956-1777, offers two-hour walking tours. Shows such as *Entertainment Tonight* and *Hard Copy* are made here. No reservations are necessary—just queue up 10 minutes before each tour, which begin on the hour from 9 a.m. to 2 p.m. The cost is $15. Call to get into the taping of a show, such as *Frasier*.

To see tapings of shows at other studios besides Paramount, call or write to **Audiences Unlimited**, Universal City Plaza, Building 153, Universal City, CA 91608, 818/506-0057.

If you'd like to attend a taping of *The Tonight Show*, you'll want to get to NBC's **Burbank Studios**, 3000 W. Alameda St., Burbank, CA 91523, early in the day. For seven dollars, you'll get a two-hour tour. Get back in line at 4 p.m., and you should have a good shot at snagging tickets for the 5 p.m. taping. Call the show's 24-hour hot line, 818/840-3537, for information on scheduled guests. You can also write for tickets before you leave home. Enclose a self-addressed, stamped envelope. Requests are processed two to three weeks in advance.

Serious films buffs and autograph seekers should go to LA's **Film and Video Permit Office**, 6922 Hollywood Blvd., across from Mann's Chinese Theater. Be there at 8 a.m. when the office prints up a schedule of that day's movie productions in the city, then set out on the trail to see the big shots shooting on location.

in the world, including New York. More than 4 million theater tickets are sold in LA every year.

Expect innovative, satirical comedy from the **Groundling Theater,** 7307 Melrose Ave., 213/934-9700, LA's equivalent of Second City in Chicago. This is where Jon Lovitz, Phil Hartman, and Pee-Wee Herman got their starts.

For jazz, try LA's oldest jazz club, the **Baked Potato,** 3787

Cahuenga Blvd. W., 213/937-9630. It's a small place in North Holly-wood that seems to never shut down. The cover charge is $5 to $10.

A hot spot for Cubano music is the **El Floridita,** 1253 N. Vine St., 213/871-8612, in Hollywood. It has good Cuban-Nicaraguan cuisine.

The Los Angeles Music Center is made up of three performance halls. The **Dorothy Chandler Pavilion,** Los Angeles Music Center, 135 N. Grand Ave., 213/972-7200, is the largest and is the home of the LA Philharmonic. The **Mark Taper Forum,** Los Angeles Music Center, 135 N. Grand Ave., 213/972-7200, is a theater-in-the-round. And the **Ahmanson Theater,** Los Angeles Music Center, 135 N. Grand Ave., 213/972-7200, is where Broadway musicals can find a home.

CITY BASICS

The **Los Angeles Convention and Visitors Bureau,** 633 W. Fifth St., Suite 6000, Los Angeles CA 90071; 800/CATCH-LA, has two walk-in information centers: Downtown: 685 Figueroa St., between Wilshire Blvd. and Seventh St., open 8 a.m.–5 p.m. weekdays and 8:30 a.m.–5 p.m. Saturdays, 213/689-8822; Hollywood: Janes Square, 6541 Hollywood Blvd., open Mon–Sat 9 a.m.–5 p.m., 213/689-8822.

Call or write to the Visitors Bureau to receive any one of a number of guides, such as *Destination Los Angeles,* plus others on shopping, dining, and entertainment. You can also reserve hotel rooms through the Visitors Bureau.

⎯ Drive Yourself Crazy ⎯

The freeways here—the most extensive in the world—are known both by names and by numbers. The names of the freeways change as you move from one community to another. For instance, Santa Monica Freeway becomes San Bernardino Freeway. Ventura Freeway becomes Hollywood Freeway. If you don't know whether you're coming or going, you're having a genuine Freeway Experience.

Sometimes it's hard to exit a Los Angeles freeway. If you find yourself in such a predicament, just relax and enjoy the ride. Then skip over to the chapter on San Diego.

Don't get into that lane that doesn't have any traffic on it. That is the HOV (High Occupancy Vehicle) lane, which is meant for car-poolers. Minimum fine for an HOV boo-boo, such as driving by yourself, is $246.

Once you get where you hoped, and it's not San Diego, you'll need to park. Good luck. Take plenty of quarters wherever you go, or shell out for valet parking. The major hotels charge up to $20 a day for off-street parking.

Amuse Yourself

OK, if you're a kid at heart, maybe you'll want to go to one of the nearby amusement parks. Most of the parks are being constantly updated, with bigger and better thrill rides all the time, and lots of crowds.

Tomorrowland at **Disneyland**, 131 Harbor Blvd., 714/781-4565, www.disneyland.com, Anaheim, has been revamped. Check out the new Astro Orbitor, a self-piloted spaceship that soars through an animated model of planets and stars. A second park, Disney's California Adventure, will debut in Anaheim in 2001.

Knott's Berry Farm, 8039 Beach Blvd., Buena Park, 714/220-5200, has a ride that is 300 feet high. Supreme Scream will send you up as high as a 25-story building in three seconds, suspend you in midair for a few seconds, and then send you down at 50 mph. Wowie zowie.

l o s   a n g e l e s

Need tickets? Call either **Ticketmaster,** 213/381-2000, or **A Musical Chair,** 310/207-7070. **Times Tix,** located inside Jerry's Famous Deli in West Hollywood, 8791 Beverly Blvd., 310/659-3678, is the discount ticket outlet where you can get half-price tickets to more than 50 live theater performances.

Disabled visitors can get information on specially equipped buses by calling the **Los Angeles County Metropolitan Transit Authority,** 213/626-4455. General information is also available from the **Commission on Disabilities,** 213/974-1053 or 213/974-1707 (TDD).

For up-to-date information on entertainment options, look in the *LA Weekly* or the *New Times LA*, both alternative weeklies. The major dailies are the *Los Angeles Times* and the *Orange County Register.*

to go ▶

San Diego—not Los Angeles or San Francisco—is the kind of place that those in other parts of the world are most likely to think of when they picture California: a bucolic setting of sunshine and water, not yet shrouded in smog or grown into anonymous infinity, still full of dreams, still obsessed with the hope of greatness tomorrow.
—Neil Morgan, *San Diego Union-Tribune*

There's only one thing wrong with this city: There's nothing really wrong with it. You're going to come here, have a perfectly wonderful time, and come home with nothing much to complain about.

Bummer.

Part of the fun of travel is coming home with tales of travel travail and feeling superior about your hometown. You know: "Yeah, Paris has some great art museums, but at least good old Des Moines doesn't have such rude waiters." What are you going to say bad about San Diego?

The weather is as close to perfect as a place can be. A desert warmth combined with ocean breezes keeps winters and summers temperate (mid-60s in winter, mid-70s in summer), and skies almost always clear—no snow, no sleet, no hurricanes; and an average of 10 inches of rain a year.

It's easy to get around. People are friendly. A strong Hispanic influence adds to the cultural vitality—you're less than 30 minutes away from another country. The tourist attractions—San Diego Zoo, Balboa Park, Old Town—are world-class.

Oh, to heck with this getaway idea. Let's just move here.

Downtown San Diego

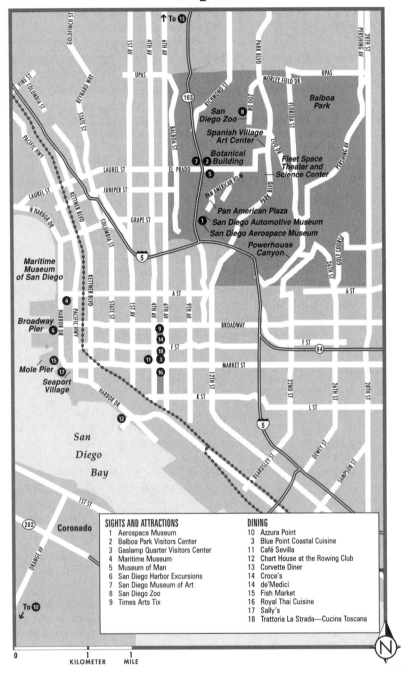

SIGHTS AND ATTRACTIONS
1 Aerospace Museum
2 Balboa Park Visitors Center
3 Gaslamp Quarter Visitors Center
4 Maritime Museum
5 Museum of Man
6 San Diego Harbor Excursions
7 San Diego Museum of Art
8 San Diego Zoo
9 Times Arts Tix

DINING
10 Azzura Point
3 Blue Point Coastal Cuisine
11 Café Sevilla
12 Chart House at the Rowing Club
13 Corvette Diner
14 Croce's
14 de'Medici
15 Fish Market
16 Royal Thai Cuisine
17 Sally's
18 Trattoria La Strada—Cucina Toscana

GETTING AROUND

With a population of 1.2 million, San Diego is America's seventh largest city and California's second largest.

The airport that serves all of these people is **San Diego International Airport, Lindbergh Field,** 619/231-2100, which has recently undergone a complete renovation—including the updating of both terminals, the addition of a pedestrian overpass, and the improvement of parking facilities.

The airport is only three miles northwest of downtown, with the major tourist areas just a bit farther. **Harbor Drive** is the scenic route to downtown, Balboa Park, and the rest of the good stuff. Along Harbor Drive is the **Embarcadero,** an area of wharves at the edge of the bay, and a great place to stroll.

For taxi service from the airport, call **Orange Cab,** 619/291-3333. The average rate for one to five persons is $2.00 for the first mile and $1.40 for each additional mile thereafter. Credit cards are accepted. Several airport shuttles are also available. Try **Cloud 9 Shuttle,** 800/9SHUTTLE.

You'll find that it's easy to move around in San Diego. The freeway system is manageable, and parking isn't a problem. Therefore you'll probably want a car, especially if you plan to take some short trips to some of the many interesting sights in San Diego County.

To the south and across the bay from the city is Coronado, which has the beach, some great hotels, and interesting shops. Farther south—less than an hour's drive—is Tijuana, Mexico. North of San Diego, up the coast, you'll find some beautiful seaside scenery, plus the towns of Mission Bay (home of Sea World) and the ritzy resort enclave of **La Jolla** (pronounced *la HOY-ya*).

Or what about a motor home for your excursions? Rent one of these dudes, see all the sights, and then just park it. **Norm's R.V. Rentals,** 12538 Poway Rd., 800/NORM-4-RVS, will fix you up. Naw, let's travel a little lighter. You can rent a Harley hawg at **Rebel,** 5600 Kearny Mesa Rd., 619/292-6200. They'll also take you on a guided tour.

But you don't *have* to rent a vehicle to enjoy your visit in San Diego. Although the city is too spread out for walking to make sense, public transportation works well. You can take the **San Diego Trolley,** which serves downtown's waterfront, Old Town, the Mexican border, and far into the suburbs. Shelter stops are convenient and easy to find. Fares range from $1.00 to $2.25, with a discounted rate of 75¢ for seniors and the disabled.

Day Tripper passes give riders one-day ($5), two-day ($8), and four-day ($12) unlimited access to **Metropolitan Transit System,** 619/233-3004 or 234-5005 (TTY/TTD), buses and the trolley. These tickets are available at the **Transit Store,** 102 Broadway, 619/234-1060.

SIGHTS AND ATTRACTIONS

In the heart of San Diego is **Balboa Park,** easily worth a whole day. It is just north of the central business district and, at 1,200 lush acres, is the largest cultural park in the nation.

Of the city's 90 museums, 14 are in Balboa Park. A few worth checking out include the following: The **San Diego Museum of Art,** 1450 El Prado, 619/232-7931, has an extensive collection of Italian Renaissance art, Asian art, and twentieth-century paintings. The **Museum of Man,** 1350 El Prado, 619/239-2001, has Egyptian artifacts and Mayan monoliths. And San Diego has always had a big part in aviation; the **Aerospace Museum,** 2001 Pan American Plaza, 619/234-8291, www.aerospacemuseum.org, tells about it. The museum has more than 65 aircraft and spacecraft.

You can experience 12 Balboa Park museums for $21 ($62 value) by purchasing a **Passport to Balboa Park,** which is good for an entire week. Museums in the park will have the coupon book, or get one at the **Balboa Park Visitors Center,** in the House of Hospitality, 1549 El Prado, 619/239-0512. Also try the **Times Arts Tix** booth downtown, Center Broadway Circle at Horton Plaza Park (open Tues–Sat, 10 a.m.–7 p.m.), 619/497-5000.

The **San Diego Zoo,** 2920 Zoo Dr., 619/234-3153, is another must-see, and it's also in Balboa Park. It's a 100-acre tropical garden containing 3,900 animals of 800 species. Be sure to see the Giant Pandas. The best way to see the zoo is on a three-mile guided bus tour. Once you get the lay of the land, you'll want to stroll among the lush hills and check out the bioclimatic exhibits such as Gorilla Tropics, Sun Bear Forest, and Polar Bear Plunge.

Also located in Balboa Park are the Reuben H. Fleet Space Theater and Science Center; the Simon Edison Centre for the Performing Arts (which includes the Old Globe Theatre, the Cassius Carter Centre Stage, and the Lowell Davies Festival Theatre); the Starlight Bowl; sports facilities; and the California Tower, which contains a 100-bell carillon that chimes every quarter hour.

The **Balboa Park Tram** provides convenient access to the park, beginning at the Inspiration Point parking lot and including 11 intermediate stops through the central core of the park. The tram is free.

After experiencing Balboa Park, head over to the **Gaslamp Quarter.** The Gaslamp Quarter is a 16-block historic downtown district that re-creates the spirit of Victorian times through the restoration of old buildings that now feature antiques, crafts, arts, restaurants, shops, and offices. Walking tours are held each Saturday, and audio tours are also available. Stop by the Gaslamp Quarter Visitors Center for information, 410 Island Ave., 619/233-5227.

The first European settlement in California was **Old Town,** where San Diego began. Here old adobes and other historic structures blend with restaurants and fascinating shops. Boosters of Old Town State Historic Park is a nonprofit organization that will tell you all about it in a tour. Visit the Old Town Visitors Center for details: 4002 Wallace St., 619/469-3174.

San Diego Bay practically defines the city. You can't miss it, and you shouldn't. Take a boat tour, such as one offered by **San Diego Harbor Excursions,** 1050 N. Harbor Dr., 619/234-4111. Nearby is the **Maritime Museum,** 1306 N. Harbor Dr., 619/234-9153, which includes a century-old windjammer, a steam ferry, and a steam yacht.

To the west of downtown San Diego is **Cabrillo National Monument,** Catalina Blvd., 619/557-5450, which commemorates the arrival of Portuguese explorer Juan Rodriguez Cabrillo on the coast of California in 1542. There's a spectacular view from the Old Point Loma Lighthouse. You can occasionally see California gray whales from up here.

Take a visit to La Jolla and visit the **Birch Aquarium at Scripps,** 2300 Expedition Wy., La Jolla, 619/534-FISH, which is the public education center for the world-renowned Scripps Institution of Oceanography. It's an interactive museum with more than 3,000 fish. Also in La Jolla, don't miss the stunningly beautiful **Museum of Contemporary Art,** 700 Prospect St., 619/454-3541. Just the view from all those windows is worth the price of the ticket (four dollars), but they'll throw in a provocative exhibition with it as well.

LODGING

San Diego has about 460 hotel and motel properties with over 45,000 rooms available to visitors. The average room rate is $56.50 per night,

Going Places

Highly recommended is **Old Town Trolley Tours**, 619/298-8687. The trolleylike buses make a circle through the high points of San Diego's tourist sites—the zoo, Old Town, Coronado. They also offer on-off privileges and stop beside many of the major hotels. Try this: Hop on the Old Town Trolley, take the complete circuit, and then double back to the spot that interests you. (One drawback: You'll have to put up with some pretty lame jokes from the drivers.)

But you haven't seen San Diego until you've seen it from the bay. Try **Harbor Excursions**, 1050 N. Harbor Dr., 619/234-4111. You'll get to see some of the huge U.S. Navy ships that are docked in the harbor. You can also take dinner and dance cruises or go winter whale-watching. A cheaper way to see things from the water is to take the San Diego–Coronado Ferry to Coronado, which is two dollars each way (pedestrians only).

according to Smith Travel Research. Rates are generally lower during the winter. If you're interested in staying at a B&B, call the **Bed & Breakfast Directory for San Diego,** 800/619-ROOMS, for a list of 30 homes and inns.

A hotel in the middle of things is the **Balboa Park Inn,** 3402 Park Blvd., 800/938-8181, $$. It has 26 suites, some with fireplaces and Jacuzzis, and you can almost hear the lions roar from the nearby San Diego Zoo.

The **Bristol Court Hotel,** 1055 First Ave., 800/662-4477, $$, has 102 units in a European setting, and you're within walking distance of Horton Plaza, the convention center, and the Gaslamp Quarter. The **Horton Grand,** 31 Island Ave., 800/542-1886, $$$, is a grand Victorian hotel near Horton Plaza, which pretty well explains its name. The rooms are filled with antiques in this Gaslamp Quarter beauty.

The **Hyatt Regency,** 1 Market Pl., 800/233-1234, $$$, offers a commanding, high-rise view of San Diego Bay, and that alone is almost worth the high-rise prices. It's in the middle of everything, next to Seaport Village.

A hotel with historic credentials and exquisite beauty is the **U.S. Grant,** 326 Broadway, 800/334-6957, $$$, which was built in 1910. It's in the heart of the business district. In the same league, and not too far away, is the **Westgate Hotel,** 1055 Second Ave., 800/221-3802, $$$, an elegant, European-style hotel in the center of the Gaslamp Quarter.

Sleep historically at the **Heritage Park Bed & Breakfast,** 2470 Heritage Park Row, 800/995-2470, $$, a Victorian mansion in Old Town. You get a candlelit breakfast, featherbeds, afternoon tea, and nightly film classics.

The **Hotel del Coronado,** 1500 Orange Ave., Coronado, 800/HOTELDEL, $$$$, is the grande dame of hotels in the area. This ocean-front resort has 692 units and a historical designation. It boasts 30 shops, a spa, a full-time activities program, nearby golf, sailing, and boating. If you can't afford to stay there, take a one-hour tour of the grounds or tour the history gallery.

Just down the road and way down in price is the **Coronado Inn,** 266 Orange Ave., Coronado, 800/598-6624, $. It has 30 units, free continental breakfast, a pool, and a coin-op laundry (something the Hotel del Coronado doesn't have). Also in Coronado is the European-style **Coronado Village Inn,** 1017 Park Pl., Coronado, 619/435-9318, $$. It's one block from the beach.

A hotel on a par with the Hotel del Coronado is **La Valencia Hotel,** 1152 Prospect St., La Jolla, 800/451-0772, $$$$, a pink palace of Spanish architecture perched on the cliffs and overlooking La Jolla Cove.

If you're willing to trade a bit of a drive for a place on the beach, consider the **Beach Cottages,** 4255 Ocean Blvd., 619/483-7440, $$. Actually, there are more than cottages here—also offered are suites, studios, motel rooms, and apartments.

The **Crown Point View Suites Hotel,** 4088 Crown Point Dr.,

Greater San Diego

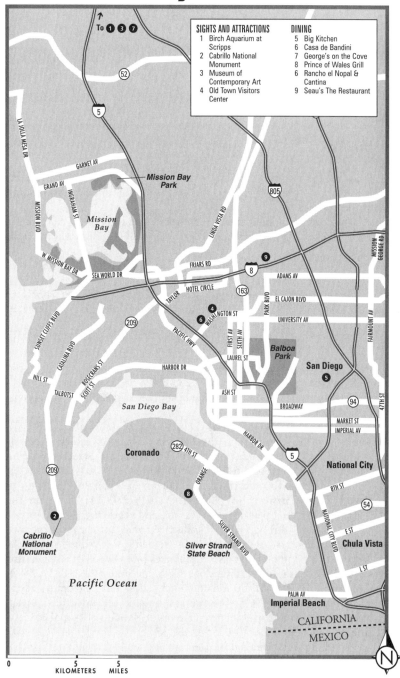

To ① ③ ⑦

SIGHTS AND ATTRACTIONS
1 Birch Aquarium at Scripps
2 Cabrillo National Monument
3 Museum of Contemporary Art
4 Old Town Visitors Center

DINING
5 Big Kitchen
6 Casa de Bandini
7 George's on the Cove
8 Prince of Wales Grill
6 Rancho el Nopal & Cantina
9 Seau's The Restaurant

LA JOLLA MESA DR
GARNET AV
GRAND AV
INGRAHAM ST
MISSION BLVD
Mission Bay Park
Mission Bay
LINDA VISTA RD
W. MISSION BAY DR
SEA WORLD DR
FRIARS RD
HOTEL CIRCLE
TAYLOR
ADAMS AV
PARK BLVD
EL CAJON BLVD
UNIVERSITY AV
FAIRMOUNT AV
MISSION GEORGE RD
SUNSET CLIFFS BLVD
CATALINA BLVD
ROSECRANS ST
SCOTT ST
HILL ST
TALBOT ST
PACIFIC HWY
WASHINGTON ST
FIRST AV
SIXTH AV
LAUREL ST
Balboa Park
San Diego
HARBOR DR
ASH ST
BROADWAY
San Diego Bay
47TH ST
MARKET ST
IMPERIAL AV
National City
HARBOR DR
Coronado
4TH ST
ORANGE
SILVER STRAND BLVD
8TH ST
NATIONAL CITY BLVD
E ST
Chula Vista
L ST
Cabrillo National Monument
Silver Strand State Beach
Pacific Ocean
PALM AV
Imperial Beach
CALIFORNIA
MEXICO

0   5   5
KILOMETERS   MILES

N

800/338-3331, $$, boasts water views of the rare bird sanctuary on Mission Bay. It offers kitchens, a buffet breakfast, and afternoon tea.

Humphrey's Half Moon Inn and Suites, 2303 Shelter Island Dr., 800/345-9995, $$$, has 182 units in a tropical setting on San Diego Bay, with harbor views, a pool, a spa, and lawn games.

The **Lodge at Torrey Pines,** 11480 N. Torrey Pines Rd., 619/453-4420, $$, overlooks the 18th green of the legendary golf course—and the Pacific Ocean, too. You'll have a bit of a drive to get to central San Diego, but maybe the view will make up for it.

DINING

Since the sea is only steps away, expect lots of fresh seafood here. Mexico, too, is only steps away, so look for the strong influence from South of the Border.

You can get oysters, sushi, and cocktails on the ground floor of the **Fish Market,** 750 N. Harbor Dr., 619/232-3474, $$, or go one floor up for the full menu. Highly recommended for its fresh seafood and low-fat California flair is **Blue Point Coastal Cuisine,** 565 Fifth Ave., 619/233-6623, $$$, in the Gaslamp Quarter.

The **Chart House at the Rowing Club,** 525 E. Harbor Dr., 619/233-7391, $$, has been around for several decades. It serves up steaks, fish, and beautiful views of the bay.

Sally's, at the Hyatt Regency, 1 Market Pl., 619/687-6080, $$$, is in a way-cool, super-sleek setting. It offers the cuisine of southern France, Italy, and coastal Spain. Kick up your heels and wash down some tapas at **Café Sevilla,** 555 Fourth Ave., 619/233-5979, $$, in the Gaslamp Quarter. The focus here is on the cuisine of southern Spain. Dinner is accompanied by a flamenco show.

Northern Italian cuisine is the specialty of **de'Medici,** 815 Fifth Ave., 619/702-7228, $$, in the Gaslamp Quarter. Another award-winning Italian restaurant nearby is **Trattoria La Strada—Cucina Toscana,** 702 Fifth Ave., 619/239-3400, $$.

If you want to dine where the Queen of Thailand dines, go to **Royal Thai Cuisine,** 467 Fifth Ave., 619/230-THAI, $$, in the Gaslamp Quarter. Specialties are seafood and vegetarian dishes.

San Diego's strong Hispanic influence comes through in some top-notch Mexican restaurants, and there are many from which to choose. A stand-out—and one that also emphasizes San Diego's other specialty, seafood—is **Casa de Bandini,** 2660 Calhoun St., 619/297-8211, $$, in Old Town. Try the shrimp and crab enchiladas. The restaurant's adobe structure, built in 1829, first served as a hotel in old San Diego. Nearby, you can get margaritas in seven flavors at **Rancho el Nopal & Cantina,** 2754 Calhoun St., 619/295-0584, $$.

Walking into **Seau's The Restaurant,** 1640 Camino del Rio N., #1376, 619/291-SEAU, $$, is like walking into a stadium, with a 25-

foot-long entrance tunnel, a football-shaped central dining area, and stadium seating. The restaurant has lots of sports memorabilia, too, and some all-American food. The owner is San Diego Charger's All-Pro linebacker Junior Seau. The restaurant is a hop, kick, and a jump from Qualcomm Stadium in the Mission Valley Center.

Ingrid Croce, widow of singer Jim Croce, established a restaurant in her husband's honor. Actually, **Croce's,** 802 Fifth Ave., 619/233-4355, $$, consists of two restaurants and three bars featuring American and southwestern cuisine and lots of memorabilia, plus live jazz and R&B nightly. It's in the Gaslamp Quarter.

The **Corvette Diner,** 3946 Fifth Ave. in Balboa Park, 619/542-1001, $, has been voted San Diego's favorite informal dining spot. You get 1950s atmosphere, American basics, a soda fountain, and rock-and-roll.

And how about an old-fashioned, two-fisted, uncomplicated breakfast? Breeze into **Big Kitchen,** 3003 Grape St. near Balboa Park, 619/234-5789, $, and get your fill for most of the day. This is where the locals hang out, and where struggling actors and musicians work. Whoopi Goldberg was one of them.

The **Prince of Wales Grill,** 1500 Orange Ave., Coronado, 619/435-6611, $$$, at the Hotel del Coronado offers top-of-the-line contemporary cuisine and jazz nightly. It's right on the ocean. Also in Coronado is **Azzura Point,** 4000 Coronado Bay Rd., 619/424-4400, $$$, in the Loews Coronado Bay Resort. The cuisine has a Mediterranean-Californian flair. *San Diego Magazine* annually cites it for "best hotel dining."

George's at the Cove, 1250 Prospect St., La Jolla, 619/454-4244, $$$, is a legendary, world-class restaurant. The cuisine is contemporary, the fish is fresh, and the view from the terrace is heart-stopping.

SHOPPING

Seaport Village, W. Harbor Dr. at Kettner Blvd., 619/235-4014, is a dining and shopping complex along the Embarcadero that is designed to depict the harborside as it was a century ago. It contains 4 major restaurants, 12 eateries, and 75 shops. While at Seaport Village you can get embroidered and imprinted sportswear, all of which features a San Diego theme, at **Crazy Shirts,** 619/595-0468.

A major center of shopping is **Fashion Valley,** I-8 and Hwy. 163 at Friars Rd. W., 619/688-9113, www.shop-fashionvalley.com, which boasts the area's only Neiman Marcus, along with stores such as Saks Fifth Avenue, Nordstorm, Macy's, Robinsons-May, and Tiffany & Co.

Another major center of shopping is **Horton Plaza,** bounded by Broadway, First Ave., G St., and Fourth Ave.—seven downtown city blocks of shopping, dining, entertainment, and award-winning architecture. It features 140 stores—including Nordstrom and FAO Schwarz—and a 14-screen theater.

Bazaar del Mundo, at the San Diego State Historical Park,

619/296-3161, www.bazaardelmundo.com, in Old Town is packed with interesting international shops and restaurants set among lush gardens and fountains with strolling mariachis.

An art gallery in the Gaslamp Quarter that specializes in Latin American furniture and art is **Galeria del Sol**, 528 Market St., 619/696-7311.

Or how about bringing something home that will leave a lasting impression. Get a genuine tattoo—the kind that San Diego sailors and Marines still get—with hula girls that wiggle with your muscles. **Tiger Jimmy,** 519 Broadway, 619/234-9419, will do it to you.

For Rodeo Drive–level shopping, go north to La Jolla. This is a good place to wander—it's a beautiful town perched on a seaside cliff. The shops of **Coast Walk** offer handmade jewelry and clothing. Stay for the sunset.

SPORTS AND RECREATION

The **San Diego Padres,** 619/881-6500, are the Major League Baseball team in town. And until April 2002, when a new ballpark is scheduled for completion, they play at Qualcomm Stadium, 944 Friars Rd. Qualcomm Stadium is also home to the **San Diego Chargers** pro football team, 619/280-2121.

San Diego is situated at the gateway to Mexico's rich fishing grounds, and it's easy to hook up with a charter fishing guide. A couple of possibilities are **Lee Palm's Sportfishers,** 619/224-3857, and **Fisherman's Landing,** 619/221-8500.

A few miles north is **Mission Bay**, a 4,600-acre aquatic playground devoted to boating, fishing, skiing, swimming, and board sailing. It has 27 miles of beaches with six designated swimming areas, plus picnic spots and lots of paths for bicycling and jogging.

Golf is big in San Diego. **Stand By Golf,** 888/825-GOLF, is a telephone reservation service that books guaranteed tee times for the following day at discounted prices.

San Diego Surfing Academy, 800/447-SURF, www.surfSDSA. com, offers personalized surfing lessons for people ages 8 to 80. It provides wet suits and surfboards.

Take a one- or three-day trip from San Diego to San Clemente with **San Diego Shark Diving Expeditions,** 619/299-8560. You'll be outfitted with scuba gear and lowered in a safety cage for a close-up view of divers in chain-mesh suits baiting the sharks, mostly blues and makos.

ENTERTAINMENT

San Diego's active theater scene is a breeding ground for Broadway hits and Broadway wanna-bes. Hits such as *Damn Yankees, How to*

Sail on San Diego Bay

Succeed in Business Without Really Trying, and *The Who's Tommy* got their start here.

The Tony Award–winning **La Jolla Playhouse,** 619/550-1010, has become one of the most respected theater companies in America. Innovative productions hit the stage from May through October at the Mandell Weiss Center for the Performing Arts, on the campus of the University of California—San Diego.

The **Lamb's Players Theatre,** 1142 Orange Ave., Coronado, 619/437-6050, has a year-round season of productions in a theater featuring intimate European-style seating. The **Old Globe Theatre,** in Balboa Park, 619/239-2255, produces 12 or more works annually on three stages. It puts the emphasis on Shakespeare in the summer. Special events such as the Mainly Mozart festival, musicals, and plays are presented at the historic **Spreckels Theatre** downtown, 121 Broadway, #600, 619/235-9500.

Or make theater a meal at dinner theaters in which the audience is invited to help solve the murder mystery. San Diego has two such offerings: **Mystery Café,** 619/544-1600, and **Murder Mystery Dinner Theater,** 619/295-5435.

The **Fern Street Circus,** 2469 Broadway, 619/235-9756, is a single-ring, theatrical circus group that performs at various outdoor settings.

The **California Ballet Company,** 8276 Ronson Rd., 619/560-5676, is dedicated to presenting a full season of professional ballet each year.

If playing pool is your thing, do it amid history in the **Gaslamp Billiard Palace,** 370 Fourth Ave., 619/230-1968. Cocktails are available.

Or how about a one-hour cruise by gondola? The gondolier will be dressed in the traditional striped shirt and hat with ribbon. Each gondola can carry up to six passengers, and the one-hour ride includes Italian music, hors d'oeuvres, and wine upon request. Call **Gondola di Venezia,** 619/221-2999.

South of the Border

Just 17 miles to the south of San Diego is a whole new world: Mexico.

More than 60 million people cross the border at Tijuana each year. You can take the San Diego Trolley in downtown San Diego for just $2.25; or you can drive, park on the U.S. side, and either walk across or take a bus that will pick you up in the parking lot.

If you drive across the border, Mexican insurance is recommended and is readily available on the border.

Tijuana is a great place to wander. The *mercados* (markets) and old-fashioned bazaars are full of colorful native crafts. Ask the price, then offer less. Dickering over prices is expected. Tijuana is a duty-free zone, and the devaluation of the peso makes finding bargains a snap.

Head for the main streets of Avenida Revolucion, Caliente Boulevard, and Paseo de Los Heroes for lots of shopping and restaurants. This is also where the high-tech discos rock the night away.

If you'd prefer to take a package tour of Mexico, many are available. Try Daytripper Tours, 800/679-8747. Gray Line, 800/331-5077, is another option.

Times Arts Tix, Center Broadway Circle at Horton Plaza Park (open Tues–Sat, 10 a.m.–7 p.m.), 619/497-5000, has half-price, day-of-performance tickets and full-price, advance-sale tickets for theater, music, and dance attractions. Call for daily listings. Also, tickets for Sunday events are available for half-price on Saturday; cash only is accepted. You can also get discounted admissions for the San Diego Zoo, Wild Animal Park, Sea World, and Gray Line Tours.

CITY BASICS

For more information on what to do and see in San Diego, contact the **San Diego Convention & Visitors Bureau** or check out their Web site: 401 B St., Suite 1400, San Diego, CA 92101-4237; 619/236-1212; www.sandiego.org. While in San Diego, visit the **International Visitor Information Center,** 11 Horton Plaza at First Ave. and F St. The disabled can get information on specialized tours and transportation through **Accessible San Diego,** P.O. Box 124526, San Diego, CA 92112-4526; 619/279-0704.

The *San Diego Union-Tribune* is the major daily newspaper. You can find entertainment news in *San Diego Secrets* and *San Diego Source*, two weeklies, plus *San Diego Magazine*.

⑱ LAS VEGAS
....
to go ▶

I came to Las Vegas in a $10,000 Cadillac and went home in a $100,000 Greyhound bus.
—Milton Berle

If you haven't been to Las Vegas lately, you haven't been to Las Vegas. The place is growing and reinventing itself almost hourly.

Something around 4,000 people a month are moving here, making Las Vegas the fastest growing city in the United States. And then there are the 30-million–plus visitors who come here annually, which is more than the annual attendance of all of America's major amusement parks combined.

The reason for all this growth and reinvention is simple: Competition. And the stakes are high.

Other states have seen the revenue potential in gambling, and have made it legal. So it's become a lot easier, and quicker, for Americans to get to a gaming table. Las Vegas has figured that out. So in order to keep the vacationers coming, the city's casinos have made sure that people will have a lot more to do than just pull the arm of a one-armed bandit.

High-end shopping, world-class restaurants, and first-class shows are everywhere. And the resorts have become kingdoms of entertainment in themselves, creating themed fantasy lands, or what others have called a Disneyland for adults.

Instead of mouse characters, however, you'll be greeted by pirates or pharaohs or showgirls in feathers. Just like at the most popular rides, you'll have to stand in line, but this time it's for the buffet. Lots of

Las Vegas

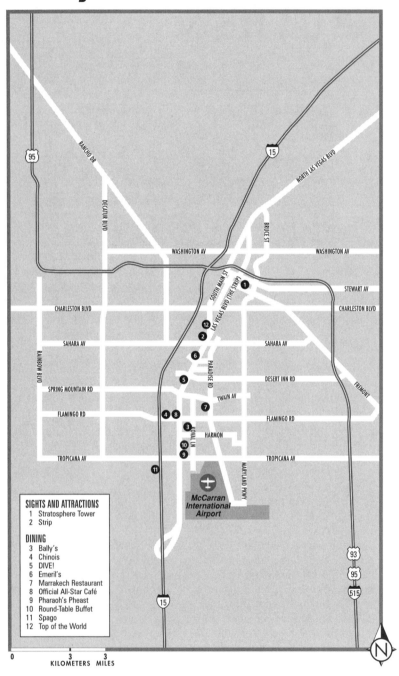

SIGHTS AND ATTRACTIONS
1 Stratosphere Tower
2 Strip

DINING
3 Bally's
4 Chinois
5 DIVE!
6 Emeril's
7 Marrakech Restaurant
8 Official All-Star Café
9 Pharaoh's Pheast
10 Round-Table Buffet
11 Spago
12 Top of the World

McCarran International Airport

0   3   3
KILOMETERS MILES

shops will take your money. And the wildest ride will be watching your fortunes rise and fall at the roulette table.

In the end, more than likely, the last of your stash will get raked in by the croupier. It's a sinking feeling, kind of like a roller coaster, except it costs a lot more.

Welcome to the American Dream. Please fasten your seat belts.

GETTING AROUND

Welcome to the madhouse.

When you step off your plane and into **McCarran International Airport,** 702/261-5743, you'll know at once that you aren't in Kansas anymore. The first thing you'll hear is the ringy-dingy of slot machines, and the first thing you'll notice is a whole lot of people who've brought a whole lot of energy to expend, and it might seem that all of them are in the airport at once.

Dive in. And hold on to your hat.

The airport is one of the busiest in the world. A recent addition is the D concourse, a little piece of architectural drama (including a 45-foot-tall panoramic window) that will get you ready for the sensory drama to come. You'll notice shops and restaurants with beckoning neon—something to whet your appetite for what's just outside the airport.

Las Vegas is easy for the quick visit. You really only have to remember two places, the **Strip** and **Downtown.** And you'll have only one problem: getting from here to there.

Getting out of the airport won't be easy. Be patient. As big and wonderful as the expanding airport is, it's not growing fast enough to handle the glut of passengers, something of which you will probably be a part. Relax. Vegas wants your money, and its entrepreneurs act like it. This whole town is customer-friendly. Finding a ride to your hotel is not as difficult as it seems.

Unless you're wanting to get out of town to visit some of the other, smaller resort towns or attractions, don't get a car. Traffic on Las Vegas Boulevard—the Strip—is horrendous. A taxi ride to a Strip hotel will cost you from $7 to $10; to Downtown, it will be between $10 and $18, depending on the route. Many taxis are available. One company to look for is **Yellow Cab,** 702/873-2227. If you'd prefer using a shuttle service, one such provider is **Gray Line,** 702/384-1234. Just step out of the airport and get a Gray Line ticket. Then get in line in front of the sign for your hotel. Or you can go in style with a Lincoln limo. Call **On Demand Sedan,** 702/876-2222.

For moving up and down the Strip, you can take a city bus. The fare is $1.50. By the way, because traffic is heavy most of the time, that bus is going to get you there about as fast as a taxi.

Another way to get around—and it's the most fun—is to move from resort to resort along the Strip, walking through the casinos and beside the shops and restaurants. It's like moving from mall to mall, but the scenery is more interesting. And you can travel across the world and through history—from an Italian villa to Monte Carlo to ancient Egypt to New York City, all within a few blocks.

Some of the resorts make it easy for you. For instance, there's a monorail from Bellagio to the Monte Carlo (same owner, naturally), so you can save some shoe leather if you want. A mile-long monorail links the MGM Grand and Bally's. Another links Mandalay Bay with Excalibur and Luxor.

SIGHTS AND ATTRACTIONS

It's hard to know if the megacasinos should be listed under Sights and Attractions, Lodging, Dining, or Entertainment. They are meant to be all of the above, and designed to hold you in their grasp for the duration of your vacation. And, honestly, if you pick the one that fits your needs, you won't need to go anywhere else. Each is a world unto itself.

Get yourself in the right mood with a pre-trip view of *Viva Las Vegas*, Elvis Presley's hunka hunka burnin' schlock. Race car driver Lucky Jackson has an unlucky moment and must work as a waiter in a casino. Here comes Ann-Margret, and his luck changes. Guess who wins the big race at the end?

Only 35 miles from Las Vegas is one of the engineering wonders of the world—**Hoover Dam**. It's an amazing place. The 726-foot-high dam on the Colorado River was completed in 1935 and formed Lake Mead, which is a water source for 25 million people.

Tours are available daily, which take visitors deep inside the monolith. A new $125 million visitors center, with some amazing views, was opened in 1995. Ask your hotel concierge about transportation to the dam.

And here are a few tips on tips: Bartenders and cocktail waitresses generally receive $1 per round for parties of two to four, and more for larger groups. It's customary for winners to tip keno runners, slot machine change persons, or casino dealers. Some gamblers who play for long periods tip casino personnel whether they're a winner or not. Many showrooms sell assigned seating tickets, which may include the tip. In showrooms that accept restaurant-style reservations and seating, it is customary to tip the maitre d' $5 to $20 to improve seating.

City Survival Tips

The biggest attraction in Las Vegas is the **Strip** itself, Las Vegas Blvd. from around Reno Ave. to Saraha Ave. The Strip is a trip, and you simply must, by walking or riding, take in the length of it and marvel at the magnitude of its displays of imagination, its chutzpah, its sheer over-the-top-ness. It is a masterpiece of mixed metaphors.

Cities, civilizations, and eras are re-created, each cheek-by-jowl to the next—New York City, Egypt, ancient Rome, Venice, Paris, New Orleans, Monte Carlo, pirates, a showboat, a South Seas island, flamingoes, an erupting volcano, dancing water, Rio, King Arthur, a circus, Bugs Bunny, Bugsy Siegel, Barbary Coast, and who knows what might be next. Hotel Monica, featuring an Oval Office–themed revolving restaurant?

Among the many wonders, check out the 1,149-foot-high **Stratosphere Tower,** 2000 Las Vegas Blvd. S. at Main St., 702/380-7777 or 800/998-6937, which is America's tallest free-standing observation tower and the tallest building west of the Mississippi. It features a revolving restaurant, indoor and outdoor observation decks, a shopping mall, and a G-force–defying thrill ride at the top of the tower called **Big Shot.** The world's highest roller coaster, **High Roller,** circles the top of the tower. You can't miss it, just like you can't miss all these other worlds of fantasy.

LODGING

The major resorts and hotels are listed below in two categories—the Strip and Downtown. Generally, the less expensive places are downtown. For help with reservations, call the **Las Vegas Convention and Visitors Authority,** 800/332-5333 (Mon-Sat 7 a.m.-7 p.m. Pacific Time; Sun 8:30 a.m.-6 p.m.). Another resource is **Hotel Reservations Network,** 800/511-5323, www.vegashotel.com.

Hotels stay pretty well booked-up, especially during the major conventions, so calling ahead is a good idea. That's how you'll get the best discounts, too. But if you just wheeled into town and started calling around, we bet you could find something—Las Vegas has more than 130,000 hotel rooms.

The Strip
Recluse billionaire Howard Hughes lived on the ninth floor of the **Desert Inn,** 3145 Las Vegas Blvd. S., 800/634-6906, $$$$, in 1967 when he was asked to vacate to make room for high rollers. To keep that from happening, Hughes simply bought the hotel and then began a series of renovations that continued after his death and that have put the Desert Inn at the top of the heap. Today it is a top-notch, 715-room hotel with a legendary golf course.

Julius keeps adding to his digs, making **Caesars Palace,** 3570 Las Vegas Blvd. S., 800/634-6661, $$$$, one of the premier hotels. It is 85 acres of extravagance in the heart of the Strip. It recently expanded to 2,471 rooms with a bigger casino. It also includes a $100 million mall called Forum Shops, as well as numerous restaurants, a huge health spa, and the 4.5-acre Garden of the Gods outdoor area with three swimming pools and many statues.

Circus Circus, 2880 Las Vegas Blvd. S., 800/444-CIRCUS, $$, besides having the usual casino and 3,744 rooms, also contains a whole floor of carnival games, arcade games, and a free circus arena in which trapeze fliers, high-wire daredevils, acrobats, jugglers, and clowns perform. It also includes the Adventuredome, America's largest indoor theme park.

Visitors to **The Mirage,** 3400 Las Vegas Blvd. S., 800/627-6667, $$$, walk into a Polynesian paradise of lush gardens under a 90-foot-high, glass-enclosed atrium. Out front, a giant volcano erupts every 15 minutes at night. This is where famed magicians Siegfried and Roy and their white tigers hang out.

Actually it kind of makes sense that a giant pyramid could find a home in the desert of Las Vegas. But a pyramid with room service? Well, why not. To get to your room at **Luxor,** 3900 Las Vegas Blvd. S., 800/288-1000, $$, after walking beneath a massive sphinx on the outside, you take an inclinator, not an elevator, which travels up the slopes of the 350-foot pyramid at a 39-degree angle.

The **MGM Grand,** 3799 Las Vegas Blvd. S., 800/929-1112, $$$, calls itself the "City of Entertainment." You'll see why. It has all kinds of restaurants, three live theaters, shops, pools, four lighted tennis courts, a 16,000-seat arena, and more than 5,000 rooms, including a new luxury addition called The Mansion.

Almost next door is "the best city in Las Vegas," also known as **New York-New York,** 3790 Las Vegas Blvd. S., 800/NY-FOR-ME, $$. A replica of the Statue of Liberty is the resort's signature, and it is backed by 12 New York City–styled hotel towers, including knockoffs of the Empire State Building (at 47 stories) and the Chrysler Building (at 40 stories). A Coney Island Cyclone-styled roller coaster, named the Manhattan Express, travels at speeds up to 65 mph.

Four major resorts have sprouted on the Strip in the last couple of years. **Bellagio,** 3400 Las Vegas Blvd. S., 888/987-1111, $$$, is the first, with 36 stories of opulence inspired by the village of Bellagio on the shores of northern Italy's magnificent Lake Como. The signature of the hotel is its eight-acre lake in the front, where an extraordinarily choreographed ballet of water, music, and lights performs several times a day. The resort is also home to a $300 million art collection that specializes in treasures of Impressionism.

Say "Oui!" from atop a replica of the 50-story Eiffel Tower at the **Paris-Las Vegas Casino Resort,** 3655 Las Vegas Blvd. S., 888/266 2687, $$$, next to Bally's. There's a gourmet restaurant up there, or you can take a look from the observation deck. Also part of the re-creation are the Arc de Triomphe, the Champs Elysees, and the Paris Opera

The Strip beckons at night

House. The hotel has almost 3,000 rooms, 8 French restaurants, and the largest ballroom in Vegas.

With 6,000 suites, the **Venetian Casino Resort,** 3355 Las Vegas Blvd. S., 888/2-VENICE, $$$, is the world's largest resort hotel, where you can paddle down the canals or walk in wonder through a replica of St. Mark's Square. Included is a 63,000-square-foot fitness club.

The newly opened **Aladdin Resort and Casino,** 3667 Las Vegas Blvd. S., 702/736-0111, www.aladdincasino.com, $$$, has all the expected amenities of the megaresort wrapped in a Middle Eastern aura. It combines two hotels for a total of 3,600 rooms, and it has a health spa and fitness center, 7 restaurants, the 7,000-seat Aladdin Theater, and a 10,000-square-foot casino—plus a European gaming salon for high rollers.

If you don't enjoy the razzle-dazzle of the casinos, you might want to consider staying at the quietly plush **Four Seasons,** 877/632-7700, $$$$, a resort inside the 3,700-room **Mandalay Bay** hotel/casino, 3950 Las Vegas Blvd. S., 877/632-5200, $$$. The Four Seasons has its own entrance and 424 rooms on the 35th through the 39th floors, plus all the amenities you expect from the high-end chain. And you're only minutes away from the bright lights of the casinos and the big hair of the Elvis impersonators. Mandalay Bay features a 10-acre tropical lagoon complete with a sand-and-surf beach, a lazy river ride, and a swim-up shark tank.

The Strip has more than just the super-duper expensive resorts. In their shadows are plenty of less expensive places to stay, and you're still free to walk through the casinos and lobbies of the big boys.

Try the **Algiers Hotel,** 2845 Las Vegas Blvd. S., 800/732-3361, $$, which is across the street from Circus Circus and four blocks from the convention center. It offers hotel accommodations at motel rates.

The **Imperial Palace,** 3535 Las Vegas Blvd. S., 800/634-6441, $$, is in the heart of the Strip. Here you'll get all the expected stuff—

restaurants, bars, swimming, big casino—at less expensive rates. It's across the street from Caesars Palace.

Downtown
The center of hotels and casinos downtown is the **Fremont Street Experience.** It's a 90-foot-high canopy over four acres of the casino-lined (and traffic-free) street. Moving images created by 2.1 million lights dance overhead. The canopy comes to life hourly after dark in a

—Chancing It————

There's only one way to win at the casinos of Las Vegas: Have fun. If you're not having fun, you might as well stay home. Then for sure you won't come home a sore loser.

Face it: The odds are against you. If they weren't, lots of smart people with big money wouldn't be betting against you. We're talking about the casino investors.

A city that was built on dreams can be a rude awakening if you aren't careful, and it can be a lot of fun if you are careful. It's a matter of attitude.

Las Vegas doesn't take itself too seriously, and neither should you. If you've come to make a profit—if visions of jackpots dance in your head—you're going to get in trouble pretty quickly

Remember that Las Vegas is a city built by losers, hence Milton Berle's nickname for the place, "Lost Wages." When you first see it, you'll see that it took a lot of losers to make this place what it is, and what it keeps becoming. The trick is to contribute as little as possible to the city's bottom line, but just enough to have a good time, too.

So, then, how can you come home with less money than you started with and still have fun?

1. Give yourself a spending limit. You know your own comfort zone. Stay on this side of it and stay comfortable. When you cross that imaginary line for the day, go do something else, or watch somebody else lose.

2. Winning is more fun than losing. If, somehow, you hit it big—let's say 240 quarters from a slot machine—quit while you're ahead. Cash in your coins and spend your winnings in the mall, or go to a nice restaurant and get the biggest steak. You're a winner! Act like it!

3. Before you go, do your homework. You'll have a lot more fun if you know what you're doing, or at least have an inkling. The Internet has lots of information on the games—try **www.casinogambling.com**. Ask for the *Las Vegas Gambling Guide* from the city's Convention and Visitors Authority Visitor Information Center, 3150 Paradise Rd., Las Vegas, NV 89109-9096; 702/892-7575, **www.lasvegas24hours.com**. Also, some hotels offer free gaming lessons. Ask the concierge.

Las Vegas puts on its running shoes each February with the **International Marathon**, 702/892-7575.

The **International Black Heritage Festival**, 702/454-1212, is held in August. Music, dancing, and folklore are just part of the two-day event. Put on your life jackets and come to the **Formula One** boat races, 864/261-7777, held each September at nearby Lake Mead.

Western heritage runs deep in Vegas. Each December you can attend the **National Finals Rodeo**, 702/895-3900.

events HORIZON

six-minute, computer-driven show that also includes wrap-around sound and music.

The **Golden Nugget,** 129 E. Fremont St., 800/634-3454, $$, with 1,907 rooms and suites, has recently been remodeled. Giant crystal chandeliers and marble make the place shine. It has five restaurants and a huge casino.

Lady Luck, 206 N. Third St., 800/523-9582, $, features a 24-story luxury tower, in-room refrigerators, suites with Jacuzzis, and three restaurants. Rates start at about $50, but sometimes you can do better.

Boasting of downtown's only microbrewery is **Main Street Station,** 200 N. Main St., 800/465-0711, $, a hotel with a Victorian theme containing $4 million in antiques.

Lots of motels downtown make Vegas an inexpensive destination if you're willing to walk a bit or ride a bus to get to the center of the action. Try the **Downtowner Motel,** 129 N. Eighth St., 800/777-2566, $, which offers free breakfast, snacks, and coffee all day.

DINING

As with everything else, Las Vegas is going out of its way to give you a reason to visit. Dining has become a big part of the lure. The bigger hotels have hired chefs with international reputations, making high-end restaurants easy to find. At the same time, the traditional bargain buffets are still around, as are all sorts of restaurants in the middle.

DIVE!, 3200 Las Vegas Blvd. S., 702/369-DIVE, $$, takes its submarine sandwiches seriously. You'll feel like you're under water when you order your sub, and that's the whole idea. They offer salads and pizza, too.

Spago, in the Forum Shops of Caesars Palace, 3570 Las Vegas Blvd. S., 702/369-6300, $$$$, is about as good as it gets. Wolfgang Puck has brought Las Vegas his signature American cuisine—fresh and

Desert Days

Want an almost sure bet? Put your money on sunshine. On average, Las Vegas has 320 clear days per year. Average rainfall is 4.19 inches per year.

Summer days are often over 100 degrees Fahrenheit. The air is dry, but that doesn't mean you aren't going to sweat if you get outside (or if you get into a heated game of craps on the inside). Some resorts provide misters to cool the air as you walk down their sidewalks.

That dry air is just as prevalent in the winter, so if you're subject to itchy skin, bring your lotion. You'll notice the dryness in your voice, too, so stay close to a source of liquid, which won't be that hard here. And although high temperatures average between 50 and 60 in the winter, don't forget your jacket. Temperatures drop precipitously at nightfall, and the wind can make things even more uncomfortable.

In the milder fall and spring, temperatures average in the 70s. This is the ideal time if you want to enjoy the desert landscape. But if all you want to do is eat, shop, and gamble, like most folks, the weather will be manufactured to your liking. At the **Forum Shops** mall of Caesars Palace, they'll even provide a perfect sky for you, with a sunrise and sunset every hour.

---

lively ingredients combining European and Asian influences. Also here is **Chinois,** 702/737-9700, $$$$, Puck's Chinese and Japanese restaurant where sushi and sashimi are specialties.

Traditional favorites such as burgers, buffalo wings, and salads are available among the sports memorabilia at the **Official All-Star Café,** 3500 Las Vegas Blvd. S., 702/795-TEAM, $$.

You'll be on **Top of the World,** 800/99-TOWER, $$$$, at the restaurant atop the 833-foot-high Stratosphere, 2000 Las Vegas Blvd. South. Steaks, fish, and lobster are specialties. You'll revolve once an hour.

The buffets are ubiquitous in Las Vegas. Why not try the one at **Bally's** (3645 Las Vegas Blvd. S., 702/739-4930, $$)? It features all-you-can-eat shrimp at brunch and special Chinese selections at dinner. The **Round-Table Buffet** at the Excalibur, 3850 Las Vegas Blvd. S., 800/979-1379, $$, is fit for a King Arthur, with royal-size portions. You can stick with the regal theme at **Pharaoh's Pheast** at the Luxor, 3900 Las Vegas Blvd. S., 800/288-1000, $$.

Specialty food is easy to find. **Emeril's,** at the MGM Grand, 2799 Las Vegas Blvd. S., 800/929-1111, $$$$, has brought its taste of New Orleans to the MGM Grand.

And if you just can't get enough of the famous Las Vegas jiggle, try the **Marrakech Restaurant,** 3900 Paradise Rd., 702/737-5611, $$, which offers belly dancing along with the Moroccan cuisine. It's open for dinner only.

SHOPPING

Las Vegas has figured out that visitors put shopping near the top of their list of fun things to do. (All you have to do is add up the receipts to figure this out—$25 billion in 1997.) Las Vegas makes it easy for you.

Convenience is a priority. In the big resorts, shopping is right there, between your room and the casino or the restaurant or the theater—in fact, you can't get from here to there without passing some of the world's top franchises.

Probably the best example is the **Forum Shops of Caesars Palace,** which features 140 specialty retailers and upscale restaurants, and it's all right there just beyond the casinos. Stores include an FAO Schwarz toy store, a Virgin Megastore, and Caviarteria, which specializes in caviar and other delicacies.

The **Bellagio** resort features Chanel, Hermes, Armani, and Tiffany. The **Paris** resort has 31,000 square feet of upscale French retail shopping. You'll walk down cobblestone streets among boutiques, a garden shop, a wine and cheese shop, men's and women's apparel, and more.

At the Venetian Resort Hotel, wander through 500,000 square feet of retail space among the **Grand Canal Shoppes.** There are 90 shops and boutiques along a quarter-mile Venetian street. The **Aladdin** has a Middle East–theme shopping and entertainment area of 450,000 square feet.

Beyond the resorts, the **Fashion Show Mall,** Las Vegas Blvd. and Spring Mountain Rd., features stores such as Neiman Marcus, Saks Fifth Avenue, Macy's, Dillard's, Robinsons-May Co., and more than 140 other boutiques and shops.

Not far out of town, on the well-traveled Interstate 15 that leads to southern California, is the **Fashion Outlet Mall.** Behind a facade of sky-wide fashion ads is 400,000 square feet of retail space that includes such stores as Williams-Sonoma, Brooks Brothers, Calvin Klein, Tommy Hilfiger, Jhane Barnes, Last Call from Neiman Marcus, Kenneth Cole, Escada, and Donna Karan. Their wares are all 20 to 70 percent off. It might be worth a trip.

SPORTS AND RECREATION

Ready for some fun? **Rebel Adventure Tours,** 702/380-6969, www.localslovelasvegas.com/rebel, will take you on a desert adventure in a Hummer. Or take it a little slower on a bicycle. **Escape the City Streets,** 6221 W. Charleston Blvd., #101, 702/596-2953, offers bike tours of Red Rock Canyon, plus daily wilderness tours. They'll even throw in a shirt.

Take a raft down the mighty Colorado River with **Black Canyon Raft Tours,** 1297 Nevada Hwy., Boulder City, 800/696-RAFT. You'll float from Hoover Dam to the Willow Bay Resort and Marina, and they'll pick you up at your hotel beforehand.

You can go bowling on one of 56 lanes and place a bet, too, at **Sam's Town Hotel & Gambling Hall,** 5111 Boulder Hwy., 800/634-6371.

The **Richard Petty Driving Experience,** 800/BE-PETTY, at the Las Vegas Motor Speedway, 7000 Las Vegas Blvd. N., 702/644-4443, allows you to hop into a genuine stock car and take it for a three-lap spin around the racing oval. Also, you can watch NASCAR and NHRA races there.

OK, so you lost your life savings at the casino and you're ready to jump . . . why not take a parachute along? Call **Skydive Las Vegas,** 806 Buchanan Blvd., 800/SKYDIVE. You'll jump from two miles up, free-fall for 46 seconds at 120 miles per hour, and then get a 6-minute parachute ride, all with an instructor. Rates run from $115 to $200.

Golf is the major outdoor sport in Las Vegas, and there are lots of courses available. The city's courses are home to the Las Vegas Invitational, the ITT LPGA Tour Championship, and the Las Vegas Senior

⎯Neon Nuptials⎯

Look, marriage is a crap shoot anyway, so why not acknowledge the fact and get hitched in Vegas? More than 100,000 couples do it every year.

And why not? It's simple and cheap.

You both have to show up at the Clark County Courthouse, and you'll have to shell out $35 for the license. There's no blood test, no waiting. Just make sure you're 18 years old. (But remember that you must be 21 to enter the casinos in town; you can gamble away your life, but not your money.)

Las Vegas has more than 60 wedding chapels in town, but that's barely enough during the most popular times for weddings—New Year's Eve and Valentine's Day. At the courthouse, couples will be waiting around the block for licenses then.

But once you've got the license, the rest is easy. If you're in a hurry, check out one of the drive-through chapels. An Elvis impersonator will help you tie the knot in some places. Or you can do it on a mountain, diving from a plane, or in a faux jungle, Tarzan-style.

If the urge to merge hits you at an inopportune time, remember that many of the chapels are open 24 hours.

The **Little Church of the West**, 3960 Las Vegas Blvd. S., 800/821-2452, has been performing services at the Hacienda Hotel since 1942. They've got flowers, music, and photographers available.

An Elvis minister will perform your service at **Viva Las Vegas Wedding Chapel**, 272 S. Ninth St., 800/574-4450. You can also go for a beach party, Camelot, Victorian, or gangster theme, or come up with your own idea.

Classic. Green fees vary from $15 to $100, and reservations are advised. Ask your hotel concierge for help.

Vegas doesn't have much in the way of professional sports. However, the minor-league **Las Vegas Stars,** 702/386-7200, play baseball at the Cashman Field Center, 850 Las Vegas Blvd. N. For basketball, the **University of Las Vegas Runnin' Rebels,** 702/895-3900, play at the Thomas and Mack Center, 702/895-3761.

ENTERTAINMENT

If you like your entertainment over the top, Las Vegas is the place for you. There's no such thing as too many sequins or feathers in this town.

All the major resorts have long-running shows or rotating headliners. Call ahead for information and tickets to the particular hotel, or request a free copy of *Showguide* from the Las Vegas Convention and Visitors Authority, 702/892-0711.

Most hotels use a ticket-only policy, but some take reservations on the phone similar to calling a restaurant. Prices range from $9 to $100 or more per person depending on the entertainer or the lavishness of the production. Some showroom tickets include drinks, tip, and tax; others don't. Sometimes a show can include dinner. So call ahead for policies and prices.

Some of the shows that have been running for years, and will probably be running for even more years, are *Jubilee,* 800/237-SHOW, a tribute to American music that climaxes with the sinking of the *Titanic.* It's at Bally's. Or see the surrealistic circus called *Mystere,* 800/392-1999, www.cirquedusoleil.com, by the Cirque du Soleil at The Mirage. A similarly fantasy-driven, acrobatic show over water is *O,* 888/488-7111, www.cirquedusoleil.com, also by the Cirque du Soleil and featured at the Bellagio. Not to be forgotten are **Siegfried and Roy,** 702/792-7777, who make an elephant disappear at their super-glitzy magic show at The Mirage.

And finally, he was Mr. Las Vegas. No, not Elvis . . . Liberace. The **Liberace Museum,** 1775 E. Tropicana Ave., 702/798-5595, shows off his glittering costumes, jewels, piano (with candelabras), and exotic cars. This place is a must. Understand Liberace and you'll understand Las Vegas.

CITY BASICS

One of the most comprehensive Web sites for Las Vegas information is the one sponsored by the **Las Vegas Convention and Visitors Authority,** 3150 Paradise Rd., Las Vegas, NV 89109-9096; 702/892-7575; www.lasvegas24hours.com. There you'll find an events calendar, maps, and information about lodging, attractions, dining, and weddings. For $4.95 you can get a **CD-ROM,** 877/MY-VEGAS, with the same kind of information, plus you get a slot-machine game to tide you over until you arrive. Call for details.

What's On in Las Vegas and the *Las Vegas Weekly* are a couple of sources for entertainment news in town. Another is *Neon*, the Friday entertainment supplement in the *Las Vegas Review Journal.*

⑲ DENVER

to go ▶

> *There were smokestacks, smoke, railyards, red-brick buildings, and the distant downtown graystone buildings, and here I was in Denver. He let me off at Larimer Street. I stumbled along with the most wicked grin of joy in the world, among the old bums and beat cowboys of Larimer Street.*
> —Jack Kerouac, *On the Road*

One word sums up this city: *Fresh.*

Fresh faces, fresh ideas, fresh money (the U.S. Mint), Rocky Mountain streams, and snow-kissed breezes.

Those fresh faces come from the young population—Denver is the baby boomer capital of America, with the highest percentage (one-third) of its population between ages 35 and 54.

Those hard-driving boomers like to play hard, and Denver's near-by mountains beckon, helping make the city the thinnest in America. (We're not sure who lined up and weighed all these people, but it's an interesting statistic nonetheless.)

Denver is also the most educated city in the United States—more than 90 percent of its metro population of 2.2 million has a high school diploma. The national average is around 80 percent.

All those smart, thin, active people want a place to have fun, and downtown Denver is their playground, with clubs and restaurants, lots of boutiques and boutique hotels, and a mile-long pedestrian promenade.

The Mile High City sits tall in the saddle. It's a great place for a getaway.

Denver

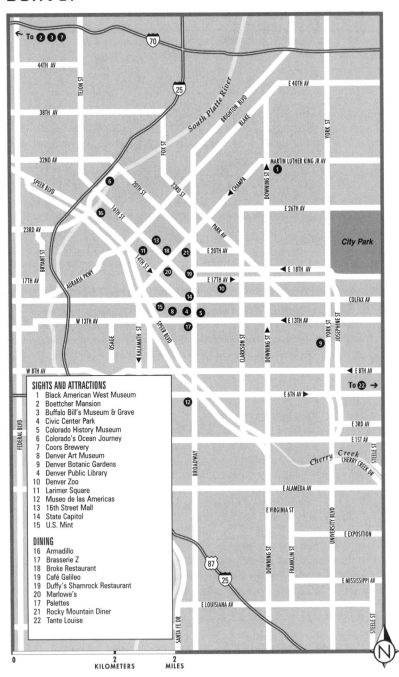

GETTING AROUND

You'll be arriving in one of the aviation wonders of the world—**Denver International Airport,** 303/342-2200, www.info-denver.denver.co.us/ ~aviation.com. It opened in 1995 and cost $4.3 billion to build. It had a few bugs to work out (the high-tech luggage distribution system developed an appetite for suitcases, dozens of which were chewed up and spit out), but all that's fixed now.

The roof of the main terminal is made of Teflon-coated fabric that is shaped into 34 peaks, just like the Rockies that you see from the huge windows. Soft light filters through the Great Hall from the roof—and that Great Hall is pretty great. It's as big as four football fields.

Should you get a car? Probably not. Denver is a congested city, especially the freeways at rush hour. But if you do have a car, one suggestion is to park it at the RTD (Regional Transportation District) station at Interstate 25 and Broadway and ride the light rail into downtown.

Without a car, the cheapest way into town is to take the **RTD Sky Ride** bus. Fares range from four dollars to eight dollars, with discounts for round-trip tickets. Call for information on this bus and all other public transportation needs.

If you choose to take a taxi, you'll pay a $35 flat rate for airport service. One company to try is **Denver Yellow Cab,** 303/777-7777. And by the way, don't try to flag down a taxi. It won't work. You'll have to call for one. Operators such as **SuperShuttle,** 303/370-1300, offer airport service for about $15 one way.

Denver has a terrifically lively **downtown,** with 5,200 hotel rooms, a performing arts complex, and lots of shops, restaurants, and nightspots. You'll want to find a hotel near the **16th Street Mall,** a mile-long pedestrian walkway that is surrounded by parks and plazas and runs right through the heart of everything.

Mall buses provide free rides up and down 16th Street every 90 seconds (those buses are the only vehicles allowed), which is the best way to get around. From there you can connect to the **light rail system,** which is about five miles long and runs from south of the city, through downtown, and to the north.

Another great way to get around is the **RTD Cultural Connection Trolley,** 303/299-6000, which runs from the end of May to Labor Day. For three dollars, you can get an all-day pass for rides to the Denver Arts Complex, the State Capitol, and the Denver Zoo, among others.

Within reach of the trolley and the 16th Street Mall are several days of fun. Just don't neglect **LoDo** (Lower Downtown), which is the northern edge of downtown and includes a concentration of Victorian buildings and refurbished warehouses. Restaurants, shops, art galleries, and brew pubs are in abundance.

The **Mile High Trail** is a series of six walking tours downtown. Get a copy from the Denver Metro Convention & Visitors Bureau

Information Center in the Tabor Center, located on the 16th Street Mall, 1668 Larimer St., 303/892-1112.

A great way to see the sights in downtown Denver is to float down Cherry Creek in a punt, which is something like gondola. Call **Punt the Creek** for details; 1666 S. University Blvd., 303/398-1322.

SIGHTS AND ATTRACTIONS

The place to be is the mile-long **16th Street Mall,** between Market St. and Broadway along 16th St., which features 10 outdoor cafés and dozens of benches, fountains, plazas, street performers, chess players, pedicabs, and horse-drawn carriages. Orient your trip from this area.

Larimer Square, 1400 block of Larimer St., just a block west of the mall, is a restored section of Denver's oldest street. This block of Victorian buildings houses restaurants, outdoor cafés, shops, comedy clubs, and nightspots.

The **State Capitol,** Broadway and Colfax Ave., 303/866-2604, is only two blocks from the eastern end of the 16th Street Mall. It's modeled after the U.S. Capitol, with a dome covered in 200 ounces of pure gold. The rotunda affords a beautiful, 150-mile-wide view of the entire front range of the Rockies, from Pikes Peak to the south all the way north to the Wyoming border. Free tours are given on weekdays from 9:30 a.m. to 2:30 p.m.

Not too far from the State Capitol is the **U.S. Mint,** W. Colfax Ave. at Cherokee St., 303/405-4761, where 5 billion coins are made each year. After Fort Knox, this is the second largest storehouse of gold bullion in the United States. The gift shop has some coins not available anywhere else. Also at the mint is a small museum on the history of money. Free tours are offered on weekdays.

Between the U.S. Mint and the State Capitol is **Civic Center Park,** the centerpiece of Denver's greenspace. In it are 25,000 square feet of flower gardens.

A Titanic Resident

Molly Brown was the wealthiest woman in Denver in the 1800s, but she didn't come from a wealthy family. Rather, she began life poor and married a man who hit pay dirt in the silver boom. She got her "Unsinkable" nickname after surviving the *Titanic* disaster. Debbie Reynolds plays her with boundless energy in the Broadway musical adaptation of *The Unsinkable Molly Brown* (1964). Run through a chorus of "I Ain't Down Yet" and then go see her house. The **Molly Brown Museum House**, 1340 Pennsylvania, 303/832-4092, has been restored to its Victorian splendor, and tours are conducted by period-costumed guides.

View of Denver from City Park

Just south of the park is the **Denver Art Museum,** 100 W. 14th Ave., 303/640-4433, which houses an extensive collection of art objects in such areas as Asian, Pre-Columbian, and Spanish Colonial art. However, the museum's main claim to fame is its stunning collection of American Indian art, which many critics consider to be the finest such collection in the world.

Not far away is the **Colorado History Museum,** 13th Ave. and Broadway, 303/756-4873, which traces the history of Indians, explorers, gold miners, cowboys, and pioneers. Dioramas and rare photos help tell the story.

The **Denver Public Library,** 10 W. 14th Ave., 303/640-6200, is something to behold. This $64 million structure was opened in 1995 with 47 miles of bookshelves and more than 5 million items, making it one of the largest libraries in the nation. The building has a three-story atrium and a huge rotunda that offers a stunning view of the Rockies.

Did you know that as many as a third of all the cowboys on the great cattle drives of the old days were black? The **Black American West Museum,** 3091 California St., 303/292-2566, tells the whole forgotten story of how African American men and women helped settle and develop the American West. The museum is housed in the home of Denver's first African American physician, Dr. Justina Ford.

The **Denver Botanic Gardens,** 1005 York, 303/331-4000, has a tropical conservatory and outdoor gardens that include rose, Japanese, and rock gardens. It's 1 of 506 public gardens in Denver where more than 240,000 flowers are planted each year.

The **Denver Zoo,** 17th Ave. and Colorado Blvd., 303/331-4100, is rated among the top 10 in America, with 3,500 animals on lots of land in City Park. Tropical Discovery is a glassed-in rain forest that feels like a walk in the jungle.

Located in the heart of Denver's Latino community is the **Museo de las Americas,** 861 Santa Fe Dr., 303/571-4401, a celebration of the art, culture, and history of Latin American countries and the southwestern United States.

Golden is a suburban city on the western side of Denver, and several sights worth seeing are there. Get free samples and a free tour at the **Coors Brewery,** 13th and Ford St., Golden, 303/277-2337, which is the single largest brewery in the world. Colorado brews more beer than any other state, and this brewery brews more beer than any other place on the planet. It's just a few miles from downtown via the Sixth Avenue Freeway.

Boettcher Mansion, 900 Colorado Rd., Golden, 303/526-5519, is a Craftsman-style retreat atop Lookout Mountain. It's full of Stickley furniture and other examples of the arts and crafts movement.

Also on Lookout Mountain is **Buffalo Bill's Museum & Grave,** take Exit 256 on I-70, Golden, 303/526-0747, which is full of original guns, posters, and costumes from the showman's Wild West Show.

One more attraction you might want to check out is **Colorado's Ocean Journey,** 700 Water St., 303/561-4450, a $93 million world-class aquarium that opened in 1999 in Denver's Central Platte Valley. It features everything from an outdoor trout stream to a coral reef.

LODGING

Denver has 23,000 hotels rooms in the metro area—5,300 of which are within walking distance of the downtown attractions.

No place in Denver is finer than the **Brown Palace Hotel,** 321 17th St., 800/321-2599, $$$. It's not named for the color, but for Henry Brown, an early settler who was the original owner of the land under it. Since 1892 the hotel has been accommodating presidents and cowboys. It was the hotel of choice of Molly Brown (no relation), who took singing lessons in Room 629 and whose voice, said her hotel neighbors, was an unsinkable screech. Today the music of choice is from the harp, which accompanies guests in the lobby at afternoon tea. Black-caped doormen will greet you, and your room will be graced with Victorian antiques.

Denver's mile-high altitude makes life a little different. Watch it when you drink alcohol. It's absorbed into the blood quicker. You'll probably also experience some shortness of breath when you first arrive, so give your body a day or two to adjust. Another thing to watch out for is sunburn. The high altitude means Denver receives 24 percent more ultraviolet radiation than a city at sea level. Sunscreen and sunglasses are a must.

City Survival Tips

Aaaw, you've come to town without your pet pooch Poopsie, and you miss him terribly. What to do? Check into the **Hotel Monaco,** 1717 Champa, 303/296-1717, $$$, and they'll lend you a bowl of goldfish to keep you company. Name them if you wish, and see them again upon your return. The hotel has in-room CD players and coffee makers, as well as a spa, a salon, and complimentary wine in the afternoons.

You could call the **Oxford Hotel,** 1600 17th St., 800/228-5838, $$$, the Brown Palace Lite. It was designed by the same architect—Frank Edbrooke—and has the same emphasis on natural lighting and art-deco styling. Its eight rooms are furnished in French and English antiques, and it has two restaurants and a spa. It's in the LoDo district, not far from Coors Field.

The Warwick, 1776 Grant St., 800/525-2888, $$$, is a deluxe European hotel downtown. Rooms are bigger than normal because this originally was an apartment building. The hotel offers complimentary breakfast, with refrigerators and balconies in most rooms.

A moderately priced all-suite hotel is **The Burnsley,** 1000 Grant St., 303/830-1000, $$, which is just five minutes from downtown. It's a place that was once co-owned by Ella Fitzgerald and Kirk Douglas. Breakfast is included.

Housed in a beautifully restored 1892 brownstone mansion near the heart of downtown Denver is the **Holiday Chalet,** 1829 Colfax Ave., 303/321-9975, $$. Rooms have lots of lace curtains and flowered carpets, and breakfast is self-serve. The B&B is in a commercial strip in central Denver.

The **Castle Marne,** 1572 Race St., 303/331-0621, $$$, is an A-plus B&B. The decor is high-end Victorian. All rooms have private baths, some with jetted tubs for two. Afternoon tea is available, and you'll feast on a gourmet breakfast.

Another of the top-ranked B&Bs downtown is the **Merritt House,** 941 E. 17th Ave., 303/861-5230, $$$. This 1889 Victorian mansion was designed by Frank Edbrooke, architect of the Brown Palace, who lived next door. The place has 10 rooms with private baths, cable TV, and telephones.

DINING

Buffalo meat is a Denver specialty. Other city cuisine highlights include Rocky Mountain trout, beef, and lamb, all of it predominant in the area.

The in-spot in Denver is Kevin Taylor's **Brasserie Z,** 815 17th St., 303/293-2322, $$, (the locals call it Brazz Z), with one of the city's loveliest dining rooms. Specialties are the pasta dishes, but many think the restaurant's burgers are the best in town.

Listen, that Kevin Taylor must be a busy guy. Another of his places is **Palettes** at the Denver Art Museum, 100 W. 14th Ave., 303/629-0889, $$$. This contemporary American restaurant overlooks a handsome courtyard. It's a great place for lunch after a morning in the museum. Recommended is the poached asparagus with roast onions and mushroom ragout.

It's a rich experience when you dine in a former bank vault. At **Broke Restaurant,** 821 17th St. at Champa, 303/292-5065, $$$, you get a complimentary shrimp bowl, plus great steaks and seafood. And you won't break the bank to dine there. It's just a block from the 16th Street Mall.

Denver 101

Denver was born in 1859 with the discovery of a few flakes of gold where the South Platte River and Cherry Creek meet. Word of the gold find brought a stampede of people, but when the gold discovery turned out to be a bust, people stayed anyway. Maybe it was the good weather.

More valuable discoveries of gold were made in the mountains, and Denver became a good place for supplies and settlements because of its mild climate. Railroads eventually came through, and Denver grew into a Wild West boomtown full of gamblers, drifters, gunmen, and silver barons.

Booms and busts have made Denver's history a bumpy ride. After years as a sleepy little western city, Denver's population doubled in the years since 1960. The last big rise in fortunes came with the oil boom in the 1970s and early 1980s, but then all that collapsed.

In the last few years Denver has been booming again with a more diversified economy. Being half-way between Mexico and Canada has made it a trading hub. It has also become the telecommunications capital of the country.

Each January is the **National Western Stock Show and Rodeo**, 303/297-1166, which is one of the nation's biggest and best. Festivities include a big parade. One of the nation's largest Native American gatherings is the **Denver PowWow**, 303/377-3724. held each March. Dancers and artisans from 70 tribes are represented.

The **Capitol Hill People's Fair**, 303/830-1651, attracts 300,000 each June to the city's most eclectic neighborhood festival. Included are more than 550 arts-and-crafts booths. Dance, theater, music, opera, and more are part of the **Colorado Performing Arts Festival**, 303/642-2678, which is held each October at the Denver Performing Arts Complex.

events
HORIZON

Duffy's Shamrock Restaurant, 1635 Court Pl., 303/534-4935, $, located downtown, has seafood, steaks, sandwiches, and Mexican food in a casual, neighborhood-bar atmosphere.

Marlowe's, 511 16th St., 303/595-3700, $$$, is one of the best of the restaurants on the 16th Street Mall. Steaks, chops, and seafood are tops. Ask for a table on the patio. Or if you're in a mad dash down the 16th Street Mall, dash into **Café Galileo,** 353 16th St., 303/573-7600, $. It offers hot panini, exotic salads, gourmet pizza, and fresh baked goods—and all of it in a hurry.

What you've always wanted, but didn't know it, is buffalo meatloaf. Get that, or try the duck enchiladas, at the **Rocky Mountain Diner,** 800 18th St., 303/293-8383, $$. Don't forget to play the jukebox.

Tante Louise, 4900 E. Colfax Ave., 303/355-4488, $$$, offers intimate dining in a renovated bungalow. The specialties are Colorado lamb, range-fed veal, and pheasant.

A Mexican restaurant should have family tradition, and you'll find that at **Armadillo,** 2401 15th St., 303/477-5880, $$, which has been serving authentic Mexican cuisine for 30 years. Get a giant margarita and then be careful—you're already a mile high; this could put you in the stratosphere. The food is traditional Tex-Mex.

SHOPPING

Like everything else in Denver, the best shopping is along the 16th Street Mall or nearby in either Larimer Square or the fast-developing LoDo area.

On the mall is the **Denver Pavilion,** 500 16th St., 303/260-6001, a two-block-long complex featuring a store that is a real Denver crowd-pleaser—Nike Town. Not only can you try *on* basketball shoes in the megastore, but you can try them *out*, too. The store has its own basketball court. Also at the Denver Pavilion are a Hard Rock Cafe, a Virgin Records store, and many more retailers, as well as six restaurants and 15 movie screens.

Another store on the mall is the **Tabor Center,** at Lawrence St. on the 16th Street Mall, 303/572-6868, which has more than 65 specialty shops and restaurants in the glass-enclosed, two-block galleria.

Stadium Walk, 18th and Blake Sts., in LoDo is a square-block complex built into historic buildings that preserve the ambiance of this historic district. The retail shops are on the street level, with residences above. Also in the 26-square-block LoDo area surrounding Coors Field are 65 bars, restaurants, and brewpubs, as well as 40 art galleries. And you're within walking distance of 4,800 hotel rooms.

Larimer Square, 1400 block of Larimer St., is Denver's most historic block, and within its Victorian buildings are 28 shops, seven restaurants, two nightclubs, and a microbrewery. One shop there is **Squash Blossom Gallery,** 1400 Larimer St., 303/534-2367, which sells both antique and contemporary jewelry and crafts of the Americas.

The **Cherry Creek Shopping Center,** 3000 E. First Ave., is an ultra-upscale mall fearing 140 stores that include Neiman Marcus, Saks Fifth Avenue, and Lord & Taylor. Just being there is a treat—the center has sculptures, skylights, and beautiful public spaces, plus one of the best bookstores in the world.

The bookstore we're talking about is the **Tattered Cover Bookstore,** in the Cherry Creek Shopping Center, 303/322-7727; 1628 16th St., 303/436-1070, one of the largest independent bookstores in the nation—with over 500,000 volumes and its own restaurant. The atmosphere is warm and comfortable, and the emphasis is on personal service. They also have a second, smaller location in LoDo.

Because of the mountains and all the outdoor activity associated with them, Denver has many sporting goods stores. One is **Grand West Outfitters,** 810 Broadway, 303/825-0300, which has in-line skates, mountain bikes, and climbing equipment, as well as a rock climbing wall.

Runner's Roost, 1001 16th St., #1128, 800/95-ROOST, has running, trail, cross-training, walking, and even snowshoes.

The largest Orvis dealer in the Rockies is **The Flyfisher,** 120 Madison St., 303/322-5014. It has an on-site casting area and a flytying bar where you can put your own lures together. It's three blocks east of the Cherry Creek Shopping Center.

Mudhead Gallery features museum-quality art of the Southwest, including Hopi kachinas, western pieces, wildlife bronzes, and silver jewelry. The gallery also offers Navajo rugs and pueblo pottery. It has two locations: at the Hyatt Regency Hotel, 555 17th St., 303/293-0007; at the Brown Palace Hotel, 321 17th St., 303/293-9977.

You can find authentic Colorado gifts, foods, and collectibles at

What's Brewing

If you love beer, Denver is your kind of town. Not only does the suburb of Golden contain the world's largest brewery (Coors), but Denver is also famous for its brewpubs. The city has more than 50 of these establishments, which make their own beer and serve food, too. By the way, a brewpub is a restaurant that brews its own beer—less than 15,000 barrels a year—and serves it fresh from the keg. A microbrewery bottles its own beer.

Something not to miss is the **Great American Beer Festival**, held each October. It attracts more than 300 American brewers who compete for prizes and hand out free samples. The all-Colorado version—**the LoDo BrewFest**—is held each June.

The fun is in the sampling. You can try a wide variety of beers by asking for a sampler—a four-ounce tasting of five or six beers. When sampling, start with the light beers and work up to the strong dark stouts.

Wynkoop Brewing Co., 1634 18th St., 303/297-2700, is Colorado's first brewpub, and the world's largest in terms of the amount of beer produced. It's in a turn-of-the-last-century building across from Union Station and has a comedy club, a pool hall, and an excellent restaurant.

Try the **Rock Bottom Brewery**, on the 16th Street Mall at 1001 16th St., 303/534-7616, for its large outdoor café and jazz groups.

The Sandlot Brewing Co., 2001 Blake St., 303/292-0200, is the only brewpub in the world located inside a baseball stadium. It's built into the side of Coors Field, with its own entrance into the ballpark. Try the Squeeze Play Wheat beer.

Made in Colorado, 4840 W. 29th Ave., 303/480-9050. For professional and college team apparel and gifts from jackets to caps, try **Sportsfan,** 1720 Federal Blvd., 303/455-6303.

SPORTS AND RECREATION

The big news in town is the **Denver Broncos'** (303/649-9000) new football stadium, which is scheduled to open in the fall of 2001. The new stadium, which will be adjacent to the current Mile High Stadium, 2755 W. 17th Ave., and will be part of the "triple crown" of sports facilities. The Pepsi Center, 200 Chapa Dr., opened in 1999 for the NBA **Denver Nuggets,** 303/893-6700, and the NHL **Colorado Avalanche,** 303/893-6700. The 50,000-seat Coors Field, 23rd and Blake St., which is in the LoDo district, was completed in 1995 at a cost of $215 million. It hosts the MLB **Colorado Rockies,** 303/ROCKIES.

The **Colorado Xplosion,** 303/832-2229 are the professional

Mild at a Mile

You'd think that mile-high altitude would mean way-low temperatures with scattered blizzards in the winter, but that's not the case at all. All of Denver's seasons are relatively mild.

Because the city lies behind a mountain barrier, the bitter north winds can't reach it and the clouds don't have much of an opportunity to bunch up into rain clouds. Denver's climate, consequently, is mild and arid, with 300 days of sunshine a year and only 8 to 15 inches of precipitation, a surprisingly small amount of which is snow.

The average temperature in the winter is 45 degrees Fahrenheit. What snow that falls doesn't last long, and warm winds called chinooks can bring 60-degree weather to Denver at any time in the winter. Golf courses are open year-round.

A lack of humidity keeps summers mild, but the best time to come is in the fall. The aspens get their vivid fall foliage from mid-September to mid-October.

women's basketball team in town. Watch them play at Denver Coliseum, 4600 Humbolt.

Denver is a real outdoors kind of place, and not just for skiing. The city has an average of 300 days of sunshine a year, and much of those bright days are mild. Golf courses are open year-round.

To get yourself involved in all the sporting fun, take a rafting ride right on the outskirts of Denver with the **River Heritage Society,** 2060 W. Colfax Ave., 303/595-0770. The society is only six blocks from Union Station.

Breeze Ski Rentals Central Reservations, 800/525-0314, has nine Denver locations, plus others at ski resorts throughout the state. They offer a complete selection of ski and snowboard equipment.

Trails and Rails Downhill Mountain Biking, 1111 Rose St., Georgetown, 303/569-2403, will get you to the top of the hills so you can coast down. Available are guided tours that include lunch and a ride on the Georgetown Loop Railroad.

ENTERTAINMENT

In the Old West boom days, Denver had 12 theaters before it had a hospital. The city is still big on the arts, with a **Performing Arts Complex,** entrance at 14th Ave. and Curtis, 303/893-4100, that claims to be the second biggest in the United States, right behind Lincoln Center in New York. Denver's center has eight theaters offering 9,212 seats, and it presents symphony, opera, theater, and dance performances year-round. The complex covers four city blocks and is just two blocks from the 16th Street Mall. Additionally, Denver has 30 other theaters and more than 100 cinemas.

The **Red Rocks Amphitheatre** is a natural outdoor area that seats 9,000 people among red sandstone cliffs. Not only is it a geological wonder, but its setting provides wonderful natural acoustics. It has played host to everyone from symphony orchestras to the Beatles, and it serves as the background in musical videos for *U2 Under a Blood Red Sky* and the *John Tesh at Red Rocks* concert. And even if there are no concerts available, the amphitheatre area is a great place for a hike and a picnic. It's 15 miles from Denver; take I-70 West to Exit 256, and follow the signs.

The **Historic Paramount Theatre,** 1631 Glenarm St., 303/825-4904, has been presenting music, comedy, dance, and films since 1929. **Theatre on Broadway,** 13 S. Broadway, 303/860-9360, specializes in regional premieres of new Broadway and off-Broadway productions.

Every weekend the **Swallow Hill Music Association,** 1905 S. Pearl St., 303/777-1003, hosts concerts featuring blues, bluegrass, Cajun, Celtic, cowboy, and acoustic music. Or sing along with your favorite rock 'n' roll tunes at **Sing Sing,** 19th and Wynkoop, 303/291-0880, which features a dueling piano bar. It's next to Coors Field.

The place to play is **LoDo** (Lower Downtown), an area of restored warehouses and Victorian houses just to the north of downtown. In its 26 square blocks are more than 80 sports bars, brewpubs, saloons, restaurants, and cafés; more than 30 art galleries; and lots of shops. Today the area is alive with people strolling through the streets, and lots of them are looking at the art galleries. On the first Friday of each month all those 30 galleries stage special events and are open late. For general LoDo info: 303/628-5428.

If you need tickets to concerts and sporting events, you can get them through **TicketMan,** 6800 N. Broadway, #103, 800/200-TIXS.

CITY BASICS

The **Denver Metro Convention & Visitors Bureau,** 1555 California St., #300, Denver, CO 80202; 800/393-8559; www.denver.org, is your source for general visitor information. You'll find two **Information Centers** in Denver: in the Cherry Creek Shopping Center, 3000 E. First Ave.; on the 16th Street Mall, 1668 Larimer St.; 303/892-1112. Both centers have lots of brochures and helpful volunteers, plus T-shirts and hats with the center's "5280" logo (because of Denver's altitude).

Check out the "Visiting Denver" site at **www.denver.com,** which offers live TV shots of the city. This Web site also has information helpful to the gay/lesbian visitor.

The Web site for **Arts to Zoo Colorado,** www.artstozoo.org, has links to all the cultural attractions in Denver. It has a calendar, plus a button that will direct you to last-minute great deals at performances.

For events information, go to **www.denver.sidewalk.com.** Another site, **www.diveindenver.com,** gives current weather information and five-day forecasts in addition to the usual restaurant reviews and such.

The *Denver Post* and the *Rocky Mountain News* are Denver's major daily newspapers. You can find more entertainment news in *5280: Denver's Mile High Magazine. Westword* is an alternative weekly with lots of advice on nightlife and other goings-on.

⓴ DALLAS–FORT WORTH
to go ▶

Progress has caused Fort Worth to be tied to Dallas,
and neither city particularly is happy about it.
That hyphen is at best a yoke for the two cities.
—Jerry Flemmons, *Plowboys, Cowboys, and Slanted Pigs*

These two don't call themselves Twin Cities. They don't even call themselves siblings. They're more like in-laws.

The chambers of commerce would like to put a good face on the partnership, but the truth is, these cities hate each other's guts. It's been that way for years. The reason lies in the profound differences between the two cities, and the result is good news for visitors. Only 30 miles apart are two distinct destinations. For the traveler, it's a twofer.

Fort Worth is where the West begins, and Dallas is where the South peters out. Fort Worth is home to big hair and big hearts, and Dallas is home to the big rich. Fort Worth is blue collar or no collar, and Dallas is white collar all the way. Dallas is known as Big D, and Fort Worth has always been called Cow Town.

But then there are the similarities, and the surprises.

If there's one thing Texas cities know how to do, it's sprawl, y'all. Fort Worth and Dallas have largely—and we mean largely—grown together, linked by smaller cities that have been swallowed by the blob. The region has something like 4.5 million people, and a name that perfectly matches its characterless nature—the Metroplex. Among the vast, freeway-ribboned, franchise-riddled land, you're not going to be

Greater Dallas

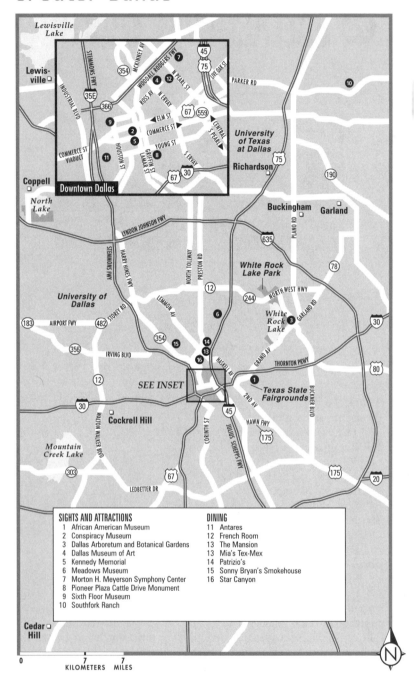

Lewisville
Lake

Lewis-
ville

Coppell

North
Lake

Buckingham Garland

White Rock
Lake Park

University of
Dallas

White
Rock
Lake

SEE INSET

Texas State
Fairgrounds

Cockrell Hill

Mountain
Creek Lake

Cedar
Hill

Downtown Dallas

McKINNEY AV

STEMMONS FWY

INDUSTRIAL BLVD

WOODALL RODGERS PWY

ROSS AV

ELM ST

COMMERCE ST

YOUNG ST

GRIFFIN ST

LAMAR ST

HOUSTON ST

COMMERCE ST
VIADUCT

N PEARL ST

N ERVAY

S PEARL

S ERVAY

CENTRAL

LIVE OAK ST

PARKER RD

University
of Texas
at Dallas

Richardson

LYNDON JOHNSON FWY

STEMMONS FWY

HARRY HINES FWY

NORTH TOLLWAY

PRESTON RD

PLANO RD

STOREY RD

LEMMON AV

NORTH WEST HWY

GARLAND RD

AIRPORT FWY

IRVING BLVD

GRAND AV

THORNTON PKWY

HASKELL AV

2ND AV

BUCKNER BLVD

WALTON WALKER BLVD

CORINTH ST

JULIUS SCHEPPS FWY

HAWN FWY

LEDBETTER DR

SIGHTS AND ATTRACTIONS

1 African American Museum
2 Conspiracy Museum
3 Dallas Arboretum and Botanical Gardens
4 Dallas Museum of Art
5 Kennedy Memorial
6 Meadows Museum
7 Morton H. Meyerson Symphony Center
8 Pioneer Plaza Cattle Drive Monument
9 Sixth Floor Museum
10 Southfork Ranch

DINING

11 Antares
12 French Room
13 The Mansion
13 Mia's Tex-Mex
14 Patrizio's
15 Sonny Bryan's Smokehouse
16 Star Canyon

0   7   7
KILOMETERS MILES

N

able to tell one urban area from the next. The traveler has no reason to spend time there.

But both cities have a heart, and both hearts have their delights. Dallas is a rich city, rich with culture. The museums are top-rated, and the city's large population brings in the best entertainment. But more than anything, Dallas has attracted an ethnic mix of people that gives it the typical richness of diversity that you'll find in most of America's biggest cities. It has a strong gay community that adds depth to the mix, and the result of it all is a heightened sense of sophistication. For interesting dining and shopping, Dallas is your destination.

On the surface, Fort Worth seems much less sophisticated. Any place that celebrates its very cowness—from its stockyards to the fact that it is home to the biggest honky-tonk in the world—doesn't seem like it's the place for world-renowned culture. But it is. Fort Worth is the home of the Kimbell Art Museum, one of the top small museums in the world. It brings in exhibits that rival anything anywhere. Fort Worth's new Bass Hall is also very highly regarded, and has been ranked among the top 10 opera houses in the world. Likewise, the Van Cliburn International Piano Competition draws the world's best classical pianists to the city every four years. Van Cliburn himself lives here.

Added together, hyphenated or not, Dallas and Fort Worth make for a singularly special getaway.

GETTING AROUND

More than likely you'll arrive at **Dallas/Fort Worth International Airport** (DFW), 972/574-8888 (airport information), 972/574-4420 (airport assistance center), 972/574-2227 (ground transportation); which is larger than the island of Manhattan and is one of the busiest airports in the world. You'll probably get lost in the terminal, and if that happens, look for people wearing green coats and cowboy hats. They're volunteers who will help you find your way. It's also possible that you'll land at **Dallas Love Field,** 214/670-6080, the home of Southwest Airlines and a nice little airport close to the city.

Taxis to either Dallas or Fort Worth from DFW airport are going to be about $40. **Cowboy Cab Co.,** 214/428-0202, and **Yellow Cab,** 214/426-6262, are two companies that operate in the area. Airport shuttle services, such as **SuperShuttle,** 817/329-2000, are going to cost a bit less.

You could get along without a car, especially if you confined your getaway to downtown Dallas, but you'll have a much better time if you get one. Dallas has a light rail system that can get you to the major points of interest in the city, but Fort Worth has no transportation system designed for tourists. Currently, no easy way exists for traveling between the cities, but that is scheduled to change soon with the completion of **Railtran,** a commuter railway that will link Fort Worth with Dallas/Fort Worth Airport.

The **DART** (Dallas Area Rapid Transit) light rail system, 214/979-1111, runs electric trains in a north-south line through downtown Dallas. The trains connect downtown hotels, the convention center, the historic West End, and the zoo. The system is designed more for residents than for tourists, but tourists can use it well enough. Supplementing the light rail system, however, are DART buses that operate a shuttle system known as **Rail Runner.** Rail Runner connects with the rail stations and has routes designed to get the visitor to the Arts District, the West End, and Union Station. Fares are 50¢, and correct change is required. The cost is the same for the light rail if you stay within downtown, or one dollar each way if you go out from there. Call DART for information or routes and schedules for both systems. Additionally, you can take a **vintage trolley,** 214/855-0006, from the downtown Arts District to the restaurants and specialty shops on McKinney Avenue. The fare is $1.50 round-trip.

SIGHTS AND ATTRACTIONS

Dallas is known the world over for two unfortunate things: It is where John F. Kennedy was assassinated. It is also where J. R. Ewing lived. The national tragedy and the prime-time soap opera are responsible for two of the most popular attractions in Dallas.

The **Sixth Floor Museum,** 411 Elm St. at Houston St., 214/653-6666, is situated on the sixth floor of the old Texas School Book Depository, where Lee Harvey Oswald fired the shots that killed Kennedy. The museum runs a film, displays many photographs, and offers a scale model of Dealy Plaza. Nearby are **Dealy Plaza National Historic Landmark District,** where JFK was assassinated; the starkly beautiful **Kennedy Memorial,** Main and Market Sts.; and the odd **Conspiracy Museum,** 110 S. Market St. between Main and Commerce Sts., 214/741-3040, www.conspiracymuseum.com, which uses a film and displays to argue that someone other than Oswald killed Kennedy.

The **Southfork Ranch,** 3700 Hogge Rd., Parker, 972/442-7800, served only as an exterior shot for the long-running *Dallas* TV series (1978–1990). J. R. never lived here; he was in Hollywood, where the show was filmed. But here you can tour the ranch grounds, see an exhibit recounting the show, shop in the western store, or grab a meal at Miss Ellie's Deli.

Dallas claims to have the largest urban arts district in America, with more than 160 museums, galleries, and artistic attractions. The crown jewel is the **Dallas Museum of Art,** 1717 N. Harwood St., 214/922-1200, which has an extensive collection of contemporary art and an Art of the Americas collection that contains an array of work from the Mayan and Aztec people, among others. Particularly impressive is the Reves Collection, an assemblage of paintings, decorative arts, and correspondence from Sir Winston Churchill that is housed in a replica of the Reves' French Riviera villa.

Dallas skyline at night

In the same Arts District is the impressive **Morton H. Meyerson Symphony Center** (the natives call it The Mort), 2301 Flora St., 214/670-3600, a beautiful building designed by I. M. Pei that has been acoustically tuned for the finest of musical performances. It's home to the Dallas Symphony, the Dallas Wind Symphony, and the Turtle Creek Chorale.

Housing one of the largest collections of African American folk art in the country is the **African American Museum,** 3536 Grand Ave. in Fair Park, 214/565-9026. Besides culturally and historically significant works pertaining to the black experience in America, it also has a collection of African art.

Also worth a visit is the **Meadows Museum** of Southern Methodist University, in the Owens Fine Arts Center, Bishop Blvd. and Binkley Ave., 214/768-2516. This museum has the most significant collection of Spanish art outside of Spain.

One of the most beautiful places in Dallas is the **Dallas Arboretum and Botanical Gardens,** 8525 Garland Rd., 214/327-8263. It is situated on White Rock Lake and consists of 40 acres of extensive gardens and the DeGolyer Mansion, a historic home of 21,000 square feet that was built in 1940 and that has an amazing library.

If you want to see the largest bronze monument in the world, that would be in Texas, pardner. The **Pioneer Plaza Cattle Drive Monument,** Young and Griffin Sts. between the Convention Center and City Hall, portrays a herd of longhorns being driven through a flowing stream in this Dallas plaza park.

Fort Worth has been blessed with some fabulously wealthy families who have reinvested their money in the community. Grain magnate Kay Kimbell and his wife Velma handed over their entire fortune to make the **Kimbell Art Museum,** 3333 Camp Bowie Blvd., 817/332-8451, live up to its nickname, "America's Best Small Museum." Its building is a perfect work of art in itself—long vaults of limestone with

Greater Fort Worth

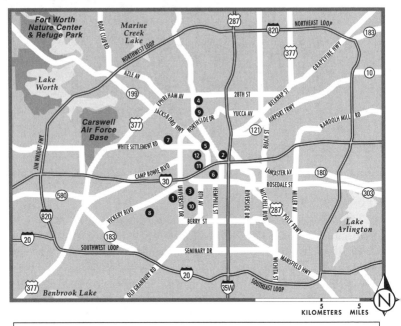

barrel ceilings that let in a suffusion of natural light to perfectly enhance the works of art within. The museum attracts the best shows of the art world, and its permanent collection is the envy of much bigger museums. It has a gift shop and a buffet-style restaurant that is of matchless quality in both food and surroundings. A lunch here and a tour of the museum will not disappoint.

Two other museums of the district are in flux. The **Amon Carter Museum,** 3501 Camp Bowie Blvd., 817/738-1933, housing a fine collection of American art, is being doubled in size and was closed at press time. It's next door to the Kimbell. Call ahead to be sure that it has reopened, which is scheduled for the fall of 2000. Similarly, the **Modern Art Museum,** 1309 Montgomery St., 817/738-9215, across the street from the Carter is moving to a new location next to the Kimbell. So call ahead—its art could be off the walls and into a moving van.

So enough about art. Where's the beef? It's in the **Stockyards Historical District,** on North Main St. at Exchange Ave., an area where cattle were once held in acres of pens, then auctioned, sold, and turned into steaks. The area has a fine little museum (131 E. Exchange Ave., 817/625-5087), the restored *Tarantula* **steam train** (817/625-RAIL), plenty of barbecue places, and shops that are heavy on the western motif. The city recently acquired its own herd of longhorns, and the cowboys who tend them will tell you about the giant cattle drives of long ago.

Sundance Square downtown, bounded by Throckmorton and Calhoun Sts. from Second to Fifth Sts., www.sundancesquare.com, is 14 blocks of restored turn-of-the-last-century buildings that now cater to modern shoppers and browsers. Don't miss seeing the new **Bass Performance Hall,** 555 Commerce St., 817/212-4200, the $60 million art-deco opera house that has been rated one of the 10 best in the world.

The **Fort Worth Zoo,** 1989 Colonial Parkway off University Dr., 817/871-7050, is also ranked among the best in America. It is the oldest in Texas and one of the biggest anywhere, with 5,000 animals that include lowland gorillas in a rain forest exhibit and the rare Komodo dragons, which are fierce-looking lizards.

If you've got time, stop by **Thistle Hill,** 1509 Pennsylvania Ave., 817/336-1212. It's a mansion built in 1903 by cattle baron W. T. Waggoner for his eccentric daughter Electra. It has 18 rooms, a 14-foot-wide staircase, and Tiffany-style windows. Electra lived lavishly—she

I t gets so hot in the summer that some dogs have been known to go into a permanent pant. Their tongues hang out all the time, night and day and winter. It's been known to happen to people, too. Be careful.

Just because it's hot as hell in the summer doesn't mean that the winters have no teeth. From December to February, mostly, is when "northers" come through—walls of cold air from the north that can turn a typical low-70s mild winter day into a subfreezing, sleet-spitting, gut-wrenching winter day. Temperatures can fall 40 degrees in an hour, an ice storm can move in, and the whole Metroplex shuts down. Schools close; drivers turn their cars into ice-skating elephants; and the enormous, chain wrecks are always the lead item on the local news. The best time to visit is in October, when the summer has finally run out of steam. Spring can be pleasant, but it's also tornado season.

City Survival Tips

took a three-hour milk bath every day and set a record at Neiman Marcus by being the first person to spend more than $20,000 in one day.

LODGING

Dallas offers a grand array of lodging options, and none is finer than the venerable and highly regarded **Adolphus,** located in the heart of downtown, 1321 Commerce St. between Field and Akard St., 214/742-8200, $$$$. The hotel was built in 1912 by beer baron Adolphus Busch and has managed to retain much of its Old World charm. Afternoon tea is served in the Grand Lobby, and fine dining is available in the French Room. The Adolphus has been rated one of the best hotels in the United States by *Condé Nast Traveler's* recent Readers Choice Awards.

If you love opulence but want cozier surroundings, you will like the **Hotel St. Germain,** 2516 Maple Ave. near Cedar Springs Rd., 214/871-2516, $$$$, a European-style luxury hotel. There are seven suites on three floors of this elegant Victorian home built in 1906, and each suite is decorated in French antiques. A continental breakfast is included. The gourmet French restaurant is reservations-only Thursday through Saturday.

Only one hotel in Texas earns a five-star rating from AAA and Mobil—the well-known **Mansion on Turtle Creek,** 2821 Turtle Creek Blvd., 214/559-2100, $$$$. The hotel is a nine-story building; the adjacent hilltop "Mansion" was once owned by a cattle baron and now houses the hotel's highly regarded restaurant.

The **Melrose Hotel,** 3015 Oak Lawn Ave. at Cedar Springs Rd., 214/521-5151, $$$, is an eight-story building located in the heart of a near-downtown neighborhood known as Oak Lawn. Rooms are spacious, and the staff is friendly.

Located in the prestigious Turtle Creek area near downtown Dallas is the 11-story **Stoneleigh Hotel,** 2927 Maple Ave., 214/871-7111, $$$. Operating in the classic European tradition, the Stoneleigh has hosted guests since 1923 in a setting that combines historic charm with modern amenities.

For the shopper, there's the **Westin Hotel,** 13340 Dallas Pkwy., 972/934-9494, $$$, with the Galleria literally at your doorstep. Shop 'til you drop, and then drop into the luxurious hotel.

Dallas has a number of bed-and-breakfasts that won't cost you an arm and a leg. For information, contact **Bed & Breakfast Texas Style,** 972/298-8586.

Fort Worth has **Etta's Place,** 200 W. Third St., 817/654-0267, $$$, a small, boutique hotel tucked away right in the middle of downtown. Rooms are pleasantly spacious with wicker and antique furniture. Common areas, including a well-stocked library, have lots of wood and brass and leather. Expect a glorious breakfast. The hotel is named for Etta Place, Butch Cassidy's girlfriend.

In Fort Worth, you don't want to miss the **Southwestern Exposition and Livestock Show and Rodeo**, 817/877-2400, the oldest in the nation—it's been around for more than a century. For two weeks, from late January to early February at Will Rogers Memorial Center, you'll see the judging of thousands of head of livestock raised by farm kids, a midway, and one of the best and roughest rodeos in the world.

Dallas Blooms each March in a profusion of color at the Dallas Arboretum, 8525 Garland Rd., 214/327-8263.

Fort Worth's next **Van Cliburn International Piano Competition**, 817/738-6536, which is held every four years, will be in May of 2001 at Bass Hall. Fort Worthians root for their favorite pianists as if they were bronc riders hanging on for dear life—and when those pianists take a ride on one of Rachmaninoff's great entanglements, believe us, they're hanging on for dear life.

The State Fair of Texas, 214/565-9931, is held in late September and early October at Fair Park in Dallas. It's the largest state fair in America. Eat a corny (what locals call a corn dog), see the cows, and watch the quick-talking guy sell you a slicer-dicer.

events
HORIZON

The **Renaissance Worthington Hotel,** 200 Main St., 817/870-1000, $$$$, is the twelve-story, three-block long trapezoidal centerpiece to Sundance Square. Rooms combine sophistication and warmth and are decorated in cherrywoods with art-deco flourishes. The hotel recently joined the Marriott chain.

If you find yourself enchanted by Fort Worth's western heritage, then the **Stockyards Hotel,** 109 E. Exchange Ave., 817/625-6427, $$$, is the place for you. It's where Bonnie and Clyde stayed when they came to town, and many of the rooms come complete with weapons. (Don't worry, they're unloaded.) The restaurant, bar, and common areas are decorated with longhorn horns and various taxidermic *objets d'art.*

Courtyard by Marriott, 601 Main St., 817/885-8700, $$, has recently renovated the former Blackstone Hotel. Built in 1929, it was Fort Worth's first skyscraper. And until World War II it was the tallest building in town. In the lobby area the art-deco design has been preserved, but the guest rooms have been thoroughly updated.

A B&B in the Stockyards area is **Miss Molly's,** 109 W. Exchange Ave., 800/99-MOLLY, $$, a former bordello above some stores. Rooms are designed to re-create a Victorian boarding house, but nicer. A big breakfast is served in the common area.

⸺ Neighborhood Watch ⸺

Dallas has three areas on the edge of downtown where you'll want to concentrate your visit. Some fine hotels are in the center of town, and they're all within walking distance of any of these three neighborhoods.

The **West End** is the historic district—guess where—on the west end of downtown. It's a 20-block area full of restaurants, clubs, and shops. The "Old Red" 1892 courthouse is there, which now houses the Visitor Information Center. The Kennedy Memorial, Sixth Floor Museum, and Reunion Arena are nearby.

The **Arts District** is on the northern edge of downtown. The Dallas Museum of Art, Morton H. Meyerson Symphony Center, and other performing arts venues are here.

To the east of downtown is **Deep Ellum**, along Elm Street. Nightclubs, shops, galleries, and restaurants are all over.

A couple of other notable areas are **McKinney Avenue**, north of downtown and just past the Arts District, where old homes have been converted into restaurants and neat shops. **Greenville Avenue**, northeast of downtown, has some interesting small shops and ethnic restaurants on its south end.

Fort Worth has three centers of interest: **Sundance Square** is a restored 14-block area downtown that is full of shops, restaurants, and movie houses. Among red-brick streets on the north side along North Main Street at Exchange Avenue are the **Stockyards**, a restored area of cattle pins, historic hotels, a steam train, and interesting shops. West of downtown near Camp Bowie Boulevard is the **Arts District**, where the city's three major art museums are clustered.

DINING

Here's a statistic to chew on: Dallas has four times more restaurants per capita than New York City. Burp.

For a bird's-eye view of Dallas, go to **Antares,** 300 Reunion Blvd., 214/712-7145, $$, located atop gently revolving Reunion Tower 50 stories above the street. New American cuisine is featured, with menu choices including a wide array of beef and seafood.

Dine in the **French Room** at the Adolphus, 1321 Commerce St., 214/742-8200, $$$, and you'll think you've gone back in time to King Louis XV's court. The setting is opulent and the service sophisticated. Cuisine is classic French cooking adapted to contemporary American taste buds. Lump crabcakes are the specialty, but the tomato-lobster consommé is something to brag about as well.

Even if you decide not to stay at its accompanying hotel, you may want to treat yourself to a fabulous meal at **The Mansion,** at the Mansion on Turtle Creek, 2821 Turtle Creek Blvd., 214/526-2121, $$$, which is the only restaurant in Texas to consistently earn five stars from AAA and Mobil. The southwestern cuisine, directed by award-winning executive chef Dean Fearing, is delightfully creative and varied. Mansion favorites are tortilla soup, warm lobster tacos, sugarcane-glazed salmon, and pan-seared ostrich filet. Save room for banana-coconut cake topped with ice cream and caramelized pineapple. Yum.

Wanna try Tex-Mex, Dallas-style? Head on over to **Mia's Tex-Mex,** 4322 Lemmon Ave., 214/526-1020, $. This small, family-owned, neighborhood eatery serves up all the classics—from enchiladas to chimichangas, tacos to fajitas. Be sure to try the wonderful, chunky guacamole.

If you're doing the Highland Park Village shopping scene, save some time for **Patrizio's,** 25 Highland Park Village at Mockingbird Ln. and Preston Rd., 214/522-7878, $$. Expect wonderful pizza and pasta of all kinds served in a lovely setting.

Sonny Bryan's Smokehouse, 2202 Inwood Rd. near Harry Hines Blvd., 214/357-7120, $, has been smoking meat for Dallasites since 1958. Tuck into a piece of tender brisket, ribs, sausage, or all three. The onion rings are some of the best in the city.

Star Canyon, 3102 Oak Lawn Ave. at Cedar Springs Rd., 214/520-7827, $$$, starring Stephan Pyles' New Texas cuisine, is so popular that it's wise to make reservations six to eight weeks in advance. Worth planning ahead for are the southwestern Caesar salad with jalapeño polenta croutons and the house-smoked barbecued pork porterhouse steak with bourbon-mustard sauce.

Fort Worth has many places where you can enjoy great Tex-Mex food, but none more well-known than **Joe T. Garcia's,** 2201 N. Commerce St., 817/626-4356, $$, host to many a debutante party. If it's nice outside, patio dining is the way to go. All the standards are on the menu—tacos, enchiladas, fajitas, chile rellenos. Strolling mariachis and great margaritas complete the picture. Enjoy.

For barbecue lovers, **Angelo's,** 2533 White Settlement Rd., 817/332-0357, $, has been serving up delicious hickory-smoked brisket since 1958 and enjoys a cultlike following among veteran Fort Worthians.

It's getting increasingly difficult to locate real chicken-fried steak, but **Paris Coffee Shop,** 704 W. Magnolia, 817/335-2041, $, has been turning out this Texas delicacy since the 1950s. This hometown café also dishes up some great chicken and dumplings, liver and onions, black-eyed peas, and cornbread. If you've still got room, snag a piece of chocolate pie. The café is open for breakfast and lunch only.

We don't want you leaving Cow Town with the idea that there are no sophisticated dining options here. Fairly new on the culinary scene but recently voted number one in the *ZAGAT Survey* is **Bistro Louise,** 2900 S. Hulen St., Suite 40, 817/922-9244, $$$. This beautifully decorated restaurant features a wide array of entrees executed with a decidedly Mediterranean flair. And be sure to save room for one of the exquisite desserts.

Another popular addition to Fort Worth's dining options is **Reata,** located on the 35th floor of the Bank One Building, 500 Throckmorton St., 817/336-1009, $$. The restaurant offers expansive views of Fort Worth and is decorated in ranch motif, with cowhide chairs and branding irons covering the walls. Food is southwestern in flavor, employing many varieties of chiles in the preparation. With a swagger in your voice, order the calf fries, and they'll think you're a native.

Finally, if you're staying at the Worthington—or even if you're not—you'll want to make a date for dinner at **Reflections,** 200 Main St., 817/882-1660, $$$$. The food is beautifully prepared and presented in a sumptuous dining room. Try the rack of lamb or roasted breast of pheasant. End the meal with one of the fabulous chocolate soufflés—your choice, white or dark.

SHOPPING

Offering more shopping centers per capita than any other U.S. city, Dallas is shopper's paradise.

The high holy temple of the Dallas shopping scene would have to be the original **Neiman Marcus** store located downtown, 1618 Main St. at Ervay Street, 214/573-5800. The store opened in 1907 and became successful by convincing wealthy Texans who could afford to shop in New York or Paris to shop here instead. A permanent exhibit on the fifth floor tells the history of "The Store." You'll want to have lunch in the sixth floor's Zodiac Room, a gathering place of Dallas socialites for decades.

Also not to be missed is **The Galleria,** LBJ Freeway (I-635) at Dallas Parkway N., Dallas, 972/702-7100, a four-level shopping extravaganza featuring over 200 stores built around an indoor ice rink. Notable tenants include Macy's, Nordstrom, and Saks Fifth Avenue.

Dallas's answer to Rodeo Drive is **Highland Park Village,** Preston Rd. at Mockingbird Ln., 214/559-2740. Built in 1931, it was one of the country's first shopping centers and has been continuously updated. It offers an eclectic collection of upscale stores and restaurants.

Another very upscale shopping mecca can be found at the **Shops and Galleries of the Crescent,** 200 Cedar Springs Rd. at Maple, Dallas, 214/871-8500. This center features a number of specialty and antique shops, including Lady Primrose and Stanley Korshak's.

Inwood Trade Center, on Inwood Rd. two blocks west of I-35E, Dallas, is a several-blocks-long strip of outlet stores. A great selection of fine products can be found along this corridor, including Crate & Barrel Outlet, AtCost Warehouse, Accessory Mart, and Shoe Fair.

Maybe you just want some great souvenirs to take back to the kids. Head over to **West End Marketplace,** 603 Munger Ave. at Market St., Dallas, 214/748-4801, a combination shopping and entertainment complex with four floors of unique shops, restaurants, and nightclubs.

Talk Like a Texan

Y'all: More than one you, as in, "When are y'all plannin' to get y'all's horses saddled?"

Bob war: Those who don't know better call it barbed wire. Men should be very, very careful climbing over it.

Tar: The rubber cushion around a car wheel, as in, "I run over some bob war back yonder and got a flat tar."

Far: A conflagration, as in, "Bubba just used some gasoline to get the barbecue grill started, and now somebody better call the far department. And by the way, has anybody seen Bubba?"

Fur piece: Nope, not a mink stole, but rather a long, long way, as in, "It's a fur piece from the ranch house to the outhouse."

Tarred: Same as plumb tuckered, or very weary.

Toad-strangler: A bigger than normal rain.

Tump: Usually with over, as in, "Daddy just tumped over the ladder and now he's hangin' from the edge of the roof by his fingernails."

Fort Worth offers many interesting shopping options, and downtown is probably the best place to start. If you're looking for the perfect travel outfit, why not give **Kasal's,** 316 Main St., 817/870-1737, a chance. Their expert personnel will put you in something wonderful with just the right accessories, too.

The **Modern at Sundance Square,** 410 Houston St., Fort Worth, 817/335-9215, has some wonderful home accessories, gifts, and jewelry from which to select. Take a look at the art exhibit while you're there.

Love a bargain? **Fort Worth Outlet Square,** Throckmorton and Third Sts., 817/415-3720, is the place for you. It's located in the Tandy Center next to Sundance Square and features over 40 upscale outlet stores such as Spiegel, Mikasa, and Nine West.

You really shouldn't come to Fort Worth and leave without something western. Head to the Stockyards. They'll fix you right up at **Maverick Fine Western Wear and Saloon,** 100 E. Exchange Ave., 817/626-1129. Why not have a beer while you're at it?

If you want to be a real cowboy (not just the rhinestone variety), mosey on over to **M. L. Leddy's Boot & Saddlery,** 2455 N. Main St., Fort Worth, 817/624-3149. They'll outfit you in the real deal.

Born to shop? On your way from Fort Worth to Dallas via State Highway 121, check out **Grapevine Mills,** 3000 Grapevine Mills Parkway, Grapevine, 972/724-4910, the Metroplex's newest value-oriented megamall. It's located two miles north of DFW Airport and features such outlet stores as Bed, Bath & Beyond; Off 5th (a division of Saks Fifth Avenue); Burlington Coat Factory; and Brooks Brothers. And if all that shopping makes you hungry, try the trendy Rainforest Cafe.

Look Like a Texan

Urban cowboys wear 10-gallon hats that are at least 3 gallons too big and swallow their ears. Real cowboys wear straw in the summer, felt in the winter, and the sweat bands are sweaty. They take their hats off in church and at Mama's. Most of the time they wear a gimme cap (a free baseball cap with advertising on the front).

Urban cowboys wear stitched shirts with fancy embroidery and fake pearl snap-on buttons. Real cowboys wear whatever's on sale.

Urban cowboys wear polished, stitched snakeskin boots. Real cowboys wear whatever's comfortable and snake-proof. If those boots have stitching on them, you can't see it for the mud.

Urban cowboys go on guided trail rides on horses named Percy. Real cowboys drive Ford F150s.

SPORTS AND RECREATION

Dallas and Fort Worth are big on spectator sports, and they generally share their teams and facilities with equanimity. Probably the cities' best-known team is the **Dallas Cowboys,** 972/579-5000—also called America's Team, or God's Team. They play at Texas Stadium, 2401 E. Airport Freeway, in the bedroom community of Irving, which is near Dallas. Good luck getting tickets to a home game; you'll need to call way in advance.

Fort Worth's claim to fame is the new **Texas Motor Speedway,** 3610 State Hwy. 114, 817/215-8520, the second largest sports facility in America and the home of NASCAR racing, giant concerts, and auto shows.

The **Texas Rangers,** 817/273-5100, play Major League Baseball at a beautiful new facility in Arlington, 1000 Ballpark Way, halfway between Fort Worth and Dallas. Check out the Legends of the Game Baseball Museum inside.

The **Dallas Mavericks,** 972/988-3865, play NBA basketball and the **Dallas Stars,** 214/GO-STARS, play NHL hockey in Reunion Arena, 777 Sports St., near the West End historic district in Dallas.

Horses race six days a week at the brand-new **Lone Star Park,** 1000 Lone Star Pkwy., 972/263-PONY, in Grand Prairie, which is halfway between Dallas and Fort Worth. The horses go in an entirely different direction—usually up—at the **Mesquite Championship Rodeo,** 1818 Rodeo Dr., 972/285-8777, which offers western fun in a covered facility from April through October. It's in Mesquite, which is closer to Dallas than to Fort Worth. The National Cutting Horse Association Super Stakes, plus lots of other horse shows, take place at the **Will Rogers Equestrian Center,** One Amon Carter Sq., Fort Worth,

817/871-8150. If you want to get on a horse yourself, try the **Benbrook Stables,** 10001 Hwy. 377 S., Fort Worth, 817/249-1001.

Golf is big in this neck of the prairie, and the Metroplex is home to lots of public and private courses. The **Tenison Park Golf Course,** 3501 Samuell Blvd., 214/670-1402, is a 36-hole public course in Dallas, and **Brookhaven Country Club,** 3333 Golfing Green Dr., Dallas, 972/241-2761, has one of the top private courses in the city. The **Colonial Country Club,** 3735 Country Club Dr., Fort Worth, 817/927-4243, hosts the famed MasterCard Colonial Golf Tournament each May. It is also where native son Ben Hogan cut his teeth.

ENTERTAINMENT

Country music is a big draw around here, but so are the more sophisticated kinds of arts. Dallas–Fort Worth is not a one-note, twangy, nasal wonder.

The place everybody's heard about is Fort Worth's **Billy Bob's Texas,** 2520 Rodeo Plaza, 817/624-7117, which bills itself as the biggest honky-tonk in the world. That's no brag, it's the truth. It's got room for 6,000 patrons, and it has 40 bar stations and its own indoor rodeo for bull riding on the weekend. The top hot acts of country music perform on weekends, with lesser known acts performing weekdays. Billy Bob's Texas is in the Stockyards area.

A much more intimate spot for country music is a couple of blocks away. The **White Elephant Saloon,** 106 E. Exchange Ave., Fort Worth, 817/624-1887, has been around for more than a century and was the site of a legendary shoot-out between bar owner and gambler Luke Short and former marshal Jim "Long Hair" Courtright. Long Hair came up short. He died on the street. Today the bar looks much like it did in 1887, and the live music is good.

The **Caravan of Dreams** in downtown Fort Worth, 312 Houston St., 817/877-3000, is the place for a variety of music, especially jazz and blues, in an intimate atmosphere.

Elm Street in downtown Dallas is the place to go club-hopping. Lower Greenville and McKinney are other hot streets. Try **Club Dada,** 2720 Elm St., 214/744-3232, for a variety of cutting-edge musical styles, especially Texas blues and rock. Another great place for national rock acts is **Trees,** 2709 Elm St., 214/748-5009. And **Dallas Alley,** 2019 N. Lamar St., 214/720-0170, contains a string of nightclubs in the West End historic district, including everything from karaoke to disco to a quiet piano bar.

Frank Lloyd Wright designed the **Kalita Humphreys Theater,** 3626 Turtle Creek Blvd., Dallas, 214/526-8210, which is the only theater in the world that was built to his design. Its architecture is reminiscent of the Guggenheim Museum in New York. The theater presents a range of productions, from musical comedies to classic plays.

Another theater of note, both for its architecture and for the quality of its live productions (a little of everything, Broadway to individual musicians), is **The Majestic,** 1925 Elm St., Dallas, 214/880-0137, which is located downtown and started life in the 1920s as a vaudeville palace.

The opera, symphony, and ballet perform at the **Bass Performance Hall,** 555 Commerce St., Fort Worth, 817/212-4200. The **Texas Boys Choir,** 2925 Riverglen, 817/924-1482, which is a Fort Worth institution and is known throughout the world, also performs at Bass and at its own venue in west Fort Worth.

The most popular tourist attraction in the state is in Arlington, a suburban city halfway between Dallas and Fort Worth. It's **Six Flags Over Texas,** I-30 and State Hwy. 360, 817/640-8900, a 200-acre theme park with more than 100 rides and shows. It's a madhouse in the summers (it attracts more than 3 million visitors annually), and it's not cheap (adult admission is over $30)—but if roller coasters are your thing, this place has some wild ones. The Texas Giant is the world's tallest wooden roller coaster and reaches speeds over 60 mph.

CITY BASICS

Contact the **Dallas Convention and Visitors Bureau,** 1201 Elm St., Suite 2000, Dallas, TX 75270; 214/571-1000; www.dallascvb.com, for more information on visiting the city. There are three **Dallas visitors centers**: "Old Red" courthouse at Houston and Commerce Sts.; West End MarketPlace, 603 Munger Ave.; NorthPark Center, 8950 North Central Expressway. Dallas also offers a hot line on special events in the city, 214/571-1301.

Likewise, contact the **Fort Worth Convention and Visitors Bureau** for details on events, attractions, and more: 415 Throckmorton St., Fort Worth, TX 76102; 817/336-8791 or 800/433-5747; www.fortworth.com. You can also stop by or call the Stockyards Visitor Center, 130 E. Exchange Ave., 817/624-4741, for information and assistance.

Transportation for the disabled is available through **DART Paratransit Service,** 214/515-7272. Information for disabled visitors is offered by the **DFW Assistance Center,** 972/574-4420.

An entertainment guide is available Fridays in the *Dallas Morning News.* Free entertainment publications include *The Met* and the *Dallas Observer.* In Fort Worth, Friday's Startime in the *Star-Telegram* has entertainment listings, as does the free *FW Weekly.* Magazines include *D, Fort Worth, Where Dallas,* and *Where Fort Worth.*

㉑ AUSTIN

to go ▶

*There's a freedom you begin to feel the closer you get to Austin . . .
it's a great place to live.*
—Willie Nelson

Think of Seattle, but with a Texas accent and without all that rain.

Think of Willie Nelson with a laptop.

That's Austin—high-tech, musical, and ever so slightly askew from the rest of the state. Heck, the city even has its own distinct aroma, something a bit smoky and a little sweet all at the same time. Part barbecue. Part marijuana.

Austin has the most college-educated people per capita among America's 50 largest cities. It also has the most computer-literate— 60 percent of the populace uses computers. And Austin's bookstore sales are the highest per capita among those same top-50 cities.

So what do all of these highly educated people do for fun, besides read books and surf the Web?

They commune with nature. They hike and bike and sail and fish around and upon the string of lakes that begin in town and snake up the Colorado River into the rolling Hill Country of LBJ Ranch fame. They swim in the cool, natural waters of Barton Springs, or they go down to Town Lake and watch a million Mexican free-tail bats take flight at dusk, rising into the sky like swirls of smoke. Or they visit the Lady Bird Johnson Wildflower Center.

Greater Austin

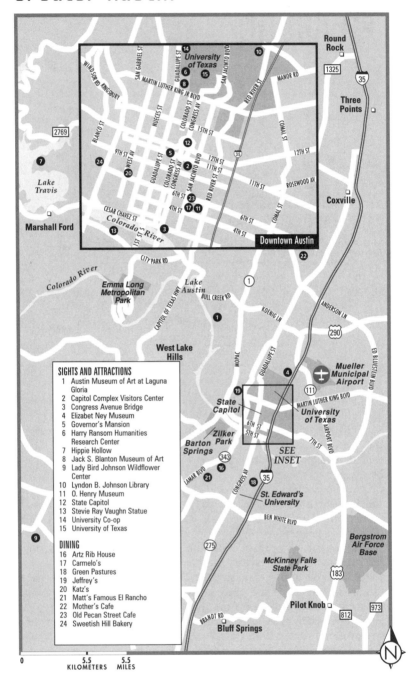

They listen to music. This is where Willie Nelson, Jerry Jeff Walker, Stevie Ray Vaughn, and Janis Joplin got their careers going. Today, this little city of just over a million (metro) has 100-plus live music venues (the city is known as the Live Music Capital of the World), plus the South by Southwest Music and Media Conference and Festival, which brings the best of the new talent to fans and producers. If you've ever watched the musical variety show *Austin City Limits*, on public television, you know what we're talking about.

They sit in traffic. Unfortunately, the word is out that Austin is hot (and we're not just talking about the weather). Austin is the second-fastest-growing city in the United States, and road construction, among other city services, hasn't been able to keep up.

But what the heck? You're a tourist. You don't need to get out during rush hour. Find a good club, get a good table, and wait. Before you know it, the crowd will have freed itself from the traffic and will be joining you; the guitarists will be tuning up; and another cold Lone Star longneck will be on its way to you.

GETTING AROUND

We warned you about the traffic. Unfortunately, one of the reasons for all that traffic is lack of a decent public transportation system. You're going to have to rent a car when you arrive at the new **Austin-Bergstrom International Airport,** 512/530-6510, www.ci.austin/tx.us/newairport, and hope for the best.

The new airport, converted from the former Bergstrom Air Force Base, is on the southeast side of the city. And upon arriving, you'll instantly get a taste of Austin. The recorded voices of Willie Nelson and Lady Bird Johnson welcome visitors to the airport. Music on the intercom is by such Austin notables as Tish Hinojosa, Sarah Hickman, and Stevie Ray Vaughn. In the men's restroom, when you look in the mirror, you can see what you'd look like wearing a cowboy hat. In the women's restroom, the mirrors come equipped with painted images of big hair. And in the huge new Barbara Jordan Terminal, you can pick up food from such Austin restaurant stars as Matt's Famous El Rancho, the original of which was a favorite of Lyndon Johnson's.

The center of the action in Austin is **Sixth Street,** which is approximately in the middle of town. Long ago Sixth Street was the center of Austin's business life, then fell into disrepute, and has since been revived. Hotels nearby and around the Capitol Complex are the place to stay. Some of the best hotels are on **Town Lake,** which is on the south end of town.

The traffic on Sixth Street can be horrendous. Get several blocks away, pay too much to park at one of the private lots, and then come back to Sixth Street and wander, although you probably won't want to stay here long. Like Bourbon Street, Sixth Street has been ruined by huge, pukey gangs of college kids who don't know how to drink, and who dare themselves into a stupid stupor. The later you stay on Sixth Street, the more you may regret it.

The place to go to is the warehouse district, several blocks away. (See the Entertainment section for details.) Everything else worth seeing is scattered about. You'll need your car to get there.

SIGHTS AND ATTRACTIONS

Officially at least, Austin has two major components—the University of Texas, with its nearly 50,000 students; and the State Capitol Complex, with its interesting buildings and beautiful Governor's Mansion. But Austin's main attraction is the music scene, and that is covered in the Entertainment section.

The **University of Texas,** I-35 and Martin Luther King Jr. Blvd., 512/471-3434, is a city unto itself, and because of all the students there, it is a center of vitality. It's a good place to stroll, with buildings dating back to the turn of the last century, and it's a very busy place if classes are in session. Visitor parking is available in the lot at Red River Street and Manor Rd. near the LBJ Library. You can get a free guide of things to see and do on campus, called *Forty Acres of Fun*, at the **University Co-op,** 2246 Guadalupe St., 512/476-7211.

The **Lyndon B. Johnson Library,** 2313 Red River St. near E. 23rd St., 512/916-5136, is one of the most-visited presidential libraries in the nation, and it's definitely a must for the Austin visitor. Within the library are a full replica of the Oval Office, a display of campaign paraphernalia and ceremonial gifts, and four stories worth of archives about LBJ.

The **State Capitol,** 11th St. and Congress Ave., is a Renaissance Revival palace, and it's naturally (would Texans have it any other way?) the biggest building of its kind among the states. It's made of native pink granite and was extensively remodeled and restored a few years ago. The rotunda is open daily. The place to get oriented is the **Capitol Complex Visitors Center,** 112 E. 11th St., 512/305-8400, where you will receive literature to help you with your tour and watch a 20-minute film narrated by Texan Walter Cronkite.

The **Governor's Mansion,** Colorado and W. 11th Sts., 512/463-5516, is a Greek Revival masterpiece that has been around since 1856. It has been recently restored and furnished with nineteenth-century Texan and American works of art. Tours are available Monday through Friday in the morning; afternoon tours are by appointment only.

One of Austin's famous residents was O. Henry, the masterful short-story writer. He lived in Austin around 1894 and worked as editor and humorist for the weekly *Rolling Stone*. Now the Victorian cottage where he lived with his family houses the **O. Henry Museum,** 409 E. Fifth St. at Neches, 512/472-1903, and it contains mementos from their life. It's open Wednesday through Sunday, noon to five.

The **Austin Museum of Art at Laguna Gloria,** 3809 W. 35th St., 512/458-8191, is an architectural wonder—a Mediterranean villa set on a 28-acre peninsula on Lake Austin. Exhibits keep the focus on the twentieth century.

The **Jack S. Blanton Museum of Art,** 21st and Guadalupe Sts., 512/471-7324, is considered one of the top 10 university art museums in the country. Collections range from contemporary to ancient art. Part of the collection is in the **Harry Ransom Humanities Research Center,** which also houses a monumental collection of literary material, including a Gutenberg Bible.

Formosa was the original name of the **Elizabet Ney Museum,** 304 E. 44th St., 512/458-2255, the home and studio of the renowned sculptor. On display are many of her works, plus her furnishings and tools, all of which lends an air of authenticity to this "working" museum.

In the far southeast side of town is the **Lady Bird Johnson Wildflower Center,** 4801 La Crosse Ave., 512/292-4200. On a 42-acre tract are wildflower meadows and a restored native prairie, plus a gift shop and café. The buildings are beautiful, made of native limestone and sandstone, and an observation tower offers a panoramic view of the Hill Country.

Each year from April to October, a million Mexican free-tail bats make a nightly commute from beneath the **Congress Avenue Bridge,** across Town Lake. The best viewing, however, is in July and August. At dusk, thousands of people come to the bridge, or stake out a spot on the nearby bike trails, to see the bats rise in a 15-minute whoosh for a night of foraging for mosquitoes. In the winter, the bats go to Mexico.

A place that draws a crowd is the **Stevie Ray Vaughn Statue,** on the southern shore of Town Lake between S. First and Lamar Blvd., which memorializes the late blues guitarist. Fans leave flowers, notes, and guitar picks. Stevie Ray faces south toward the site of the old Armadillo World Headquarters, the famed musical venue where he learned the ropes of the business.

LODGING

If you long to be in the thick of things and appreciate a sense of history, then the **Driskill Hotel,** 604 Brazos at Sixth St., 512/474-5911, $$$, which has been in operation since 1886, is where you need to be. LBJ kept a suite here when he was president. The location is wonderful—in the middle of the happening Sixth Street scene. The hotel also sports a grand, ornate lobby, although rooms can be slightly faded. Nevertheless, if character and location count, this is a great place to stay.

You'll want a lake view at the **Four Seasons Hotel,** 98 San Jacinto at E. Cesar Chavez St., 512/478-4500, $$$$. The hotel, decorated in a southwestern theme, is only yards away from the convention center. It offers the standard amenities including heated pool, indoor whirlpool and saunas, exercise room, and popular restaurant, the Cafe at Four Seasons.

Also close to the convention center and offering a good view of Town Lake is the **Radisson Hotel, Austin,** 111 E. Cesar Chavez St. at Congress Ave., 512/478-9611, $$$. The hotel is 12 stories with 283 rooms and is only minutes away from the Town Lake Hike and Bike Trail.

The **Omni Hotel,** 700 San Jacinto, 512/476-3700, $$$$, looks sleek with its chrome and glass and polished red granite walls arranged around a 200-foot-tall atrium. The hotel offers 315 rooms in 14 stories and is home to a locally popular eatery, Ancho's Restaurant, which is known for its southwestern cuisine.

The twin-towered **Holiday Inn, Town Lake,** 20 N. I-35, 512/472-8211, $$, features standard Holiday Inn amenities and is conveniently located on Interstate 35.

If you find comfort in a babbling brook, consider staying at the **Hyatt Regency Hotel,** 208 Barton Springs Rd. at Riverside, 512/477-1234, $$$$, where a creek flows through the Branchwater Lounge located in the lobby. Again, this hotel is on Town Lake, so you'll want to ask for a lake-view room.

If B&Bs are more to your liking, why not try **Carrington's Bluff,** 1900 David off W. Martin Luther King Jr. Blvd., 512/479-0638, $$, a two-story Greek Revival house built in 1877. The house is perched on a tree-shaded bluff near the UT campus and has eight rooms furnished with English and American antiques. Breakfast and afternoon tea are served on lovely English china.

The **Inn at Pearl Street,** 809 W. Martin Luther King Jr. Blvd., 800/494-2261, $$$–$$$$, is another B&B located near the UT campus. This turn-of-the-last-century inn has four beautifully appointed rooms with private baths. Some rooms have porches, and all have access to some stunning common areas. This B&B was a former Designer Showhouse.

Finally, you may want to consider getting out of the hustle-bustle and traffic snarls of Austin at **Lake Travis Bed and Breakfast,** 4446 Eck Ln., 512/266-3386, www.laketravisbb.com, $$$. Located just 20 miles from downtown Austin, this fabulous B&B offers amazing 75-mile views from just about any vantage point. Each of the four guest rooms (all with private baths) is exquisitely furnished and has its own private deck where you will be served a gourmet breakfast.

DINING

Austin offers a dizzying array of dining options ranging from sophisticated to down-home, from barbecue to fusion.

Green Pastures, 811 W. Live Oak, 512/444-4747, $$$, has been an Austin institution for decades. Housed in a grand white Victorian home, with peacocks strutting about the grounds, this place sets the

The biggest musical event in Austin is the **South by Southwest (SXSW) Music and Media Conference and Festival**, www.sxsw.com, which is held every March. At a recent conference, more than 5,500 musical professionals attended seminars, schmoozed, and listened to rising talent at 42 Austin clubs.

Spamarama, usually in April, celebrates the mysteries of the famed mystery meat with a contest for best dish made with Spam. Showmanship and imagination play a big part. Spam pancakes, anyone? In May the **O. Henry Pun-off** is held at the O. Henry Museum, 409 E. Fifth St. In something like a spelling bee, contestants must come up with the best spontaneous play on words.

And last, the **Armadillo Christmas Bazaar** is a December gathering of craftspeople who sell every kind of doodad from the sacred to the profane. It's held at the Austin Music Hall, 208 Nueces St.

For details on these and other events, contact the Austin Convention and Visitors Bureau, 800/926-2282.

events
HORIZON

standard for southern hospitality and for food, with offerings such as grilled boneless duck breast wrapped in bacon and stuffed with a mild poblano pepper. Sunday brunch is especially memorable.

For the white-tablecloth treatment in a low-key setting, you'll want to try **Jeffrey's,** 1204 W. Lynn, 512/477-5584, $$–$$$. The menu successfully mixes continental, southwestern, and Asian cuisines. For an appetizer, try the poblano corn chowder with orange cream and herbed chicken. Entrées include Thai curried lamb, venison loin and duck breast, and sea bass with red pepper linguine.

The **Old Pecan Street Cafe,** 310 E. Sixth St., 512/478-2491, $$, is a Sixth Street institution that's been turning out great steaks, seafood, pasta, and chicken in the continental style for years. Fabulous desserts are produced by the in-house bakery.

Did you wake up hungry, or do you just want a treat to take home on the plane? Stop at **Sweetish Hill Bakery,** 1120 W. Sixth St., 512/472-1347, $, Austin's oldest European-style bakery featuring a great selection of cookies, cakes, breads, and lunchtime sandwiches.

If you just gotta have some good ol' Texas barbecue, head on over to **Artz Rib House,** 2330 S. Lamar Blvd., 512/442-8283, $, for chicken, brisket, sausage, and of course, its namesake—ribs. Side dishes are above average, and the charbroiled burgers are excellent. Still not full? Have a crack at sweet potato pecan pie or banana pudding.

Missing New York? Austin has the answer—**Katz's,** 618 W. Sixth St.

and Rio Grande, 512/472-2037, $–$$, as in "Katz's never closes." It's a New York–style deli (but it's not an offshoot of the Katz's in NYC) where you can cozy up to a huge pastrami sandwich. Be sure to try the fried pickles.

Austin has a way of bringing out the "old hippie" in a person. If you find this happening to you, you'll want to pay a visit to **Mother's Cafe,** 4215 Duval, 512/451-3994, $, for some great vegetarian fare. The emphasis is on wholesome Tex-Mex and Italian food, as well as stir fries.

In an Italian frame of mind? Give **Carmelo's,** 504 E. Fifth St., 512/477-7497, $$, a try. They serve homemade pastas plus the standard veal, beef, chicken, and seafood dishes, in a romantic setting. Don't forget cappuccino and dessert.

You just can't come to Austin and not go to a Tex-Mex restaurant, and the granddaddy of them all has to be **Matt's Famous El Rancho,** 2613 S. Lamar Blvd., 512/462-9333, $. You can count on a good meal and great service with all the Tex-Mex standards from which to choose. Specialties include chile relleno and shrimp a la Mexicana.

SHOPPING

Most of Austin's best shopping is contained in the **Central West** section of the city, bounded by Town Lake (south), I-35 (east), 45th St. (north), and city limits (west), an area that includes downtown. So let's get going!

Northern bears hibernate in the winter. Texans hibernate in the summer. They get in under the air-conditioner in early June and don't come out until mid-September.

You don't want any first-hand knowledge of how hot it gets. But if you make the mistake of coming to Texas in the summer, here are a few tips: (1) Don't even think about renting a non–air-conditioned car. (2) Drink plenty of liquids. Margaritas are recommended, but lots of water is better. (3) It's true about being able to fry an egg on the sidewalk. But seriously, you can also poach your brain in that same heat. If you jog, go out early in the morning (predawn) and take plenty of water. (4) If your car breaks down on a remote highway, don't just head out. It might be a long way to get help, so just sit there with your hood up and look pathetic. The good news is that the rattlesnakes won't be out in the heat. They'll be deep in the ground, waiting it out. You'll be safe, unless you run out of water.

City Survival Tips

Sail around the string of lakes surrounding Austin

If your time is limited and you want the most bang for your buck, head to Central Park, home of famed Central Market, venerable Austin department store Scarbrough's, Dr. Chocolate, and Clarksville Pottery.

With over 100 varieties of olive oil, 150 varieties of pasta and pesto sauces, and a mind-boggling array of cut flowers and organic produce, **Central Market,** 4001 N. Lamar Blvd., 512/206-1000, is the most upscale grocery store imaginable. It's also big, so your first time through you'll want to get one of the maps provided by the store. Bring an ice chest to carry your perishables if you can.

For the chocoholic in all of us, **Dr. Chocolate,** 4001 N. Lamar Blvd., 512/454-0555, provides a fix. You'll find loads of yummy home-made chocolates (you can watch them being made), chocolate-dipped strawberries, and even chocolate pizza.

For unusual gifts by local artisans, head to **Clarksville Pottery and Galleries,** 4001 N. Lamar Blvd., 512/454-9079. The store features everything from chip-and-dip bowls to hummingbird feeders. In addition to pottery, they have glass and wood jewelry and art.

The "Drag" refers to Guadalupe Street, the University of Texas's westernmost border. For those of you who never quite got over the sixties, this is the place to be. Two not-to-be-missed stores are University Co-op, the mother of all Austin bookstores, and The Cadeau, a Drag institution for over thirty years.

University Co-op, 2246 Guadalupe St., 512/476-7211, has served Austinites and UT students for over a hundred years. Textbooks are located in the basement, but the upstairs General Books department is well-stocked, too. Usually there are great bargains to be found here. Warning: it's unlikely that you'll walk away without something orange (the school color), longhornish (the official school critter), or both.

The Cadeau, 2316 Guadalupe St., 512/477-7276, is a fascinating gift shop featuring everything from fine china to fashion accessories—upscale, but with an edge.

If you're really into the sixties scene, you're gonna need some beads. Also on the Drag is **Nomadic Notions,** 2426 Guadalupe St., 512/478-6200 for all sorts of beads, strung and unstrung.

No doubt the great Austin music scene has you hankering for some new CDs, so cruise on over to **Waterloo Records,** 600 N. Lamar Blvd., 512/474-2500. The knowledgeable staff can help you find your favorites in their well-stocked store.

Finally, if you're a bargain hunter, particularly of the upscale sort, **Last Call from Neiman Marcus,** Brodie Oaks Shopping Center, S. Lamar Blvd. at Ben White, 512/447-0701 oughta get the juices flowing: Neiman's quality merchandise is offered at drastically reduced prices. The store is located in the southwest end of Austin in the Brodie Oaks Shopping Center.

SPORTS AND RECREATION

Austin is not big enough to have much in the way of professional spectator sports. But the city more than makes up for that deficit with its abundance of parks and lakes and its opportunities for recreational sports.

The only team worth noting in the city is the **Austin Ice Bats,** 512/469-7469, a regional hockey team that plays at the Travis County Exposition Center, 7311 Decker Ln.

The Town Lake Greenbelt is the focal point for bicyclists, joggers, and walkers. It contains 25 miles of trails that circle the lake. For a hiking and biking guide, contact **Austin Parks and Recreation,** 200 S. Lamar Blvd., 512/499-6700.

Other recreational options include renting a mountain bike at **Bicycle Sport Shop,** 1426 Toomey Rd., 512/477-3472. Or do the Texan thing and get on a horse. **Bear Creek Stables,** 13017 Bob Johnson Ln., Manchaca, at the southern edge of Austin, 512/282-0250, will take you on a trail ride. Also, the **Texas Sailing Academy,** 512/261-6193, rents sailboats and gives instruction.

A place not to miss, especially if you made the mistake of visiting Austin in the very deadest dead of summer, is **Barton Springs,** in the west end of Zilker Park at the end of Barton Springs Rd., Texas's most famous swimmin' hole. The water that rises through the limestone is crystal clear and a constant 69 degrees Fahrenheit, which will cool off even the most overheated tourist.

The truly adventuresome outdoorsperson will not want to miss MacGregor Park on Lake Travis, better known as **Hippie Hollow.** You're free to go skinny-dipping here, but be prepared for peepers who buzz by in boats. No one under 18 is allowed. The park is about 15 miles west of Austin. Perhaps climbing is your thing. If so, **Pseudo Rock,** 200 Trinity St., 512/474-4376, has more than 5,000 square feet of sculpted indoor surface for beginner to advanced rock climbers. It's across from the convention center.

Finally, one great way to see the Hill Country is to golf in it. Try the **Highland Lakes Course,** 12 miles west of Cedar Park on RR 1431, near Lake Travis, 512/267-1685.

ENTERTAINMENT

You're in the cultural capital of Texas. But Texas culture is not necessarily refined. It's not leather-bound or catalogued, it doesn't wear a tutu, and you don't need to get dressed up to find it. The culture is in the music, and the music is down the street in the corner bar, aching and celebrating with steel guitars and fiddles and pianos. It's a lot more fun than a moribund museum.

Austin has more than 100 live music venues that are mostly confined to the following styles: country, blues, folk, alt rock, jazz, and Latin. Most of the clubs are in the Sixth Street entertainment district (east of Congress Ave.), in the warehouse district just west of the central business district (Fourth St. west of Congress Ave.), and on Congress Avenue itself. But other great clubs are scattered all over town.

The best clubs and pubs are in the warehouse district. Try **Fadoo,** 214 W. Fourth St., 512/457-0172, an Irish pub that can be very busy on weekends, and where the prices can be upscale. **Ringside,** 300 Colorado St., 512/474-1870, is a jazz and cigar bar not too far away. And the **Speakeasy** jazz club, 412 Congress Ave., 512/476-8017, is, as they say in Austin, tray chick.

Stubbs, 801 Red River St., 512/480-8341, has excellent barbecue and an outside venue for concerts. This is where the best bands play, and the Sunday gospel brunch is a real uplift.

Or sit on the deck among beautiful trees and listen to a variety of music at the **Cedar Door,** 910 W. Cesar Chavez St., 512/473-3712.

The premier place for the blues in Austin is **Antone's,** 213 W. Fifth St., 512/320-8424, which has been around for two-plus decades, presenting such legends as Muddy Waters, Buddy Guy, and of course, Stevie Ray Vaughn.

For country music, no place is better than the **Broken Spoke,** 3201 S. Lamar Blvd., 512/442-6189. This place has been around for decades, serving up legends such as Johnny Bush, the Geezinslaws, and Gary P. Nunn, whose tune *London Homesick Blues* is the theme song of *Austin City Limits.* The chicken-fried steak here is pretty good, too.

Folk music is alive and kicking, and some of the best is served up at the **Cactus Café,** in the Student Union Building, 24th and Guadalupe Sts., 512/475-6515, a smoke-free, intimate listening venue on the University of Texas campus. It books some of the top Texas and national acts.

Liberty Lunch, 405 W. Second St., 512/477-0461, is the place to find the top rock acts, but you might find funk, reggae, and zydeco music there as well. It used to be an open-air place, but then it bought the roof of the old Armadillo World Headquarters.

You want variety? The place to hear such local and national notables as chanteuse Toni Price or the zany Asylum Street Spankers is the **Continental Club,** 1315 S. Congress Ave., 512/441-2444. Tuesday evening's Happy Hour shows are an Austin tradition.

Road shows find their way to these favorite Austin venues (plus lots more): The **Austin Music Hall,** 208 Nueces St., 512/469-7469, is a renovated warehouse that hosted a tribute to the late Stevie Ray Vaughn featuring Bonnie Raitt, Eric Clapton, and others. And bring the bug spray when you go to hear such luminaries as John Prine, Joni Mitchell, and Tori Amos at the oak-shaded amphitheater known as **The Backyard,** Texas Hwy. 71 at RR 620, 512/263-4146. When Willie Nelson comes to town, this is where he plays. Also noteworthy is **Southpark Meadows,** 9600 S. I-35, 512/280-8771, in south Austin, where such recent touring acts as the Lollapalooza tour, R.E.M., the Lilith Fair, and Hootie and the Blowfish have played.

For the classic arts, the options are plentiful. Check out the musical productions, classic movies, and other performance-art shows at the refurbished pre-WWI vaudeville house known as the **Paramount Theatre,** 713 Congress Ave., 512/472-5470.

For sheer zaniness you can't beat **Esther's Follies,** 525 E. Sixth St., 512/320-0553, which presents some of the best off-the-wall Austin-type humor. Next door, hear stand-up comedy and improv at the **Velveeta Room,** 521 E. Sixth St., 512/469-9116.

The **Performing Arts Center,** E. 23rd St. at E. Campus Dr., 512/471-1444, on the UT campus is a complex of five buildings with a concert hall and a theater hall that presents everything from Broadway shows to classical music recitals.

You can get half-price tickets to some same-day theatrical performances at the **Visitors Center,** 201 E. Second St., 512/454-HALF. It's a good idea to call ahead to see what's available.

CITY BASICS

The **Austin Convention and Visitors Bureau,** 201 E. Second St., Austin, TX 78710; 800/926-2282; www.AustinTexas.org, is the general resource for all of your questions regarding a visit to Austin. You can also get information on Austin restaurants, clubs, and accommodations from **www.austin360.com.**

The *Austin Chronicle* and the weekly entertainment supplement to the *Austin American-Statesman* will get you up-to-date on what's happening in the clubs.

㉒ NEW ORLEANS

to go ▶

Don't you just love those long rainy afternoons in New Orleans when an hour isn't just an hour—but a little piece of eternity dropped into your hands—and who knows what to do with it?
—Tennessee Williams, *A Streetcar Named Desire*

Here's how we'd spend our little piece of eternity in New Orleans: we'd eat.

It's the most worthwhile thing you can do here. The food will stick to your memory. (Here's our menu: Oysters Rockefeller, blackened redfish, café au lait, and bread pudding.)

The unfortunate thing about New Orleans is that other people have different ideas on how they're going spend their piece of eternity: they're going to drink, and not just during Mardi Gras.

It won't take long for them to get drunk. (One of those Hurricanes will blow you away in nothing flat.) It's a pretty good bet that they're going to be rude. At certain times, there are so many drunks in New Orleans that they can't be avoided.

"Laissez les bon temps rouler"—let the good times roll, they say. But being around a bunch of college punks who are rolling-down drunk is not our idea of a good time.

So you can either roll with it—get drunk with them—or chart a different course.

Try this: New Orleans in the morning.

Let's have a courtyard breakfast. Pull up a wrought-iron chair.

New Orleans

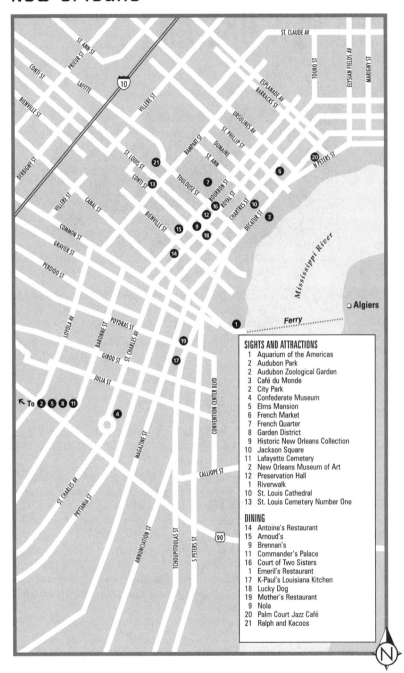

ST. CLAUDE AV

SIGHTS AND ATTRACTIONS
1 Aquarium of the Americas
2 Audubon Park
2 Audubon Zoological Garden
3 Café du Monde
2 City Park
4 Confederate Museum
5 Elms Mansion
6 French Market
7 French Quarter
8 Garden District
9 Historic New Orleans Collection
10 Jackson Square
11 Lafayette Cemetery
2 New Orleans Museum of Art
12 Preservation Hall
1 Riverwalk
10 St. Louis Cathedral
13 St. Louis Cemetery Number One

DINING
14 Antoine's Restaurant
15 Arnoud's
9 Brennan's
11 Commander's Palace
16 Court of Two Sisters
1 Emeril's Restaurant
17 K-Paul's Louisiana Kitchen
18 Lucky Dog
19 Mother's Restaurant
9 Nola
20 Palm Court Jazz Café
21 Ralph and Kacoos

The wet air is cool. You can hear the birds. Pleasant people are about. The drunks are passed out and gone, and the smutty T-shirt shops are closed. The new sun shines down the balconied streets, and the smell of frying beignets and percolating coffee escapes from the kitchen.

A sense of otherness prevails. You are in a place, a very real place, far, far away from the ordinary. It's a little piece of Europe, you think, but it has the refreshing rough edges of America.

For a few hours—for a little piece of eternity—you are in the most exquisite city of them all.

GETTING AROUND

New Orleans International Airport, 225/357-4165, is 12 miles west of the central city. A taxi into the city is going to cost you something over $20, not the best option. And forget the car. New Orleans is a walking city.

Instead, try the city-sponsored **Airport Shuttle,** 504/592-0555. It's $10 each way to downtown. In the airport is an information desk where you can buy tickets and get help, and it's staffed 24 hours a day. The shuttle leaves every 10 minutes. Also consider getting downtown via the **city bus,** 504/737-9611; the cost is $1.50. Within the city itself, most bus fares are $1.00.

Streetcars, 504/248-3900, are $1.00 (St. Charles Ave./Carrollton Ave.) or $1.25 (Riverfront). Exact fare is required, and you can transfer to a city bus for a dime. You can also get unlimited ridership with a Visitor Pass, which is available at hotels and stores. The passes cost four dollars for one day or eight dollars for three days.

If you ignore our advice and decide to use a car, be warned: parking is expensive, and the rules are strict. Metered parking is a quarter for 12 minutes—and you better be careful about parking in "rush hour zones" (no parking from 7 a.m.–9 a.m. and 4 p.m.–6 p.m.) or during special events such as parades. Also, if you park in front of driveways, in fire lanes, on sidewalks, in loading zones, at corners and crosswalks, or near fire hydrants, you're going to get towed.

For the quick visit to New Orleans, there are three musts, in order of importance: the French Quarter, the Garden District, and the parks and museum area.

Stay in the **French Quarter,** or next to it in the central business district. But unless you're one of those party-hardy people and are going to be up all night anyway, don't stay on Bourbon Street. The noise is stupendous. Plenty of nice hotels are nearby, almost all of them charming and within walking distance to an abundance of interesting sights.

Canal Street is the main dividing line of the city. To the east of it is the French Quarter (downtown), and to the west is uptown. To the north is Lake Pontchartrain, and to the south is the Mississippi River.

SIGHTS AND ATTRACTIONS

The **French Quarter** (also known as the Vieux Carre, or "old squared off area") is a rectangle comprising 72 city blocks, bounded by Iberville Street (paralleling Canal Street), N. Rampart Street, Esplanade Avenue, and the Mississippi River. You can have a grand old time without ever leaving this area. And if you miss it, you haven't been to New Orleans.

The heart of the French Quarter is **Jackson Square,** bounded by Chartres, St. Ann, St. Peter, and Decatur Sts., one-square-block of iron-gated parkland where a statue of Andrew Jackson stands. It's surrounded by wide, pedestrian-only streets where artists set up their easels, impromptu bands play, and the Mississippi goes rolling along just below. Take a long look and bring in a big, easy breath. Go ahead and swat that mosquito that just landed on your neck. This is New Orleans.

Just to the north of Jackson Square is the **St. Louis Cathedral,** 504/525-9585, a Spanish-style structure that is the oldest cathedral in the United States. A church has been on this spot since 1718, but the current one, replacing one destroyed by a hurricane and another by a fire, was built in 1793. It's a mix of architectural styles, just like the city and its inhabitants. The facade is Spanish; the altar is from Belgium; and the markers identifying those buried within it are in French, Spanish, Latin, and English. Tours are available during the day.

Just to the east of Jackson Square is the **French Market,** Decatur St. and Ursulines Ave. It's been a trading place since the days when American Indians lived here, but most of the current buildings are from the eighteenth and nineteenth century. Stalls are everywhere, full of interesting crafts and foods. Get a shellacked alligator head. It might come in handy.

Nearby and bordering Jackson Square on Decatur Street is **Café du Monde,** 800 Decatur St., 800/772-2927, an open-air eatery where beignets and café au lait are staples. You've got to stop here and get something. But be warned: Dress appropriately for beignet-eating. These little lumpy fried donuts are covered with powdered sugar, and unless you want to look like you just got back from a cocaine orgy, you better not wear black. Also remember that this is an open-air coffeehouse, and you don't want to eat downwind of your own beignet.

And of course there's **Bourbon Street,** which is named for the royals and not for the booze. If you're going to see it, see it early in the day before the crowds move in. It's mostly tacky, with souvenir shops, fast-food places, and come-on-in-sailor-and-see-the-transvestites places. Then go back at night. Wade through the crowds. See if you can find some good music. Watch where you step.

Just off Bourbon Street is **Preservation Hall,** 726 St. Peter St., 504/522-2841. Here's the real deal. Old-timers of the music world come here to make the sounds of jazz and Dixieland just like the old days. You'll have to fight for a spot to see, and the seats are uncomfortable. But if you love music, you won't care.

Going Places

The *Cajun Queen* **Riverboat**, 504/524-0814, is an authentic replica of a nine-teenth-century passenger steamboat that will take you on a Mississippi River cruise past the French Quarter, plantations, and the site of the Battle of New Orleans during the War of 1812. The boat departs three times a day from the Aquarium of the Americas dock.

You can go from the Aquarium of the Americas to the Audubon Zoological Garden aboard the *John James Audubon* **Riverboat**, 800/233-BOAT.

Get a tour of the surrounding bayous in a seaplane with **Air Tours on the Bayou**, 504/394-5633, www.bayou-airtours.com. Or see the same areas in an air boat with **Wild Side**, 800/975-9345.

You can see all the best of New Orleans nightlife and music with **New Orleans Tours** by taking either its Pete Fountain's Jazz Extravaganza tour or its New Orleans Nightlife tour, 504/592-0560, www.visitnola.com.

Haunted History Tours, 888/6GHOSTS, www.hauntedhistorytours .com, will tell you all about ghosts, vampires, and voodoo in a walking tour of cemeteries and the Garden District.

Similarly, the **New Orleans Historic Voodoo Museum**, 724 Rue Dumaine, 504/523-7685, www.voodoomuseum.com, will help you experi-ence authentic voodoo altars, artifacts, readings, and rituals, all in the capable hands of the museum's spiritual mother, Queen Margaret, and her assistant, Bloody Mary.

Gray Line, 504/587-0861, will take you on a tour of downtown shopping centers and art and antique shops. Hop on or off as you like for one price.

One block over is **Royal Street,** where the French Quarter looks most like the French Quarter should. Much of this street, like Bourbon Street, is closed to traffic most of the time. Here you'll see the rows and rows of apartments with French grillwork. The street also has loads of antique shops.

You've got to see at least one New Orleans cemetery, and **St. Louis Cemetery Number One,** Basin and St. Louis Sts., is in walking distance, about a block from North Rampart Street. Here you'll see the aboveground tombs (the ground is too wet for burials) that date back to 1800. One of the notable residents here is Marie Laveau, the voodoo queen. This is not a good place to go at night. But it's muggers, not ghosts, that you need to worry about.

Near the French Quarter is the **Riverwalk,** Canal and Poydras Sts. along the river, a huge, two-story structure fashioned from old ware-houses that contains lots of shops and restaurants. You must stop by the **Aquarium of the Americas,** 1 Canal St., 504/581-4629, to see the Gulf

If your idea of fun is a drunken, colorful brawl, you'll love **Mardi Gras**, 504/887-3199. Literally, it means "Fat Tuesday"—the day before Ash Wednesday when the Lenten season of penitence begins in preparation for Easter. In other words, before the fasting comes the blowout. And New Orleans knows how to do a blowout.

Carnival season actually begins on Twelfth Night—January 6—and ends on Mardi Gras, a day that varies on the calendar because Easter is a moveable feast set by the Church.

Mardi Gras really gets going the two weeks prior to Fat Tuesday, with costume balls and parades aplenty, where masked members of "krewes" (clubs) ride on floats and throw down souvenirs such as miniature footballs, cups, bikinis, beads, and doubloons. People go nuts scrambling for these trinkets, and therein lies the brawl.

You'll need to phone ahead months in advance to get a hotel room during Mardi Gras.

A unique way to combine a vacation and the Mardi Gras is to contact one of the clubs that sponsors floats in the parade. For instance, the Krewe of Pegasus will get you to the Mardi Gras Ball and let you ride in the parade. The deal includes hotel, costume, throws (the trinkets tossed to the crowds), and two parties.

Another major event in town is the **New Orleans Jazz and Heritage Festival**, 504/522-4786, www.nojazzfest.com, a 10-day extravaganza of music, crafts, and cooking. Some of the greatest musicians in the world perform here. It usually takes place in late April, and it really, really draws a crowd—so again, book way ahead.

events
HORIZON

of Mexico exhibit, a 400,000-gallon tank holding species native to the area. It also has exhibits featuring the aquatic life of the Amazon and the Mississippi.

The **Garden District,** bounded by St. Charles Ave., Jackson Ave., Magazine St., and Louisiana Ave., is 65 blocks of amazingly beautiful and varied houses. You can get there on the St. Charles streetcar. Most of the houses are from the mid-nineteenth century and are antebellum in style, with huge old live oaks and stunning gardens. Go in the early spring if you can, when the camellias and azaleas are blooming. The 1300 block of First Street has some of the most beautiful homes, several in the Greek Revival style. Also, the **Lafayette Cemetery,** near Washington Avenue, 504/947-2120 (for group tours), was the inspiration for Anne Rice's *Vampire Chronicles* series.

Finally, farther uptown is the **Audubon Zoological Garden,** 6500 Magazine St., 504/581-4629, a first-class zoo with some interesting habitats, such as the Louisiana Swamp, where a marsh comes alive with 'gators and birds. And don't miss the nearby **Audubon Park,** between Magazine St. and St. Charles Ave., where jogging, bicycling, and picnicking are ideal. Both places are named for the famed naturalist, who lived in New Orleans between 1821 and 1830. Next, go north to **City Park,** near Lake Pontchartrain at 1 Palm Dr., an equally beautiful area for the nature lover. The **New Orleans Museum of Art,** which is within City Park, is an important repository for a variety of great art, especially Oriental porcelains and some fine French Impressionist works.

Some other interesting sights that you may want to visit include the following places:

The **Elms Mansion,** 3029 St. Charles Ave., 504/895-5493, is a post–Civil War house that features marble fireplaces, original tapestries, and Flemish oak carvings. Stop by and take a tour.

The **Confederate Museum,** 929 Camp St., 504/523-4522, is the oldest museum in Louisiana. It contains Civil War memorabilia including uniforms, weapons, flags, and personal effects of great Southern leaders.

Also of note is the **Historic New Orleans Collection,** 533 Royal St., 504/523-4662, which is located within a complex of historic buildings and is a research center for state and local history. You can get a guided tour of the buildings and see the history galleries.

LODGING

You can't beat the **Maison de Ville,** 727 Toulouse St., 800/634-1600, www.maisondeville.com, $$$$. This is where Tennessee Williams worked on *Streetcar*. It has 16 stunning rooms with antiques and with balconies overlooking both the street and the courtyard. Out back are the former slave quarters, which were built in 1742. A short walk away Maison de Ville offers its guests another option: the luxuriously furnished **Audubon Cottages,** where the naturalist lived in 1821. Service is impeccable. Breakfast is served on a silver tray.

Here's another nineteenth-century townhouse-turned-hotel in the French Quarter refurbished with elegant antiques and period paintings. The **Soniat House,** 1133 Chartres St., 800/544-8808, www.soniat house.com, $$$$, offers breakfast in its tropical courtyard. Expect first-rate, personal service. It doesn't get any better—or any more southern—than this.

A French Quarter gem and one of our favorite places in New Orleans is the **Saint Louis Hotel,** 730 Bienville St., 800/535-9111, www.stlouishotel.com, $$$$, a charming luxury hotel with a magnificent courtyard and a first-class Creole restaurant.

A bit less expensive and still quite elegant is the **Dauphine Orleans Hotel,** 415 Dauphine St., 504/586-1800, $$$. It offers a guest library, minibars, continental breakfast, and afternoon tea.

The **Lamothe House,** 621 Esplanade Ave., 800/367-5858, $$$—a 150-year-old townhouse—sits among mossy oaks at the edge of the Vieux Carre. Breakfast is served at long banquet tables.

A grand old hotel, and the largest one in the French Quarter, is **The Montelone,** 214 Royal St., 800/535-9595, $$$. It has three restaurants, a rooftop patio, and a grand view of the city.

The **Edgar Degas House,** 2306 Esplanade Ave., 800/755-6730, $$$, is just that—the place where the Impressionist master stayed when he was in New Orleans. It offers six rooms and six suites in the French Quarter.

Another French Quarter hotel, this one with a European feel but without the European prices, is **Le Richelieu,** 1234 Chartres St., 800/535-9653, $$. Its rooms have hair dryers and refrigerators, and room service is available.

The **Grand Boutique Hotel,** 2003 St. Charles Ave., 800/976-1755, $$, is an art-deco gem on the Mardi Gras parade route in the Garden District. The hotel features all suites and offers valet parking. Microwaves and coffee makers are also provided.

The **Chateau du Louisiane,** 1216 Louisiana Ave., 800/734-0137, $$, is a B&B in the Garden District. It's an 1885 mansion with private baths, phones, and dataports.

DINING

The cream of the crop is Creole cooking—very European, elegant, and complicated, but with regional spices that can really turn up the heat. Some of the finest restaurants in the world are in New Orleans and in this category. You'll pay top dollar, and you'll remember the meal forever.

Antoine's Restaurant, 713 St. Louis St., 504/581-4422, $$$$, has been doing it right since 1840. Fifth-generation proprietor Bernard R. Guste knows his business—and his oysters Rockefeller, which were invented here. The place looks like a museum that ran out of room about a century ago.

Try the oysters in cream at **Arnoud's,** 813 Bienville St., 504/523-0611, $$$. Heck, try everything. This is a huge place that really is a museum, too.

You'll find some adventuresome cooking and surroundings at **Emeril's Restaurant,** 800 Tchoupitoulas St., 504/528-9393, $$$, in a converted warehouse with exposed water pipes. Ask about the duck and mushroom etouffee.

Nola, 534 St. Louis St., 504/522-NOLA, $$$, is Emeril Lagasse's spin-off of the original, with similar food but in a much more casual, contemporary atmosphere.

The Sunday jazz brunch is a tradition at **Commander's Palace,** 1403 Washington Ave., 504/899-8221, $$$, which is located in a Garden District mansion and is noted for its bread pudding soufflé. Men are required to wear jackets. Call way ahead.

French Quarter street performers

For a daily jazz brunch featuring a buffet of 60 dishes, head to the **Court of Two Sisters,** 613 Royal St., 504/522-7261, $$$. In the evenings, the restaurant—which features a large courtyard—is a top-of-the-line sit-down establishment.

You'll find classic New Orleans cuisine and even better jazz at the **Palm Court Jazz Café,** 1204 Decatur St., 504/525-0200, $$$. Some of New Orleans's legends play here.

The seafood is fresh and the best of it is fried at family-owned **Ralph and Kacoos,** 519 Toulouse St., 504/522-5226, $$. Ask for the seafood platter, and get some of everything.

For breakfast, go to **Brennan's,** 417 Royal St., 504/525-9713, $$$—but you can get their famous poached eggs any time of day. It's in a beautiful, high-style nineteenth-century building.

Mother's Restaurant, 401 Poydras St., 504/523-9656, $, is home of "Mother's Best Baked Hams." It's been serving po-boys for over 50 years, and also specializes in breakfast, with southern basics such as biscuits, grits, and of course, Mother's Ham.

For good old Cajun cooking, you've got to go to Chef Paul Prudhomme's **K-Paul's Louisiana Kitchen,** 416 Chartres St., 504/524-7394, $$$. This is the guy who made the blackening thing famous years ago, and he still does it best. Expect long lines and the likelihood that you'll have to share a table with strangers. Here's a hint that worked for us: Skip breakfast; then get in line for lunch at 11:30 or so, and you won't have to wait nearly as long.

You can't leave New Orleans without trying a **Lucky Dog,** 504/524-6010, hot dog. The hot dog–shaped food carts are everywhere in the French Quarter.

And finally, why not learn how to do it yourself? The **Creole Delicacies Gourmet Shop & Cookin' Cajun Cooking School,** in the

Accent on Food

As do the architecture and the big-city accents of the friendly people, New Orleans cooking will instantly give you a sense of otherness.

The European influence is strong, and shows itself in what is known as Creole cooking. (A New Orleans Creole is a descendant of an early French or Spanish settler.) Cajun is quite different. Sure, these folks are strongly French, but several centuries in America—spent far back in the swamps eating just about anything that moved because that's all there was—puts a different spin on things. There's a sense of desperation in the pot.

Pieces of alligator, whole crawdads, okra, tomatoes—my word! It takes some courage to eat something like that, and lots of hot sauce. That's Cajun cooking.

So you put all that together, and you get some Italians and Haitians and former slaves and aristocrats involved, and that's New Orleans cuisine. It's a divine mess.

Here's a quick glossary:

Andouille (ahn-DOO-ee) is a spicy Cajun sausage.

Beignet (bin-YAY) is a lump of dough, fried and dunked in powdered sugar. Eat it with . . .

Café au lait (ca-FE oh-LAY), half-milk and half chickory-spiced coffee. Chickory is a bitter herb that, when added to coffee, doubles the force of its kick.

Etouffee (ay-too-FAY) is a tomato-based sauce used to cover, and enhance, things like crawfish and shrimp and Lord knows what else—possibly a water moccasin. Literally, it means "smother."

Gumbo is a spicy soup, usually made with okra and sausage, shellfish, or whatever got caught in the net last week.

Muffuletta is a huge sandwich served on a loaf of bread and stuffed with Italian meats, cheeses, and olive spread. You probably can't eat a whole one by yourself. A po-boy is of similar size, often containing fried oysters and stuffed with mayo, lettuce, and tomato.

Praline (PRAW-leen) is a candy made from pecans and a sugary concoction so sweet that it will curl your teeth.

Turtle soup is not always what you expect. If the kitchen has run out of turtles, it will use alligators.

Riverwalk, 1 Poydras St., 504/586-8832, will teach you how to cook and serve it to you for lunch, all for $15. Or try the **New Orleans School of Cooking**, 524 St. Louis St., 504/525-2665, where you'll get plenty of tall tales, laughs, and recipes along with a meal in a historic French Quarter setting.

SHOPPING

Antiques are the thing in New Orleans. There are more than 200 antique shops here, some of them offering some of the finest items in the world, from tapestries to furniture and objets d'art, all in the nineteenth-century homes of Creole aristocrats.

Most of the shops are centered in two areas—Royal and Chartres Streets in the French Quarter, and uptown on Magazine Street. Here is a small sampling:

Boyer Antiques & Doll Shop, 241 Chartres St., 504/522-4513, has dolls, toys, and related items of the 1800s and 1900s, plus dollhouses, miniatures, and porcelain. For estate jewelry that includes garnets, hat pins, and cameos, stop by **Joan Good Antiques,** 809 Royal St., 504/525-1705, www.joangood.com.

M.S. Rau, 630 Royal St., 504/523-5660, specializes in American cut glass and Victorian furniture. They've been in business since 1912. **Philip B. Lam,** 2727 Prytania St., 504/899-7491, offers collectibles from the Civil War South, including antique jewelry, photographs, and slave items. It's in the Garden District.

Jon Antiques, 4605 Magazine St., 504/899-4482, is located in a historic home. It has over 4,000 square feet of English and French eighteenth- and nineteenth-century furniture.

A Gallery for Fine Photography, 322 Royal St., 504/568-1313, offers rare photos and books from Ansel Adams, Alfred Stieglitz, and William Wegman. Fine original graphic art with selections of work from the 1930s and 1940s can be found at **Stone & Press**, 238 Chartres St., 504/561-8555.

Beckham's Bookshop, 228 Decatur St., 504/522-9875, has been selling old and second-hand books and classical records in the French Quarter for 30 years.

Get your candy at **Aunt Sally's Praline Shop,** 810 Decatur St., 504/944-6090. Watch it being made and get a free sample.

If you're dressing up for Mardi Gras, you'll need what the **Mardi Gras Center,** 831 Chartres St., 504/524-4384, has—costumes, makeup, hats, wigs, plumes, crowns, and beads.

Bourbon French Perfumes, 525 St. Ann St., 504/522-4480, on Jackson Square has been hand-blending fragrances since 1843. Get the scent that's just right for you.

SPORTS AND RECREATION

Take a fishing charter with **Capt. Nick's Wildlife Safaris,** 800/375-FISH. The dock is about a half-hour from New Orleans, and all equipment is provided.

The area also has many other guide services for fishing and for photo expedition, too. Both Capt. Nick's and **Papa Joe's Cajun**

Native Tongue

You'd expect a long Southern drawl here, but you won't find it unless you happen to run into a tourist from Savannah. The New Orleans accent sound more like the "dem" and "dose" of Brooklyn.

Here's a sampling of the native language:

New Orleans. The natives say New OY-uns. You'll be labeled an outlander if you say New or-LEENS.

Chartres. Throw away your freshman French book. The street name is pronounced Charters. Other streets: **Esplanade** is ES-plaine-ADE. **Burgundy** is Burr-GUN-dee. **Carondelet** is Care-on-da-LET. And, the biggie: **Tchoupitoulas** is Chip-a-TOOL-us.

Vieux Carre is Voo Car-RAY.

The French Quarter is pronounced by the natives as Da Franch Kwatas.

A **banquette** (ban-KET) is a sidewalk.

Neutral ground is a term describing the median in a road. It derives from the old days when the wide strip of land that is now Canal Street divided the French Quarter from the American Sector.

Lagniappe (lan-yap) means "a little bit more," something like a baker's dozen.

A **Creole** is a person descended from a French or Spanish settler who was born in America. A **Cajun** is a person descended from the French settlers in Nova Scotia, who were expelled by the British in the eighteenth century. Most of them settled in the swampy territories of south Louisiana.

Picayune (pick-y-UNE) means small or trifling. It comes from the Spanish coin, valued at about six cents, which was the original price of the local newspaper. Thus the name of the paper, the Times-Picayune.

Gris-gris (GREE-GREE) is an amulet worn for luck or used to conjure evil on enemies of voodoo worshipers.

Wetland Guide Service, 504/392-4409, will also take you on a photography expedition into the coastal marshes.

In the mood to bowl? Check out the **Mid City Lanes Rock 'n Bowl,** 4133 S. Carrollton Ave., 504/482-3133, which has been around since 1941. You get live music with your spares and strikes.

The tropical climate makes golf a year-round sport in the area. **Oak Harbor Golf Club,** 201 Oak Harbor Blvd., Slidell, 504/646-0110, is a Pete Dye–inspired course and is rated the number one public course in New Orleans. Another championship course is at the **English Turn Golf & Country Club,** One Clubhouse Dr., 504/392-2200, home of the Compaq Classic.

If you'd rather head to the gym, daily rates are available at the **Downtown Fitness Center,** 380 One Canal Pl., 504/525-2956. The center has all the major fitness equipment and is within walking distance of the major hotels.

Contact **Southern Runner Productions,** 504/899-3333, for information on the running/walking events of many distances that they produce almost weekly.

If you feel more like being a spectator, catch a home game of the **New Orleans Saints** football team, 504/733-0255. They play in the Louisiana Superdome, 1500 Poydras St.

ENTERTAINMENT

Find out what's happening at the **Contemporary Arts Center,** 900 Camp St., 504/523-1216, which has 10,000 square feet of gallery space with 24 exhibitions each year. It's home to artists' bold experimentation in painting, theater, photography, performance art, dance, music, and video.

To see free daily demonstrations of glassblowing and other arts, go to the **New Orleans School of Glass Works & Printmaking Studio,** 727 Magazine St., 504/529-7277.

New Orleans has plenty of casinos, none of them anything special. But if you're in the mood to gamble, try **Bally's Casino Lakeshore Resort,** One Stars & Stripes Blvd., 504/248-3417, which has lots of slots and gaming tables.

And at some point in your travels around the city, you've got to stop by **Pat O'Brien's** for one of those famous Hurricanes. It has a main bar, a sing-along patio bar, and a patio with a flaming fountain. Another noteworthy drink is the Hand Grenade, said to be New Orleans's most powerful drink. You can pull the pin on one at the **Tropical Isle** bar, 721 Bourbon St., 504/529-4109.

One of the most famous nightclubs in town is **Pete Fountain's,** in the Hilton Hotel, Third Floor, 2 Poydras St., 504/524-6255—where the legendary jazz clarinetist still plays. To hear some of the city's best contemporary jazz, stop by **Snug Harbor,** 6236 Frenchmen St., 504/949-0696. Likewise, you'll find traditional jazz at the **Palm Court Jazz Café,** 1204 Decatur St., 504/525-0200. And if you still need more jazz, check out the music behind **Famous Door,** 339 Bourbon St., 504/522-7626. **Fritzel's,** 733 Bourbon St., 504/561-0432, is the place to hear Dixieland jazz in a unique European setting.

The **Storyville District,** 124 Bourbon St., 504/410-1000, is named for the nightclub called Storyville that opened in 1897 and is considered to be the birthplace of jazz. This new complex features multiple rooms that offer constant music from noon until 1 a.m.

The **Funky Pirate,** 727 Bourbon St., 504/523-1960, features Big Al Carson, the 550-pound international blues star, plus lots of other great blues music.

The **Southern Rep Theatre,** One Canal Pl. at Canal and N. Peters Sts., 504/861-8163, features Southern dramas, playwrights, and actors in an intimate theater. It's at the Shops at Canal Place on the third level.

For Broadway shows, concerts, gospel music, and more under the stars, go to the **Saenger Theatre,** 143 N. Rampart St., 504/525-1052.

Finally, to experience New Orleans's original supper club, go to the **Red Room,** 2040 St. Charles Ave., 504/528-9759, featuring fine dining with live jazz and dancing. It has cocktail lounges and a cigar lounge.

CITY BASICS

For French Quarter room reservations, try **877/SAV-CASH.** You can also get information on the Internet from www.bigeasy.com or www.visitnola.com. Contact **Bed and Breakfast,** 800/729-4640, for B&B reservations in the French Quarter and Garden District.

For information on the arts, contact the **Arts Council of New Orleans,** 225 Baronne St., Suite 1712, 504/523-1465. And learn about all the big events happening during the year by contacting **French Quarter Festivals,** 100 Conti St., 504/522-5730, www.fqfestivals.org.

Offbeat is New Orleans's monthly guide to the city's music and entertainment scene. You'll find it free at most hotels. The city's oldest weekly tourist magazine is *This Week in New Orleans.*

Information is also available from the **New Orleans Convention and Visitors Bureau,** 800/672-6124, www.neworleanscvb.com. In addition to the Web site offered by the visitors bureau, consider checking out www.orleansnet.com.

The *Times-Picayune* is the major daily newspaper in New Orleans. A weekly that has lots of entertainment information in it is the *GambitWeekly.* Also, a free magazine that can help you around the local scene is *Where New Orleans.*

㉓ MEMPHIS

to go ▶

Memphis After Midnight (James Carr)
Letter to Memphis (The Pixies)
The Memphis Blues (W.C. Handy)
Memphis Hip Snake (The Cult)
Memphis Rhythm (Bob Marley)
Memphis Exorcism (Squirrel Nut Zippers)
Stuck Inside of Mobile with the Memphis Blues Again (Bob Dylan)
—Songs with Memphis in the title

Is Memphis a one-note wonder? Ain't it nothin' but one big Elvis impersonator?

Oh no, no. You've got it all wrong. This place plays lots of different notes.

It's the home of the blues, for one thing, and the birthplace of rock 'n' roll. Then there's gospel, jazz, rap, and soul, and plenty of rockabilly and good old country-western (not all of it is across the state in Nashville).

Did you know that Memphis is mentioned in more songs than any other city in the world? Yep, 389 times, according to the latest count from *Billboard* magazine.

Here's a few of Memphis's famous names in music (minus Mr. Presley), all of whom were born or spent serious time here: Isaac Hayes, B.B. King, Kirk Whalum, Otis Redding, Johnny Cash, Jerry Lee Lewis, Carl Perkins, Wilson Pickett, Howlin' Wolf, Ike Turner, Charlie Pride, Tina Turner, opera stars Marguerite Piazza and Kallen Esperian, Carla "Queen of Soul" Thomas, Billy Gibbons of ZZ Top,

Downtown Memphis

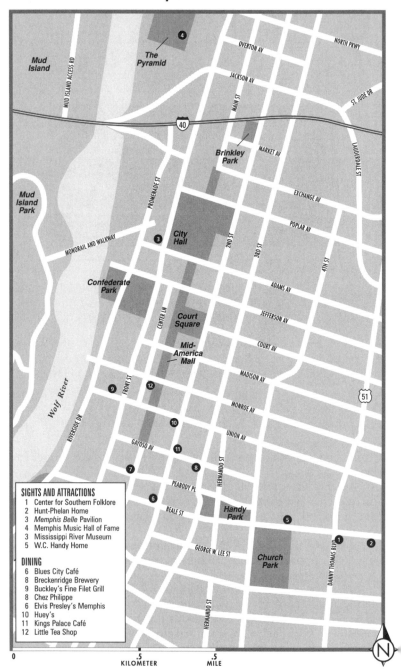

The Pyramid ④

Mud Island

MUD ISLAND ACCESS RD

OVERTON AV

NORTH PKWY

JACKSON AV

MAIN ST

ST. JUDE DR

40

Brinkley Park

MARKET AV

LAUDERDALE ST

Mud Island Park

PROMENADE ST

MONORAIL AND WALKWAY

City Hall ③

EXCHANGE AV

POPLAR AV

2ND ST

3RD ST

4TH ST

Confederate Park

CENTER LN

ADAMS AV

Court Square

JEFFERSON AV

Mid-America Mall

COURT AV

Wolf River

RIVERSIDE DR

FRONT ST

MADISON AV

⑨

⑫

MONROE AV

51

⑩

UNION AV

GAYOSO AV

⑪

HERNANDO ST

⑦

⑧

PEABODY PL

⑥

Handy Park

BEALE ST

⑤

GEORGE W. LEE ST

Church Park

DANNY THOMAS BLVD

①

②

HERNANDO ST

SIGHTS AND ATTRACTIONS
1 Center for Southern Folklore
2 Hunt-Phelan Home
3 *Memphis Belle* Pavilion
4 Memphis Music Hall of Fame
3 Mississippi River Museum
5 W.C. Handy Home

DINING
6 Blues City Café
8 Breckenridge Brewery
9 Buckley's Fine Filet Grill
8 Chez Philippe
6 Elvis Presley's Memphis
10 Huey's
11 Kings Palace Café
12 Little Tea Shop

0 .5 KILOMETER .5 MILE

N

"Sam the Sham" Samudio, Rita Coolidge, Sam and Dave, and Sun Studio founder Sam Phillips.

Add in the rich, sweet taste of pork barbecue, a vision of that rolling, muddy Mississippi, and the plaintive memory of Martin Luther King Jr.'s last days, and it sounds to us like a lot more than just one note. Sounds like a whole symphony.

GETTING AROUND

With a city population of about 650,000 and a metro population of just over a million, Memphis is not unmanageable. Although most of the attractions are concentrated around Beale Street downtown, you still may want a car.

Memphis International Airport, 901/922-8000, is about 15 minutes from downtown. For passengers it's not terribly busy, but remember that because of the city's central location in the United States, MIA has become the world's busiest cargo airport. You may get in an airplane traffic jam because of the Federal Express planes and 25 other freight carriers. This is FedEx's home port.

Cab fare from the airport to downtown is about $15. Try **City Wide Cab Co.,** 901/324-4202, or **Yellow Cab Co.,** 901/577-7777.

The main concentrations of Memphis attractions and hotels are in three areas—downtown near Beale Street, where the nightlife is active and the blues hardly ever stop; the Poplar Ave., I-40, and U.S. 240 interchange, which is about 17 miles to the east of downtown; and the Graceland area on Elvis Presley Blvd., which is about 10 miles to the south of downtown.

We recommend downtown as the place to concentrate your visit. The downtown trolley system (Memphis Area Transit Authority's "showboat" bus, 547 N. Main St., 901/274-6282, 901/274-1757, TTY) runs a five-mile loop route down Main Street Mall and Riverside Drive from Auction Street near The Pyramid to Calhoun Street and the National Civil Rights Museum. Fares are 50 cents each way, with a daily lunch-hour rate of 25 cents between 11 a.m. and 1:30 p.m. The trolley system is accessible to people with disabilities.

The **Memphis Area Transit Authority** (MATA), 901/722-7100, also operates a tourist-friendly bus service. You can get a special tourist pass with unlimited rides for one low price. Call MATA for details. You can also catch a bus at the baggage claim area of the airport to get downtown, but you have to transfer at least once.

SIGHTS AND ATTRACTIONS

Beale Street, is the heart and soul of the city and the place to begin and end your visit. It is really a bit hard to classify—the whole area is a

⸺ Civil Rights Site ⸺

The **National Civil Rights Museum**, at 450 Mulberry St. downtown, 901/521-9699, www.civilrightsmuseum.org, is a must for any tourist. It's housed in the Lorraine Motel, site of the slaying of Dr. Martin Luther King Jr. Inside are exhibits and interactive displays that trace the history of civil rights activity and its leaders—including the Little Rock school integration of 1954, Rosa Parks' Montgomery bus incident, and the March on Washington. All of this culminates in the emotional scene of the Lorraine, where King was assassinated on April 4, 1968.

living, breathing, toe-tapping museum, so it also belongs in the Entertainment section. The area should likewise be classified under Dining because of all its good barbecue places, and under Shopping because it is home to such unique places as A. Schwab, which is just as much a museum as a department store.

The centerpiece of Beale Street is the modest little **W.C. Handy Home,** 352 Beale St., 901/522-1556, where the musician gave birth to the blues and helped raise six children besides. In 1909 Handy wrote a campaign song for a Memphis mayoral candidate, and it won such praise for its sound that its words were rewritten and the song became *Memphis Blues*, the first blues song to be published. He also wrote *St. Louis Blues*. A statue of him overlooks Beale Street from the shady park named in his honor.

Beale Street rocked with nightlife until the Depression years, when it fell on hard times. But $500 million in redevelopment has put new life into the area. Now it's like Bourbon Street, filled with music every night, and it has lots of shops, restaurants, boutiques, nightspots, theaters, and parks.

Walk along the street and you'll be walking over history. The **Beale Street Walk-Of-Fame,** which is near the Orpheum Theatre at Beale and Main Streets, consists of brass notes in the sidewalk honoring those who have contributed to America's blues music.

Another major attraction on Beale Street is the **Center for Southern Folklore,** 209 Beale St., 901/525-3655. It has several films about the area, such as *If Beale Street Could Talk*, plus a distinctive gift shop of regional items and a performance space featuring blues, jazz, and gospel music.

The **Hunt-Phelan Home,** 533 Beale St., 800/350-9009, is one of the oldest homes in Memphis. It was built in 1828 and contains a treasury of Civil War artifacts. Each room has been restored to its original splendor. Included are antique silver and china, an 1874 rosewood grand piano, and a library that General Ulysses S. Grant used as his office when Union soldiers took over Memphis during the Civil War.

Not far from Beale Street is the **Memphis Music Hall of Fame,**

97 S. Second St., 901/525-4007, which features 24 video and six continuous audio presentations on Memphis's music legends from W.C. Handy to Elvis Presley and Charlie Rich. You can view video biographies of Memphis's music legends, plus a re-creation of the P. Wee Saloon on Beale Street, where Handy wrote the *St. Louis Blues.*

Another must-see sight downtown is **Sun Studio,** 706 Union Ave., 901/521-0664, the birthplace of rock 'n' roll. Here's where Elvis Presley, Jerry Lee Lewis, Johnny Cash, Roy Orbison, and many others launched their careers. Tours are conducted by day, and the studio is a real studio at night. Next door is the **Studio Café,** and above it is a museum/gallery featuring rare recordings and memorabilia of the great era of American pop music.

See the other sections of this chapter for others sorts of things to do on Beale Street. Just don't miss this street!

After undergoing a $30 million renovation, the **Memphis Zoo,** 2000 Galloway, 901/276-WILD, www.memphiszoo.org, has attained world-class status. Its specialties are exhibits on the African veldt, Asian temple ruins, Peruvian rain forests, and Jamaican caverns.

Mud Island, an island in the Mississippi that's easy to get to on a monorail and walkway from Adams Avenue downtown, has the 18-gallery **Mississippi River Museum,** 125 N. Front St., 800/507-6507, with its Mississippi River Walk—a five-block-long scale model of the river that includes its own faux Gulf of Mexico and a beach. Also there is the *Memphis Belle* **Pavilion,** 125 N. Front St., 800/507-6507, which contains World War II's most famous airplane—the first U.S. bomber to complete 25 missions against Nazi targets and return to the United States. It was the subject of a famous documentary in 1943 and also a more recent film.

One of the country's finest small museums is the **Dixon Gallery and Gardens,** 4339 Park Ave., 901/761-5250. Featured are major Impressionist works by Renoir, Degas, and Monet; eighteenth-century porcelain; and gorgeous gardens.

The **Mallory-Neely House,** 652 Adams Ave., 901/523-1484, is a carefully preserved Italian villa–style mansion dating to the 1850s. This 25-room house contains antiques and furnishings spanning 100 years. Additionally, several other historic houses can be viewed in the same midtown neighborhood known as the Victorian Village.

The oldest and largest fine arts museum in Memphis is the **Brooks Museum of Art,** 1934 Poplar Ave., 901/722-3500. It features paintings, sculptures, prints, drawings, and photographs from antiquity to the present. Major exhibitions also rotate through the museum.

The **Pink Palace Museum and Planetarium,** 3050 Central Ave., 901/320-6320, includes natural and cultural history exhibits from dinosaurs to the stars. It's housed in a mansion built in 1923 for Piggly Wiggly founder Clarence Saunders. If you've always wanted to see an exact replica of the original Piggly Wiggly, this is the place for you. It's included in one of the wings of this multifaceted museum complex.

Central Memphis

To 2

Chickasaw Garden
6

BUNTYN ST

Frank T. Tobey Park

SIGHTS AND ATTRACTIONS
1 Brooks Museum of Art
2 Dixon Gallery and Gardens
3 Mallory-Neely House
4 Memphis Zoo
5 National Ornamental Metal Museum
6 Pink Palace Museum and Planetarium
7 Studio Café
7 Sun Studio

DINING
8 Anderton's
9 Erling Jensen, The Restaurant
10 Half Shell
11 Neely's Bar-B-Cue

POPLAR AV

HOLLYWOOD ST

EAST PKWY

AVERY AV

Christian Brothers University

Mid-South Fairgrounds

SOUTHERN AV

JACKSON AV

Rhodes College

SUMMER AV

Overton Park Municipal Golf Course

MONROE AV

MEDA ST

UNIVERSITY ST

COOPER ST

Municipal Zoo
4

MC LEAN BLVD

REMBERT ST

COWDEN AV

NELSON AV

YOUNG AV

1

8

EVERGREEN ST

BELVEDERE BLVD

CENTRAL AV

LAMAR AV

Glenview Park

WILLETT ST

PEACH AV

POPLAR AV

COURT AV

UNION AV

WILLETT ST

WATKINS ST

CLEVELAND ST

EASTMORELAND AV

PEABODY AV

MONTGOMERY ST

BELLEVUE AV

51

ELVIS PRESLEY BLVD

NORTH PARKWAY

240

40

JEFFERSON AV

MADISON AV

NEPTUNE PL

LINDEN AV

E.H. CRUMP BLVD

MISSISSIPPI BLVD

9

51

3

11

ORLEANS ST

7

10

ADAMS AV

JEFFERSON AV

MARSHALL AV

BEALE ST

VANCE AV

WALKER AV

AUCTION AV

3RD ST

5

DANNY THOMAS BLVD

MILE
KILOMETER

N

The only museum in the United States dedicated to preserving the craft of fine metalwork is the **National Ornamental Metal Museum, 374** Metal Museum Dr., 901/774-6380. Exhibits range from jewelry to outdoor sculpture, and the museum also has a working blacksmith shop overlooking the Mississippi River.

LODGING

The **Peabody Hotel,** 149 Union Ave., 800/PEABODY, $$$, is all it's quacked up to be, and more. This is the place to make your nest. In comparison, all other hotels in Memphis are decoys.

The Peabody is as grand and eccentric as an ancient southern lady. You get all the expected amenities—afternoon tea in the elegant lobby, overstuffed furniture, floral displays as big as bushes, several high-end restaurants, an athletic club, and, from the roof, a wonderful view of Old Man River. Likewise, the hotel is downtown near all the action.

And then there's the duck parade. Nothing else in America is like it. At 11 a.m. each day, to the tune of John Philip Sousa's *King Cotton March*, a small fleet of mallards marches off the elevator, down a red carpet unfurled for them in the lobby, and into the gorgeous Travertine marble fountain, where they splash about all day. At 5 p.m., it's reverse course—back down the red carpet to the elevator and up to their penthouse pond for the evening. The display really draws a crowd.

The **Ridgeway Inn,** Poplar Ave. and I-240, 800/822-3360, $$, is owned and operated by the Peabody Hotel Group—the same good service at a much lower price, but without the ducks, unfortunately.

A small, intimate hotel in the heart of downtown and across the street from the Peabody is the **Talbot Heirs Guesthouse,** 99 S. Second St., 901/527-3700, $$. It has nine rooms and no dining facilities.

If your heart belongs to Elvis, now you can sleep next door to the King. **Elvis Presley's Heartbreak Hotel,** 3677 Elvis Presley Blvd., 901/332-1000, $$, opened in the summer of 1999 across the street from Graceland mansion. You get free in-room Elvis movies and packages that can include Graceland tours.

The **Days Inn Graceland,** 3839 Elvis Presley Blvd., 901/346-5500, $$, has a swimming pool shaped like a guitar and 24-hour-a-day Elvis movies on its Elvis Channel. Talk about total immersion.

In the heart of downtown Memphis, within walking distance of Beale Street, is the **Radisson,** 185 Union Ave., 800/333-3333, $$$. It has an outdoor pool, a whirlpool and sauna, plus exercise facilities. Free morning coffee and newspaper are included.

Another of the well-situated hotels downtown is the **Marriott,** 250 N. Main St., 800/228-9290, $$. It has 400 rooms on 18 floors, with an indoor pool, health club, and in-room movies. The hotel is located right on the trolley line.

Just 25 minutes south of Memphis is the **Bonne Terre Country**

Inn, 4715 Church Rd. W., Nesbit, Miss., 601/781-5100, $$, which sits on a 100-acre rolling estate. A Greek Revival mansion features 10 guest rooms with fireplaces, Jacuzzis, and balconies that overlook the lake and pool.

If you really want to meet some interesting folks, hook up your Winnebago at the **Elvis Presley Boulevard RV Park,** 3971 Elvis Presley Blvd., 901/332-3633, $. They've also got tent sites and showers, a coin laundry, and a dump station. You're also within walking distance of Graceland.

DINING

Let's remain on Beale Street, or thereabouts in the downtown area. There's no sense going far off if we don't have to.

Elvis Presley's Memphis, 126 Beale St., 901/527-6900, $$, is a restaurant operated by the Presley folks that offers southern cuisine along with Elvis artifacts, live music, and a gospel brunch.

Besides the usual southern delicacies such as huge steaks and slathered slabs of barbecued pork ribs, you can get homemade hot tamales and seafood gumbo at the **Blues City Café,** 138 Beale St., 901/526-3637, $$. Also try **Kings Palace Café,** 162 Beale St., 901/521-1851, $$, featuring award-winning gumbo.

You'll get more beef for the buck at **Buckley's Fine Filet Grill,** 117 Union Ave., 901/578-9001, $—the famous Buckley filet is just $9.99. The restaurant is also noted for its homemade pastas.

The **Breckenridge Brewery,** 145 S. Main St. at Peabody Pl., 901/524-1080, $$, is a microbrewery and restaurant with standard pub grub in the historic Majestic Theater building, which dates to 1914.

Let's go upscale southern with some hushpuppies served with shrimp Provençale. Or try the roasted veal loin breaded with artichokes, vegetable puree, and a light-roasted garlic sauce. **Chez Philippe,** 149 Union Ave., 901/529-4000, $$$, is top of the line in Memphis, and it's in the famed Peabody Hotel. For fine dining, try **Erling Jensen, The Restaurant,** 1044 S. Yates, 901/763-3700, $$$$. Start with the foie gras and end with the warm chocolate tart.

The best burgers downtown are at **Huey's,** 77 S. Second St., 901/527-2700, $. It's got live music on Sunday afternoons and live blues bands on Sunday nights. The locals are nuts about **Neely's Bar-B-Cue,** 670 Jefferson, 901/521-9798, $$, especially those ribs.

The **Little Tea Shop,** 69 Monroe Ave., 901/525-6000, $$, is Memphis's oldest restaurant, dating back to 1918. It's a lunch-only establishment, 11 a.m. to 2:30 p.m., featuring southern cooking such as biscuits, fried chicken, and peach cobbler made from scratch. You'd better get there early to get a seat.

The freshest seafood in town is at the **Half Shell,** 688 S. Mendenhall Rd., 901/628-3966, $$, a Memphis landmark. The shrimp dinner

The Glories of Graceland

Say what you want about Elvis, he was a phenomenon. People from around the world—approximately 750,000 a year—come here to see where he lived and got his start.

Elvis is a major industry in Memphis, kind of like cotton used to be. The headquarters of that industry is Graceland, the Presley mansion. Some call it America's down-home version of the Palace of Versailles. The two are about equally gaudy.

The mansion was built in 1939 with music in mind. The daughter of the first owner, Ruth Marie Cobb, was musically inclined, and grew up to be principal harpist for the Memphis Symphony Orchestra. Many of the rooms were designed for performances.

Elvis paid $100,000 for the mansion and its 14 acres of grounds in 1957, when he was 22. He lived there 20 years.

Today, groups of about 14 people are taken through the mansion at a time. You get a tape recorder to listen to as your guide, and then away you go through the wild blue-suede yonder of Elvis's home.

There's the kitchen, where those fried peanut butter and 'naner sandwiches were made. The dining room, with a stained-glass partition of peacocks, Elvis's favorite bird.

The staircase, completely mirrored. The pool room, TV room, and then the Jungle Room, in African motif with a waterfall. And the Hall of Gold, with 37 gold albums on the wall. Outside is the Meditation Garden and the graves of Elvis; his mother, Gladys; his father, Vernon; and his grandmother, Minnie Mae Presley.

After the house tour, they take you in a van to see his private jets (one is named after his daughter, the *Lisa Marie*; it has gold buckles on the seat belts). The tour ends where you started, smack dab in the middle of Graceland Plaza, where you can conveniently buy everything from Elvis stamps to Elvis watches; an Elvisopoly game; or an interactive CD-ROM tour of Graceland.

Graceland is at 3734 Elvis Presley Blvd., a mile south of I-55; 800/238-2000, www.elvis-presley.com. Tickets are $18.50 for adults.

or the Gulf oysters are tops. **Anderton's,** 1901 Madison Ave., 901/726-4010, $$, has been a Memphis tradition since 1945. Ask about its lobster dainties and the hot apple dumplings.

SHOPPING

A great place for shopping on Beale Street is **A. Schwab's,** 163 Beale St., 901/523-9782, a department store that has been run by the same family since 1876. The store's slogan is, "If you can't find it at Schwab's, you're better off without it." Well, there's not much in the world that you'd be better off without, because Schwab's has just about everything, including voodoo powders, clerical collars, magic potions, 99¢ neckties, handcuffs, church usher badges, hardware, clothing, tools, and toys. Don't neglect the second floor, which is a mini-museum full of artifacts from Beale Street's heyday.

The **Cooper-Young District**, S. Cooper St. and Young Ave., located in historic Midtown near Victorian Village, is filled with antique shops, vintage clothing boutiques, and art galleries, plus several popular restaurants.

Memphis Music, 149 Beale St., 901/526-5047, has a huge selection of blues recordings, T-shirts, and music books. Now that you've heard the music, you need something to learn to play it on. You'll find what you need at **Rod and Hank's Vintage Guitars,** 45 S. Main St., 901/525-9240.

You'll need a drummer, too. Equip her or him at the **Memphis Drum Shop,** 878 S. Cooper St., 901/276-2328. They've got drums, cymbals, and other percussion instruments, and they'll give you a lesson, too.

And of course you'll need to look the part. Get funky with vintage clothing from **Vintage Mania,** 2151 Young Ave., 901/274-2879, which has clothes from the 1930s to the 1970s, specializing in psychedelic fashions. They've also got art-deco glassware and furnishings.

The **Village Boutique,** 300 S. Main St., 901/521-0466, specializes in imported authentic African fashions, carvings, and accessories.

With more than 70 shops in one place, you're likely to find what you've always been looking for at **Palladio Antique and Interior Marketplace,** 2169 Central Ave., 888/276-3808. It's been compared to the French Quarter for its ambiance, complete with a courtyard crowded with garden antiquities.

Finally, for your Memphis souvenirs, head over to **Y-Not,** 333 Beale St., 901/527-9084.

SPORTS AND RECREATION

Memphis isn't big enough for the big leagues, but there are still plenty of sports to keep you interested. The **Memphis Redbirds,** 800 Home-run Ln., 901/721-6000, are the Triple-A baseball affiliate of the St. Louis Cardinals. Also, the **University of Memphis,** 901/678-2331, has a basketball team that draws huge crowds to The Pyramid, One Auction Ave., 901/521-9675. The Tigers are frequently nationally ranked. And the **Memphis RiverKings,** 901/278-9009, play hockey at the Mid-South Coliseum, 996 Early Maxwell Blvd. They were the Eastern Division champs in 1996–97.

Memphis has 182 parks totaling 6,000 acres, with everything from small riverside walking parks to fitness trails and garden centers. The

Take a moonlight excursion on a paddlewheel riverboat

Parks Commission, 901/454-5200, also operates two 9-hole and five 18-hole golf courses. One of the best golf courses in the area, the **Cherokee Valley Golf Club,** 6635 Crumpler Blvd., Olive Branch, Miss., 601/893-4444, is only 10 minutes south of Memphis.

The **Fogelman YMCA,** 245 Madison Ave., 901/527-9622, offers an eight-dollar day pass, with discounts from some hotels. It has an extensive collection of exercise equipment, a running track, and a pool.

If you brought your boat, you can launch it into the Mississippi from the **Meeman-Shelby State Park.** Call the **Riverside Park Marine,** 901/525-3808, for information.

Elvis loved fast cars, and there are plenty of them at the **Memphis Motorsports Park,** 5500 Taylor Forge Rd., Millington, 901/358-7223, which features drag racing, road racing, and oval track competition. It's only 10 minutes from downtown Memphis in suburban Millington.

Southland Greyhound Park, I-40 and I-55, West Memphis, Ark., 870/735-3670, has live and simulcast greyhound racing and thoroughbred horse racing. It's open year round. Call for racing schedules.

ENTERTAINMENT

Again, Beale Street is the place to be.

The **Orpheum Theatre,** 203 S. Main St., 901/525-7800, is the premier venue near Beale Street. This former vaudeville palace, built in 1928, has gotten a $5 million facelift and has been transformed into one of the South's top performing arts centers.

B.B. King's Blues Hall, 143 Beale St., 901/524-5464, features the best in blues nightly, with memorabilia from the blues legend's past and some pretty good ribs and fried catfish.

The folks in Memphis voted the **Black Diamond,** 153 Beale St., 901/521-0800, as the best new club in town. It has live music nightly plus pizza and po-boys. Also, the **Hard Rock Cafe,** Beale and Hernando Sts., 901/529-0007, is the only one of the chain that offers live music. The food is all-American, from burgers to brownies.

The **Overton Square Entertainment District,** Madison Ave. at Cooper, 901/278-6300, is a three-block, architecturally diverse area in the heart of Memphis that includes restaurants, live music, comedy, dancing, and theater.

The Pyramid, One Auction Ave., 901/521-9675, is a 32-story stainless steel sports and concert facility serving as a tribute to Memphis's Egyptian namesake. Inside is a 20,000-seat, multipurpose arena. It's at the northern end of downtown.

Adjacent to The Pyramid is the **Pinch Historic District,** N. Main St. from the convention center to North Parkway, the newest entertainment area in downtown Memphis. It's a turn-of-the-last-century neighborhood first settled by Irish immigrants and Jewish merchants. Within it are six restaurants/bars offering live entertainment every weekend.

The **Germantown Performing Arts Centre,** 1801 Exeter Rd., 901/757-7256, in the suburb of Germantown, presents the best in music, dance, theater, and opera. The **Memphis Symphony,** 901/324-3627, performs at various venues throughout Memphis, including outdoors. Memphis's only professional live theater is **Playhouse on the Square,** 51 S. Cooper St., 901/726-4656. It offers everything from drama to Broadway musicals.

CITY BASICS

For information on visiting the city, contact the **Memphis Convention & Visitors Bureau,** 47 Union Ave., Memphis, TN 38103; 901/543-5333; www.memphistravel.com. Also, the city's **Visitor Information Center** is located inside the Memphis Police Museum, 119 Riverside Dr. Call 901/543-5333 for a *Safety Tips for Tourists* brochure or 901/751-0158 for a **trolley map.**

The **Memphis Hotline,** 901/57-ELVIS, can give you up-to-date information on what's happening in the city. Likewise, **weather information** is available by phone, 901/522-8888.

The *Memphis Commercial Appeal* is the city's major daily newspaper. You can also get entertainment news from *Memphis* magazine.

⓷ ATLANTA

to go ▶

I want to say to General Sherman . . . that from the ashes he left us in
1864 we have raised a brave and beautiful city; that somehow or other
we have caught the sunshine in the bricks and mortar of our homes.
—Henry W. Grady, *The New South*, 1886

The Old South—or at least the part of it around Atlanta—is long gone
with the wind. Atlanta today is an up-to-the-minute, vital, vibrant big
city with one foot planted firmly in the future and only a toe hanging
back in the past.

You could call it the second burning of Atlanta and call it a shame,
because most of the old buildings—those that weren't torched by that
horrid General William Tecumseh Sherman in 1864—have been
shoved aside by the McFranchised present. To find the past, you're
going to have to hunt for it.

The future is easy to find. Downtown Atlanta is a shiny jumble of
postmodern skyscrapers and is busy with postmodern people running
from task to task, just like you. The 20-county metro population is 3.6
million, with newcomers streaming in by the dozens daily. Atlanta is a
boomtown, the capital of the New South, with a go-man-go mentality.

Something that gave Atlanta new life was the 1996 Olympics.
Between 1990 and the Games, Atlanta spent $2 billion on Olympic-
related and other construction. Two million visitors came to see the
games, and 3.5 billion watched the Olympics—and Atlanta—on television that summer. Big bucks and lots of exposure have given Atlanta a

Atlanta

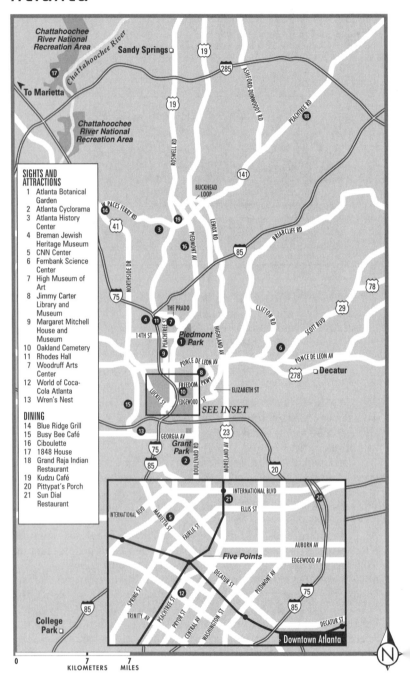

Chattahoochee River National Recreation Area

Sandy Springs

19

285

ASHFORD-DUNWOODY RD

To Marietta

17

19

PEACHTREE RD

18

Chattahoochee River National Recreation Area

ROSWELL RD

141

BUCKHEAD LOOP

SIGHTS AND ATTRACTIONS
1 Atlanta Botanical Garden
2 Atlanta Cyclorama
3 Atlanta History Center
4 Breman Jewish Heritage Museum
5 CNN Center
6 Fernbank Science Center
7 High Museum of Art
8 Jimmy Carter Library and Museum
9 Margaret Mitchell House and Museum
10 Oakland Cemetery
11 Rhodes Hall
7 Woodruff Arts Center
12 World of Coca-Cola Atlanta
13 Wren's Nest

DINING
14 Blue Ridge Grill
15 Busy Bee Café
16 Ciboulette
17 1848 House
18 Grand Raja Indian Restaurant
19 Kudzu Café
20 Pittypat's Porch
21 Sun Dial Restaurant

W PACES FERRY RD

14

41

LENOX RD

BRIARCLIFF RD

85

3

19

PIEDMONT AV

16

NORTHSIDE DR

75

78

CLIFTON RD

SCOTT BLVD

29

THE PRADO

4 11 7

14TH ST

PEACHTREE ST

Piedmont Park

1

HIGHLAND AV

6

PONCE DE LEON AV

9

PONCE DE LEON AV

278

□ Decatur

8

FREEDOM PKWY

10

ELIZABETH ST

LUCKIE ST

EDGEWOOD ST

15

SEE INSET

13

GEORGIA AV

23

75

Grant Park

BOULEVARD RD

2

MORELAND AV

85

20

INTERNATIONAL BLVD

21

ELLIS ST

20

INTERNATIONAL BLVD

MARIETTA ST

5

FAIRLIE ST

AUBURN AV

Five Points

EDGEWOOD AV

DECATUR ST

PIEDMONT AV

75

SPRING ST

PEACHTREE ST

12

PRYOR ST

CENTRAL AV

WASHINGTON ST

85

85

College Park □

TRINITY AV

DECATUR ST

Downtown Atlanta

N

0   7   7
KILOMETERS MILES

new sense of sophistication; visitors have some new things to see and do, along with easier ways to get there and an overall safer city to visit.

But behind the bustle are lots of easy-going, friendly people and a sometimes gentle, sometimes brutal past—Margaret Mitchell's mint-juleped South; the trampled fields where Americans killed Americans; and the place from which one man with a dream, the Rev. Martin Luther King Jr., changed the world forever.

GETTING AROUND

You'll be arriving at **Hartsfield Atlanta International Airport,** 404/530-6600—one of the world's busiest airports—and you'll be a long way from anything worth seeing. You can get to the center of things by bus, taxi, shuttle, or a rapid-rail service called **MARTA** (Metropolitan Atlanta Rapid Transit Authority), 404/848-4711 or 404/848-5389 (information for disabled passengers), which is a good, clean, convenient way to get around. The system has 36 stations served by 238 rail cars and 704 buses.

If you decide to take the train from the airport, you can hop on at baggage claim. The trains offer a place to store your luggage, but it's a good idea to keep an eye on it. The subway's two lines make an easy cross pattern, with the intersection occurring downtown at Five Points, a huge underground station that is the only place you can switch from the north-south to the east-west line. For your $1.50 you get two transfers, in case you need to connect with one of the buses. Turnstiles accept exact change or MARTA tokens, which are sold in vending machines. Buses operate the same way—accepting only exact change or tokens.

All MARTA stations and cars are fully accessible to the disabled. MARTA also can provide vans with wheelchair lifts.

If you decide to take a taxi, 404/658-7600 (rate information), from the airport to downtown, the ride will cost you about $18. Two taxi companies in the area are **Atlanta Lenox Taxi Co.,** 404/885-1662, which accepts major credit cards, and **Checker Cab Co.,** 404/351-1111.

The **Atlanta Airport Shuttle,** 404/524-3400, also provides transportation from the airport to downtown ($10, one-way; $17, round-trip).

Everything is so spread out here (think of Atlanta as Los Angeles with a southern accent), that even though MARTA is good for short hops within town, the best way to get to many outlying points of interest is by freeway. You need a car. Rent one.

If you don't hit Atlanta at peak commute time, you'll be just fine. Interstate 20 runs east and west, Interstate 75/85 runs north and south, and Interstate 285 loops around. Easy as peach pie, darlin'.

But for getting around *within* that loop of concrete called Interstate 285, the good news is the bad news: The good news is that you have only one street to remember—**Peachtree Street,** which runs

Going Places

Pennyman Specialty Tours puts the emphasis on African American and Atlanta history tours; 800/833-2844. If your interest is the War Between the States, **Civil War Tours** will get you to the battlefields in the Atlanta area, 770/908-8410. **Gray Line** will also show you Atlanta. It has a tour office in Underground Atlanta; 800/965-6665.

through the center of the city and is the major east-west dividing line. The bad news is that it seems like just about *every* street is named Peachtree Street. In fact, there are 55 different Peachtree Streets around Atlanta, and even the major one becomes Peachtree *Road* in the north of the city. So just because you're on Peachtree doesn't mean you're not lost.

SIGHTS AND ATTRACTIONS

You're going to want to see "the Dump." This is what Margaret Mitchell affectionately called the modest apartment where she spent several years writing the world's most popular novel—*Gone With the Wind.* Now known as the **Margaret Mitchell House and Museum,** 999 Peachtree St., 404/249-7012, Mitchell and her husband John Marsh lived there from 1925 to 1932. Mitchell did most of her writing at a little sewing table and would hide the manuscript under a large towel to protect her privacy, something she guarded to the very end.

The **CNN Center,** Marietta St. at Techwood Dr. NW, 404/827-2300 (tour reservations), is headquarters of the global village, and the most visited site in Atlanta. Here is Ted Turner's vision in all its gleaming glory. Do consider signing up for a tour—you'll get to see studios in action and newsgatherers at their desks, probably yakking around the coffee pot and talking about their golf game instead of Kosovo. Make reservations for the tour to guarantee a spot, but walk-up tickets are available at 8:30 each morning for that day only.

In 1866 an Atlanta pharmacist named John Pemberton invented a "brain tonic" that consisted of extracts from the coca plant and kola nuts. A customer's request to have his **Coca-Cola** served with soda water is what eventually led to the creation of Atlanta's most famous product. Today evidence of Coke's impact on Atlanta is everywhere, but of most interest to the visitor is the **World of Coca-Cola Atlanta,** 55 Martin Luther King Jr. Dr. just behind Underground Atlanta, 404/676-5151, which demonstrates the marvel of marketing behind the drink. The place is actually a short course in the history of advertising, and an interesting look at how our culture is reflected in those ads.

For a change of pace, stop by the **Atlanta Botanical Garden,** in midtown above Piedmont Park, 404/876-5859, which consists of 30 acres of outdoor display gardens and a 15-acre urban forest.

The world's largest oil painting revolves around you in **Atlanta Cyclorama,** 800-C Cherokee Ave. SE, 404/658-7625, which depicts the 1864 Battle of Atlanta. The audience sits on a tiered viewing platform and watches as the painting—brought to life with computerized narration and sound effects—turns slowly around.

The **Atlanta History Center,** 130 W. Paces Ferry Rd. NW, 404/814-4000, includes an opulent Atlanta mansion, a farmhouse, and 33 acres of gardens, all of which tells the story of the city and the South.

See a life-size replica of the Oval Office at the **Jimmy Carter Library and Museum,** 441 Freedom Parkway, 404/331-0296. Also here are a collection of replicas of gowns worn by past first ladies and a gift shop that has lots of Carter campaign memorabilia.

Oakland Cemetery, 248 Oakland Ave. SE, 404/688-2107, which was established in 1850, is a treasure trove of Victorian funeral statuary. Buried here are Confederate soldiers, Atlanta mayors, Georgia governors, and Margaret Mitchell.

The **Breman Jewish Heritage Museum,** 1440 Spring St. NW, 404/873-1661, is the largest of its kind in the Southeast. It consists of two galleries—one on Atlanta's Jewish heritage, another on the Holocaust.

Joel Chandler Harris was the author of the Uncle Remus tales, and you can see his Victorian era home, the **Wren's Nest,** 1050 R.D. Abernathy Blvd. SW, 404/753-7735, here in Atlanta.

Also here in the city, at the **Fernbank Science Center,** 156 Heaton Park Dr. NE, 404/378-4311, is one of the nation's largest planetariums. It also has an observatory, exhibit hall, and 65-acre forest.

The $20 million **High Museum of Art** in midtown Atlanta is high-tech yet classical in architectural effect, with its rounded glass walls and gleaming white color. Start at the top and curve your way down the ramps through contemporary and classical paintings, African art, folk art, and photography. The museum is part of the **Woodruff Arts Center,** 1280 Peachtree St. NE, 404/733-4400, which includes the Alliance Theatre Co., the Atlanta College of Art, and the Atlanta Symphony.

Rhodes Hall, 1516 Peachtree St., 404/885-7800, a 1904 Romanesque mansion, was the home of furniture magnate Amos G. Rhodes. Inside is an elaborately carved mahogany staircase, as well as stained glass panels that depict the glorious, unreconstructed history of the Confederacy.

LODGING

Like everything else in Atlanta, the best hotels are concentrated in three areas—Buckhead, midtown, and downtown. We recommend that you aim toward the middle. Midtown is a quiet area near the major museums and is convenient to both ends of Peachtree.

You can't get much more convenient to midtown favorites such as the Fox Theatre and the Woodruff Arts Center than the 11-story **Wyndham Midtown Atlanta,** 125 10th St. NE at Peachtree St., 800/996-3426, $$$. The hotel is home to the Midtown Athletic Club, which has an indoor lap pool. This is where rock and country music stars like to stay.

Downtown, inside the CNN Center, is the swanky, high-dollar **Omni Hotel,** 100 CNN Center, 404/659-0000, $$$$. Stay here and you'll be next door to Ted Turner—he keeps an apartment in the CNN Center. The Omni has 458 deluxe rooms and 15 suites.

You won't spend much money and you'll be part of the nerve center of Atlanta's African American community if you stay at **Paschal's Motor Hotel** downtown, 830 Martin Luther King Jr. Dr., 404/577-3150, $$. The hotel is home to a famous fried-chicken restaurant, and some of the big R&B singers perform in the lounge.

The **Westin Peachtree Plaza,** 210 Peachtree St. NW, 800/228-3000, $$$$, at 73 stories, claims to be the tallest hotel in the Western Hemisphere. The hotel is located downtown and has three restaurants and an indoor/outdoor pool with a complete health club.

The **Granada Suite Hotel,** 1302 W. Peachtree St., 404/876-6100, $$$, was built in 1924 in a Spanish Colonial style and was originally designed as a garden apartment building. Renovations have turned it into an all-suite hotel with wet bars, refrigerators, microwaves, and coffee makers. The breakfast buffet is complimentary.

D on't wear an antebellum hoop skirt on the subway. They charge you extra for taking up three seats. But if you must wear one, Atlanta law states that on the back of the skirt, the wearer must attach a red reflector and a sign that says, "WIDE LOAD."

Take extra deodorant if you go to Atlanta in the summer. It's a steambath. The winters are quite changeable—a balmy day can be trampled by a winter steamroller, so be prepared for anything. Spring, of course, is azalea season, but that's when the crowds come out, too. We recommend Atlanta in the fall. This is a heavily wooded, hilly city, and the whole place becomes a patchwork of reds and oranges and yellows after the first cool spell. Fall comes late to Atlanta; the year we were there, Atlanta's foliage was burning brightly in mid-November.

Whatever you do, don't ask for Pepsi here. We can't guarantee your safety if you do. Atlanta is the birthplace and world headquarters of Coca-Cola. Coke built this city, and continues to serve it well through charitable investments and jobs.

City Survival Tips

You'll feel like a southern squire at midtown's **Ansley Inn,** 253 15th St. NE, 800/446-5416, $$$, a three-story Tudor mansion that's now a B&B. You'll also love the antique elegance. Breakfast is at a huge table in the formal dining room, and in the evening you'll find hors d'oeuvres and iced tea in the living room. Every room has a private bath and whirlpool.

The **Woodruff Bed and Breakfast Inn,** 223 Ponce de Leon Ave., 404/875-9449, $$, also in midtown, spent much of its life as a brothel operated by Miss Bessie Woodruff. It has 12 rooms and 14 suites, one of which has a hot tub. This turn-of-the-last-century Victorian home is near the historic Fox Theatre and many restaurants and bars, and it's only a short stroll away from Piedmont Park.

Not too many blocks away is the **Shellmont Bed & Breakfast,** 821 Piedmont Ave. NE, 404/872-9290, $$$, a home built in 1891. All rooms in this moderately priced inn have private baths, and a full breakfast is included.

Buckhead's only B&B is the **Beverly Hills Inn,** 65 Sheridan Dr. NE, 404/233-8520, $$$. It has 18 guest rooms, each with a kitchen, a balcony, and a private bath. You'll get a bottle of wine upon your arrival and complimentary breakfast in the garden room each morning.

DINING

Cosmopolitan Atlanta has it all, but what you probably can't get at home is southern cuisine. What's southern cuisine? We'd describe it as down-home uptown cooking, as if the chef went to culinary school in Paris without ever forgetting what he learned at his Mama's knee back home in Athens or Rome—Georgia, that is.

One place that shines is the **Blue Ridge Grill,** 1251 W. Paces Ferry Rd., 404/233-5030, $$$, with a stacked-stone fireplace and timbers from an 1890s cotton mill. This is upscale southern, with an emphasis on hickory-grilled meats and fish. They don't have possum on the menu, but a nice side dish is the tomato, corn, and okra cobbler.

The **Kudzu Café,** 3215 Peachtree Rd. NE, 404/262-0661, $$$, in Buckhead continues to win raves for its southern comfort food such as hickory-smoked pork chops and fried green tomatoes. Much of the fare isn't heavy on the fat, but the Kudzu Moon Pie will destroy your diet.

Scarlett O'Hara had an aunt named Pittypat Hamilton, and here she's gone and opened a restaurant across from the Westin Peachtree Plaza called **Pittypat's Porch,** 25 International Blvd., 404/525-8228, $$. Feast on the Savannah crabcakes, venison pie, and Twelve Oaks barbecue ribs, with a little peach cobbler to top it off, and your diet will be gone with the wind.

If you're gonna eat southern, then the restaurant should look the part, and you can't get any more authentic than the **1848 House,** 780 S. Cobb Dr., 770/428-1848, www.1848House.com, $$$, one of the few antebellum Atlanta houses left standing because it was used as a Union hospital. Specials include pan-roasted quail and saddle of venison. Consider the jazz brunch. The restaurant is 20 minutes from downtown.

You can watch the chef through the open kitchen at midtown's **Ciboulette,** 1529 Piedmont Rd. NE, 404/874-7600, $$$, an upscale restaurant that specializes in modern French cooking. Try the roast squab with cabbage au jus.

Can you get tandoori catfish in Atlanta? Probably not, but you can get tandoori chicken and all those other spicy kinds of dishes at **Grand Raja Indian Restaurant,** 2919 Peachtree Rd., 404/237-2661, $$, in Buckhead.

You can get the best of soul food without paying top dollar at the **Busy Bee Café,** 810 Martin Luther King Jr. Dr., 404/525-9212, $$. It's been in business for over 50 years.

——— King of Atlanta ———

If Atlanta is black America's capital city, then the old **Ebenezer Baptist Church** is its capitol building, and the heart and soul of the Civil Rights Movement. It is here that the memory of Dr. Martin Luther King Jr. remains most vividly alive. He was pastor of the church from 1960 until his assassination in Memphis in 1968.

The church is part of the 42-acre **Martin Luther King Jr. National Historic Site**. To get yourself oriented and to gain a historical perspective, start across the street from the church at the Visitors Center, 450 Auburn Ave., 404/331-3920. Here, through stunning exhibits and a film, you'll learn about Atlanta, segregation, and King the man, the preacher, and the world leader.

From there you can visit King's birth home, which is just down the street (although it's free, you'll need a ticket for the tour); the **Martin Luther King Jr. Center for Nonviolent Social Change**, where the movement continues; King's gravesite, amid a tranquil reflecting pool; and old Ebenezer Baptist, which was founded in 1886. (The present building was erected in 1922.)

Recently the congregation completed a new sanctuary across the street, and the old building has become a living museum where tours take place and ecumenical services are held. Consider yourself fortunate if you should happen to be in town during one of Ebenezer's monthly gospel choir concerts.

Down the street are the Big Bethel African Methodist Episcopal Church, 220 Auburn Ave., with its giant "Jesus Saves" sign on the steeple, and the Royal Peacock Club, 184–86 Auburn Ave., which was built in 1922 and has hosted such luminaries as Cab Calloway, Louis Armstrong, and Aretha Franklin.

The Atlanta History Center showcases the history of the South

If you're willing to pay top dollar to feel like a top dog on top of the world and get a top-notch meal in the bargain, go to the **Sun Dial Restaurant,** 210 Peachtree St. NW, 404/589-7506, $$$$, atop the Westin Peachtree Plaza Hotel. As the whole place rotates and the metropolis of Atlanta glitters at your feet, rotate down the menu through some fine continental cuisine. The smoked prime rib wouldn't be a bad choice.

SHOPPING

As a major commercial hub, Atlanta has the whole scale of goods, from posh boutiques to malls to tiny, interesting shops.

Perhaps the center of the city's shopping is at **Underground Atlanta,** 55 Upper Alabama St., 404/523-2311, a six-block collection of more than 100 shops and 12 restaurants that have found a home in the old viaducts beneath the city. The area is just east of the Five Points MARTA station, and it's a great place for strolling and watching people.

One thing to check out in Atlanta is the offering of antiques. **Bennett Street,** in the SoBuck section of the upscale neighborhood of Buckhead, is the place to go. Or try the **Buckhead Design Center,** 2133 Piedmont Rd., 404/876-2543, where 140 antiques dealers and interior designers show their stuff in a southern Victorian environment.

For authentic African artifacts handcrafted from stone and wood, pay a visit to **African Pride,** 88 Upper Alabama St., Suite 194, 404/523-6520. Or to check out the South's largest collection of Birkenstocks, make your way to **Abbadabba's,** 421-B Moreland Ave. NE, 404/588-9577.

The **Swan House,** 3130 Slaton Dr. NW, 404/261-0224, the impressive 1928 mansion that presides over the grounds of the Atlanta History

Neighborhood Watch

If you want to get to know Atlanta, get in a car and drive through its neighborhoods. Here's a suggested circle.

Start at **Buckhead**, the most exclusive area of Atlanta and the home of some high-end housing, nice restaurants, boutiques, and trendy nightspots. Also here, on West Paces Ferry Road, are the Governor's Mansion and the Atlanta History Center. Buckhead is at the upper end of Atlanta's east-west dividing line, Peachtree Street. (But it's called Peachtree Road in Buckhead.)

To the south is **Ansley Park**, which is about three miles from downtown, just off Peachtree Street at 15th Street. Beautiful, historical homes are nestled among the trees.

Just east is **Virginia-Highlands**, an area of 60- to 80-year-old homes that have been renovated by young professionals. It has a shopping district of family-owned, unfranchised restaurants and stores.

To the south is **Little Five Points**, Atlanta's equivalent of New York's Greenwich Village. Here you'll find many free-wheeling shops and galleries. And the Star Community Bar, 437 Moreland Ave. NE, has a shrine to Elvis in a former bank vault. 494/681-9018.

Inman Park is just west. Built in the early 1900s, this was Atlanta's first planned suburb, and it catered to the well-to-do. Victorian-style homes with gazebos and scalloped awnings are set among huge willow trees.

A bit farther west is **Sweet Auburn**, a popular residential area for African Americans and the center of black history in the city. Here is the Martin Luther King Jr. Center for Nonviolent Social Change; King's birth home; a visitors center that houses the civil rights museum; and the famed Ebenezer Baptist Church, the birthplace of the American Civil Rights Movement.

Now move west, to **downtown**, which has become a neighborhood in itself. Lots of people have moved here to loft apartments. Also here are many art galleries and shops, plus helpful Downtown Ambassadors who patrol the streets offering security and assistance.

Center, has a gift shop in the coach house where you can find antique porcelain and unusual gifts. It also has an art gallery and tea room.

For specialty Georgia gifts that capture the flavor of the place, go to **Eventz over Georgia,** 1219 Oakdale Rd., 800/880-LARK. Pick out a gift basket, and they'll ship it for you.

In the center of downtown and connected to the major hotels is the **Peachtree Center Shopping Mall,** Peachtree St. and International Blvd., 404/654-1296, with more than 60 restaurants and shops. Another shopping center is the **Phipps Plaza**, 3500 Peachtree Rd. at the Buckhead Loop, 404/261-7910, at the other end of Peachtree. It has upscale stores such as Gucci and Lord & Taylor.

SPORTS AND RECREATION

For spectator sports, Atlanta has been in the big leagues for years. Baseball's **Braves** (404/577-9100), football's **Falcons** (404/223-8000), and basketball's **Hawks** (404/827-3800) have all had their winning seasons in the last few years, and the fans have rewarded them with full stadiums. And then there was the biggest sports extravaganza of all time, the Olympics, and Atlanta is still feeling the effects of its afterglow.

Catch a Braves game at Turner Field, 755 Hank Aaron Dr., 404/522-7630; a Falcons game at the Georgia Dome, One Georgia Dome Dr. NE, 404/223-9200; or a Hawks game at Philips Arena, 100 Techwood Dr.

The 21-acre **Centennial Olympic Park** downtown, International Blvd. and Techwood Dr., 404/223-4412, is a good place for a walk or a jog and a little serenity, especially around the Fountain of Rings, which has 25 water jets and is the world's largest fountain utilizing the Olympic symbol of five interconnecting rings.

If golf is your game, reserve your spot at more than 35 top golf courses in Atlanta and the surrounding area through **Great Georgia Golf,** 770/565-5642.

For something on the wet and wild side, **Appalachian Wildwaters,** 3165 Highland Dr., Smyrna, 800/USA-RAFT, offers rafting on nine rivers in the area. Or get a behind-the-scenes look at the **Atlanta Motor Speedway,** 770/707-7970. You may even get lucky and see a race. The speedway is in the suburb of Hampton.

ENTERTAINMENT

Atlanta has always been a hub, of course, but those train tracks and airports and long-haul truck routes have been bringing in more than tires and tomatoes and lumber. Artists and entertainers have been coming in, too, making Atlanta an arts hub as well.

This is a young city, a place filled with yuppies who are working hard, who like to play hard, and who don't mind spending money. Atlanta knows how to party.

If you go to one entertainment place in Atlanta, go to the **Fox Theatre,** 660 Peachtree St. NE, 404/881-2100. This opulent showplace opened in 1929 and has become the place for the biggest and best performances of Broadway shows, concerts, and summer movies. A massive organ plays the pre-show audience sing-alongs. The ceiling, with thousands of bulbs, imitates a night sky as viewed from a desert. When you call, ask about tours. If a show's not available, you can still see the theater.

The **Atlanta Ballet,** 404/894-ARTS, the oldest ballet company in the United States, presents classical and contemporary works at the Fox Theatre and at the Robert Ferst Center for the Arts at Georgia Tech, 349 Ferst Dr. NW. Atlanta's largest theater is at the **Atlanta Civic Center,** 395 Piedmont Ave., 404/523-6275, where the biggest of Broadway hits are performed.

For a real slice of the South, try to catch a performance of the **Southern Order of Storytellers,** 770/391-9844. Call for information on the next event.

Blind Willie's, 828 N. Highland Ave. NE, 404/873-2583, welcomes you with a neon alligator and lots of Delta and New Orleans–style blues. It has live entertainment every night, and Sundays are often acoustic.

One of the most popular sports bars in Buckhead is **The Lodge,** 248 Buckhead Ave., 404/233-3345. It offers pool, shuffleboard, widescreen TVs, and an entrance into the East Village Grille next door, where the chicken wings are extra hot.

Tongue & Groove, 3055 Peachtree Rd., 404/261-2325, is an upscale cocktail lounge and sushi bar where the truly cool of Atlanta collect. If you want to fit in, you'll have to look chic.

CITY BASICS

Call ahead to the **Atlanta Convention & Visitors Bureau,** 800/ATLANTA, for a map and brochures. Likewise, **visitor information centers** are located in the north terminal of the airport; in Underground Atlanta, 404/222-6688; at Lenox Square, 3393 Peachtree Rd.

Get same-day half-price tickets to Atlanta events at **AtlanTIX,** 770/772-5572. The booth located in Underground Atlanta is open Tuesday through Saturday from 11 a.m. to 6 p.m. and Sunday noon to 5 p.m. You have to show up in person; no reservations are taken.

The city's major daily newspaper is the *Atlanta Journal-Constitution.* You can pick up tips on entertainment from *Atlanta* magazine, *Jezebel* magazine, or *Where Atlanta.* **Creative Loafing Network,** www.creativeloafing.com, is another neat place for interesting tidbits on what to do in Atlanta. Check out their Web site.

㉕ MIAMI

to go ▶

Miami Beach is where neon goes to die.
—Lenny Bruce

For the quick getaway, Miami Beach is where you want to be. It's where the action is—the sand, the water, the sun, the warm breezes; boiled crabs and broiled tourists; art-deco hotels painted in a rainbow of pastels; the babes, the hunks, the 88-pound models; skimpy swimsuits and skimpy lunches in chi-chi sidewalk cafés; and all that neon, which actually is far from dead.

The city of Miami and its rich, palm-shaded suburbs are interesting enough, but most of the fun is on that slip of sand to the east. Rent a car, find the right freeway, and head for the beach.

South Beach (SoBe)—America's version of the Riviera—is the southern portion of Miami Beach where everybody who's anybody is trying to get a tan. It is full of small to medium-size European-style hotels, most of an art-deco style, that have been recently restored. Also there are nightclubs that know how to rock and restaurants that are willing to take a chance on their cuisine. If you don't stay in this area, you've at least got to see it.

Walk down Ocean Drive. Tromp around in the sand. Stroll along that wavy ribbon of concrete called the Promenade, and smile. Pretend you're Somebody. Somebody might believe you.

Downtown Miami

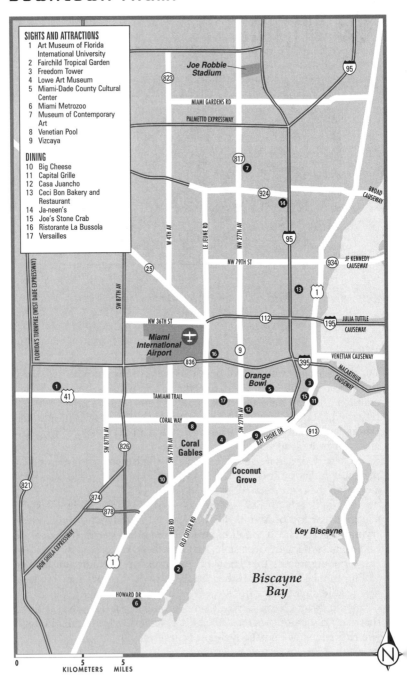

SIGHTS AND ATTRACTIONS
1 Art Museum of Florida International University
2 Fairchild Tropical Garden
3 Freedom Tower
4 Lowe Art Museum
5 Miami-Dade County Cultural Center
6 Miami Metrozoo
7 Museum of Contemporary Art
8 Venetian Pool
9 Vizcaya

DINING
10 Big Cheese
11 Capital Grille
12 Casa Juancho
13 Ceci Bon Bakery and Restaurant
14 Ja-neen's
15 Joe's Stone Crab
16 Ristorante La Bussola
17 Versailles

Joe Robbie Stadium

MIAMI GARDENS RD

PALMETTO EXPRESSWAY

BROAD CAUSEWAY

JF KENNEDY CAUSEWAY

NW 79TH ST

NW 36TH ST

JULIA TUTTLE CAUSEWAY

Miami International Airport

VENETIAN CAUSEWAY

MACARTHUR CAUSEWAY

Orange Bowl

TAMIAMI TRAIL

CORAL WAY

Coral Gables

Coconut Grove

Key Biscayne

HOWARD DR

Biscayne Bay

W 4TH AV

LE JEUNE RD

NW 27TH AV

SW 87TH AV

SW 57TH AV

SW 27TH AV

BAY SHORE DR

RED RD

OLD CUTLER RD

FLORIDA'S TURNPIKE (WEST DADE EXPRESSWAY)

DON SHULA EXPRESSWAY

0   5   5
KILOMETERS   MILES

N

GETTING AROUND

Miami International Airport, 305/876-7000, is seven miles from downtown and less than a half-hour from the beaches. It's a busy airport—the sixth busiest in the United States—with lots of business as an international hub and as the place where cruise passengers arrive.

Miami is a widespread town, so you need a car here. Traffic is bad but not fierce; parking is difficult but not impossible. Getting from here to there without a car is worse.

You can get there in style (don't forget your dark glasses) in a luxury rental car from **Excellence,** 3950 NW 26th St., 888/526-0055, www.excellenceluxury.com. **ExotiCars,** 1490 NE LeJune Rd., 888/541-1789, www.bnm.com/exotic.html, can also put you in an upscale seat. Or you can always stretch out in a stretch limo. Try **Dolphin Limousine Service,** 800/344-7002. All of the usual car rental agencies are also available at the airport. **Dollar,** 800/800-4000, www.dollarcar.com, offers low rates, unlimited free mileage, and no drop-off fees within Florida.

You can get to your Miami Beach hotel for about $11 on the **SuperShuttle,** 305/871-2000. Taxi rates are $1.75 per mile; to downtown the cab fare is $15 to $18, and to Miami Beach the cost is about $22. Try either **Flamingo Taxi,** 305/885-7000, or **Metro Taxi,** 305/888-8888. You can also get around Greater Miami and the beaches via **water taxis,** 954/467-6677, www.watertaxi.com, which hold 27 to 49 passengers each and are available for one-way or all-day transportation.

Public transportation is available through the **Metrobus** system, 305/770-3131 or 305/654-6530 (TDD), which can get you around town and to the beaches for $1.25 each way. You can also get around on the **Metromover,** 305/770-3131, individual motorized cars that run atop a 4.4-mile elevated track around downtown. The Metromover cars connect to the **Metrorail,** 305/770-3131, an elevated rail system that extends into the suburbs. The Metromover is 25 cents each way, and the Metrorail is $1.25. Exact change only is accepted.

SIGHTS AND ATTRACTIONS

The **Art Deco District** of South Beach is an attraction unto itself. It contains more than 800 buildings designed in this distinct style of the Roaring '20s, all within a single square mile. Within the area are a bouquet of boutique hotels and boutiques themselves, plus the Bass Museum, the Jackie Gleason Theater, a vast shopping district, and the great people-watching beaches of Lummus Park and South Pointe Park.

One of the most comprehensive collections of art in the southeastern United States is housed at the **Bass Museum of Art,** 2121 Park Ave., 305/673-7530. Besides special exhibits, the permanent collection features Old Master paintings, sculptures, textiles, period furniture, and ecclesiastical artifacts.

The **Art Deco Welcome Center,** 1001 Ocean Dr., 305/672-2014, sponsored by the Miami Design Preservation League, offers art-deco tours Saturdays at 10:30 a.m. and Thursdays at 6:30 p.m. You can also go on your own with an audio tour ($5 to rent the cassette), or you can take a bike tour the first and third Saturdays of each month. The bike tours are offered by the **Miami Beach Bike Center,** 601 Fifth St., 305/674-0150; a two-hour tour is $15 and includes the bike rental.

Also in South Beach is the **Wolfsonian,** 1001 Washington Ave., 305/531-1001, which houses a dramatically displayed collection of 70,000 European and American objets d'art produced between 1885 and 1945, including furniture, glass, ceramics, paintings, and sculpture.

The **Holocaust Memorial,** 1933–45 Meridian Ave., 305/538-1663, is a tribute by Miami Beach Holocaust survivors to the 6 million Jews who were victims of Nazi terrorism in World War II. It features a photographic mural and a Memorial Wall of names. The *Sculpture of Love & Anguish* is a huge arm cast in bronze with a concentration-camp number on it. Surrounding it are smaller sculptures of concentration-camp victims trying to reach out of the same hell from which the arm seems to be reaching. The detail of horror on the faces is stunning.

The **Ziff Jewish Museum of Florida,** 301 Washington Ave., 305/672-5044, is housed in a beautifully restored synagogue built in 1936 that has 80 stained-glass windows, chandeliers, and art-deco features. A permanent exhibit is *MOSAIC: Jewish Life in Florida,* which depicts more than 230 years of life among Florida's Jews.

Worth a look is the **Freedom Tower,** 600 Biscayne Blvd., in downtown Miami. It was built in 1924 as the city's first skyscraper and became the gateway to freedom for almost half a million Cuban refugees in the 1960s—the Ellis Island of the South.

The **Miami–Dade County Cultural Center,** 101 W. Flagler St., 305/375-1700, with its Mediterranean plaza and myriad fountains, contains a state-of-the art library and a historical and fine-arts museum.

The **Art Museum of Florida International University,** SW Eighth St. and 107th Ave., 305/348-2890, features national traveling and self-curated exhibitions including the acclaimed American Art Today series. Stroll through the museum's outdoor sculpture park called ArtPark.

North Miami's newest art institution is the **Museum of Contemporary Art,** 770 NE 125th St., 305/893-6211, a state-of-the-art facility that opened in 1996. A gift shop features handcrafted jewelry and objects that are one of a kind.

South of Miami, a must-see is **Vizcaya,** 3251 S. Miami Ave., 305/250-9133, the architectural wonder built in 1916 by industrialist James Deering on the banks of Biscayne Bay. The house combines elements of an Italian Renaissance villa with native materials. The formal gardens are similar— Italian statuary is nestled among southern live oaks dripping with Spanish moss. It is an island of serenity and beauty amid busy Miami.

High-rise hotels dominate Miami Beach ....

The **Lowe Art Museum,** 1301 Stanford Dr., 305/284-3535, in Coral Gables is next to the University of Miami. On permanent display are treasures of the Renaissance and Baroque periods, as well as Greco-Roman antiquities and Native American, Asian, and African art.

Another must-see in this suburban area south of downtown Miami is **Fairchild Tropical Garden,** 10901 Old Cutler Rd., 305/667-1651, 83 acres of gardens that were established in 1938. Take the tram tour among the palms, flowering trees, and lily pools. Also featured is a fascinating gatehouse museum, a 16,000-square-foot conservatory, and an interesting garden shop.

The **Miami Metrozoo,** 12400 SW 152nd St., 305/251-0400, has more than 900 animals on a 290-acre habitat that is strong on jungle life.

And in Coral Gables is the **Venetian Pool,** 2701 DeSoto Blvd., 305/460-5356, which some consider to be the world's most beautiful swimming pool. It's a spring-fed body of water with waterfalls, caves, and moorings that will remind you of—where else?—Venice. You can take a dip Tuesday through Sunday year-round.

LODGING

There are a number of reservation services for the Miami area. One to try is **Central Reservation Service.** Another that also offers help with condos, rental homes, and resorts is **Florida SunBreak,** 800/SUN-BREAK. And **Hotel Reservations Network,** 800/964-6835, promises hotel reservations at a discount of up to 65 percent.

If you want to stay in the Deco District, you aren't going to have a problem. Many choices exist, and many of them are of the intimate, European variety.

Mıamı Beach

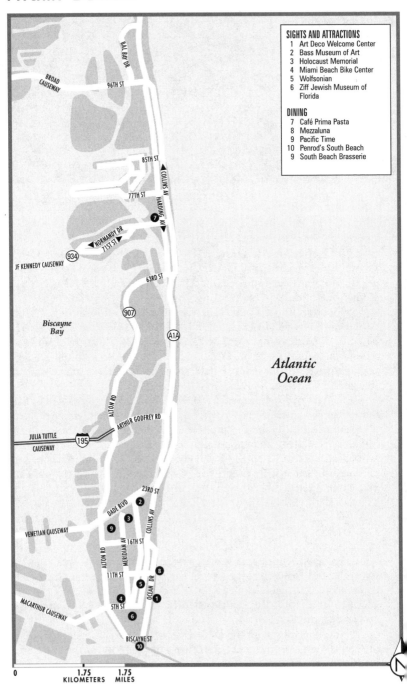

SIGHTS AND ATTRACTIONS
1. Art Deco Welcome Center
2. Bass Museum of Art
3. Holocaust Memorial
4. Miami Beach Bike Center
5. Wolfsonian
6. Ziff Jewish Museum of Florida

DINING
7. Café Prima Pasta
8. Mezzaluna
9. Pacific Time
10. Penrod's South Beach
9. South Beach Brasserie

BAL BAY DR.

BROAD CAUSEWAY

96TH ST

85TH ST

77TH ST

COLLINS AV

HARDING AV

NORMANDY DR.

71ST ST

JF KENNEDY CAUSEWAY

(934)

63RD ST

(907)

(A1A)

Biscayne Bay

Atlantic Ocean

ALTON RD

ARTHUR GODFREY RD

JULIA TUTTLE CAUSEWAY

(195)

23RD ST

DADE BLVD

COLLINS AV

VENETIAN CAUSEWAY

ALTON RD

MERIDIAN AV

16TH ST

11TH ST

OCEAN DR.

MACARTHUR CAUSEWAY

5TH ST

BISCAYNE ST

0   1.75   1.75
     KILOMETERS   MILES

N

The **National Hotel,** 1577 Collins Ave., 800/327-8370, $$$, must rank at the top. Its 106 rooms have been restored with historic correctness from the hotel's 1939 origins, and the result is a work of art. One of the many dramatic architectural elements is the hotel's 203-foot-long swimming pool, a narrow span of water that draws the eye out to the Atlantic beyond. Rooms feature wall safes, TVs with VCRs, and 24-hour room service with free continental breakfast.

Next door is the super-cool **Delano,** 1685 Collins Ave., 800/555-5001, $$$$. (Madonna is part-owner of the restaurant here, to give you an idea of the coolness factor.) Minimalism is the order of the day—you won't find a whole lot of furniture in your room, and that sleek, slack look will cost you. In the pool out back, they pipe in classical music that you can only hear when you're submerged.

The Avalon, 700 Ocean Dr., 800/933-3306, $$, is a little less cool and not nearly as expensive. It has 108 restored deco-style rooms and offers free continental breakfast, in-room refrigerators and safes, ceiling fans, air conditioning, and VCRs.

The **Park Central,** 640 Ocean Dr., 800/727-5236, $$, has a rooftop deck where you can watch all the fab action of Ocean Drive below. Ask for the Vampire Lestat room, which Anne Rice described in one of her vampish novels, *Tale of the Body Thief.*

Singer Gloria Estefan wanted only the best (and she got it) for her art-deco–style **Cardozo Hotel,** 1300 Ocean Dr., 800/782-6500, $$$, which features large rooms, hardwood floors, and handmade furniture.

The **Blue Moon** hotel, 944 Collins Ave., 800/724-1623, www.bluemoonhotel.com, $$$, has a sort of split personality. First, it's a Mediterranean-style villa with gardens galore. But then the new owner, Merv Griffin, bought the art-deco building next door and put everything together into one hotel. Somehow the culture clash all works out. The hotel is one block from the beach.

Another boutique hotel of the highest order is **The Impala,** 1228 Collins Ave., 800/646-7252, $$$. Rooms have large tubs and CD players. This is another Mediterranean-style building with original artwork throughout. A continental breakfast is included.

Moving out of the Art Deco District, the **Indian Creek Hotel,** 2727 Indian Creek Dr., 800/491-2772, $$, comes highly recommended. It, too, is a deco restoration project, with none of the pretentiousness built in. (Case in point: room keys are attached to rubber alligators.) The staff is as friendly and helpful as any we've encountered. Also, you're only 10 minutes away from the SoBe scene, and in a much quieter location.

You'll be back in the '50s at the **Eden Roc Resort,** 2525 Collins Ave., 800/327-8337, $$$. The ambiance is relaxed, and amenities include a rock-climbing complex, an Olympic-size pool, and a health club.

You can't miss the **Fontainebleau Hilton Hotel & Resort,** 4441 Collins Ave., 800/548-8886, $$$$. This landmark originally opened in 1954. Later it was taken over by the Hilton and restored and expanded.

You'll love driving far north up Collins Avenue toward what looks like two large pillars surrounding the hotel's pool. Surprise, it's a trompe-l'oeil mural. The hotel includes a wonderful pool (a real one), shopping, restaurants, the works.

The Biltmore, 1200 Anastasia Ave., Coral Gables, 305/445-1926, www.biltmorehotel.com, $$$$, is one of the finest resort hotels in the world. It has golf, tennis, opulent rooms, five-star dining, and America's largest hotel pool. Its Old World character has been preserved in its Mediterranean architecture, Roman columns, handpainted ceilings, and sparkling fountains.

DINING

South Beach is where the Beautiful People like to congregate, of course, which means the Beautiful Chefs will be there to serve them. They'll serve you, too, if you've got the money. Other centers of dining are Little Havana, where the rich flavors of Cuba are abundant, and the toney communities of Coral Gables and Coconut Grove, where many of the restaurants have been rated four-and five-star for their Floribbean, New World, and Cuban cuisines.

When the stars go out to eat, they like to go to the **South Beach Brasserie,** 910 Lincoln Rd., 305/534-5511, $$$, actor Michael Caine's restaurant in South Beach. Try the bouillabaisse, the ahi tuna, or the lobster salad.

Penrod's South Beach, One Ocean Dr., 305/538-1111, $$, has something for everyone in one location—the Seafood Grill, which overlooks the Atlantic; the Barefoot Beach Café, a more casual place right on the sand; and Café Nikki, a garden-style restaurant with fountains.

Mezzaluna, 834 Ocean Dr., 305/674-1330, $$$, puts the emphasis on the Mediterranean, with upscale trattoria cooking. The building is powder blue inside, with fluffy clouds painted on the ceiling.

One of the area's most famous restaurants is **Joe's Stone Crab,** 227 Biscayne Blvd., 305/673-0365, $$$, which has been around since 1913. Prepare to feel a definite pinch in the pocketbook, though, and remember that the restaurant is open only during stone crab season—October 15 to May 15.

Winning raves for its inexpensive Italian food—pizza, pasta, and subs—is the **Big Cheese,** 8080 SW 67th Ave., 305/662-6855, $, in South Miami.

Back in Miami Beach and tucked away in a shopping center is an Italian restaurant that's a step above the ordinary. It's so genuine we could barely understand the owner and his descriptions of the specialties for that day. It doesn't matter; it's all good at the **Café Prima Pasta,** 414 71st St., 305/867-0106, $$.

Asian fusion is the specialty at the **Pacific Time,** 915 Lincoln Rd., 305/534-5979, $$$, in the Lincoln Road Shopping District. Recommended is the grilled ginger chicken with sweet "sake-yaki" vinaigrette and tempura sweet potatoes. And for dessert, have the broiled pink grapefruit with wildflower honey.

The **Capital Grille,** 444 Brickell Ave., 305/374-4500, $$, serves aged steaks, chops, and seafood downtown.

You'll get strolling troubadours performing the native songs of Spain, plus oak-grilled fresh game and seafood, at **Casa Juancho,** 2436 SW Eighth St., 305/642-2452, $$. And just down the street is a Cuban restaurant with a French name, **Versailles,** 3555 SW Eighth St., 305/444-0240, $$. It's been serving Cuban food, such as chicken and

⎯Neighborhood Watch⎯

The **Miami–Dade County** area covers almost 2,000 square miles and contains about 2 million people. Its neighborhoods and suburban cities are a rich stew of flavors. You'd be mistaken if you went to just the southern end of Miami Beach and thought you'd seen it all. There's so much more than South Beach.

Right next door and up the beach is the rest of Miami Beach. Here you'll see some massive resort hotels, miles of condos serving a huge retirement community, and two important museums—the Wolfsonian and the Holocaust Memorial. A bit farther up is **Bal Harbour**, a rich community with some of the finest shopping in the world. **Downtown Miami** also has its charms and is certainly worth a visit.

Just west of Brickell Avenue is **Little Havana**. This vibrant neighborhood is alive with the flavors of Cuba. The streets are lined with shops, casual sidewalk cafeterias, and supper clubs that rock with the sounds of salsa and danzon at night. Stop at a café and order a café con leche—molasses-thick coffee with heavy cream. If you need a pick-me-up, this will pick you up and spin you around.

Little Haiti is a vibrant community of refugees who have embraced the American way without really blending in. Check out the Caribbean Marketplace, which resembles the Iron Market in Port-au-Prince.

The African American communities of **Overtown** and **Liberty City** are enjoying a rebirth. You'll want to see the colorful murals on the buildings that celebrate African American history and heroes.

Just south of Miami are the communities of **Coral Gables** and **Coconut Grove**, which are as beautiful as their names imply. Coral Gables is a neighborhood that has been meticulously preserved from its birth in the 1920s as a suburban tribute to the Old World city of Venice. Among the palm-lined streets and magnificent golf courses are houses that evoke images of Spain, Italy, thirteenth-century France, and even China. Coconut Grove has a similar feel.

yellow rice with fried plantain, for more than a quarter-century. You won't believe the glitzy decor.

Ristorante La Bussola, 264 Giralda Ave., 305/445-8783, $$, has won raves for its northern Italian cuisine. This is a white tablecloth kind of place with Renaissance decor and piano music.

How about Haitian? The **Ceci Bon Bakery and Restaurant,** 5934 NE Second Ave., 305/759-2326, $, specializes in Haitian bread and pastries.

If you've got a hankering for curried goat, **Ja-neen's,** 1272 NW 119th St., 305/688-0521, $$, can fix you up. Oxtail is another specialty of this Jamaican restaurant.

SHOPPING

The **Lincoln Road Shopping District** in South Beach is a mall only in the sense that it's a nice place for walking. Otherwise it does not resemble the usual two-story, franchise-heavy suburban version. It's a mall with an imagination.

The pedestrian concourse contains cafés, restaurants, nightclubs, boutiques, and art galleries. This eight-block stretch has unique pavement designs, fountains, and shade structures all put together in a modern, funky way.

The **Bal Harbour Shops,** Bal Harbour, 9700 Collins Ave., 305/866-0311, is a glitzy mall offering shopping on a scale equal to Rodeo Drive or Fifth Avenue. It's in Bal Harbour, in the northern part of Miami Beach.

The **Bayside Marketplace,** 401 Biscayne Blvd., 305/577-3344, is a must-shop place in downtown Miami. This is a refurbished, open-air version of the old Pier 5 fishing pier, where tourists used to congregate under the famous neon sailfish in the 1940s and '50s. A multitude of shops are here to suit every taste and budget. You'll also find more shops in the nearby commercial district from SE First Street to NE Third Street west of Biscayne Boulevard.

You should take in the **Miracle Mile** of Coral Gables, where designer boutiques and department stores line the red-brick street of Coral Way. Coconut Grove's best shopping is around **Grand Avenue,** which offers everything from haute couture to haughty kitsch.

You can get vintage autographs of sports figures, movie stars, and rock stars, plus historical documents, at **Gotta Have It! Collectives,** 504 Biltmore Wy., Coral Gables, 305/446-5757.

Watch a master cigar-roller do his thing at the **Cigar Connection,** 534 Lincoln Rd., 305/531-7373, in the Lincoln Road Shopping District (a pedestrian concourse between 16th and 17th Sts. from Washington Ave. to Alton Rd.). You can buy domestic and imported hand-rolled premium cigars, as well as humidors and cigar accessories.

X-Isle Surf Shop, 437 Washington Ave., 305/673-5900, is the place to go for a large variety of surfboards, body boards, wet suits, and beach accessories.

African masks and carvings are available at **Out of Africa,** 2911 Grand Ave., #402, 305/445-5900.

SPORTS AND RECREATION

Even if you don't like horse racing, or if you miss the season (March to May), you should see the **Hialeah Park** racetrack, E. Fourth Ave. between 21st and 32nd Sts., Hialeah, which is just northwest of Miami. The track was built in 1925 and has been called one of the most beautiful in the world. It's listed on the National Register of Historic Places.

If you're interested in spectator sports, Miami has plenty of offerings. The **Florida Marlins,** 305/626-7400, are making a splash in Major League Baseball at Pro Player Stadium, 2269 NW 199th St. The **Miami Dolphins,** 954/452-7000, are always making waves, too, and are no stranger to the Super Bowl. They also play at Pro Player Stadium. Likewise, the **Miami Heat,** 305/577-4328, are hot to trot and can be found running all around the Miami Arena. Call to get the latest word on the NBA team's schedule.

Bet on the fast, fast game of jai-alai at **Miami Jai-Alai.** Jai-alai is a handball-like game using a rubber ball and a wicker basket attached to the player's arm.

The Miami area is a golf mecca. Courses of all kinds—at resorts, at country clubs, and for the public—are everywhere, among the swaying palms and warm ocean breezes. Check out the famed **Doral Golf Resort and Spa,** 4400 NW 87th Ave., 305/591-6453. A central reservation service for golfers is provided by **Tee Times USA,** 904/439-0001. And you can get some help with that swing with golf lessons from **Visual Edge Systems,** 561/750-7559, in Boca Raton.

Blue Water Sports, 800/ISLAND-HOP, will take you on a chartered boat for skin diving, sailboating, fishing, or sightseeing. Swim with the dolphins or take a hop down to the Florida Keys. You can also reel in the big ones from the charter boat *Striker-1,* 888/REEL-IT-IN. Half-day and full-day charters are available.

ENTERTAINMENT

The club scene on South Beach is amazing. This is where the need-to-be-seen get seen, and these models-to-be and actor wanna-bes are out there on the dance floor, in front of the band, and at the restaurant tables, working hard. You'll never see so many perfect teeth anywhere else in one place.

Part of the entertainment is trying to spot celebrities, and your odds are pretty good. Movies are constantly being filmed here. Consid-

— Welcome to the Tropics —

Tropical weather will feel pretty good to you if it's February and you're a Chicago Popsicle. But if it's summer and you're looking for a temperate ocean breeze to waft away a big-city heat stroke, you're out of luck. Miami can be as stifling as any jungle city in the world. You'll have to learn to take the good with the bad:

1. Rain showers, which often roll in during the afternoons, keep things lush, but they also keep the humidity lush.
2. Sunshine is plentiful, and so is sunburn. Wear a hat. Bring the sun block.
3. Air-conditioning is plentiful, but it might prove to be too cool for you sometimes. Bring a light jacket.
4. Hurricanes happen, and you don't want to be anywhere near the place when they do. (The average elevation of Miami is 12 feet.) Hurricane season is roughly mid-summer to late fall. Keep an eye on the weather. If it looks threatening, either cancel your plans or pack some canned goods.

er these: *The Birdcage* with Robin Williams and Nathan Lane; *Something About Mary* starring Cameron Diaz and Matt Dillon; and *Up Close and Personal* starring Robert Redford and Michelle Pfeiffer.

Television is constantly bringing Miami into focus. There are more than 35 modeling agencies in the area. Film festivals and fund-raisers bring out the VIPs, and many celebrities are attracted to the area for the same reason you are—balmy weather and beautiful surroundings.

Music is in the air from all the recording studios in the area. The multiculturalism that enlivens the cuisine does the same thing for song, which is what brings artists such as Gloria Estefan, Julio Iglesias, and Aretha Franklin here to record albums.

All of this makes the SoBe nightclub scene hot, hot, hot. Following are some of the hottest places.

Amnesia, 136 Collins Ave., 305/531-5535, is a good place to dance the night away, especially out on the courtyard under the stars. Dancing both inside and out is the big thing at **Bash,** 655 Washington Ave., 305/538-2274.

One of the hottest of the hot is **Groovejet,** 323 23rd St., 305/532-2002, which doesn't really get hopping until after 2 a.m. For live jazz, blues, and Brazilian music seven nights a week, try the **Van Dyke Café,** 846 Lincoln Rd., 305/534-3600.

The best of Broadway comes to the **Jackie Gleason Theater,** 1700 Washington Ave., 305/358-5885. This is where the Jackie Gleason TV show was originally taped, and it has since become the home for the Florida Philharmonic, the Miami City Ballet, and the Concert Association of Florida.

The **Concert Association,** 305/532-3491, oversees performances of classical music and dance in the Greater Miami area. Call for information and tickets.

Try the **Coconut Grove Playhouse,** 3500 Main Hwy., Coconut Grove, 305/442-2662, for some of the best live theater in the area. It is recognized nationally for a tradition of innovative and original productions. The **Gusman Center for the Performing Arts,** 174 E. Flagler St., 305/374-8762, located downtown, is home to the Miami Film Festival and performances of all kinds. This 1925 building is considered an architectural treasure.

The **New World Symphony,** 800/597-3331, ext. 140, is one of the best orchestras in the world. It performs full-orchestra concerts, chamber music, and a new South Beach Sound series at the Lincoln Theatre, 555 Lincoln Rd., and elsewhere.

You'll find the **Florida Grand Opera** performing in Miami at the **Miami Dade County Auditorium,** 2901 W. Flagler St., 305/547-5414, an art-deco jewel that is a popular facility chosen by many international touring acts.The Gusman Center often hosts the **Florida Philharmonic Orchestra** while the **Miami City Ballet** regularly dazzles audiences at the Jackie Gleason Theater.

To get you into the Latin spirit of Miami, seek out the **Ballet Flamenco La Rosa,** 305/672-0552, which is sponsored by the Performing Arts Network. They'll even give you a flamenco dance lance lesson. (Consider it something like a Latin blood transfusion.) Call for details on concerts and lessons.

CITY BASICS

For free maps, guides, and brochures, call the **Greater Miami Convention & Visitors Bureau,** 800/283-2707, www.miamiandbeaches.com. You can also contact the **Miami Beach Hotline,** 305/673-7400, for information and assistance. For information on more than 100 hotels in the area, call the **Greater Miami & the Beaches Hotel Association,** 800/SEE-MIAMI. People with disabilities can get assistance from **Miami-Dade Disability Services,** 305/547-5444.

Ticketmaster, 305/358-5885, sells tickets to major sports and entertainment events at outlets throughout the area.

The **Black Archives, History & Research Foundation of South Florida,** 5400 NW 22nd Ave., 305/636-2390, is a nonprofit organization that promotes black heritage research and cultural activities throughout the area. **Hispanic Heritage Council** can be reached at 305/541-5023.

The *Miami Herald* is the major daily in the area. *Miami New Times* is the city's premiere alternative weekly. You can also find entertainment news in the magazine *Where Miami.*

INDEX

World of Coca-Cola Atlanta: 300
Wreck Beach: 149
Wren's Nest: 301
Wright, Frank Lloyd: 100
Wynkoop Brewing Co.: 239

Yerba Buena Center for the Arts:
187

Ziff Jewish Museum of Florida: 312

PHOTO CREDITS

page 1, Times Square at night, New York—© Andre Jenny/Unicorn Stock Photos; page 15, Philadelphia—© Bob Krist/Greater Philadelphia TMC; page 29, Memorial Bridge to Lincoln Memorial—© Chad Ehlers/International Stock; page 43, Rowers and sailboats on the Charles River, Boston—Massachusetts Office of Travel and Tourism; page 57, Montreal under the snow seen from the Mont-Royal— © Daniel Choinére/Tourisme Montréal; page 69, Skydome next to Gardner Expressway—© Andre Jenny/International Stock; page 81, Rock & Roll Hall of Fame—© Jonathan Wayne; page 91, Architecture next to the Chicago River— Peter J. Schulz/City of Chicago; page 105, Missouri Botanical Gardens—Gail Mooney/St. Louis CVC; page 117, J.C. Nichols Fountain—© CVB of Greater Kansas City; page 127, St. Paul's Landmark Center—© St. Paul CVB; page 139, Pacific Starlight Dinner Train—British Columbia Rail; page 151, The Monorail—© John Elk III; page 163, Old Town historic district—© John Elk III; page 175, Trolley in front of Grace Cathedral—San Francisco CVB; page 189, Palm–lined street in Beverly Hills— Michele and Tom Grimm/Los Angeles CVB; page 203, Balboa Park—© James Blank/San Diego CVB; page 215, Fremont Street Experience—Las Vegas News Bureau; page 229, 16th Street mall—Denver MC & VB; page 243, Exchange Ave. in the Historic Stockyards—Fort Worth CVB; page 259, Carriage ride in front of the capitol building—© J. Griffis Smith/Austin CVB; page 271, Pat O'Brien's—© Alex Demyan/New Orleans CVB; page 285, Trolley—Memphis CVB; page 297, Fountain of Rings at Centennial Olympic Park—Georgia DITT; page 309, Art Deco district—© Robin Hill/Miami CVB

Guidebooks that really *guide*

City•Smart™ Guidebooks
Pick one for your favorite city: *Albuquerque, Anchorage, Austin, Calgary, Charlotte, Chicago, Cincinnati, Cleveland, Denver, Indianapolis, Kansas City, Memphis, Milwaukee, Minneapolis/St. Paul, Nashville, Pittsburgh, Portland, Richmond, Salt Lake City, San Antonio, San Francisco, St. Louis, Tampa/St. Petersburg, Tucson.* US \$12.95 to 15.95

Retirement & Relocation Guidebooks
The World's Top Retirement Havens, Live Well in Honduras, Live Well in Ireland, Live Well in Mexico. US \$15.95 to \$16.95

Travel•Smart® Guidebooks
Trip planners with select recommendations to *Alaska, American Southwest, Arizona, Carolinas, Colorado, Deep South, Eastern Canada, Florida, Florida Gulf Coast, Hawaii, Illinois/Indiana, Kentucky/Tennessee, Maryland/Delaware, Michigan, Minnesota/Wisconsin, Montana/Wyoming/Idaho, New England, New Mexico, New York State, Northern California, Ohio, Pacific Northwest, Pennsylvania/New Jersey, South Florida and the Keys, Southern California, Texas, Utah, Virginias, Western Canada.* US \$14.95 to \$17.95

Rick Steves' Guides
See *Europe Through the Back Door* and take along guides to *France, Belgium & the Netherlands; Germany, Austria & Switzerland; Great Britain & Ireland; Italy; Scandinavia; Spain & Portugal; London; Paris;* or *Best of Europe.* US \$12.95 to \$21.95

Adventures in Nature
Plan your next adventure in *Alaska, Belize, Caribbean, Costa Rica, Guatemala, Hawaii, Honduras, Mexico.* US \$17.95 to \$18.95

Into the Heart of Jerusalem
A traveler's guide to visits, celebrations, and sojourns. US \$17.95

The People's Guide to Mexico
This is so much more than a guidebook—it's a trip to Mexico in and of itself, complete with the flavor of the country and its sights, sounds, and people. US \$22.95

JOHN MUIR PUBLICATIONS
A DIVISION OF AVALON TRAVEL PUBLISHING
5855 Beaudry Street, Emeryville, CA 94608

Please check our web site at www.travelmatters.com for current prices and editions, or visit your local bookseller.

Cater Your Interests on Your Next Vacation